The Million Dollar Lawyers

Books by Joseph C. Goulden

THE BEST YEARS 1976
H. L. MENCKEN'S LAST CAMPAIGN 1976
THE BENCHWARMERS 1974
MEANY 1972
THE SUPERLAWYERS 1972
THE MONEY GIVERS 1971
TRUST IS THE FIRST CASUALTY 1969
MONOPOLY 1968
THE CURTIS CAPER 1965

The Million Dollar Lawyers

By Joseph C. Goulden

A behind-the-scenes look at America's big money lawyers and how they operate

G.P. Putnam's Sons • New York

Portions of this book were published in different form in *Penthouse* and *The Texas Monthly*.

 Published simultaneously in Canada by Longman Canada Limited, Toronto.

SBN: 399-12239-7

Library of Congress Cataloging in Publication Data

Goulden, Joseph C
The million dollar lawyers.

Includes index
1. Lawyers—United States. 2. Practice of law—United States. I. Title.
KF300.G645 340'.0973 78-4680

PRINTED IN THE UNITED STATES OF AMERICA

For Maureen R. Mylander, who cared for a bear when he needed it; kindness is never forgotten.

Contents

Acknowledgments

Several hundred persons—lawyers and laymen—provided the interviews and documentation that went into this book. I am especially grateful to Truman M. Talley, who had the original idea from which the book evolved, and nurtured it through its early stages. As stated in the Prologue, many persons who gave me interviews did so with the guarantee of anonymity. As a journalist I dislike using unnamed sources. However, bar canons on self-publicity and professional criticism being what they are, many attorneys felt they had no choice. In any event, the following individuals were of assistance to me during the past two years when this book took shape:

Professor James Frierson of East Tennessee State University. John D. Craigie of the Insurance Information Institute. Davida Maron of the Legal Resources Center, Washington. Baxter Ward of the Los Angeles County Board of Supervisors and Margaret Carrell of his staff. Stanford Shmukler, Rose DeWolf and B. A. Bergman of Philadelphia. Pike Powers, Jr., of Beaumount, Chris Harvey of Dallas, Scott Baldwin, Franklin Jones Jr., and Franklin Jones, Sr., of Marshall, all in Texas. Jack Abercrombie of Orlando, Florida. Raoul Lionel Felder of New York. Jack and Stephanie Biddle and Bob Negrin of the Computer Industry Association, Rosslyn, Virginia. Stanley Sporkin, Theodore Sonde, Richard Patterson, Bobby Lawyer and Sally Hamrick of the Securities and Exchange Commission. Marion Jay Eply III of White & Case, New York. Richard E. Cheney of Hill & Knowlton, New York. Robert J. Militana of Bethesda, Maryland. Milton Freedman of Arnold & Porter, Washington. Kenneth J. Bialkin of Willkie, Farr & Gallagher, New York. Monroe Freedman of Hofstra Law School. Art Mielke of the Bureau of the Census. Ed Garvey and Pat Eubank of the National Football League Players Association. Theodore R. Cubbison of Youngstown, Ohio. Walter W. Morrison, Frank A. Orban III, Neill H. Hollenshead and James L. Arnold of The Research Group, Charlottesville, Virginia. Fred Grabowsky, counsel of the District of Columbia Bar. Roger Wheeler, John H. Clark, Jack Bailey and Serge Novovich of the Telex Corporation. Floyd Walker and Louis and Liz Jansen, all of Tulsa. Robert Aitken and Anthony J. Murray of Long Beach, California. Arthur Cecelski of Virginia Common Cause, Springfield, Virginia. Betsy Barley of *Medical World News*, New York. Millard Ruud and Nancy Jones of the Association of American Law Schools. Dean Bunch of the University of Florida law school. Professor James Clark of Indiana University, special consultant to the ABA on legal education. Gary Sellers, Ralph Nader, Joan Claybrook and Mark J. Green, all of Washington. Leonard Ring of Chicago. Peter Shuck of Consumers Union, Washington. Mike Pertschuk, Lynn Sutcliff and Chris O'Malley of the Senate Commerce Committee. Jane Lakes Frank and Doug Lea of the subcommittee on constitutional rights, Senate Judiciary Committee. Fred Smith, legislative assistant to Rep. Larry McDonald (R., Ga.). Sol Z. Rosen of Washington. John E. Lama, executive director of the Michigan State Bar, Detroit. Greg Staple, Andrew Watson and Bob and Linda Burt, all of Ann Arbor, Michigan. Vicki Toensing, Victoria Heldman, Sheldon Miller, Harry Okren, Albert Lopatin, Richard Goodman, Ivan Barris, Richard M. Goodman and Harriett and Norm Rotter, all of Detroit. Daniel J. Demslow, chairman of the Michigan State Public Service Commission. Michael Dively, deputy director, Michigan Department of Commerce. Ross M. Hagen, Lynn Taylor, Kathleen S. Doyle, Alice Fins, Phil Smith, Fred Franklin and LaMar Forsbee of the American Bar Association, Chicago. Robert L. Rauzi, of Mount Vernon, Ohio. Henry H. Wallace of Pittsburgh. Jerri Joy of the Senate Judiciary Committee. Richard Haas and Kurt W. Melchior of San Francisco. Bruce Gebhardt and Michael Starr of the Association of Trial Lawyers of America, Boston.

Tom Noel of Denver, Colorado. Professor Vern Countryman of Harvard Law School. Robert W. Bennett of Northwestern University School of Law. Louis G. Davidson of Louis G. Davidson & Associates, Chicago. W. David Gardner of Rockport, Massachusetts. Tom Mechling, New York. Lily Barry of the State Bar of California. John Perazick of Washington. William H. Kotlowski, Jr., of Defense Research Institute, Milwaukee. John A. Lucido of Berkeley Heights, New Jersey. William F. Alexander, A. C. and Betty Greene, Bob Compton, Billy Porterfield, Phil Burleson and Lee Clark of Dallas. Les and Roxanne Cramer, Jack and Greta Lahr, Peter and Lennie Feigl, Heather and Mike Hornberger of Arlington, Virginia. Bernard and Lillian Packer of Washington. Harriett and David Bernstein of Bethesda, Maryland. Louis and Leatrice Gevantman of Potomac, Maryland. Louise and Paul Wilson of Woodstock, Virginia. And Janice Thrace and John Adams of the U. S. Post Office, Rileyville, Virginia. Special thanks are due to Irene King, a typist who can improve upon the raw copy, and to Pat Altobello.

Prologue

A bitterly cold January afternoon, I stomped my boots on the foyer floor to shake off the encrusted snow, and stepped into the brick hundred-year-old townhouse on Jefferson Avenue in Detroit, leaving behind me on the street the near-zero winds whipping across the Detroit River from Canada. Lawyers all over the Midwest had been telling me, "If you want to see a collection of tough, honest cookies who are driving the insurance lawyers batty, go see these guys in Detroit."

"These guys" were the personal injury firm of Lopatin, Miller, Bindes & Freedman, and they occupied the townhouse. The receptionist gave me a seat and some hot coffee and a polite it'll-be-just-a-few-minutes excuse. As I settled down, a man came out of the catacombs in the rear of the building to consult with a nervous, thirtyish black woman seated across the room.

"They say $2,700 tops," he told her. "I don't think we should take it. If I go back to them and say we gotta' have more, they'll top three thou. But it's up to you. If they dig in, it could be another twelve or sixteen months before we go to trial. They'll probably settle then, but you'll be out the time. Now I recommend that you let me keep talking with them. But it's your decision."

The woman pursed her lips. This was important business. "I'm going to get *something*, anyhow?"

"Sure," the lawyer said. "No way you're gonna' be cut out. What we're talking about now is whether we bargain some more, in hopes we get extra now, or wait and see what they give us further down the pike. Any way it cuts, you are gonna' get some money."

"You the lawyer," she said. "You do what you think is right."

He nodded and disappeared down the hall, and I sipped my coffee and thumbed through a copy of *Trial Magazine*, journal of the Association of Trial Lawyers of America (ATLA), the trade association of plaintiff attorneys. I came across an editorial by the ATLA president, Robert G. Begam:

> It is an unfortunate but undeniable truth that the only effective check on great economic power is a countervailing power to inflict losses payable in dollars. Adverse verdicts have a marvelous didactic effect in assuring safer subsequent production, distribution and use of potentially deadly substances.

I liked the quotation, so I jotted it into my notebook. By the time I had finished, the lawyer was back, smiling at the woman.

"Thirty-five hundred," he said. "One phone call. They first said thirty-two; I said thirty-seven; so we split. They'll have the check over in a few days. All you have to do is come in and sign the release agreement and the settlement and the check. Okay? We'll call you when it's ready."

The woman reflexively reached out and clutched the lawyer's forearm and smiled. "You did me all right," she said. "Thanks. I mean it. I really appreciate it." They clucked some more pleasantries, and the lawyer left, and as the woman put on her coat she told the receptionist, "That's one fine man. I'm right happy I heard about you people. When I get home I gonna' tell my sister . . ."

Enter, then, a handsome man in his late thirties, shirt open two buttons down the neck, coat and slacks casual, a small pendant swinging against his chest. Sheldon Miller. My God, I thought, this is the most relaxed lawyer I've ever seen. This guy *likes* what he is doing, and he shows it.

"Personal injury, uh?" Miller said, and he grinned. "Well, you've come to the right place if you want to hear the plaintiffs' side, as opposed to the propagandistic crap the insurance companies put out.

"Man, we're public enemy number one to the medical malpractice insurance people. There are seventeen lawyers in the firm, and I think we're the largest in the country devoted exclusively to personal injury work. We've brought two hundred twenty-five malpractice suits in five years. The next largest has only one hundred ten or one hundred twenty. My partner, Al Lopatin, he sued one hospital fifty times, and it was open only eighteen months.

"This was Fairwood General Hospital, out in suburban Warren County. Fairwood was an American concentration camp with one big difference from the ones in Germany. It existed not to exterminate people, but to drain them of money. This stuff I'm going to tell you all comes out of the depositions and sworn court testimony, and you can go down to the file room when we've finished talking and check what I said.*

"What happened the very first day Fairwood opened epitomizes its entire operation. There was a snowstorm, and people stranded in cars near Fairwood sought shelter there. The owner and founder—a doctor, mind you—greeted them at the door with a stethoscope and put many of them to bed. Next thing, he was billing Blue Cross for case after case of 'treatment of possible coronary.' "

Miller talked at length of cases of unnecessary surgery; of "exploratory surgery" where the physician didn't even bother to take a biopsy; of the teenaged girl who unnecessarily lost an ovary; of the real estate agent, friend of the owner, who walked around in a white coat and was regularly paged as "Dr. ———."

"So how did it all bust open? We did it. A woman came to my partner, Al Lopatin, with a story we found hard to believe.

"Her husband entered Fairwood for a routine physical and first thing they knew he was hustled off for gallbladder surgery. Fourteen days later he was dead. The woman insisted nothing had been wrong with him. Lopatin is a good listener, and he's wise about doctors, and he thought she was a nut. But he took the case on a fifty percent contingency basis and did some investigating.

"Sure enough, the lab report showed the gallbladder had been perfectly normal, and nothing in the records supported the deci-

*I did. Shel Miller has a memory of uncanny accuracy. However, seldom does a lawyer encounter an institution as bizarre as Fairwood General.

sion to go into it. About the same time our investigator made a real find. He turned up a former nurse who kept a daily record of events, with the intention of writing a book. She had moved to California, but he found her, and what a story!

"She had been tending this patient, and one afternoon he became ashen, his pulse dropped, and his abdomen distended—classic signs of hemorrhaging. The doctor said he 'couldn't be bothered' and sent her to another doctor. This guy 'wanted to know when nurses became diagnosticians' and said 'nothing was wrong with the man.' The director of nursing told the woman to 'go and mind her own business.' She went off duty at three P.M. The man died at five P.M.

"Al tried the case, non-jury, and got a $230,000 verdict, largest ever for medical malpractice in Michigan at the time. (He cut the fee; the fifty percent was too much when you get an award like that.) At any rate, other hospital cases began coming out of the woodwork, and as I say, we ultimately sued this one hospital fifty times.

"What burns the hell out of me is that malpractice suits put this guy out of business, not the medical society. Doctors didn't blow the whistle—lawyers did, with malpractice suits.*

"Our firm is weird in the sense that we handle all types of cases. Most are the small injury cases such as whiplash that these so-called prestigious firms won't take. Lopatin's philosophy is that every one deserves a lawyer, and that you can make a good living through volume. Once the word gets around to the public that you are a hard worker, and you get results, the big cases come.

"There's another important factor, too—guts. You've got to develop a feel for how far you can carry a case to get the most for your client without blowing it." And Shel Miller told me a story.

In a rural area of Michigan, a truck carrying tons of slag ran a stop sign and crashed into a pickup truck, killing all four teen-aged boys riding in it. Miller represented families of two of the victims.

*The prosecutor's office finally forced Fairwood General Hospital to close in the late 1960s after an investigation disclosed that thirteen doctors and nurses worked there without licenses. Dr. Sanford Stone, the founder, now deceased, pleaded guilty in 1967 to criminal charges of professional misconduct. By one accounting his insurance carriers paid more than $3 million in malpractice claims.

Investigating, he found the truck had been coming up a steep incline from a gravel pit, on a road so constructed that a vehicle had to make a sharp left turn to get over the final rise. One driver said that a truck that came to a complete stop would have to go through fourteen changes of gears to regain full speed. So the regular practice was to ignore the stop sign and hope that no one was coming.

"Michigan law is disgraceful when it pertains to the death of a child," Miller said. "You could recover only 'pecuniary loss'—that is, what a child might eventually pay for the support of his parents, and nothing more. If you're going to have a fatal accident in Michigan, kill a kid; they're less expensive."

Miller first asked $150,000 to settle; the insurance carrier for the trucking company offered $35,000. Judge J. Victor Baun, the state court jurist assigned to the case, after a conference of opposing lawyers said he felt they should settle for $80,000.

"I'll turn in my law license before I settle for $80,000," Miller told the judge. "The judge kept asking me, 'What will you really take?' Hell, the insurance company wasn't even willing to pay the eighty, and he was pushing me on it. He finally accused me of going into cahoots with the two other defendants—the gravel pit and the insurance carrier for the teenagers' pickup truck—so that we could get the $1 million insurance carried by the gravel truck. In fact, that was 'deep pocket money.'"* Judge Baun, angered, even ordered an investigation of Miller, which got nowhere at all. "I told Baun later, 'My office won't appear in your court again. Good-bye, Judge.'"

The case eventually went to trial before another judge, and after five days of testimony the insurance carrier offered Miller $100,000. "The mother said, 'Take it.' I said, 'No.' I had a feeling things were going our way; it's one of those things you can't pinpoint, but you just *sense.*

"When testimony ended, the offer jumped to $157,000, and now both parents wanted to accept. I still said no. 'What *will* you take?' the insurance lawyers asked. I would just shake my head and walk away.

"Now let me tell you what the insurance company didn't

*In the jargon of personal injury lawyers, a "deep pocket" defendant is what the name implies: a defendant who is able, either through assets or insurance, to pay a multidigit settlement.

know. I was almost physically ill from tension. My stomach wouldn't calm down, I had diarrhea, I had trouble sleeping. Was I doing the right thing? Who can predict a jury? Suppose there is one screwball? Man, when you stick your neck out and reject a substantial offer for two kids' instantaneous death in an accident you best be careful."

The jury broke the tension a day later. It returned a verdict of $750,000, highest ever in such a case in Michigan. Including interest, the final payment was more than $1.1 million, of which the family received $700,000 plus.

"That," Shel Miller said, "is what makes PI [personal injury] law interesting."

By happenstance, the next morning I encountered two of Miller's partners, Al Lopatin and Harry Okren, in a corridor of the City-County Building, which houses the Detroit courts. We stopped to chat a moment. "We're ready to pick a jury in a rather interesting case," Lopatin told me. "A tunnel exploded under the Detroit River during construction and killed twenty-three people and injured a bunch more. We've already won a $4.8 million verdict in the death cases, and now we're going to trial on the injured. This would be a good one for you to watch."

"I'm sorry, but I have appointments in Buffalo tomorrow, and I can't break them."

"I'll keep you posted," Lopatin said. "Come see us again sometime."

A few hours later I was in the London Chop House in downtown Detroit with Shel Miller and one of his associates, Victoria Heldman, when Lopatin and Okren walked in. Lopatin's normal expression is neutral, even a bit on the dour side, but there seemed to be a bounce to his walk. Behind the two partners trailed a gloomy phalanx of men carrying heavy briefcases, six or eight of them.

Lopatin slapped Miller on the shoulder and winked at me and walked on. Okren lingered to give the news. "They bailed out," he said. "Two point three million dollars, right before we seated the jury. So, what the hell. We decided to buy lunch for the insurance lawyers."

Shel Miller clapped his hands above his head. "Whoopee!" he

exclaimed. "Well, Harry, we made expenses today." He beckoned to a waiter and ordered Grand Marnier.

I glanced over at the insurance lawyers sitting with Lopatin. Their drinks looked large. And strong. And they were not smiling.

Let me admit it. I am a lawyer freak. I find the breed universally fascinating, even if not consistently admirable. They are entertaining raconteurs, and I enjoy listening to them even when the story involves outrageous legal gamesmanship. They can switch from pomposity to gentle self-depreciation in the course of a sentence. They can gloat over triumph, and they can also tell, with the same outward glee, how an opposing lawyer thumped them in court. I enjoy sitting in a cubicle in a federal building in Washington and listening to an earnest government lawyer, perhaps two years distant from Duke Law School, describe taking a deposition from a corporate pooh-bah. I have looked out over the astounding number of lights in downtown Topeka, Kansas, at four in the morning from the twelfth floor office of a lawyer in his eighties as he described some complex oil patch litigation of the 1930s; despite the hour, I did not yawn. I have visited offices in New York that should be condemned by the health or safety authorities; I have also wondered how the people at Cravath, Swaine & Moore manage to come up with the wintertime fresh flowers on the polished wooden coffee table in its 57th floor reception area at One Chase Manhattan Plaza in Wall Street.* I am likewise impressed with the partners' luncheon of the four-man firm of McLin, Burnsed, Austin & Cyrus, in Leesburg, Florida (population 12,000)—a table in the back room of a roadhouse restaurant on the outskirts of town, with hamburgers, cold beer and conversation.

Lawyers can be bastards to their subordinates, and especially secretaries; what woman cares to be treated with the same impersonal coldness which one would direct to an IBM typewriter

*Other Cravath, Swaine & Moore amenities must be noted. Someone comes around during the day and sharpens everyone's pencils. A shoeshine man visits the office several times daily; he services lawyers while they are in conference, on the telephone, doing dictation. Luncheon interviews are conducted not over brown-bag sandwiches, but in the Wall Street Club upstairs, with double-digit entrees and a view of New York harbor.

or a file cabinet? But at their best, lawyers can massage the sensitivities of aggrieved clients to an extent far beyond the call of professional duty. Here is an example of what I mean:

I spent five days in Dallas in the autumn of 1975 with Phil Burleson, an old friend who worked days and attended school nights to obtain his law degree, and who, now, in his early forties, is earning a six-figure annual income. Burleson is a good criminal appeals man. It was his brief that persuaded the Texas Court of Criminal Appeals to reverse the death-sentence conviction of Jack Ruby, the killer of presidential assassin Lee Harvey Oswald. Criminal lawyers put Burleson on their team in major trials (i.e., when the client has money) so that he can shape the case for appeal while it is in progress. When I visited him, Burleson's four-man firm also was building a business clientele. But at the outset of my visit he related embarrassing news.

"You asked to spend time with me to see how a medium-sized city firm looks in operation," he said. "Well, this week isn't going to be typical by any means, and I almost called and asked you to give me a rain check.

"This is the situation. An associate who is no longer with me took on a case where a fella' had two guys fix up his car for him. They all work out at a truck terminal. My man wasn't satisfied with the work, so he refused to pay. So we're going to trial in county court Tuesday morning."

How much was involved? I asked.

Burleson shook his head with true chagrin. "A real big one," he said, "$450."

Jesus, can't you settle?

"No. My man is mad, he wants his day in court. So do the other people. They won't take a cent less than they claim they are owed. This is what you could call a grudge suit."

So the next morning I sat with Burleson in an anteroom off the court while he reviewed the case with the client, a stocky man in his twenties. There wasn't much to talk about, for it was soon obvious the man had no grounds for refusing to pay for the repairs. Burleson talked earnestly, pleadingly, desperately. But the man refused to settle, either for all or any fraction of the disputed sum.

Judge Robert E. Day frowned when Burleson said his client insisted on trial. "Hell, Phil, why don't you pay the $450 out of your own pocket? You're going to lose that much time out of your practice."

"Don't think I wouldn't like to do just that," Burleson said. "Anyway, let's pick a jury."

They did, and the trial dragged over two days, surely one of the duller proceedings ever conducted in any court. I took notes periodically to keep myself awake. Suffice to say that when the testimony ended, the jury barely had time to close the door of their room before they reached a verdict: Burleson's client had to pay the full amount.

The guy still didn't look satisfied. "I still think I'm right," he said, "but that jury thing, that's final, isn't it?"

"Yeah," Burleson said. "Unless you want to appeal to district court." (He immediately looked as if he wished he could bite his tongue for making a suggestion that could prolong a lost cause even further.)

The guy shook his head. "Nah," he said, "I don't think I could take off any more time from work." He paused. "Hey, how much do I owe you anyway?"

"Well, as I told you, my fee during trial is $100 an hour, and you could add it up as easily as I could."

"Man, I don't have that kind of money." The man's face registered the first spread of an expression of acute alarm; his mouth tightened, and his eyes blinked and darted sidewards, as if he were announcing to himself, "What I done got myself into?"

Burleson let him squirm a minute. "'Course, now, I realize you probably don't have that kind of money . . ." Repeated bobs of the head, the face saying, "You so right." Burleson continuing, "so I tell you what you do. See what you can scrape up, and call me tomorrow, maybe the next day. You come up with a couple of hundred, I think we can settle okay."

They agreed, and Burleson and I walked down the hall toward the elevator.

"Hey." We stopped. "Mr. Burleson, I just want to say thanks for getting me my day in court." Burleson waved his hand in mock salute, and we strolled on.

My day in court. In essence, Americans expect nothing more from their legal system and the men who run it—that is to say, the lawyers. When an affair arises that requires the intervention of an attorney, the citizen deserves someone to represent him who is competent, who gives his case serious attention and who is tolerably observant of the bounds of decency and common sense. He is entitled to expect the same of the courts, if indeed his case goes there, and of the attorney for the opposing party.

In their lodge meetings and trade journals, attorneys talk about the law as the glue that holds civilization together. So how well are these fellows doing their work? What can the citizen expect of them when his car is smashed by a falling tree or he gets into a business dispute? Does he, in fact, receive his "day in court"?

As was the case with my earlier books on the legal profession,* *The Million Dollar Lawyers* benefited from innumerable hours of interviews with lawyers and their clients, happy ones and angry ones, throughout the United States. Fortunately, bar associations are beginning to relax the somewhat silly rule against lawyer "self-publicity" which in some areas was so strictly enforced that an attorney could say nothing more than good morning to a journalist without risk of professional censure or worse. An hour deep into one interview a lawyer in the Southwest broke me off and said, "I'm not sure I should be talking to you about my practice." He telephoned the executive director of his state bar, and together we explained my project. The director responded, "Go ahead and talk with him. You might get a reprimand, but the publicity will probably be worth it." However other lawyers (and bar officials) remain chary of the publicity rule; hence some of my interviews had to be on a no-attribution basis. In some instances I disguised specific details of particular cases still in progress so as to avoid my lawyer sources' being cashiered from their profession. A more formal recitation of sources is in the chapter notes.

Rileyville and Arlington, Virginia
April 1976–February 1978

***The Superlawyers* (1972) and *The Benchwarmers* (1974), both published by Weybright & Talley, New York.

Chapter One

The Bombers

I did not like the neighborhood, a shabby commercial side street just off the Loop in downtown Chicago. A saloon with an "early bird special" whitewashed on the window—a shot and a beer for 79¢. A porn shop. A cut-rate jewelry store (TRANSISTOR RADIOES $3.99 THIS WEEK ONLEY). [sic] A dank restaurant featuring fried chicken wings and bean soup. I found the address and stepped around two drunks arguing in the doorway and walked up the stairs.

I did not like the office. Frosted glass, the lawyer's name in flaking black paint, one letter scratched off but still distinguishable. Dust balls outside the adjacent office, a "collection referral service."

I did not like the secretary. A brittle blond in her late twenties, fuzzy aqua sweater and knit white skirt. She was on the phone, and she slipped her hand over the mouthpiece and said, "With you in just a minute, hon," and resumed the conversation, which had to do with someone named Deborah and Chuck, and wasn't it just awful, and Thursday night would be fine, but Friday would be just as good and yes, she had heard about Freddy and wasn't it just awful . . . I sat down and began reading a two-day-old *Chicago Tribune*, and the secretary smiled at me again and did the hand-mouthpiece thing and said, "Just a few more seconds, hon," and I read the first section and the sports pages and part of the financial section.

I did not like the lawyer. He arrived about fifteen minutes after I did, a short, balding fellow in his late forties, two manila file folders and a bulky envelope tucked under his arm. He smiled. I saw dirty teeth and a patch of whiskers on his lip that had escaped the razor, one, two, maybe more mornings. He looked down at his secretary, who was saying into the phone, "Gotta' run now, baby, so . . ."

"Hang the fucking thing up," the lawyer said.

"See you later, baby . . ."

"NOW, GODDAMNIT! NOW!"

She did. A thirtyish brunette had followed the lawyer in the door, and she halted at the sound of the shouts, as if uncertain as to whether she wanted to walk any further. The lawyer turned to me. "You must be Mr. Closkey. I'm going to have to have you wait a moment, because I'm running late, but I'll get you squared away. She can't get away with that."

"No, I am not Closkey, I am Goulden, the writer from Washington who spoke with you on the phone earlier and . . ."

"Oh, yeah, yeah, I remember now. You're writing about the superlawyers practicing outside of Washington. Well, you've sure come to the right place, because we do some super things around here. Don't we, Rose?" The last, to the secretary, who was handing him a sheaf of phone message slips

"No, this isn't exactly a book on superlawyers, but more a book on how . . ."

"I don't care, call it what you want, I don't mind the publicity. In fact, I want the publicity. Come on in and watch how I work. This here is Mrs. Smith,* and she won't mind talking in front of you, will you Mrs. Smith?"

He did not wait for an answer. He walked into the inner office. "Rose, get us some ice. If that guy Closkey comes in, tell him I'm going to be busy for a while, that I have a very important person here from Washington for a conference. He's going to have to wait. He will. He's in a jam." Mrs. Smith followed us, hesitantly.

A cluttered desk. An overstuffed chair. Two straight chairs. A leather couch with a red pillow and a fuzzy aqua blanket—the same hue as Rose's fuzzy sweater. A plethora of framed certificates and diplomas, whatever collective prestige they might sig-

*For reasons that should be becoming obvious, real names are not used in this section.

nify obscured by dust. A Rabelaisian print of a seventeenth-century lawyer with a counseling arm around a woman's waist.

"Stella here has a problem," the lawyer began, jerking his head toward Mrs. Smith. "She's married to this jerk who drinks and beats hell out of her and screws around, and we're getting ready to cream his ass, aren't we, Stella?" She started to say something but the lawyer did not pause. "She gave me the basic story when we met last week and what we're going to do today is nail down some of the particulars. Did you get the letters, Stella?"

Mrs. Smith had been watching me, and she was uncomfortable. "Some of this is pretty personal, Mr. ———, and I wonder if . . ." I arose, but the lawyer waved his hand for me to sit down. "Mr. Goulden isn't using any names, and he's a professional, too, and you can talk in front of him, Stella, just like he was another lawyer."

Mrs. Smith didn't look happy, but she said, "Okay, it's okay with me, I guess." I did not like myself for doing so, but I sat back down. She handed some papers with handwriting across the desk, and the lawyer began reading them.

"Your sister writes here she's heard him use abusive language towards you. The judge is going to want to know specifically. What does he call you, Stella?"

She glanced at me, and I would not make eye contact. "He calls me a 'worthless cunt' and a 'stinking asshole' and stuff like that. He does this even in front of my mother. She says if my father was alive, he'd kill him."

"Take this back to your sister. Have her write it down, and use the words. Okay?"

"I don't think she will. She don't like the words."

"She want to help you get away from this jerk? You tell her to do as I say."

The lawyer was at the next letter. "Your friend Shirley, she was around when he was bragging about this other woman. Again, Stella, you get this damned language here that doesn't really say anything. *What* did he say? What words did he use?"

Enter Rose, welcome relief both to me and Mrs. Smith. Three glasses and a plastic container of ice. The lawyer looking into a desk drawer, emerging with a fifth of Four Roses. Glug glug glug. "Rose, get us a little water, this stuff needs it." She did, and she also carried a fourth glass, into which she poured a glug of her own. The lawyer glared at her. "Oh, shit," she said, "come off it, it's four-thirty and I've worked my ass off today. I'm not going to get drunk and run off with a typewriter." The lawyer said nothing, and she snatched up the glass, and she banged the door when she left.

The whiskey was awful, but we sipped it, and I even did a semblance of a toast to Stella Smith. "To a happier future," I said, and she looked puzzled, and then she smiled.

The lawyer again. "Stella, exactly what did he say that your sister heard?"

"Is this something I'm going to have to say in court, too?"

"Yes, you are. Now do you want a divorce, or do you want to stay with this guy? I am your lawyer, Stella, and I'm doing my goddamnest to get you out of this marriage, which is what you said you wanted to do. Now what did he say to your sister that is proof he was playing around?"

"Well, it was a Saturday afternoon, and he had been drinking beer since that morning, when he worked on the car outside the house. He was high, and he was mean, like, he was saying bad things to me all day long. He hadn't come in until late the night before, real late, like after midnight, and when I asked about the bowling league he said, 'Yeah, I bowled all right, and it was damned good bowling, too.'

"When Shirley came over he got even nastier, because he doesn't like her. She's good, but she's fat, and she ain't so pretty, and he's always saying I 'run around with dogs like her.' But she is my best friend.

"Anyway, what happened was this. Shirley and I was in the kitchen drinking coffee when he come in and popped another can of beer. I said something like, 'Remember, we're going to Momma's for dinner tonight.' I didn't want him to get bombed, but he don't like me to gripe about him drinking.

"He started cussing me. He called me 'bitch' and 'cunt' and all kinds of nasty names, and finally Shirley, she spoke up and said, 'Oh, leave her alone, Harry, she's done a lot for you.'

"This just got him madder. 'Done a lot for me, shit,' he said. 'I got better pussy last night the first time out with this girl than I got from this dead head the whole nine years we're married.'

"What he said didn't soak in right away, but Shirley started crying and shouting and saying, 'It's bad enough you screw around, you bastard, but do you have to brag about it right in front of her?' "

Mrs. Smith was beginning to cry now, and her shoulders shook as she tried to suppress the sobs. All I could think to do was hand her her glass. She shoved it back. The lawyer sat impassively. He has seen too many clients cry to waste empathy on yet another anguished woman. Mrs. Smith finally continued.

"He laughed. He said, 'What's the fun of getting good ass if nobody knows about it? This gal last night wasn't the first, and she damned well won't be the last, and if you two bitches don't get off my back, I'll bring her over here right now and hump her in the living room.'

"Shirley and I left then. I got a small suitcase and a few things and spent the night at her house, and Sunday night too. He didn't call or nothing, and when I went home Monday, after time for him to go to work, all his clothes and stuff was gone. I tried to talk to him on the phone once later, to get some money, and he just cussed me and hung up."

The lawyer: "Shirley can tell about all this?"

Mrs. Smith: "She don't like coming to court, but she said she'd do whatever necessary to help me get away from him."

The lawyer: "How much screwing around did you do yourself before all this happened?"

Mrs. Smith, puzzled: "What do you mean?"

The lawyer: "You know what I mean. How many guys did you ball yourself after you married Harry?"

Mrs. Smith, stunned: "Now, listen, no way. I'm *not* that kind of woman, and I *never* have been. *He* was the one who . . ."

The lawyer, smiling: "Okay, okay, don't get excited. I wanted to be sure that you had clean skirts before we charged him with adultery. Otherwise, he comes back with a story of his own and we get zapped. Follow?"

Mrs. Smith, still ruffled: "I suppose so, but you sure shook me."

They talked about the technicalities of how to end the marriage: Mrs. Smith would get her sister and her friend to rewrite the statements. The lawyer would file petitions for divorce and ask for temporary support in the interim. "His take-home pay is $168 weekly? We'll go for half of it. We won't get that much, you being healthy and childless and still young enough to work, but we'll shake him around a little bit anyway."

"I don't want his damned money. I just want to get rid of him."

"You let me worry about the strategy, honey," the lawyer said. "Asking for money is a bargaining chip. You always ask for things you know you can't get, just so you'll have some throwaways. He'll be so relieved when we hold off on the money demand that he won't give you any trouble on the divorce itself. Okay?"

Mrs. Smith nodded. "If you say so."

"That pretty well wraps it up except for one thing. You paid me $100 last week, and I told you I thought I could handle everything for $550 or $575, plus maybe $200 for the court costs. How much more do you have?"

"Right now, not much. He left me with the bills, and the rent was due two days later, and you know I don't make much money at the restaurant."

"Hey, let's don't spend time on the details. You didn't answer my question. How much more money do you have? Now? Today? In this room?"

"Well, certainly not $450 or $500. What I'm carrying today, I need to get through until Friday, when I get paid."

"Forget that. When are you going to have my $500? Would your mother come up with it for you?"

"She might, but she wouldn't like it. You know, she don't have so much herself, just the pension and her little sick fund at the credit union, what she's saving for an emergency."

Deep, dark frown. "Damn, woman, this *is* an emergency. You want to get away from this bastard, and I run a law office, not a legal aid society. I pay my rent and groceries, too, and all I got to sell is lawyering. We've been in here almost an hour, and that's valuable time. A lawyer could charge you seventy-five, a hundred, even a hundred and a quarter dollars for an hour of time. Mr. Goulden here, he's an expert on lawyers, he knows what you pay them. Isn't that right, Mr. Goulden, I could be charging this lady one hundred and twenty-five dollars for this consultation?"

Impulse: Lady, get the hell away from this jerk. He is a crude, vulgar money-grubber, and he violates your very dignity each time he opens his mouth.

I put down the impulse. I am an observer of lawyers, not a monitor of lawyers, and I had stated my intention in advance: to watch how this attorney went about his business. I turned to Mrs. Smith: "Yes, *some* lawyers *could* charge $125 for what you are receiving here today." I don't think she understood the stressed words.

"I'll talk to my mother and my brother; we'll come up with it, somewhere."

"You ever do any go-go dancing?"

"What?"

"Go-go. You know, topless."

"Me? What gives you an idea like that?"

"You're built enough for it. Listen, this guy I do some investments with, he puts girls into places up in Old Town,* sort of like a booking agent. He's always looking for new talent, and you could make, two, maybe three times as much a week doing that as you can waiting tables." He stopped and his eyes dropped from Mrs. Smith's face to her bust, and then came up again.

"The work isn't bad. Shake and bounce a bit to the music. Who knows, you might even make some extra money. Get me paid off in two or three weeks, without having to bother your mother. Let me get this guy on the phone right now . . ."

Mrs. Smith interrupted him. "No," she said, "that won't be necessary. I'll find your damned fee, and I'll have it here by Friday." She was putting papers back into her purse, and she was working her jaw in a way that hinted she wanted to say something about this man's "lawyering" but was ready to swallow perhaps one more potion of bile if necessary to get her divorce.

"I'll be in court most of the day, Friday, so just leave those revised statements with Rose—and the money. Okay?"

"Yes, I understand."

The lawyer rose, but he did not escort Mrs. Smith to the door. She simply turned and left without a further word to either of us.

"Cold-headed cunt, that one is," the lawyer said. "About as

*A nightclub section north of downtown Chicago.

much personality as a goddamned dead fish. I don't blame old Harry for hustling outside pussy. Man, this is one I'll handle with relish, because *nobody* should be married to a woman that stiff."

We talked about my book, and I explained that I was interested in the nuts and bolts of a big-city divorce practice, the realities, as opposed to what is taught in law schools and discussed in the legal journals.

"Man, you've come to the right place, because I'm a realistic son of a bitch," the lawyer said. Using his hand he fished out new ice cubes for our drinks and poured more Four Roses. "I've been divorced three times myself, and I'm coming up on number four. So I'm not sentimental about the institution of marriage. When two people want out of it, I'm happy to help them get the best deal possible.

"Further, it's my living. I'm a lawyer, not a social worker. When an adult asks me to perform a piece of work for him, and agrees to pay me in U.S. currency, we have a deal. I tell the party what's required for him or her to get out of a marriage, and what kind of settlement we can get away with.

"That dame who just left is typical of the stuff I do—a dumb-ass Polack who is essentially a dumb person, and who marries a jerk who loses interest in her once he's banged her a few times. Both of them made a bad deal—she, probably the worst deal, because now she's seven years older, and that many more miles down the track.

"She thought I was insulting her, asking if she'd like to dance go-go. Best thing in the world that could happen to her—get out and loosen up a little bit, make some money and find a boy friend who would give her some fun. Sure, I have a selfish motive. I want to make sure she comes up with my fees, and that's a way she can do it in a hurry.

"I'll tell you something else you can put in your book, but don't use my name or the city, because I don't want any crap with the bar association. You know ———, the singer?"

By name, I certainly did, for she gets into the papers, and onto the TV and movie screens.

"Twelve, fifteen years ago, when she was a nobody, she married a jerk musician who played at a club on North Clark Street.

Man, she was *nothing*—playing with dope, doing real crap engagements, really, a tramp.

"Anyway, she finally had it up to here with this musician, because he was pissing away what little money she made, and beating up on her besides. At the time, I did labor negotiation work for some of the clubs, and she got my name and asked me to handle her divorce.

"Sure, no problem, the musician didn't give a rat's ass about staying married, so it would go through like cream. Only thing is, this chick ——— didn't have more than a few hundred dollars saved, and she wanted to use it to get out of town, get out to Vegas and try some of the clubs there.

"So she asked me, real sweet like, was there any way she could handle the fee without spending any of her money. I said, 'Sure, baby, you come up to Wisconsin with me for a weekend, we stay at this lodge I know, and you can forget about the fee.'

"Oh, she bargained. She would give me a night at her place, or a night at mine, but I didn't budge. The upshot was that we went to Wisconsin, and I had a helluva' time with her, and she relaxed and enjoyed it too."

The lawyer paused and tilted his head so he was staring at the ceiling, and I knew he was deciding whether to share yet another part of the memory with me. He was, and he did.

"In fact, it was so fun that I halfway got the idea she'd do it again, even after she got to be a name. She was here four or five years later, playing one of the hotels, and I called and got a secretary, some dame who travels with her. She took a message, and I didn't hear nothing for two days, so I called back. The secretary assured me she had given ——— the message, and I said, 'Remind her who I am, that I handled her divorce here a few years back.' And the secretary says, 'Oh, she remembers you all right, and to save you some time, I wouldn't bother calling her again.' "

A tight, sour laugh. "I don't care. Everytime I see her on TV, I say to myself, 'Man, I've had that, in every way a man can.' "

I had heard sotto voce comments about "couch fees" from other lawyers (and not all of them divorce specialists, either), but this Chicagoan was the first to boast about taking sex from a client in lieu of money. "How often does this happen?" I asked.

Refills from the bottle of Four Roses. The secretary in with three letters for the lawyer to sign; as he did so she went to the outer office, returned with her glass and filled it again. He scowled and she stuck out her tongue at him. "Wise ass," he said. "A hell of a lot smarter than yours," she replied, and left.

"That's one right there," the lawyer said after the door closed.

I am not a fast thinker. "One what?"

"A couch fee. That's how we got started. She couldn't pay, so I took it out in ass, and I liked her so much I put her in the office. She had been working at some real estate firm out on the west side, and she's a good secretary, and we understand one another. She gets more money than she would as a straight secretary, and we spend one, maybe two evenings a week together.

"Plus, of course, whatever we manage to squeeze in here at the office on slow afternoons when nobody's around."

We talked perhaps half an hour more, chiefly on how the lawyer coaches clients to give the right answers in court to win a divorce on grounds of threats of physical violence by their spouses. I had heard the same scripts, in variant form, so many times that I became bored, and I made an excuse to say I had to get back to my hotel.

"Where you staying?"

I named a small commercial hotel off the Loop, cheap and obscure, but clean and close to the downtown law offices. The lawyer wrinkled his nose. "Yeah, I know it. What you got on tonight?"

I did not want to have dinner with this man, and I mumbled something about making some phone calls, and typing notes, and maybe arranging an interview with another lawyer. He broke in. "Let that stuff go. You need some relaxation. Here it is after six o'clock and you're still working.

"Tell you what. You saw Rose. She has a smart mouth, but she's one hell of a woman. What say I fix you two up for the night? You'd have some fun, and you wouldn't have to stay in that kind of hotel tonight." He paused and attempted an apparent lascivious smile. "You won't get any notes typed, though, because Rosie will f—— your brains out, that's for sure."

"What would Rose think about such an arrangment? After all,

she is an adult, and obviously a woman with a mind of her own."

"Rose does what I say Rose does," the lawyer said. "She gets extra because she does extra. Let me call her; I'll show you."

I stopped him with a wave of my hand. "I think you are a slimy bastard," I said, "and the sooner I get away from you and your schlock operation, the happier I'll be."

The lawyer was standing, spluttering. "You can't talk to me like that. Who the hell . . ."

"I *did* talk to you like that. So long."

When I walked through the outer office Rose said, "You must be hard up for material if you have to write about guys like that."

I smiled and nodded as I left, and as I walked down the dark stairs to the street I thought, *Oh, Rose, I don't know, jerks are more interesting when they are self-revelatory.*

Let's be blunt about it. Few citizens who have professional contacts with divorce lawyers think kindly, or highly, of them. One reason, of course, is that the subject of discussion—dissolution of a marriage—is not as happy an occasion as, say, a merger of two corporations or the purchase of a new home. But divorce lawyers bring much of the general opprobrium upon themselves. "Divorce is to the practice of law as proctology is to medicine," scoffs Michael Wheeler, a professor at the New England School of Law in Boston who has done extensive work in the field.[1] Judge Paul Alexander of Toledo, Ohio, who has heard thousands of divorce cases during three decades on the bench, feels that divorce lawyers are produced by a sort of reverse Darwinism—a "survival of the unfittest" that is responsible for the "greed and corruption" he sees in divorce practice. Indeed, Judge Alexander accuses lawyers of pushing people into divorces that were "unwanted, unnecessary and undesirable." The lawyers' motive is economic greed:

> . . . divorce is their rent, their stenographer's salary, their baby's shoes, sometimes their solid gold Cadillac. The simplest uncontested case is generally worth a couple of hundred dollars; a case involving even a moderately well-to-do husband accused (not necessarily guilty) of infidelity is ordinarily worth a few thou-

sand to the lawyers. How unrealistic to expect them to forgo anything like that for mere considerations of ethics or morals.[2]

"Family law" is a backwater of the legal profession. Robert Drinan, of Boston, who edited the *Family Law Quarterly* before his election to Congress, recognized the low status of his specialty when he wrote:

> The fact is that the American bench and bar have never really been interested in the law of domestic relations. Lawyers have tended to avoid divorce cases and have allowed a "divorce bar" to grow up in each metropolitan area. Similarly judges, at least until very recently, have acquiesced in the fact that the divorce court enjoys the least prestige of all the courts.[3]

"There is no doubt that when a couple sees red, lawyers see green," wrote Rose DeWolf, a Philadelphia *Bulletin* columnist whose book on divorce grew from the fire and brimstone her husband endured in coming out of a bad first marriage.[4] Divorce is a jolting experience, even when love has long since left a marriage. And a lawyer with his eye on a higher fee need only give an angry client a nudge to tilt him out of control. Consider:

—Norman D., a political scientist for a think tank in the Washington area, left home one night after a series of arguments convinced him his marriage was at an end. "I was mad, but I wasn't vindictive. Mary and I had discussed separation earlier, and we agreed we wouldn't screw one another, that we would make a civilized settlement. The first thing my lawyer said was, 'Get down to the bank and clean out your account. Also the credit union and the stocks.' I told him that wasn't fair, because she needed money for living expenses. 'It's your loss, for she'll do it,' he said. I didn't believe him. Well, she did, and I didn't know about it until I had four checks bounce in one day. When I called her to raise hell she said, 'My lawyer told me to grab the money before you did.' The net result was to make us distrustful of one another, and I'm sure the bad feelings dragged out our settlement negotiations by many, many hours. We paid $45 an hour."

—Helen P., a Dallas area college professor, felt she was heading for an amicable settlement with an adulterous, drunken husband when he suddenly tried to impose a limitation on the fees he had agreed to pay her lawyer.* "He talked to lawyer friends, and they told him $300 and court costs were enough for an uncontested separation. I had already agreed to pay the lawyer $375. My lawyer became furious, and before I knew it he had persuaded me to forget the separation and file formal divorce papers. I had a tailor-made case for adultery, for my husband had been rather open with a woman around people who knew me. Right away this doubled the fee. But the lawyer didn't stop there. He had my husband—and *his* lawyer—running to court almost every week to answer some kind of motion. In the end, my husband paid more than $2,000 and he hated me for every penny of it. I admit I went along with my lawyer. But I'm ashamed of myself now. The last time we left court my lawyer said, 'That cheap so-and-so, he'll never quibble about $75 again.' "

—Debbie B., secretary in a Manhattan publishing house, was ready to split from her husband, who, although Protestant, held a high position with a Catholic organization. "My lawyer's eyes literally lit up when I told him where ——— worked. We hadn't been getting anywhere in negotiations for a settlement. The lawyer said, 'Call him right now and tell him that you intend to file for divorce, on grounds of adultery, and that a deputy sheriff will serve the papers on him this week at his office.' I protested. I said, 'That will cause ——— all sorts of embarrassment, and maybe even cost him his job.' The lawyer said, 'We won't have to go through with it; the threat will knock him off dead center.' Well, I wouldn't do it. I thought it was dirty. I got another lawyer."

Bar ethical canons essentially put the burden of what's right and what's wrong on the conscience of the divorce lawyer. The American Bar Association's Code of Professional Responsibility binds a lawyer to "represent his client zealously within the

*A brief digression: Many states require as a matter of law that the husband pay the legal bills. There are interesting local variations. In Arizona for instance, a divorce isn't final until the lawyer files routine papers with the clerk, the judge's "order" notwithstanding. Lawyers won't file these papers until they are paid. According to Michael Wheeler in *No Fault Divorce*, one lawyer, a man named V. L. Hask, had scores of unfiled decrees in his files when he died in 1972, some dating back almost half a century. At least one client had unwittingly committed bigamy three times in the belief that Hask had gotten "final" divorces for him.[5]

bounds of the law." Later, there is a cautionary note: "The duty of a lawyer to represent his client with zeal does not militate against his concurrent obligation to treat with consideration all persons involved in the legal process and to avoid the infliction of needless harm."[6] Given such contradictory admonitions, the best—which is to say, the toughest and most successful—divorce lawyers go for the jugular, and without apology or hesitation. Raoul Lionel Felder, a Manhattan divorce attorney, wrote in his definitive book *Divorce*,[7] "If it comes to a fight, it is the lawyer's function, using all ethical, legal and moral means, to bring his adversary to his knees as fast as possible. Naturally, within this framework the lawyer must go for the 'soft spots.'" Herbert A. Glieberman, of Chicago, a leader of the American Academy of Matrimonial Lawyers, extends the hardboiled attitude even to opposing lawyers on occasion, if their behavior does not meet his expectations:

> It has been wisely stated that ignorance breeds arrogance. Often when you encounter an arrogant opponent you must deal with him accordingly. If your opponent does not cooperate in trying to solve the problems which are troubling both of your clients, you have no alternative but to utilize every legal device necessary to bring him to his knees. Do not hesitate to bring a motion to dismiss or to strike, to use extensively all discovery and deposition procedures and motions, and petitions as applicable to win victory for your client and to help educate your arrogant opponent as to the fact that his arrogance has been costly to himself as well as to his client. . . .[8]

States a Dallas lawyer who earns perhaps half his income from divorce cases: "This is a rough field because you are dealing mainly with nutty people. Divorce is inherently acrimonious, and people who have fought and hated one another for years see the proceeding as their 'last chance to take a shot at the SOB.' The wife is grimly determined to clean out the husband, financially, so that the rest of his life will be miserable. The husband is grimly determined not to give a dime to a nagging harridan who has blighted his life. Man, they come in loaded for bear. I've had actual fist fights and slapping matches in this very office during settlement negotiations." Ivan Barris, a former president of the Detroit Bar Association, who does upper-crust divorces in his city, says, "Just give me a good clear-cut murder case any day of the week; emotions never run as high as they do in divorce. This is especially true when you have a woman who is, say, forty-five years old. Her beauty is fading. She knows she is not going to get another man. Her husband is with another gal. They become absolute maniacs. Men can be just as bad. Fighting the divorce case becomes their entire life."

Barris spoke from bitter personal experience, for he spent nine years on a case involving a couple named Rose which he described in a formal brief to the Michigan Supreme Court with these words:

> Historians advise that the First War of the Roses was fought, at least intermittently, over a period of some 30 years (1444–1485). It is but a slight exaggeration to state that if Mr. Rose has his way [in an appeal then before the court] the instant "War of the Roses" will span a period which, relatively speaking, will make the First War of the Roses appear to be only slightly longer than the so-called Six Day War fought in the Middle East in 1967.

The case, as related in court papers, went this way: Jack Rose, son of a wealthy builder and financier, had a personal fortune of some $4 million. His marriage lasted about a year before she started divorce proceedings. Rose resisted, and she failed because of legal deficiencies in her court pleadings. Barris got into the case at this point and tried again. "She would have settled initially for $75,000 to $100,000, reasonable in view of his fortune and the short term of the marriage. But Rose would have none of it."

Barris got a court order requiring Rose to support his estranged wife, and the fighting began in earnest. Rose refused to pay support, and Barris repeatedly had him cited for contempt; several times he was jailed briefly. Rose filed laborious appeals of any order entered against him—more than two dozen, in all—and took them to the Michigan Court of Appeals, the Michigan Supreme Court and the U.S. Supreme Court. "We finally won at trial on the grounds of cruelty, and the judge awarded Mrs. Rose $650,000, plus $85,000 to me for legal fees. Rose went completely out of control. He issued scurrilous diatribes against me and everyone connected with the case," Barris said. In one petition Rose called the judge "an extortionist, a fraud-feasor, a blackmailer and a racketeer . . . merely a grotesque caricature of a judge—a cheap, shabby, corrupt little man who sits in black robes behind a bench."

The courts finally appointed a guardian for the erratic Rose, but he was undeterred. He subpoenaed Supreme Court justices in an attempt to prove bias. He entered law school, flunked out, and kept attending classes anyway until school authorities had him ejected for trespass. He printed announcement cards and hired an office and passed himself off as an attorney.

Months after the final judgment, when Rose had lost his final appeal and paid Mrs. Rose the $650,000, Barris' mail one morning contained an astounding document: an order from the Michigan Court of Appeals overturning every past decision and ruling for Rose on each point he had raised. "I was stunned," Barris said, "because I knew that no appeal was even pending. I hurriedly called the court clerk, who was mystified as well. We did some checking, and sure enough Jack Rose had forged the order. He obtained some papers with the judges' signatures, and masked out the body, and typed in a new decision. That was enough. They put away Jack Rose. The Second War of the Roses finally ended."[9]

Client zaniness is more than many lawyers can endure, and hence they refuse to have anything to do with divorce cases. William Saunders, of Honolulu, a few years back abandoned a thriving divorce practice with the suggestion that any lawyer who spent his time handling such cases was not entirely sane. Saunders listed four reasons:

—Both husband and wife blame the opposing lawyer for the other party's behavior and bad-mouth him to anyone who will listen.

—Both husband and wife blame their own lawyer for their financial plight after divorce. The husband's lawyer "sold me out for a quick settlement." The wife's lawyer "rolled over and played dead for the other side."

—Because of the emotional volatility of divorce, clients call their lawyer at any hour of night or day— often to ask a question he had answered earlier. A stock instruction of divorce lawyers is, "Don't listen to what people tell you at cocktail parties. They don't know law, and they'll only confuse and scare you." The admonition is regularly ignored. So, too, is the lawyer's plea that the client write down what he is told and follow instructions.

—Once the divorce is over, both parties are so drained financially that it's difficult for them to pay the lawyers what they feel they have earned.[10]

"A divorce lawyer needs to know more Krafft-Ebing than Blackstone," says a Denver lawyer. "I'm pretty broad-minded. I spent two summers on the San Francisco docks, as a college student, and I worked in West Germany for the CIA in the years when being a spook gave you access to some, ah, *interesting* circles. In a single year I handled divorces for a guy whose wife had screwed not one but *three* of his brothers; for a woman whose husband made her first prize in a lottery at his fraternal lodge, without her knowledge, and with the expectation she would 'pay off' the winner; for another woman whose husband wrote love letters to a high school basketball player, a seventeen-year-old boy. There was another one involving a bathtub and drinking twelve bottles of beer that's so gamey I'm not even going to mention it. I'm not a square—but I am shocked at the stories I hear across this desk." Herbert Glieberman, the Chicago divorce expert, has come onto cases so "horribly gross" that the evidence is euphemized in the court records or omitted altogether. In his autobiography, *Confessions of a Divorce Lawyer,*[11] Glieberman matter-of-factly ticks off examples of the cases that spice his career. An Italian housewife, limited to two or three sexual sessions monthly with her husband, "took the family dog 'as her lover.'" An overweight man in his fifties became suspicious of his twenty-seven-year-old wife and, with the help of a detective, tracked her to a motel. They found her in bed with a rock musician. "Caught in the throes of mutual oral intercourse, utterly naked, she lifted her head and, with unbelievable cool, said, 'What in the hell are *you* doing here? You know I hate to be interrupted during my sensitivity sessions.'" A prosperous architect, curious about his wife's proclivity for oral sex and gaps in her personal schedule, tapped her phone and recorded hours of her torrid conversation with a woman lover, including mutual masturbation inspired by words over the lines of Illinois Bell Telephone Company. Then there was the Chicago educator ("ultra-liberated," in Glieberman's words) who told his wife, "I want to stay married to you, Bonnie. But only if you'll let another couple in bed with us." Glieberman, who is a conventional man, won each of these cases, with personal as well as professional pride. Of the educator-swinger, for instance, he wrote, "A contract is a contract, and he'd broken the most sacred one of all. And he'd broken one of society's still-sacred taboos to do it."

Richard "Race Horse" Haynes, a Houston divorce lawyer, says a particularly mean trick he has seen on more occasions than he cares to remember is for an angry wife to accuse her estranged husband of "deviant sexual practices" once she starts divorce proceedings.[12] The woman derives two satisfactions: she has an excuse for the failure of her marriage (and truth is irrelevant; she simply wants something self-exculpatory to tell her friends), and she is able to take a vicious parting shot at her husband. Haynes said, "A common accusation is that the husband is a homosexual. It's impossible for a guy to defend himself against something like that. If he has a sensitive job or if he's in politics, the accusation alone can be devastating. The people who pass this kind of 'information' along on the cocktail-party circuit figure that if the wife says it, it must be true. Who would know better than she? 'Where there's smoke, there must be fire—right?' Even if she later gets the divorce on other grounds and he remarries, some of the smear she spread will stick to him."

Accusations of sexual kinkiness can be even more damaging when they go into formal court pleadings. A case in point: in the early 1960s an enormously popular Texas politician was serving his fifth term and regularly being reelected by comfortable margins. Then, disaster. During a hate-tinged divorce proceeding the politician's wife filed court papers alleging, among other things, that after an election-night party he forced her to watch him have intercourse with a Mexican-American prostitute. He denied the allegation, and a divorce was finally granted on other grounds. The local newspapers, editorially supportive of him in his campaigns and generally undisposed to print any divorce news whatsoever, wrote about the charges in such gingerly language that a lay reader could have concluded that his wife was upset because the politician ate popcorn in bed. But photocopies of his wife's pleading rustled around town, and soon thereafter the electorate put him out of work.*

A cagier technique is to hold back gamey allegations for bargaining. Herbert A. Glieberman, who has no hestitancy in playing rough when necessary, nonetheless counsels other lawyers to avoid using inflammatory language in the first court petition. If two grounds for divorce exist, he advises, "Use the less devastating one to commence with. If all negotiation fails, you can always amend your complaint, if necessary, to include the more important ground for divorce. By holding off you may gain the gratitude of the defendant and make him more disposed to negotiate. If he fails to be appreciative of your restraint, you can use the unpleaded ground . . . as a bargaining weapon. . . ."[13]

The popular image of a divorce case has long been that of a private detective skulking through the bushes outside a window with a telephoto lens, seeking a candid snapshot of the wife *in flagrante delicto* with a lover. Such is not exactly the case. More than 90 percent of the cases that go through divorce court are not contested by either party—the marriage is dead, and both parties recognize it. For middle- and upper-income people especially, a negotiated settlement, rather than a judge, sets the terms of the divorce.

The law, sadly, was slow in coming into accord with human realities. State laws governing divorce have been so tangled, so contradictory, so varied from jurisdiction to jurisdiction, that generalizations are impossible—other than to say that too many people were left unhappy, either in or out of marriage.

The reasons for the muddle have been historical, religious and political. Society frowns upon the dissolution of marriage. The Catholic Church is devoted to the sanctity of the family. Legislators, when chin to chin with a controversial subject, prefer to do nothing. Hence some thundering absurdities. For instance, until 1966, New York law, permitting divorce only for adultery, had not been substantially changed since it was written by Alexander

*As a reporter for *The Dallas News* I was in the courtroom for hearings on the divorce. Politically, I detested his arch-conservatism; personally, I felt a twinge of pity when he leaned forward and shielded his eyes with his hands, as if to blot out the sight of his wife sitting in the witness chair, renouncing their marriage.

Hamilton in the eighteenth century. So the rich fled to Nevada or Mexico for quickie divorces, the middle class trumped up phony "adultery" cases in cheap Long Island motels, and the poor abandoned one another. Anomalies abounded. A Massachusetts woman was denied a divorce even after her husband was convicted of incest with a teenaged daughter, the court holding that the law provided remedies other than divorce for punishing this particular act. In New York a woman sought a divorce after her husband was convicted of committing sodomy with another male. No luck. New York law did not term a homosexual affair adultery. Or consider the legal doctrine called "recrimination." Roughly translated, "recrimination" means that if both parties are at fault in a marriage, they cannot be divorced—they are stuck with one another until death.

Everyone involved in the divorce industry—lawyers, judges, family counselors, social workers, above all the spouses—knew the system insulted common sense and human nature. In the words of a San Francisco lawyer, "Reality isn't always what political and religious superstitions say it should be." Given bad laws, divorce attorneys connived to find ways around them, and the truth be damned. Consider Nevada, for decades a mecca for what lawyers call "migratory divorce." A person lacking grounds for divorce in his home state moved to Nevada, lived in a motel or dude ranch for six weeks, then went to the courthouse with a lawyer and swore, under oath, that he intended to remain in the state indefinitely—a statutory requirement for becoming a legal resident. He received the divorce and caught the next plane home. Judges and lawyers alike knew all parties were lying, yet such decrees were granted by the thousands. One judge admitted to legal scholar Michael Wheeler that he once had scheduled a court hearing early in the morning so a pro football quarterback could catch a noon plane to training camp. The lawyer asked the player at the hearing, "Is it your intent to remain in the state of Nevada for an indefinite time?" "Yes," he replied, and raced for the airport, divorce decree in pocket. He has not since set foot in Nevada.[14]

In the pre-1967 days when proof of adultery was required for a divorce in New York State, perjury was rampant—and acknowledged. Milton Hutner, one of the deans of the New York divorce bar, candidly told a *New York Times* reporter in 1970,

"No question about it—they were dirty. The going to the hotel room, the raid, the whole business of private detectives." At the trial "everybody was scared because there was a great deal of fabrication." The lawyers were nervous as well. "Let's face it," Hutner said, "your witnesses were committing perjury." The district attorney's office periodically "cracked down" on divorce lawyers and private investigators, and even put several in jail—nonetheless, the system survived until 1967. (The impetus for New York reform began when Governor Nelson Rockefeller received a Nevada divorce in 1962, an action that vividly illustrated the ease with which the New York rich could shed their spouses, while the middle and lower economic classes either had to fabricate an adultery case or stay at home. Rockefeller's subsequent reelection demonstrated that divorce was not necessarily a political liability.)

But flouting of the law is not an entirely safe way for a divorce lawyer to do his business. In the 1950s Ralph D. Paonessa, a lawyer in Riverside County, California, near Los Angeles, filed some two score petitions for annulments of marriages. Each alleged, essentially, that the husband said before the marriage he wanted children, then refused to have sexual relations with his wife. The plethora of similar cases aroused suspicions, and investigators checked with the litigants. In some instances, they found, the parties involved actually had had children, a fact known to lawyer Paonessa. The State Bar of California brought charges, and the California Supreme Court suspended him for two years.[15]

A more celebrated case—because of the money and personalities involved—brought disgrace to noted New York attorney Benjamin A. Javits, brother of the Republican senator, Jacob Javits. Lewis Rosenstiel, the multimillionaire liquor magnate and head of Schenley Industries, a conglomerate, hired Javits to free him from his fourth wife, Susan Lissman Kaufmann, a blond divorcee thirty years his junior (whom a judge was to describe as "a woman with an insatiable desire and hunger for money with an appetite that could neither be satisfied or appeased"). According to his own testimony Javits didn't want the case and took it only because Rosenstiel, an old friend and business confidant, insisted. Rosenstiel was determined to shed Susan without giving her a dime in settlement, and he supposedly told Javits, "I will spend five million, ten million whatever it is! Spend it!" Javits proceeded by attacking the validity of an earlier divorce Susan had been granted in Mexico from a man named Felix Kaufmann. Money was passed to Mexican officials, and the courts there quietly started annulment proceedings, as Javits wished.

Then things fell apart. Although he had talked earlier of being willing to spend millions for a divorce, Rosenstiel balked when Javits' tab reached $410,000, fired him, hired attorney Roy Cohn and sued for the return of his money. Susan Rosenstiel, meanwhile, hired Louis Nizer, the diminutive trial lawyer, who on a talent-per-pound basis is perhaps the toughest attorney in America. Nizer went after the Mexican annulment with the feisty enthusiasm of a bulldog chewing a juicy bone. Nizer easily proved that the annulment was phony, based upon forgery and payoffs to officials as high as the attorney general of the Mexican state of Chihuahua. (For his efforts Nizer also won a court-awarded fee—to be paid by Rosenstiel—of $360,000, largest ever in a New York divorce suit.)

The bar grievance committee charged Javits with attempting "to perpetrate a fraud upon the courts of Mexico and the United States by paying moneys to Mexican public officials and a Mexican national in order to improperly obtain and subsequently defend a nullification of a Mexican divorce decree." In his 70's by this time, suffering heart trouble and cancer of the pancreas, among other ailments, Javits gaspingly protested innocence at a bar hearing, assigning blame to an office mate—deceased—who he claimed had handled the Rosenstiel matter. The disciplinary board did not believe Javits, and suspended him from practice for three years. He escaped disbarment only because of his poor health and retirement from the active practice of law.[16]

Men who serve on enough committees and carry enough titles to warrant the accolade, "a dean of the family law bar," decry the poor esteem of divorce lawyers—yet they can recognize reality. Raoul Lionel Felder, for instance, volunteered, "The lawyers in my area of law . . . run the spectrum from superb to cesspool."[17]

Yet another Manhattan divorce lawyer asks, "How the hell do you define 'effective representation' other than to try to get all your client deserves—or thinks he deserves, anyway—under the law and the facts? I don't believe in divvying it up down the middle in a case where the husband wants out of a twenty-year marriage just so he can go play house with some little braless popsy who bounces when she walks.

"Sure, I have 'ethical guidelines,' but they are mine, and not what some jerks at the bar association say I should or shouldn't do. Let me give you a couple of examples, and both of these, by happenstance, come out of the same case." He pressed a buzzer and told a secretary to get him what we'll call the "Klimers File," although this is not the name of the people involved.

"Okay, the husband is big in a publishing house, and his average adjusted gross income the past five years, according to his own 1040s—and let's talk about that in a minute—is $52,312 and some change. He's in his early fifties, married seventeen years, two kids, both in private school; Momma doesn't work. He meets a gal from another publishing house at the Frankfurt book fair, and they hit it off, and he decides he wants to go with her full time.

"Momma comes to me. Under a rule of thumb I can get her 35 to 50 percent of his gross for support. In fact, his lawyer tells me right off he's willing to go 40 percent. Of course, he's to have the benefit of this other chick's salary, and she's pretty high in her own house. Balls. That means Momma lives in Forest Hills rather than the East Seventies, or worse, and I look at her and I think she isn't going to find another Prince Charming.

"For me the fee is going to be around five thou, awarded by the court, paid by the husband. That's standard. But we have some leverage. Momma tells me that he's charged a lot of expenses to his employer that aren't really legitimate—Montauk summer entertainment that wasn't really business, and some side travel when he's in Europe. There are also some tax things that Uncle Sam might want to hear.

"I decide, let's play with this guy awhile. I strike a deal with Momma. I'll start with the offered 40 percent as a base. For that her tab runs $5,000, to be paid by hubby. Anything above that, she gives me 20 percent off the top—flat, if it's a lump settlement; for three years, if it's counted into the monthly payment. She's okay; she has nothing to lose; she tells me to go ahead.

"The look on your face tells me you know the bar says a contingency fee arrangment is a no-no in a divorce case. So what? Momma likes it, because she might get more money. I like it, because it salves my conscience for playing rough. You don't like it? Tough. Try and prove it, you can't.

"This is what happened. I told the husband, through his lawyer, that we intended to bring in the comptroller of his company for examination about the expense accounts. The reason I stated was to establish that he had effective income above that he received in annual salary. The real reason, of course, was to signal him that we were ready to do some whistle blowing at his publishing house. He was vulnerable. He had cheated, and he would be out on his ass.

"There was some yelling, but we got 58 percent of the gross. My share added another $11,000 to my fee—$4,000 I've already gotten, the rest over the next two years. Nothing in writing, but Momma is honest, and she'll pay. Why? Because the agreement stipulated that the first three years of payments go through this office.

"Now let me tell you the clinker. We were literally in the last page of the negotiations when Momma comes in one day, kind of sheepish, and tells me she's pregnant. My jaw dropped. 'How the hell can that happen?' I ask. 'You've been separated for five months.'

"She grinned and said, 'Well, there's this nice young man who gives me tennis lessons. I asked him home for lunch, and the first thing you know . . .'

"Wow, what a problem. I fixed her for an abortion within the next twenty-four hours, but I held my breath. This could really have screwed up my negotiations, and she could have come out with a lot less than 40 percent. But nothing on God's earth says I have to tell the other side my client's been committing adultery herself*—much less getting knocked up—and she was on her feet in time to sign.

"The husband thinks I'm a bastard, and he's bad-mouthed me

*The lawyer is right. The New York City bar held in 1940 that it was "proper" to represent a client who has committed adultery in a divorce action.[18] The American Bar Association, in an informal ethical opinion issued in October 1965, stated, "The attorney for a plaintiff in a divorce action is not obligated to advise the court of his client's admission that she has become pregnant by another man; he should advise his client that such adultery constitutes a defense if raised by the other party and that she must be truthful if questioned under oath or assert her constitutional right not to incriminate herself."[19] Indeed the Arizona Bar Association has gone so far as to rule that adultery committed by a client is one "crime" that may not be reported to authorities by the lawyer.[20]

around some people I know. He's living on an income of less than $30,000 and paying taxes as if he made $45,000 because of the way we split alimony and child support, and I hear that his hot little chickie doesn't think he's all that exciting now, living in a one-bedroom apartment on Central Park West. Momma is happy, though. She has almost $30,000 a year, and she's found that these guys around the East Side tennis clubs know about more things than your backhand and ground stroke.

"So what am I—a 'bomber' or a good lawyer? Momma certainly has nothing bad to say about me."

Happily for the unhappily married, divorce law in America is caught in a sweeping revolution that during the past half decade has thrown many of the legal *curiosa* of the past into the dustbin. Statutory law is finally catching up with human experience. The new concept is called "no-fault divorce," which can be simply defined as divorce on unilateral demand.[21] During the years 1971–76 no-fault divorce became virtually universal in America, with only four states (Illinois, Pennsylvania, South Dakota and Mississippi) retaining the old "fault only" grounds for divorce.* The traditional defenses are effectively eliminated, and the courts rarely deny dissolution of a marriage after a separation period of one to two years—*provided that the party who wants out of the marriage is prepared to pay the price.* The latter is the reason that divorce remains a lucrative field for American lawyers. The United States has no-fault divorce; it remains light years away from no-lawyer divorce, and in the words of Dallas matrimonial specialist Louise Raggio, "Handling your own divorce is a little like taking out your own tonsils—it's a fairly routine operation, but you'd better let a professional handle it."[22]

Credit for beginning the revolution, however, is not due the legal profession, although divorce lawyers have groused publicly for decades about the rules under which they work and loudly called for change, without doing anything to promote change. In fact, two New York divorce specialists, Dr. Doris Jonas Freed and Professor Henry Foster,** credit the Archbishop of Canter-

* As of January 1, 1978.

**Freed is with the firm of Delson & Gordon and in 1976 chaired the Divorce Laws and Procedure Committee of the ABA's Family Law Section. Professor Foster is a professor at the New York University School of Law.

bury with launching what they call the "main assault on the citadel of orthodoxy" in a 1966 pronouncement in which he proposed irretrievable breakdown of the marriage as the "appropriate ground for divorce." The Archbishop's proposal fell on fertile ears; as one English barrister put it, "the [divorce] law would do well to keep in touch with the ordinary man's idea of what is right and proper." In due course both England and Canada opted for divorce modeled along the lines suggested by the Archbishop, although in modified form. Eventually, legal reformists in California came to the same conclusion: no longer should divorce be fault-related; the standard would be "irreconcilable differences, which have caused the breakdown of the marriage." The very word "divorce" was stricken from the statutes, and replaced by "dissolution of marriage." Instead of a case being styled "Joe Doe versus Mary Doe," it is listed as "In re the marriage of Joe Doe and Mary Doe." A person can initiate a dissolution action even though he or she is having an affair—a barrier under previous law because the person would be considered "at fault." In the words of a San Diego attorney, "The new law means that a husband can get rid of his wife if he doesn't like the way she combs her hair or sweeps the dining room floor. An 'irreconcilable difference' is in the eye of the beholder—if a person swears he can no longer live with his spouse, he's out, period." Property and custody issues must still be decided—by the court or jury, if not voluntarily—but the dissolution itself is so routine that Michael Wheeler in *No Fault Divorce* cites a San Francisco lawyer, who has refined the processs to five leading questions to which he insures that the client knows that the proper answer is "yes":

Lawyer: "Have you been a resident of California for six months and of the county for two months before the filing of this petition?"

Client: "Yes."

Lawyer: "Is it true there are no children?"

Client: "Yes."

Lawyer: "Is this your signature on the marital agreement?"

Client: "Yes."

Lawyer: "And does this represent a complete accounting of all the property that you wished to have settled by the court and all your rights for spousal support?"

Client: "Yes."

Lawyer: "Is it true there have arisen in your marriage irreconcilable differences which you and your husband have attempted to remedy, but which you have been unable to overcome?"

Client: "Yes."[23]

The lawyer then steps aside, says, "I have nothing further, Your Honor," and the decree is granted.

Yet the lawyer must proceed cautiously, even in an uncontested, no-fault proceeding. Ralph B. Maxwell, who had an active divorce practice before becoming a state judge in North Dakota, counsels extensive coaching of the witness before court, and heavy reliance on questions that can be answered yes or no. "Poorly worded questions," Maxwell says, "will disrupt the presentation and upset the witness." He gave this example:

Poor: "How many issue were produced of this union?"

Better: "How many children did you and your husband have?"

Still better: "Four children were born during this marriage; is that correct?"

As a trial judge, Maxwell winces when he hears a lawyer ask a question such as, "You have alleged in your complaint that the defendant has been guilty of extreme cruelty toward you. Would you tell the court what that consisted of?" Maxwell writes:

> Now the poor client is expected to compress into a few well-chosen words a graphic picture of two decades of neglect and abuse. I have yet to see a witness adequate to the task. Generally, after the poor woman has been thoroughly humiliated by a confused, faltering, incoherent attempt, the lawyer will finally step in to help out.
>
> Some curious responses have been elicited by this type of question. They have varied from simple, stunned silence to a long-winded, acrimonious tirade of petulant or irrelevant trivia. . . .
>
> "Who, me?"
>
> "What do you want me to say?"
>
> "That's a tough question!"
>
> "Well, I can't say he was ever cruel to me. He was actually real good to me."

According to Maxwell, the lawyer was never able to overcome the last response, and his client left court undivorced.[24]

To much of the divorce bar, "no-fault divorce" is tantamount to "no-lawyer divorce," hence stringent opposition, and especially in the Family Law Section (FLS) of the American Bar Association. The rise of no-fault divorce did touch off a proliferation of do-it-yourself divorce kits—forms and an instruction manual selling for $20 or so and up—which a thrifty citizen could use to find his way out of marriage. (Many state bars fought sale of the kits on grounds they constituted the unauthorized practice of law.) But divorce lawyers used arguments other than threats to their pocketbooks in opposing no-fault divorce: in the words of an Indiana lawyer, the reform advocates "are cheating people of the professional representation, the professional advice, that a good family lawyer can provide."*

The vehicle for no-fault divorce, on a national level, was the National Conference of Commissioners on Uniform State Laws, an unofficial but nonetheless powerful advisory body that for almost a century has worked to take contrary kinks out of various state laws.[25] Although local variations remain, most states operate under fairly parallel commercial laws, a convenience for businessman and lawyer alike. The national conference put a task force to work on a model no-fault law in 1967, a panel of practicing lawyers, scholars and social and behavioral scientists. In the words of one person who worked with the panel, "This was undoubtedly the most outstanding array of family law specialists ever assembled in one room."

Following normal procedures, the panel early on established liaison with the ABA's Family Law Section. One reason was to insure that practicing divorce lawyers had a full voice in the matter. Another was to make the ABA a *de facto* cosponsor of any model code that resulted, thereby enhancing chances of accep-

*I listened to arguments pro and con over the lawyers' true motivation for opposing no-fault divorce, and I must confess I did not deduce the answer. But persons other than lawyers have an economic interest in divorce. In the late 1960s, after passage of California's no-fault law, Howard McKissick, Jr., a Nevada divorce lawyer who also happened to be speaker of the Nevada General Assembly, proposed cutting his state's residency from six to three weeks to meet the new "competition." According to Wheeler in *No Fault Divorce*, resort and hotel lobbyists beat down the idea with the argument that the number of divorces would have to double to offset the change.[26]

tance by the various state legislatures. On past issues, such a procedure brought swift, almost automatic approval by the ABA's governing body, the House of Delegates.

Not so for no-fault divorce. The panel, the Family Law Section and the House of Delegates hacked around with a model no-fault law for more than four years, with reformers unable to persuade the House to accept the test of "irretrievable breakdown" as the sole ground for dissolution of marriage. At the House's direction the Family Law Section tried to work out a specific definition for "irretrievable breakdown"; in doing so, it reverted right back to the old "fault" concept of divorce. Finally, in 1974 the National Conference of Commissioners, which had originally commissioned the no-fault panel, gave up on the Family Law Section. It did so by the rare—for the ABA—stratagem of simply ignoring the Family Law Section and taking the no-fault issue directly to the House of Delegates, where it won endorsement.

In the words of one keen student of ABA internal politics, "For the House to override the wishes of a section isn't exactly unprecedented, but it has the effect of being a rebuke. What happened, I think, is that the ABA hierarchy realized the public was getting ahead of the organized bar—not an uncommon occurrence—and that we were beginning to look rather foolish. After all, one hell of a lot of state legislatures approved the model no-fault code while the Family Law Section was still haggling over commas and community property."

What practical effect did no-fault divorce have upon lawyers' pocketbooks? Not much, according to what I've read in bar internal publications and according to lawyers I've interviewed over the past three years. Fees are down, for there's much less work in an uncontested action. Store-front law firms in Los Angeles, Dallas, Chicago and elsewhere can zip through a divorce with assembly-line ease for $100. Even in the affluent Virginia suburbs of Washington a middle-income professional can shed a spouse for less than $500. But volume is up sharply, which means that total lawyer revenues are virtually unaffected. As Bob Hope joked not so long ago, "Divorce is so commonplace these days that nobody bothers to cry at weddings."

In one area, though, the divorce lawyer remains much in demand: among the New York society and show business personalities for whom a divorce can mean a settlement in the millions of dollars.

Raoul Lionel Felder chuckled into the telephone receiver nestled into his salt-and-pepper beard. "Wow," he said, "that sounds great." Telephone clutched close, he leaned over the desk and shook my hand and motioned me to a comfortable leather chair. He continued the conversation. "Huh, huh, yeah- . . . Caught him right there in the Oyster Bay house, eh?" Pause. An exuberant laugh. "Well, did he have time to get his bathrobe? Wow!" Pause. "Yeah, they're good as witnesses. Listen, what I'll do is draw up the affidavit today for you to sign, and I'll say that the chauffeur and maid were there when you served him. I'll leave the papers with my doorman tonight, and you pick them up and sign them, okay. 'Bye now. And that was good, good work."

Felder laughed again and rummaged around on his desk and shoved over that day's *New York Daily News*, which was opened to a prominently displayed story.

"LADY" LOOT A NO-SHOW FOR LERNER

The fourth wife of *My Fair Lady* lyricist Alan Jay Lerner has tied up the royalties to his hit Broadway show in a battle to collect $64,000 that she says he owes her in back alimony and child support.

The hold on Lerner's money became known in Manhattan State Supreme Court yesterday as Micheline Lerner, a slim, attractive French-born blonde, pressed a writ of attachment against Lerner.

Mrs. Lerner, who divorced the song writer in 1965, complained that Lerner has defaulted on payments of $4,166 a month.

In the suit, Mrs. Lerner charged that Lerner is now married to his sixth wife and has moved to London, England, "where I cannot sue him. . . ."

The story went on to say that Lerner insisted he lived in Oyster Bay, Long Island, not London. The disputed residence was important because a writ of attachment—briefly, an order freezing cash or other assets—cannot be obtained against a person unless the person has a foreign address.

"That was a private investigator who just reported serving papers on Lerner that put him undisputably under the jurisdiction of New York courts," Felder said. "We'll eventually get the money, no doubt about it, because my client, Micheline, has a valid support order.

"Someone in Lerner's position is vulnerable because he makes his money publicly. What I did was file the writ of attachment against Lerner at the St. James Theater, where there's a revival of *My Fair Lady*, and at ASCAP,* where he receives royalties. Now if he was a stockbroker or a real estate developer, this could be a tougher deal, because they have ways of hiding income and assets. Oh, Lerner's lawyers will give us a chase through the courts for a bit, but in the end he'll pay."

"Why didn't Lerner face the inevitable, then, and pay up rather than waste time and money in a court wrangle that brings him bad publicity?"

Felder smiled. "For the very reason that family law is a tough trade. He's mad, and he's emotional about 'what this woman is doing to me.' Lerner hasn't been married to her for over ten years—he's gone through two other wives in that period. His notion is that he's feeding a dead horse. So he's sore, and he'll make it as rough as he can for us. But we'll get the money."

I had come to Felder's office—a pleasant, sun-filled suite on Fifth Avenue in the Fifties—because of his reputation as one of the six or so lawyers who monopolize big-money divorce cases in New York. Collectively these lawyers are known as "The Bombers," and although the person who first used the name did not intend it as a compliment, Felder called himself just that during the first five minutes of our conversation. A "bomber" supposedly does what the name implies: if necessary, he'll use any legal high explosives available to help a client with a case, even if it means blowing the opposing spouse into bits and pieces. Journalist Charles Sopkin[27] tells of the husband who during his first visit with a prominent (but unnamed) Manhattan divorce specialist mentioned that his wife was a native of England. The

*The American Society of Composers, Authors and Publishers.

lawyer's face brightened. "Well," he said, "then it's a simple matter. We'll get her deported." Appalled, the man replied, "I'd prefer something a little less, ah, violent." "Then you don't want the divorce, and naturally you don't want me," said the lawyer. He waved the prospective client out of his office.

As Felder wrote in his book *Divorce*, he is "no more in favor of divorce than, say, a general is necessarily in favor of war or a doctor in favor of surgery. But like the general and the doctor," he continues, "I know that sometimes there is no alternative to war, surgery or divorce. . . . Once the decisions have been made, once I have been hired, then . . . my sole aim is to gain victory. And in doing so, I will do anything and everything I think necessary to serve the interests of my client, to achieve his purpose—to gain him a divorce in which he will come out financially, psychologically, in every way—on top. That is what I have been hired to do and if in doing it I appear cold and calculating . . . then that's the way it has to be." Felder is especially delighted when he goes against an actor or other show business person, people who live in a world of yes-men and sycophants. He arranges a conference with the actor and his lawyer, and casually lets it be known that he has "never heard of him" and, in his words, makes "him feel I could not care less if I ever did." Subtly shorn of his self-importance, and aware that his ego faces a certain bruising if he goes into court, the actor more often than not surrenders.

Felder. William G. Mulligan. Irving I. Erdheim. Vincent J. Malone. Morris H. ("Happy") Halpern. Dr. Mitchell Salem Fisher. "Say those names," a New York divorce lawyer told me, "and you've called the roll of The Bombers. If you live in New York, and you're sued for divorce, and you see one of those names on your wife's papers, dig yourself a great big old deep hole, and keep your head down, and pray that they leave you enough money to catch the subway home from the courthouse. They completely dominate the divorce cases that mean anything."

Raoul Felder agrees. "When there's money involved, they eventually get to one of us. I suppose that 80 percent of my cases are with five or six other lawyers. This is good. There is a minimum of animosity. We know what the case is worth. Unless you have a lunatic client—and this does happen, unfortunately—we should be within the parameters when we begin talking settlement."

Felder walked around his desk and began flipping through a stack of file folders. "Here are cases that I'll be settling this week. Malone. Mulligan. Malone again. Howard Spellman. All bombers."

I am a snoop, and my eye caught a figure on a tax return in one of the folders. "Keep your hand over the name," I said, "But run that one by again. Did I see the figures I think I saw?"

Felder did as I asked, and I looked at line 15 of some anonymous divorce client's 1975 tax returns. It showed an adjusted gross income of $212,000. I made a respectful noise. Felder seemed momentarily puzzled; he sees such figures daily. "Oh," he said. "Well, that's really nothing." He went through the rest of the folders and read off annual incomes: $678,000; $119,000; $148,000; $348,000. "The low one, that $119,000, is the wife's income. She doesn't work. That's all trust money. Now that's a typical week. This is what, Wednesday? We'll settle all of these by Friday."

But what slim folders for such munificent cases. A personal injury lawyer, I remarked, can accumulate a file drawer of papers for a $2,000 slip-and-fall case.

"We do it differently," Felder said. "If I want information, they send over the tax returns. Why make me file a motion? If I'm not entitled to the stuff, they know I won't ask for it.

"God forbid that I go against an unsuccessful lawyer, the person who feels that he has to 'make a reputation' just because I'm in the case. It's a disservice to his client and to me. I feel like telling some of these people, 'Your problem isn't with me, it's with your psychiatrist.' I get involved with an amateur, and I'm tripped up with twenty-five frivolous motions, none of which should have been filed. A lawyer is a lot like a taxi driver. You make your money by turning over the meter, and you don't turn over the meter when the other side is wasting everybody's time."

Felder is a deceptively cheerful fellow—he is bitingly cynical about the abilities of many of the other lawyers who "try to practice divorce law," a bit self-deprecating and totally detached emotionally from the marital debris that is his everyday work.

"Many divorce lawyers are misfits," Felder said. "Many of my colleagues, I must report, have not mastered the English sentence. Lawyers who go into this end of the business are usually needy, emotionally and psychologically. Many have been married several times, and they carry much hostility around with them, which they vent against the opposing side when they get to court. Many are completely uncultured, with no understanding of psychology.

"Even worse, there is absolutely no way one trains to become a divorce lawyer. A criminal lawyer can work with the district attorney or the Department of Justice. A negligence lawyer trains with an insurance company or as a flunky in a personal injury firm. God knows, but your Washington lawyers learn their business in government agencies.

"I had no intention of becoming a divorce lawyer. I wanted to do litigation, so I signed on as an assistant U.S. attorney in the eastern district of New York, prosecuting organized crime cases. They say I did pretty well. I did have a reputation of being tough in court. One Mafia defendant got so mad at me he hurled a water pitcher at me, right in front of the judge and everyone. And there were the death threats, the things you expect when you put mobsters in jail.

"In 1964 this was getting sort of repetitious, and I began looking for a way to go into private practice. A rock-and-roll songwriter sought me out and asked me to handle a divorce for him. He found his wife was having an affair with the 'friend' who had been best man at their wedding. I quit government and took the case and won, and the writer was prominent enough that it got a big headline in the *Daily News*: BEST MAN KISSES AND TELLS.

"This was a fantastic break for me because it told other lawyers—men who had known me in government—that I was handling divorce cases. The big New York firms (and the same is true in other cities) stay away from divorce cases. Say you are a stockbroker, and you use a securities firm as your main business lawyer. If you ask a partner there about handling a divorce, it's almost a certainty that he'll refer you to me or one of the other half dozen. Four partners in a firm might be referring to me, the other thirty have divorce-lawyer friends elsewhere, so the referrals are spread around."

Felder went into private practice in January 1964 and his reputation swelled rapidly, although he argues, unconvincingly, that "lack of competition and default" put him at the top in an unwarranted hurry. One reason is that Felder is a cultured man in what is essentially a roughneck business. Although of modest social origins, Felder speaks the language of the big rich, and he inspires confidence among people who are inherently clannish and suspicious of outsiders. And the results Felder has obtained for clients are chatted about in Southampton and Westchester and Newport. In his book Felder almost casually mentions a settlement he negotiated for a woman client: a million dollars cash, tax-free; an income of $60,000 a year; a cooperative apartment worth $500,000; and a vast collection of paintings and jewelry. That sort of outcome, once it's talked about on the cocktail-party circuit, means that people unhappy with their marriage begin asking around for Raoul Felder's telephone number.

They had best bring money. Although Felder would not discuss specific fees, he did say $5,000 is the rock-bottom minimum for which he will handle a case—"and that has to be an uncontested action where there is a voluntary division of property."* As a rule of thumb a client who seeks out a lawyer in the bomber class needs an adjusted gross income of $150,000 annually and/or a net worth of $1 million. The bombers simply are not interested in the wife of a $25,000 junior executive whose case will drag for months and result in a court-awarded fee of $2,000.

One reason for Felder's sensitivity about fees is a wide public sentiment that divorce lawyers charge too much, and that by restricting their practices to the rich, they deny legal services to the middle class. The latter criticism Felder knocks down by pointing to his volunteer work for the Legal Aid Society. The former he answers in roundabout fashion: "When John Mitchell's law firm was taking $100,000 fees for handling a municipal bond issue, who complained?** Some of the cases we handle are just as intricate as the securities deals, and there's no reason for a lawyer to give away his time."

Felder smiled. "Another reason is that I'm doing my bit towards redistributing the wealth of America."

"Oh? From whom to whom?"

*One exception is referrals from the Legal Aid Society, persons with an annual income of less than $7,500. Felder accepts several such cases weekly; he waives the nominal fee of $10. One "charity" case that went to the appeals courts cost his firm $25,000 in out-of-pocket expenses.

**For a discussion of the law firm that formerly had President Nixon and Attorney General Mitchell as partners. see my book *The Superlawyers*.

"From rich people to me."

The high fees notwithstanding, Felder is besieged by the unhappily married demanding that he represent them. "A certain number of people will hire you even when they can't afford you, for psychic satisfaction. I once had a madam as a client—a judge referred her to me, as a matter of fact—and she told me, 'There's no such a thing as a $50 prostitute as opposed to a $200 prostitute. But certain men must have "the best." So a girl gets $50 at ten o'clock and $200 at twelve o'clock.'

"The same thinking guides people when they hire a divorce lawyer. I'll explain that their regular lawyer can handle most routine cases—divorce law isn't all that complex—and I am careful to have a detailed retainer agreement in which I note that there are 'more reasonable lawyers' in New York.

"The more you tell this to some clients, the more assertive they become about hiring you. You realize they don't want to pay you money for normal reasons—they leave the realm of the law and go into the realm of psychology. It's not normal to want to destroy a spouse. I try to stay away from these situations. And I can do it because the nature of divorce practice gives you enormous independence. Every case is a one-shot proposition. I can give back the money at any point and withdraw. You can't do that in a conventional commercial law situation."

Nuts find their way to Fifth Avenue. Not so many months ago a distraught heavyset woman appeared in Felder's office. ("You can do some screening by phone, but occasionally a real wild one slips through.") He decided after several minutes' talk he did not want the case, and referred her to an associate, who also quickly rejected her. The woman began unbuttoning her blouse. She said, "Tell him that if it's necessary for me to take off my clothes, I'll do it." Felder and the associate persuaded her to leave—still clad—and wouldn't let her back in the office. "Many women are looking for a substitute husband, emotionally and otherwise, when they begin a divorce. I won't socialize at all with a client—not even a drink or a cup of coffee. If the talk becomes suggestive, I make a point of letting them know that my wife is right over behind that door, in her own law office.*

"I had a young associate join me a few years back. The first

*Felder's wife, Myrna, is associated with his firm.

night he dated a client. I fired him the next day. A divorce lawyer runs too many risks when he socializes with clients. I have two cases now where the woman is claiming that the husband's lawyer gives her a hard time because she spurned him [the lawyer]."

In another instance Felder spent four or five minutes interviewing a prospective woman client. "I found she was just out of a mental institution, and she was too complex and confused for me." At the woman's insistence, he gave her names of fifteen other lawyers for her to consult. A few days later one of the lawyers told Felder the woman was saying that they had slept together and that she had tapes to prove it. Astounded, Felder demanded that the lawyer get the tapes from the woman and listen to them. He did. One was of the woman talking to a girl friend. At one point she said, "You know, they practically threw me out of the office. But I'll bet that if I went back and offered to go to bed with him, he'd take the case."

The woman interrupted the playing of the tape and jabbed a finger at the casette recorder. "There," she exclaimed.

"There, what?" asked the confused lawyer.

"That's the proof!" the woman said.

The lawyer ushered her out.

A distraught-sounding woman called Felder at home one evening and claimed she was in an "emergency situation" and needed a good divorce lawyer forthwith. ("One of the problems of a divorce practice is that significant events tend to happen at night. Whoever heard of a husband beating up his wife at three in the afternoon? It's always three in the morning. That's why I carry a telephone beeper, and keep it on twenty-four hours a day.") Felder doesn't like to be disturbed by strangers at night, and to dissuade the woman he said he would charge her $500 if she insisted on an immediate interview. She promptly agreed. Suspicious, Felder took his wife with him when he went to the office. "The woman came in wearing a very very low cut evening gown. She paid the $500, she talked gibberish, she left." A few days later Felder mentioned the incident to a woman client. "Describe her," she said. He did. "Heavens," she said, "that's my husband's girl friend." Deduced Felder: "They were trying to set *me* up. Sick people. Some will stop at nothing when they start trying to kill a spouse."

So why does a sharp lawyer spend his professional life engrossed in such gamey turmoil? Felder professes to be aloof from his cases, emotionally, yet his face became extraordinarily somber when he told of a custody case in which a judge ruled that one child should go with the father, one with the mother. "The little girl wanted no part of her mother, who had to physically drag her out of the courtroom and down the corridor. The scene became so traumatic, what with the child screaming and resisting, that the family service officers stepped in and effectively overruled the judge by letting the girl go with the father. My medical training helps [Felder briefly considered a medical career before turning to law]; so does my experience as a prosecutor." The long hours—7:00 o'clock in the morning until past dinnertime, plus most weekends—are another drain. A month before we spoke, Felder had bought a summer home in Montauk; he had managed to get there for brief snatches of two weekends, and had spent most of his time on the phone. He interrupted our talk to tell his wife that he probably would miss the trip the coming weekend as well, because of settlement negotiations. "Let the chauffeur take you out on Friday afternoon, and I'll join you on Saturday if I can," he said. "If I can."

So I returned to my previous question: Why? Felder fell silent a moment and then buzzed his secretary and asked her to bring copies of letters he had received recently from three clients.

A New York judge: "You were indeed a beacon light in the otherwise dreary and bleak nightmare of my matrimonial battle."

A church official: "I shall always be grateful for your never-failing patience and courtesy with me over the past several months, and for the fact that, in the midst of my sadness and loss, you have been not only trusted counsel but valued friend."

A physician: "No day has gone by in the last month without my gratitude to you being foremost in my mind. Your brilliance was apparent the first day we met. What became increasingly clear with each week you worked with me was your humanity and compassion."

"I don't like divorce, because it is a failure of relations between two human beings. In many instances, staying in a bad marriage is better than splitting, and I make that point when I talk with prospective clients. I make my living from divorce—

but I repeat: I don't like divorce. As a lawyer, however, my aim is to do the best job possible for a client. And these letters, I think, indicate that some people agree that I do."

A half hour later, at a luncheon with some publishing executives, I casually mentioned that I had just come from Felder's office. One of the men across the table involuntarily winced. "Hell, yes, I know that guy," he said. "My cousin is a doctor, and when his wife sued him for divorce she hired Felder, and let me tell you, by the time Felder had finished with him . . ."

A bombing mission, successfully completed.

Court Recess One

Attorney Phil Burleson seldom handles divorces. "It's messy, and it's emotional, and I find it more challenging to do a complicated criminal appeal." Nonetheless, a few years back, Burleson took the case of a lawyer's wife who was suing for divorce on grounds he was having an affair with a female colleague. The lawyer denied everything, and to add further insult to the wife, he hired his alleged paramour to represent him in the case. The wife had suspicions, but not proof, of adultery, and according to Burleson, "We weren't getting anywhere in the case."

Burleson is a motorcycle buff. On weekends he sheds his gray business suit for jeans and a crash helmet and buzzes away to Meridian, a small town south of Dallas where he owns a lake house. "I was riding through town one lazy Sunday afternoon when, lo and behold, the lawyer and his girl friend came out of a motel and got into his car. I quickly turned around and followed them as they did several errands, then returned to the motel and went into a room together. They thought nothing about this guy riding along behind them in a crash helmet. It concealed my face enough that they couldn't recognize me. After they closed the door I went to the motel office and picked up several match folders."

A few weeks later, during depositions, Burleson asked the lawyer whether he and the woman had ever been out of town together. They huddled, and the lawyer said, yes, they had, to West Texas, to try a case together, and on another occasion to a bar function in Fort Worth. But he insisted the travel had been strictly business. And in answer to a direct question he said they had made no "social trips" whatsoever.

Burleson reached into his pocket and flipped one of the motel match folders onto the table. The two lawyers stared at it, stunned.

"Have y'all ever traveled to any other places besides this motel?" he asked.

There was a long silence, a withdrawal for whispered conversation, then a stumbling explanation. Well, as a matter of fact they *had* gone to Meridian together, but only so that the woman could visit a relative, with whom she had stayed. The lawyer occupied the motel room alone.

Burleson listened with a dubious grin, nodding his head in disbelief from time to time. "They watched me as if they expected another match folder to hit the table at any moment. The uncertainty is what killed them. They didn't have the slightest idea how I found out about the one motel, and I wasn't about to tell them. I let them sweat. My gut feeling was that there *had* to be more than one afternoon in the country; common sense told me that."

Shortly after the deposition the lawyer offered a handsome settlement to his first wife, the divorce was granted and he married his associate. "I never did tell him where I got those matches," Burleson said.

Chapter Two

A Couple of Country Lawyers

Scotty Baldwin frowned as he tried to remember the 1975 cases. He had a piece of scrap paper on the corner of the desk, and he jotted down dollar amounts as he and his partner, Franklin Jones, Jr., recollected them.

"The biggest one we've ever had was $1,800,000 for the collapse of a storage tank up in Atlanta, Texas. A horrible thing. Six men killed, another thirteen injured, crushed under more than a million gallons of water, sheets of metal, girders, pipes, whoosh-whoom all over them. The tank was intended to store woodchips, but they tested it by filling it with water, ignoring every known law of physics. No one ran any stress analysis, even though filling the tank took weeks. It floated down like a big old Frisbee. But that was in '73. What we want is a total for 1975."

Back to the scrap paper: $560,000 for a man who lost both hands in a metal press; $770,000 for a man who lost both legs in an accident involving an outboard motor; $526,000 for a man who suffered severe burns when the "cherry picker" crane in which he was working brushed electrical wires; $450,000 for a back injury.

Jones and Baldwin poked deeper into their memories. "What about that ol' blond-headed gal in the car wreck?" Baldwin asked. "What'd we get—$125,000? That's right, but darned if I can even remember her name right off."

$90,000 in another boat accident case. $235,000 in a fatal collision. $300,000 for a man who fell from a scaffolding when the guard rail broke. $350,000 for an oil driller injured in a North Sea operation off Great Britain.

Baldwin added up the figures. "I make it $3,430,000," he said. "That's just the major ones; the odds and ends run it over $4,000,000."

"Hey, wait," interjected Jones, "we forgot all about the Penrod case.* That runs it up another $500,000 or so."

Baldwin laughed and put down his pencil. "Jesus," he said, "I'd never stopped to run out the figures before. That sounds pretty good for a couple of country lawyers, hey?"

Yes, it does, and to me the irony was where I found them: in a law office some six blocks from where I spent my childhood, in Marshall, Texas, a onetime cotton-railroad town, now turned to light industry, in the piney woods near the Louisiana border. In my quest for the big-gun lawyers of the personal injury field I had concentrated on big cities, and for several reasons. Small towns simply do not generate a steady volume of personal injury cases likely to return six-figure sums, and the occasional "big case" that does arise is apt to be snapped up by a firm in the city, either directly or through referral from a local lawyer who does not feel capable of protracted legal conflict with the likes of General Motors. Lawrence Charfoos, of Detroit, for example, receives personal injury cases from throughout the Midwest, and he says the bulk of them are "from lawyers who don't want to get in over their heads."

During a brief visit to Marshall in the fall of 1975—a familial respite from interviews in Dallas and Chicago—I saw an item in the local *News-Messenger*, the newspaper which I once served as city hall and police reporter, business-farm-youth-auto editor and second-string photographer. The story read as follows:

Large Settlement Reached Here

A settlement of over half a million dollars was reached in a case scheduled before federal court here this week, a jury verdict assessing $235,000 to the plaintiff was returned in a second case, and another $200,000 settlement was announced. . . .

A settlement of $526,757, reportedly one of the largest of its

*The plaintiffs were two men who suffered disabling injuries in an oil field accident.

> kind involving only one plaintiff, was made to Alvin Dean McDowell by A. B. Chance Co.
>
> McDowell filed suit as a result of electrical burns he sustained Feb. 15, 1973, while working on an electric transmission line near McKinney. . . . He was represented by Scott Baldwin of the Marshall law firm of Jones, Jones and Baldwin. . . .
>
> In the only case before the court this week that went to the jury, $235,000 was awarded to Mrs. William K. Grant in a suit against R. E. B. Transport Inc.
>
> Mrs. Grant filed suit after her husband was killed in a two-vehicle accident Jan. 10 at an intersection of Loop 281 in Longview. . . .
>
> Mrs. Grant was represented by Franklin Jones, Jr., of Jones, Jones and Baldwin. . . .
>
> A settlement in a third case . . . awarded $200,000 to William F. Helms in a suit against Clary Well Service. Helms was permanently disabled in an accident at a Clary well site when a pipe slipped through an elevator and fell on him, breaking his back . . .
>
> Helms was represented by Carl Roth of Jones, Jones and Baldwin. . . .

I clipped the article and said to my mother, "These guys seem to be doing okay," and I left Marshall, and in the next months I talked to lawyers in Detroit and Philadelphia and New York and Buffalo and God (and IRS) knows where else. Then, in the spring, a *News-Messenger* clipping in the mail from my mother, with a note scrawled across the top: "They never fail to win." The headline read, $686,000 AWARDED HERE AS FEDERAL COURT CLOSES.

The article mentioned only one personal injury case, that of a man whose hands were chopped off by a metal press. The jury gave him $561,200. The story noted that he was "represented by Marshall attorneys Scott Baldwin and Franklin Jones, Jr., of Jones, Jones and Baldwin." There was a $124,800 gap between the headline and the article, but no matter: a Marshall law firm deserved close attention.

A scorching hot July morning, and I took off my jacket when I left the air-conditioned car to walk across South Franklin Street in Marshall to a modernistic blackish-brick building sitting catty-cornered on the southwest side of the intersection. White pea gravel and green plants, face-nipping air conditioning beyond the plate glass door, a receptionist with the charming verbal skill of the Texas female, that of making "yeh-yus" a two-syllable word.

Into the main office suite, and a surprise. Franklin Jones, Sr., was on the couch, visiting with his son and enjoying watching his subteen grandson hustle around the office, carrying papers for the secretaries. The kid is half-English and sounds it, and Jones Senior cocked his head and tried to imitate him without noticeable success. Jones Senior is in retirement, and a cane helps him get around, and in conversation he sounds downright mellow. But beginning in the late 1920s Jones Senior terrorized railroads all over the state of Texas.

My memory of him is of a fellow who was only a cut or so above being a town character, and my only regret now is that I didn't listen to him more carefully in those days, for he made far more sense than the *Dallas News* or the *Reader's Digest*, my primary sources of "information."

People joked about Jones: "Know the best way to improve the value of an old worn-out cow? Cross it with the Texas & Pacific Eagle [the T&P's fast, main east-west train] and then hire Franklin Jones to bring your lawsuit." Millard Cope, the Bourbon editor of the *News-Messenger*, wouldn't quote Jones in the news columns when he challenged an action of the sacrosanct city government, or the archconservatives who controlled the county and state Democratic organizations. But he did occasionally permit a long letter to the editor, which many people in town thought to be odd: whyever would a grown man be so cantankerous? I remember no specifics, but Jones also reputedly had peculiar ideas on Negroes, to the grave extent that he actually thought *Brown* v. *Board of Education* should be respected as the law of the land. During these years my Texas friend Ronnie Dugger wrote, in another context, to the effect that in rural East Texas, "only the game laws protect liberals." Whatever the source of Jones' protection—the Divinity or the Texas Game and Fish Code—he survived, and he remembers those years with chortling relish.

"I handled lawsuits in an area stretching from New Orleans to El Paso, that covered by the Texas & Pacific and Southern Pacific railroads. My father, S. P. Jones, began this practice in the days when anyone who handled workmen's compensation cases was considered a cut below even a criminal lawyer. The corporate lawyers viewed us with grave suspicion.

"The law under which we operated was the Federal Employers Liability Act [FELA], which was passed in 1908.[1] During the first decade of this century, it was a commonplace saying that no trainman could, in the days of the link and pin couplers, serve his time as a brakeman and become a conductor without the loss of at least three fingers. President Theodore Roosevelt pleaded for an end to the practice of putting the entire burden of loss of life or limb upon the railroad employee, and that's why Congress passed the FELA.*

"Of course, the FELA didn't give the railroad lawyers much worry, because the courts were pretty well stacked in their favor. During the 'golden eras' of Coolidge and Hoover, before the reform of the U.S. Supreme Court, judges considered FELA as the product of meddling do-gooders who would suggest that a railroad might not construct its trestles with human bone and ballast its tracks with the flesh of its employees.

"The position of the 'responsible moderates' of the time was that the maimed employee and the wife and the children of the employee killed in service could far better bear the human overhead incident to the operation of our railroads than could the employers who were doing so much to develop the country, and who in the industrial infancy should be insulated from the economic responsibility of caring for the maimed and bereaved.

"The legal concepts were silly. The courts followed the rule that when a man took a job, he assumed the 'burden of risks normally incident to the job at hand' and also those arising from negligence which was so 'open and obvious' that he must have been aware of it. This actually *encouraged* the railroads to permit the danger of the work to become notorious, for the more obvious and greater the risk, the more reason for applying the doctrine to defeat the claims of those injured through it.

"Some of the younger lawyers find this kind of legal history unbelievable, but it is real. I know. I've sat in courtrooms all over Texas and Louisiana and heard these railroad lawyers from

*Previously, injured workmen were effectively barred from recovering damages by the doctrines of the fellow servant, comparative negligence and assumption of risk.

Dallas and Shreveport and New Orleans argue that brakeman Smith was responsible for the loss of his own leg because he knew how dangerous it was to throw a switch on a dark rainy night. The judges would go along with them on the doctrine of 'assumed risk,' and refuse to let a jury decide the case; Smith would go out of court on a crutch and that's it; he has no lawsuit, no money, no leg.

"During the decade 1923–33 the Supreme Court reviewed some thirty-five FELA cases, and ruled against the plaintiff twenty-nine times on questions of 'sufficiency of the evidence.' In other words, the court held that the trial jury—the people who had listened to all the evidence personally—should be ignored. I've given the court credit for one thing: the justices didn't attempt to conceal what they were doing. In one case the Supreme Court said it had a sacred obligation 'to give special consideration to the facts in order to protect interstate carriers against unwarranted judgments.' Well, bosh. In one case the court denied recovery to a brakeman who testified he was injured by an unusual jerk of the train on which he was working. Listen to the Supreme Court in this one: 'Wells' statement that the jerk was given by the engine was, obviously, a mere conjecture as he was then at the side of the caboose, ten car lengths away, where he could not see what occurred on the engine.'

"Of course, this poor fellow was jerked to kingdom come, and the engine was pulling the train, but in those 'golden days' of 1927, this was insufficient.

"Another loophole these railroad lawyers used was whether the train was actually in interstate commerce at the time of the injury. Interstate commerce was the key because that brought the cases under federal jurisdiction. All sorts of anomalies arose. If a locomotive needed repairs and was taken to a back shop, the courts said this wasn't interstate commerce. But if it pulled over for repairs on the road itself, you were covered.

"I went to the U.S. Supreme Court myself on one case that enlarged the law—briefly, that if intrastate commerce was moving on a main line that was used for interstate commerce, the injured person was covered.

"Congress got rid of many of these inequities with a 1939 amendment to the FELA. It completely knocked out the inhumane doctrine of 'assumed risk,' and it provided simply that so long as the employee's work substantially affected interstate commerce, he was covered by the FELA.

"These changes made it much easier to win personal injury cases, and quite naturally it became suddenly quite popular for a lawyer to become a plaintiff attorney. We've whittled away, and it's been a slow process, but the progress is being made. From the 1940s on, the Supreme Court—with some notable exceptions, such as Justice Felix Frankfurter*—held fairly consistently that a jury should be able to determine the facts in a case without the meddlesome interference of an appeals court, and that an employer's liability to his workers should bear some connection to reality.

"But I still remember those days when a southern courthouse could be a mighty lonely place for a small-town lawyer who was up against the big boys from Dallas, and the court was on the railroad's side."

Franklin Jones, Jr., sat behind a desk across the room, fidgeting with a letter opener and listening to his father. He is a lithe, sun-bronzed man in his mid-forties who keeps in shape by swimming a mile daily at his private pool. I had not seen "Soupy" Jones since an Alpha Tau Omega fraternity rush party at the University of Texas in 1952; he was a law student, I, a green freshman. He had just screwed up his wrist in a shotgun accident, and we sat on a porch and drank Schlitz from cans and talked about Caddo Lake and people we knew. Three years my senior, Jones graduated from the UT law school and returned to Marshall and joined the firm his grandfather had founded early in the century. A few years later another of the founder's grandsons, Scott Baldwin, also joined the firm. The close family ties between the two cousins—Jones Junior and Baldwin—are obvious. When an anecdote begins—and both men are vivid raconteurs—one talks a few sentences, pauses, the other picks up the story to tell his part. And these men know their territory, and the people who live in it, and what to expect of them.

"Yeah, things have changed," the junior Jones said. "But a lot depends on where you have a case. Houston, for instance, is

*Justice Frankfurter argued that the Supreme Court should devote its time to fixing national policy and not waste energy on what he once called "insignificant cases" involving death or injury, brought under the FELA.

a Baghdad for personal injury lawyers. It's an industrial city with many working people who appreciate the dangers of the work place. Juries will listen to you there, because these people have worked in the steel fabricating plants and the petrochemical complexes, and they know what it's like to drive a truck. You can get good verdicts there. The insurance companies know it, and they are prone to settle a Houston case out of court.

"Dallas, now, is a different story entirely. It's a Sahara compared to Houston. Dallas is an insurance center, and the entire community is against you in a PI [personal injury] case, because all these little clerks and file shufflers are taught to believe that if the insurance companies pay out money, it will 'hurt the company.' An insurance functionary—a guy with a big title and a small salary—loves to go back to the office and write a memo telling his boss that he 'did the right thing' and refused to vote damages.

"So, if we get a Dallas case, we do everything possible to avoid filing there. Move the trial anywhere at all, spare me Dallas.

" 'Course, you do get lucky occasionally. We recently had a case where a stray horse got onto the highway. Our man was driving at night and hit him, and was severely hurt. During pretrial the defense came in with pictures showing that the pasture fence was secure enough to have held the horse, and therefore the owner, a very rich man, could not be liable.* Not so long afterwards the insurance agent who sold our man his auto policy showed up with some pictures he had taken the morning after the accident. They showed the fence to be one heck of a mess; you could have taken elephants through it. Now, of course, this meant we caught the other side in a flatout lie, and they were quite ready to settle."

An interruption. A secretary announces the arrival of lawyers to take depositions from a Jones client, a truck service manager who suffered grave injuries when a butane truck overturned on a

*As part of their pretrial preparation Jones, Jones and Baldwin obtained aerial photographs of the rich man's estate, which stretched over scores of acres of prime real estate just north of Dallas. Scotty Baldwin showed me the pictures to demonstrate the care with which the firm prepares a case. A juror, I remarked, might get the idea that a man who owned that much land in the north Dallas suburbs is rather wealthy and capable of paying off a citizen who ran into a horse. Baldwin smiled impishly. "Well, now that you come to mention it . . ."

curve during a test drive. Chris Harvey is from the Dallas superfirm of Strasburger, Price, Kelton, Martin and Unis, which has the reputation of being perhaps the best insurance defense office in Texas; he is a small, nondescript man with spectacles, who says he's tired from several days' travel doing similar legal work elsewhere in Texas. Pike Powers, Jr., a round-faced man in his thirties, is from another insurance defense firm, Strong, Pipkin, Nelson, Parker and Powers, in Beaumont, an industrial city just east of Houston. "Here's the enemy!" exclaims Jones and goes to the doorway to greet the visitors. (The "enemy" has spent the last hour in private offices in the Jones, Jones and Baldwin building, using the telephone and reviewing files and acting at home. PI and defense lawyers fight vigorously, even viciously, in court, but in most instances they are unfailingly courteous in their personal dealings.)

Powers exchanges folksy banter with Jones Senior, saying that his partner, Charles Pipkin, "told me to be sure and say hello to you." Jones beams. "That old devil. We've been round and round in many a courthouse. He always acts nervous, as if the worst is about to happen. I was up against him once when he defended some people who had loaded a tank truck with liquid chlorine to its liquid capacity, without allowing for any expansion. It wasn't a matter of *if* but *when* it blew. He managed to shift liability over to another party, and that day he wasn't shaking at all, he was strutting. He said to me, 'I'm walking on the air of love.'

"Another thing old Pipkin was good at—tell me, how old is he now?" "Eighty-two," replied Powers—"was losing papers. You'd get into an area that was hurting him, and CRASH! a whole file of papers would fall on the floor and scatter every which way. Pipkin would be on his hands and knees, hunting them down, saying, 'I'm sorry, Your Honor,' and I'd be fumin', 'cause I knew why it happened. It'd take five minutes for things to calm down, and longer than that to get your witness back to where you had him. A sly old devil."

Everyone laughed, so Jones Senior told another story, this one about the witness who was called to the stand and asked if he swore to "tell the whole truth, and nothing but the truth." "I won't lie," the fellow replied, "I'll leave that to my lawyers."

Enough. Jones Junior and the two visiting lawyers gathered

their papers and we adjourned to a conference room where the deposition was to be taken. Jones took me around to another office to meet his client, a slender man in his thirties in a western-style knit suit; vicious scars were visible under his open-necked shirt, and others criss-crossed his face. Jones briefed him on what was to happen. "If you don't understand a question, and you answer, you are going to make a mistake. Be forthright and honest, and answer as completely as you can. Okay?"

"Okay," said the client. He took the last nervous puff off a cigarette and followed us around the corner. (Jones earlier had told me of his physical condition: back and other injuries that made him permanently unfit to work, although he had tried. The outcome of the suit, in all probability, would determine whether he had an income the rest of his life or subsisted on welfare.)

Jones had also expressed some irritation about the legal barriers to suing an employer in Texas. "Under the workmen's compensation laws, an injured person more or less automatically recovers his medical expenses, plus payments for the time he is actually out of work. But the same law protects the employer from having to pay damages for pain and suffering and compensatory damages, unless you can prove him guilty of gross negligence. As a rule of thumb, you almost have to have a death case to collect beyond the workmen's comp payments.

"One way around this little help-the-corporations gimmick is to prove that a man's injury was caused by a defective product. Under the doctrine of products liability, a manufacturer bears ultimate responsibility for the safety of a product he sells—it must be free from defect, and not unreasonably dangerous to the user.

"In this case we didn't sue the truck company that employed our man; we sued International Harvester, the manufacturer of the truck. Later on we joined in the Ross Gear Division of TRW, and we're going both ways: that the truck itself was defective, and that the steering gear mechanism was defective. Either way, the truck didn't work as it should have, and the steering wheel wouldn't respond on a ninety-degree turn, and it overturned and killed one man and injured our man."

Did the later inclusion of the gear manufacturer mean that perhaps Jones had found damaging information about the steering mechanism during his pretrial work? He smiled. "Let's talk about that later, if the case is finished before you write your book."

Depositions are tedious fare, with lawyers probing for elusive facts and trying to pin witnesses down to exact statements and to prod them into providing information that might knock the bottom from the lawsuit. Pike Powers, however, began his questioning of Jones' client as if he were chatting with a friendly neighbor. "All right if I call you Junior?" he asks. "Apparently everybody else does." Junior shrugs. "Okay with me—done it all my life."

Powers traces Junior's personal and work history, for the most part by tracking over answers that Jones had supplied earlier to written interrogatories. He gets a bit more precise on Junior's tickets for speeding and his thirty-one-day hospitalization for a back injury after an accident in the 1960s. One attempted trap Powers was unable to spring. He took Junior through a long recitation of his truck service career, from back-shop grease monkey to shop manager. Yes, Junior said, part of a manager's job was sedentary—paper and telephone work. Oh? Well, what percentage of your time was actual mechanical work? Sixty percent, Junior replied. Poof. Powers was unable to make a desk man of Junior.

But Powers did score two points: that Junior had earned about as much the few months he worked after the accident as he had the preceding ones, and that he had suffered blackout spells the year before the truck wreck. (Jones had warned me in advance: "All they can do is try to show he blacked out and rolled the truck. They'll try, but they can't do it.") But Junior survived questions about past heavy drinking: yes, he had knocked off a bottle of vodka daily at one time, but he had "quit cold" after an ulcer operation in 1965.

At noon we broke for a lunch of sliced barbecued beef, pinto beans and cole slaw, brought in by a secretary. Jones told Powers that he thought the deposition should continue without interruption: "I believe you'll wear out quicker if you don't eat." Powers laughed. "Man, I ain't been mean."

Well, he hadn't, but he had established that Junior had quit three jobs after the accident, even though the employer had said nothing about dissatisfaction with his performance. Should the case go to trial, the defense lawyers could point to Junior as an accident-prone man with a record for speeding violations, a past history of heavy drinking, and documented spells where he had blacked out without seeming cause. Was he also a malingerer who had decided to parlay an admittedly serious accident into a lifetime annuity? Such was the groundwork that Pike Powers had laid before the barbecue break. But could he overcome the rest of Junior's story—that the steering wheel "just wouldn't respond," that he had hollered, "Get out!" to his passenger and hit both the hand and foot brakes and shifted down thirteen gear stops, only to have the truck roll anyway. And that ever since his release from the hospital, in his words, "setting hurts me, standing hurts me. The pain in my back makes it unbearable at the end of any given day."

The after-barbecue questions dragged, and I thought of other things to do on an East Texas summer afternoon and said my good-byes.* Back in Marshall a week later I returned to Jones, Jones and Baldwin for a talk with Scott Baldwin. In the interim, I had asked perhaps a score other lawyers in the PI field in Texas for some opinions on why the firm did as well as it did. "Oh," said one Dallas lawyer, unhesitatingly, "It's Scotty; my God, man, Franklin Junior can't carry his briefcase." On the phone from Houston a few days later an old Austin classmate, now a defense attorney, said, "Jones, easily; Baldwin goes along to impress the juries, because he's good-looking and smiles a lot."

Baldwin has problems. A progressive spinal disease hurts him and bends him, and he is constantly in motion even as he sits in a chair, trying to get comfortable. I remember him as the darkly handsome, if somewhat diminutive, son of "Old Doctor Baldwin," a good high school athlete who always seemed to be smiling. My older sister was his contemporary, and I know at least three of her high school friends who would have sworn lasting love to him—had Scotty ever noticed them. He didn't. Now I re-

*Before the deposition I asked Jones what the case should be worth; he swore me to secrecy and said, "Six hundred thousand dollars, although they aren't saying a word about settlement at this point." In November 1976, after two hours' deliberation, a trial jury in Marshall gave Junior Walton $650,000. It awarded another $450,000 to the widow and son of the man killed in the crash. Jones Junior wrote me later, "We were successful in establishing total liability . . . on the shoulders of TRW. The jury found the defect in the steering mechanism existed when it left TRW's plant, and accordingly all of International Harvester's liability was passed through to TRW." The jury also found that International Harvester did not alter the gear while it was in their hands. Thus did the lawyers' inclusion of TRW as a belated defendant insure that the proper party was found liable.

alize that this man with the flashing eyes, with the soft-hued summer slacks and open-necked shirt, sitting in a law office across from the old site of Maranto's Grocery in downtown Marshall (population 24,000) makes probably as much money a year as a partner in Cravath, Swaine & Moore, the New York corporate firm, or even the fabled Washington superlawyers Clark Clifford and Lloyd Cutler, and certainly as much as the PI people I'd met earlier in the "hot" personal injury towns of Cleveland, Chicago and Detroit.

Scotty doesn't have the slightest idea what I am thinking about, and I don't tell him. I simply say, "Why don't you tell me what's happened since you left Austin," meaning the University of Texas law school.

"I came out of school and went into practice by myself. I did everything. I repossessed TVs, I collected debts, I looked for law business. I hired a secretary even when I didn't have any clients. I paid her $35 a week for a half a day. I'd sit in the office in the morning and answer the phone; she'd show up at noon, and I'd hit the streets.

"After a few years I threw in with my brother, Phillip, and we did a more-or-less general practice—some bank stuff, some real estate, a bit of personal injury. When Lyndon Johnson made Phillip a judge [of the Court of Customs and Patent Appeals, sitting in Washington] I came over here.

"This is getting the family back together. Old Mr. Jones, the founder, was my grandfather on my mother's side, which makes me and Franklin Junior cousins. We had the one-generation break in the law, on my side at least, when my daddy decided to become a doctor.

"How did we get where we are? By being willing to go down to the courthouse and try cases, that's how. We have tried twenty to thirty a year to jury verdicts—and I mean *jury verdicts*, and not those situations where the other side settles up at the courthouse door. You've got to earn the respect of the other side, and there's only one way to do it—earn it in the courtroom. There's only a handful of lawyers who'll get over there and try a lawsuit.

"The federal district courts in East Texas sit in a town only a week or two at a time, which means you get kind of busy during a session. Franklin and I have had situations where we'll have one jury out, deliberating; we'll be putting on evidence in a second case; and during the recesses we'll be picking a jury in a third case. It's a gut-racking experience, to have a jury verdict come in while you're trying another case. The judge puts the working jury back into the spectator seats, and receives the verdict. If it's good, okay. But oh, man, to have a bad one come in during a trial—you can't help but wonder what effect this has on your current lawsuit: I mean, you've tried one and lost it, and the other jury says, well, they brought one bad one, maybe they've brought *two* bad ones. Taking the other jury out of the courtroom doesn't do anything. In a small town, everybody around the courthouse, even the jurors, knows what happens in a trial."

So where do the cases come from? Franklin Jones, Jr., was in the room now, and he picked up on the conversation.

"Insurance companies love to deal with people who won't try a case, who will settle cheap. I know of one union—I won't name it—which persuades about 90 percent of its members to take their personal injury cases to a certain lawyer. He settles them wholesale, in bulk; I know of one instance where this lawyer literally settled a case for fifty cents on the dollar, based on what everybody involved knew it was worth, except maybe the guy who was hurt.

"My point is that when volume goes up, quality goes down—and don't fret, because I'm getting around to your question, about where our cases come from.

"East Texas is an area that turns out a lot of oil workers, both in the fields and in the offshore rigs, and even in the Alaskan pipeline. Now this is an area of law that most laymen know little about, but the offshore rigs come under admiralty law, which means they are federal cases, if you are hurt there."

Jones leaned back and looked into the ceiling and consulted his memory. "Right now I can think of cases we have where the injury was in Singapore, Trinidad and the North Sea. In fact, we have two in the North Sea. How did these people come to us? Because, somewhere back over the years, we represented a friend of theirs who mentioned our name; they remembered us and came to us.

"Just this week we received a letter from an oil company worker in Iran, who was hurt there in a taxi accident. He wanted to hire us. How? Well, this gets complicated. We once represented a person who had relatives killed in a plane crash in Alabama. The guy in Iran had been a witness in that case; he remembered us; he wrote us."

I had to interrupt. "Wait a minute. You are lawyers in Marshall, Texas. How the dickens do you go about bringing a suit in Iran? And how did you get mixed up in an airplane crash case in Alabama?"

Scotty waved his hand. "Simple. If the company the man works for is from the United States, and we can prove the taxi accident was job-related, we bring the suit either where the man lives or where the company has its corporate offices. The Alabama case? The victim involved used to work for Thiokol Chemical Corporation, out in Karnack [fourteen miles northeast of Marshall]. Her family knew us from somewhere or another, and she asked us to do the case. Running down the origin of 'where did you get this case?' is not often that complex—from Karnack to Alabama to Iran—but it gives you an idea.

"A lot of union men in the oil industry and the construction trades carry a lawyer's card with them all the time; they always assume something could happen to them."

Which is not to suggest that client relations are always totally amicable. For the past several years Jones, Jones and Baldwin have been litigating a case in which two oil field workers sustained crippling back injuries. The defendant was Penrod Drilling Corporation, whose convoluted ownership included three trusts controlled by the fabled Texas oilman H. L. Hunt ("one of ol' Hunt's play pretties," said Jones). Although the accident occurred in East Texas, Penrod claimed it must be sued in Dallas, its corporate home, but Jones, Jones and Baldwin insisted on filing in Marshall. ("Ain't no way we're going to try this suit in Big D," said Jones.) Baldwin, researching, found an old opinion by Learned Hand that said an unincorporated association could be sued anywhere it did business; he felt the definition fit Penrod, and the district, circuit and supreme courts agreed. At a non-jury trial in Marshall the judge gave the men $770,000, at which date the Fifth Circuit Court of Appeals issued an extraordinary opinion: although it agreed the workers were entitled to recover damages, it balked at permitting them to be computed on the assumption that the American economy would be subject to inflation during the thirty-odd years remaining in their life expectancy. It remanded the case back to the district court for reconsideration of the monetary award. This appeal and its accompanying side motions dragged for almost two years.

The plaintiffs, meanwhile, yelled loudly for their money, and all Baldwin could tell them was, "The circuit court usually decides these things within ninety days." After each ninety days one of the burly plaintiffs would call to inform Baldwin that he was "living on red beans and that he wanted his money." Baldwin could only repeat, "They usually do it in ninety days."

"Finally he exploded and said he was comin' over here to whip me. I'd had enough by now. I said, 'Well, goddamnit, come on and bring your lunch.' "

The man didn't appear. The case went to the Supreme Court twice, to the Fifth Circuit Court of Appeals in New Orleans three times, Jones, Jones and Baldwin finally settling for an amount near the judge's original award. "There comes a point, especially when the clients need money, as these old boys did, that it's wise to get out," said Baldwin. "But I'm still glad that old boy didn't show up, because I don't think I could have whupped him."

So how do Jones, Jones and Baldwin go about constructing a personal injury case and presenting it to a jury? Personal injury lawyers invariably assert that suits are won long before they reach the courtroom—that the side which does the best advance preparation is going to win. Another dictum is that the more money involved in a case, the higher the quality of the lawyers on each side—especially the defense. "When you go up against Lloyd's of London or Travellers Insurance," Jones said, "you see the best defense money can buy. I like it that way. I'd rather try against a good lawyer than the other kind."

I asked the cousins for a trial transcript of a case that illustrated how they go about their work, and when I flew back to Washington my suitcase contained a seventeen-pound multithousand page file entitled *Steven Paul Gandy* v. *Verson Manufacturing Company*, tried in the Marshall division of the U.S. district court on March 29-31 and April 1, 1976.[2] Gandy, at age twenty-two, was preparing to enter his final year at the University of Texas; after graduation he planned to enter the nursery business with his brother, in his hometown of Tyler. He took a summer job in 1974 at a Carrier Air Conditioning plant in Tyler, operating a brake press that stamped out finished pieces of metal. Carrier had bought the machine from Verson the preceding year for $14,064.75. It was wired to operate with either of two control switches: a foot pedal contained in a recessed box, or two push buttons located so far apart that the operator must use both hands and press them simultaneously. Carrier installed the machine with only the foot pedal.

A supervisor trained Gandy for one day; the next night he went to work on the 11:00 P.M. to 7:00 A.M. graveyard shift. The press gave Gandy problems. Several times during the night, according to his later testimony, the machine "double-stroked" —that is, the ram would come down twice, or more, when he pressed the foot pedal, rather than once. He consulted a supervisor, who tinkered with the machine and told him to keep working.

At six o'clock in the morning the press slammed down on Gandy's hands with a force of sixty to sixty-five tons. "When I saw what it had done, I screamed, I walked back and I yelled and the next thing I knew someone had come to me and laid me down on the ground and they wrapped me up. Part of me was telling me to look at them and the other part didn't, so I just vaguely glanced at them, and all I can remember was just the skin hanging off—hanging my hands onto the rest of my arms."

Gandy lost both hands. Jones, Jones and Baldwin sued the Verson company for $2,500,000, charging that the machine was dangerously defective on three grounds: that it did not have an effective guard, that it would make unplanned strokes, that the warning on the face of the machine was inadequate.

Why sue Verson, rather than Carrier? "The workmen's comp thing," said Jones. "Carrier had paid his medical bills and thousands of dollars for the work time he missed. Also, it's much harder to prove gross negligence on the part of an employer than it is for a manufacturer. Verson let the brake press out of its plant in unreasonably dangerous condition; that's all we had to prove."

No such creature exists as the "typical" personal injury case. Yet *Gandy* v. *Verson* contains many of the elements that make PI law exciting for attorneys on both sides of the courtroom—the emotion of listening to a handless young man explain how he lost his limbs and list the everday functions he can no longer perform; the frustration of defense counsel in trying to persuade the jurors to "listen to the facts," rather than be swept up in sympathy; the embarrassment of a plaintiff's "expert witness" who didn't do his homework; the defense witness who has the words of a decade-old speech dribbled back at him, a sentence at a time; the technical explanations of what makes America's modern gadgetry work. The maneuverings of the lawyers—the tactical shifts of Jones and Baldwin from emotionalism to solid technical fact and back again to Steve Gandy's maimed hands, and the countering moves of defense counsel Tom Alexander of Houston and John H. Minton of Tyler—illustrate the intensity with which a million-dollar lawsuit is contested.

Cardinal rule number one for a plaintiff's lawyer is to make maximum use of the client's disability, even if flaunting of the injury makes him uncomfortable in the courtroom. In the words of a Philadelphia negligence lawyer, "I'm not averse to making a man feel bad about himself for the course of the trial if the end result is to get him several hundreds of thousands of dollars." *

So at the opening day of trial, Gandy sat in the courtroom without his artificial hands, trying to make the stubs of his arms less visible to the inevitable glances of spectators. Psychic discomfort, to be sure, but part of his lawsuit.

Baldwin, during his opening statement, told the jurors they should be thinking about big money as the trial progressed, for the plaintiff deserved it.**

> I will ask you to consider what the value is of a man going through life without his hands and think about it during the course of this trial, at night, when you wake up, as you will because you [are] a conscientious jury. . . .

*Baldwin: "Get the money out in the open at the outset. If you wait until the closing argument to say you want umpteen millions of dollars, the amount shocks the jury. You talk about dollars at the beginning, and they'll start asking themselves, "How much would I want if I was hurt as bad as that poor feller?' "

**Melvin Belli, the San Francisco lawyer, once represented a woman butchered by a plastic surgeon. Instead of improving her breasts' appearance, in Belli's words, he left her "like a Picasso nude. Both breasts were almost square. One was obviously larger than the other, the nipples had been sliced off and transposed inches higher than they should have been and the nipples looked inward. In addition, she had a large gash running from her breasts to her pubes." Belli trapped the defense into agreeing to let the jury view her nude in the privacy of the judge's chambers. She "stood there like a statue, face scarlet, head down, her eyes filling with tears and the tears running down onto the scars on her breasts." But when she left court she had a judgment of $115,000.[3]

We take our hands for granted. The simple matter of rubbing your nose or rubbing your eye, opening a door, holding the hand of a frightened child, the list is as long as your imagination is. I can give you a hundred things now that he can't do, and that is not even a part of it. . . .

Think about it and prepare yourself for your decision, and I think that you will agree with me that he had the God-given right of going through life a whole man and that a verdict of $2,500,000 is a reasonable verdict, when you consider what this man has lost, that is, his manhood, his hands, the parts of his body he uses the most.

A San Francisco defense lawyer once told me, "You can defend sprained back cases all day long and not worry, because the jury can't see the injury. But I tell my clients [insurance companies], 'If the person suing you comes to court with a leg missing, or a big scar across his face, write out a check on the spot; don't waste our time with a jury.'" Thus the dilemma of Verson's lead defense counsel, Tom Alexander, as the jury looked at his handless opponent.

"Mr. Baldwin, who is a wonderful lawyer, has made a beautiful appeal to sympathy without much reference to the actual evidence in the case," Alexander said. "For instance, he asked each of you to think *all the time* about what Mr. Gandy can or cannot do." He said the jurors must also concentrate on whether the press was defective:

You really must steel yourself to appeals of sympathy. For instance, every time I have seen Mr. Gandy he has had prosthetic devices on his hands and he uses them very well. There can be no reason for him appearing here today without them other than a direct appeal to sympathy . . . while you are trying to discharge your duty to this court to decide the facts in this case. . . .

This machine [the brake press] is a well-thought-out machine, well-planned, has stood the test of time, and if you, as jurors, let your mind get so obscured that you don't pay attention to the evidence about the machine itself, it is going to be awfully difficult for you at the end of this case . . . to decide . . . was this machine defective when it left Verson's control?

Gandy, the first witness, described how the brake press worked. "What you do, you put a piece of metal in there, and it had a blade kind of like a guillotine, and it would come down and crush the piece of metal into a desired shape." The process was supposed to flick finished pieces of metal through the machine to a basket, but some landed off to the side. "So after they would get three or four in there I would reach my hand through and put them in the basket." A foreman told him to do it this way, Gandy said. He continued, "I was cleaning off the back of the die and my foot was out of the foot valve [the triggering mechanism] and for some reason the machine came down again and when it did I saw what it had done. I screamed. . . ."

Gandy went on to describe how he looked down and saw his hands hanging from his wrists by shreds of skin. Yes, he said, the machine had "misfired" several times during the shift, and he had complained to a supervisor, who had tinkered with it. No, he had received no briefing on safety, nor had he been given any operating manuals for the machine.

Why wasn't Gandy wearing his artificial hands to court? They were heavy and made his stumps sore, and he could wear them only about half the time. (A riposte to Alexander's suggestion that Gandy had left the hooks at home to elicit sympathy from the jury.) How did he feel? The pain was "constantly burning." There were phantom sensations that made him reach with nonexistent hands—only to realize there was nothing with which to reach, and nothing to touch if he could. There were nightmares when he awoke screaming and crying. Gandy seldom went out because of embarrassment. People would come up to him on the street and, in his words, "ask me what happened, why I am like that; they have no concern for my feelings whatsoever about it."

Baldwin put into evidence a list of 150 things that Gandy said he could no longer do. His dream of being a nursery man was over. "You have to hoe, you have to plow, you have to trim trees, you have to use snips, you have to graft, you have to bud, and quite a few things like that." None of these could be done by a man with artificial hands. Baldwin turned the witness over to Alexander for cross-examination.

A lawyer who roughs up a pitiable witness risks alienating jurors, so Alexander walked carefully. Yes, Gandy did remember a sign on the machine, "Never place any part of your body under the ram or within the die area." No, Carrier had not instructed him on proper use of the machine. Didn't his own violation of safety rules cause the accident? No, the machine "misfired," and a superior had told him to clear away the finished metal with his hands.

Whatever headway Alexander made was dashed by Baldwin with the single question he asked on direct examination:

> BALDWIN: Would you mind pulling up your sleeves and showing the portions of your arms so we can know just what parts of your arms it was that were amputated?
>
> GANDY: I can't—
>
> THE COURT: He can't hold them up, you will have to do it for him.
>
> REPORTER'S NOTE: Whereupon the witness's sleeves were pulled up and his arms exhibited to the jury.
>
> BALDWIN: I have no further questions, Your Honor.

Next, Baldwin put on two technical witnesses, Paul F. Youngdahl, a mechanical engineer from Palo Alto, California, and Richard Fox, an engineering professor from Case Western Reserve University in Cleveland. Both avowed the press should have come with a barrier guard or an electric eye to prevent the operator from putting his hands into a dangerous area; any number of fail-safe devices were available at minimal cost.

Yes, said Alexander, but was it not true that standards set both by the federal government's Occupational Safety and Health Administration (OSHA) and the American National Standards Institute (ANSI), an industry group, required that the *employer* provide guards and insure their usage? Perhaps, said Youngdahl, but the manufacturer, with his special expertise, is best qualified to design and install the guards.*

Then Alexander got tough. He depicted Youngdahl and Fox as professional witnesses who would testify to anything for a fee—and not very capably, either. He expressed surprise that Fox had appeared as a witness in 138 personal injury cases in

*Jones and Baldwin knew the defense would cite the OSHA and ANSI standards, so they primed the jury to ignore the issue. Baldwin said in his opening statement that the standards "are not enforceable, they are voluntary . . . they are largely written by industry, the very people that sell these machines. . . ." He brought out through several witnesses the distinct parallels of language in both the OSHA and ANSI standards and that of the Verson operating manual for the press in question.

five years. He was astounded that Youngdahl hadn't even visited the Carrier plant during his "investigation" of the accident.

> YOUNGDAHL: It was not important to reach an opinion about this Verson press brake.
>
> ALEXANDER: Well, sir, I wasn't talking about reaching an opinion. Actually, you reach your opinion in many, many cases right off the bat, don't you? These people know where to hunt for somebody who will say a machine is defective.

Baldwin objected, and Judge Joe J. Fisher sustained him. So Alexander tried a slightly different tack. How many cases had Youngdahl appeared in during the last year? "Perhaps fifty in the past year, in one way or another."

Alexander huffed, "Will you be surprised to know that's more cases than I have, and law is my full-time occupation?" Judge Fisher cut him off even before Baldwin objected, saying the point was "immaterial and irrelevant." Alexander could not resist a parting shot. He asked Youngdahl, "You would imagine that there are quite a few [engineers] closer to Marshall, Texas, than Palo Alto, California, who are qualified engineers and who have actually had experience with presses." (Several days later, in his closing argument, Alexander used even stronger language. Fox, he said, "has appeared as an expert witness on plastic toy horses, on bicycle seats, on Exercycles, on tailgate accidents, automobile accidents, every kind. Whenever anybody has any kind of an injury, Mr. Fox is willing to show up.")

Alexander's chief expert witness was Kirk Lunser, manager for electrical engineering for Verson. Lunser was direct. Five or six components would have to fail before the press malfunctioned. "Outside and inside experts" had checked the press immediately after Gandy's accident and found nothing wrong with it. Even when they tried they could not make it double-stroke.

"All right, sir," Alexander asked, "do you know of anybody that could perceive it better than you, who designed and built the press?"

"I don't know, sir," Lunser replied.

Unfortunately for Lunser, Jones and Baldwin had done some quiet research on patents that Verson and its engineers had obtained over the years, a laborious task that involved reviewing thousands of pages of technical documents. As Baldwin explained to me, "Patents are a good source of evidence, especially for cross-examination, because they always contain many statements acknowledging dangers and safeguards, together with overstatements of the utility and effectiveness of the device." Patents are a matter of public record at the U.S. Patent Office in Washington, a facility Baldwin visits frequently. "In fact, I imagine that we were one of the first law firms ever to use patents in the trial of products cases. One simply needs to know his subject matter sufficient enough to go to the patent office and make a 'patent search.' The patents are indexed both topically and by name of the inventor. It is a simple matter to look up, for example, all patents on press brake machines, or to be more specific, all patents relating to guards of press brake machines. Another method would be to look up all the patents in the name of a manufacturer, for example, Verson. As a matter of practice these patents usually are obtained several years before the product hits the market. Therefore, all of the dangers and exaggerated claims are well known to the manufacturer."

In the instance of Verson, Baldwin's research in the Patent Office was well worth the effort. Baldwin read language that engineer Lunser had used in a patent application for a safety device to be used on a press, but one which was *not* used on the press sold to Carrier:

> The press control circuits heretofore developed have left much to be desired from the standpoint of safety. For example, the run control push buttons referred to at the operator control station are often subject to a great deal of abuse, which can cause undesired grounding or short circuits in the various contacts operated by the control punch button.
>
> In such cases, it is readily possible that the press ram can be operated by the pressing of only one or less than all of the control buttons . . . or *the press ram can operate continuously when it is supposed to stop automatically after one cycle of operation, placing an operator in the path of the movement of the press ram in great danger.* (Emphasis added.)

"I spoke those last words loud and slow and clear," Baldwin said later, "and the jury heard me. There we had it, in Verson's own words: their presses are apt to double-stroke just the way we claimed it did when poor Steve Gandy lost his hands. This application language knocked the props out from under Verson." All Lunser could say in rebuttal was, "We protect for something that is nearly impossible, to be doubly safe, sir." Baldwin gave Lunser one last ruffle before letting him off the stand, bringing out that he was neither a college graduate nor a licensed engineer. ("My own experts had degrees festooned all over them. This was a way of suggesting to the jury that Verson wasn't the big efficient do-nothing-wrong corporation it claimed to be.")

Another Verson expert witness, Frank Holland, a "consultant engineer," also called the press brake safe. He blamed the accident on both Carrier, for not properly training operators, and on Gandy himself. Holland felt Gandy was tired at six o'clock in the morning—he, too, had once worked a graveyard shift—and had unwittingly, "perhaps even unknowingly," shifted his foot onto the press switch.

Jones did the cross-examination this time, attempting to lead Holland into a trap. First, he had Holland insist that chances of the machine's malfunctioning were "perhaps a billion to one or something like that." The questions were gentle, even innocuous. "I wanted him to think he was home free, that I couldn't touch him," Jones said. Then Jones pulled a sheaf of photocopied pages from his file.

> JONES: Let me ask you if you agree with this point, Mr. Holland, or this statement? "A good starting point in the design of a press control is to assume that each relay push button valve and limit switch is going to fail some day, in either an open or closed condition."
>
> HOLLAND: Yes, that sounds to me like a talk that I gave at the National Safety Congress in 1966.*
>
> JONES: I wondered if you would recognize it . . . Do you also recall telling them that . . . . [equipment failure] is not too unrealistic a premise because in many stamping plants there is little, if any, preventive maintenance of electrical controls?
>
> HOLLAND: Right.

*At this point, according to Jones, "Holland got a sheepish look on his face, as if he knew something awful was about to happen to him." Ridiculous, retorts Holland; as a veteran expert witness he had fully expected the talk, entitled "Electric Power Press Control," to be brought up, and he had reviewed it before going onto the stand. Indeed, Holland felt that *Jones* was the surprised party, when he quickly identified what the lawyer was reading to him.

There was more sparring as Jones led Holland through other sections of the speech: "The designer of the press control must also remember that the human mind of even the most conscientious operator is going to wander away from the job at times and that some operators would use all of their ingenuity . . . to defeat any safety control or guarding installed on a press. To them it is like a game, like Russian roulette." Then came what Jones considered the key exchange:

> JONES: Did you also tell them, sir, when foot switches are used that the dies should be shielded with suitable guards or the foot switch should be located far enough away that the operator cannot reach any . . . point in the press?
>
> HOLLAND: Yes, I said that.

Holland continued to insist that installing the safety gear was the employer's responsibility, not the manufacturer's; that no safety device was on this particular brake because the plant did not use the two-hand operating station furnished with the machine. But as Jones saw the situation, "The jury wasn't listening to him any more. They had heard *Verson's own witness* say that Verson had turned loose a machine that could maim a man. Under strict liability, that is all we had to prove."

Both sides called witnesses who gave contradictory testimony on whether the press brake did or did not malfunction. Gandy witnesses said the machine double-cycled for as long as forty-five seconds, and that repairmen had to be summoned to turn it off. Other coworkers, testifying for Verson, called the press brake safe. A rule of PI law is that if a witness hurts you in one area, have him talk about something else on cross-examination. So Baldwin did not quibble with Michael Glenn Williams, who was voluble on behalf of the defense. He simply asked about the accident scene: "You had a horrible injury there, didn't you? Did you see the flesh and the blood and bones? And he obviously was in pain, wasn't he? Were his hands hanging on by the skin?"

Now defense lawyer Alexander tried a diversion of his own, only to be trapped by his own mistaken witness.

> ALEXANDER: You had an occasion to talk with Mr. Baldwin about this accident before, have you not?
>
> WILLIAMS: Yes, sir, I have.

ALEXANDER: Where was that?

WILLIAMS: Garland [Texas, a Dallas suburb], I believe it was at the Ramada Inn.

ALEXANDER: How long ago was that?

WILLIAMS: Maybe a month, maybe a little more, I am not sure.

ALEXANDER: Were you subpoenaed to come here?

WILLIAMS: Yes, sir, I was.

ALEXANDER: You never refused to come for Mr. Baldwin or anybody else, did you?

WILLIAMS: No, sir.

Alexander's clear implication was that Baldwin had tried to keep the jury from hearing testimony damaging to his client. But, as Baldwin put it later, "The defense attorney got greedy. The fact is that I'd never seen this man before in my life."

BALDWIN: I have a few questions. What does Mr. Baldwin look like?

ALEXANDER: Well, I say Mr. Baldwin, he was—I don't see him in the courtroom.

REPORTER'S NOTE: Whereupon there was laughter in the courtroom.

BALDWIN: Thank you.

Alexander by now was clearly on the defensive, with Jones and Baldwin eliciting damaging testimony time and again from his own witnesses. Alexander put on the Carrier purchasing agent, Robert L. Wilkerson, so that he could get into evidence a letter of purchase from Verson stating that guards were not included with the press, and that it was the employer's responsibility to provide "guard devices, tools or other means" to protect workers against "serious injury." Wilkerson also said Carrier chose to install the machine without the two-hand press controls, relying instead on the foot pedal.*

In short order Baldwin had Wilkerson admit that one reason he bought the Verson machine was because it was cheaper without the safety guards.

BALDWIN: It was a savings to Verson to sell this machine without a guard, wasn't it?

*Baldwin, analyzing: "Once again Verson was trying to duck responsibility by saying Carrier was the culprit."

WILKERSON: I would think so, sir.

BALDWIN: And for whatever the reason, this machine was manufactured and sold without any character of a guard on it or safety device, wasn't it?

WILKERSON: Yes, sir . . . . they have made the policy that you buy it without the point of operation guard.

Wilkerson also said that after Gandy's tragedy, Carrier had decided to put protective barriers on all punch presses in its factory to prevent similar future accidents.

The record suggests that Alexander realized his client was in for a rough time when the jury retired, and all that he could do was to try and hold down the amount of damages. Thus, he put into the record a physician's report from the Texas Institute for Rehabilitation and Research (TIRR), where Gandy had been outfitted with artificial limbs. The report declared Gandy was adjusting well to the prosthetic devices and that he suffered no "significant pain on his stumps," which had healed well. So far, so good. The finding contradicted Gandy's testimony about his inability to use the metal limbs; if Gandy played loose with the truth on one point, could his story of the malfunctioning press be believed?

Unfortunately for Alexander—and Verson—the report discussed other matters as well, and the entire document went into the record. The report said that Gandy had planned to finish college before marrying. "Two weeks after his injury, Steven went ahead and married his fiancée because 'he needed her after what had happened.' His wife, Jane, accompanied him to TIRR. She is a sixteen-year-old high school student."

Jones said, "When Alexander read that in court, Steve went absolutely white. He leaned over and said, 'That's a lie.' I was afraid he was going to blow up, he was so shaken. I told him to calm down, that he'd have a chance to rebut the report when he went back on the stand."

The defense lawyers either did not notice Gandy's emotional reaction, or misinterpreted it. Jones and Baldwin gambled. When they recalled Gandy he was asked only about work rules; not a word was said about the physician's report. They sat back to see what Alexander would do.

Blam. Early on, Alexander asked whether the report was accurate in describing what he could do with the prosthetic devices. Gandy squirmed in his seat. "The look that came over his face is something that I've never seen before, that of a man in sheer agony," Jones said. "I thought to myself, 'Either he's going to explode, or he's going to knock this lawyer right on his ass.' " Back to the trial record:

> GANDY: Well, from listening to you, a person could be—I mean you couldn't understand it correctly, no, sir.
>
> ALEXANDER: You say the record is inaccurate.
>
> [Jones, recreating: "Steve was right on the edge of the witness chair. He was hurting. What had been said about his marriage had offended him, I think, even more than the loss of his hands."]
>
> GANDY: Well, I loved my wife, and I didn't marry her because I needed her in that effect.
>
> I married her because I loved her.

Jones glanced at the jury. Tears rolled down a woman's face. Several men cast distinct frowns towards the defense table. Gandy quivered, but he said nothing more. Alexander ended his questioning.

The jury went out at 9:10 A.M. on April 1. It broke for lunch, then returned at 2:48 P.M. with a verdict of $561,200. Judge Fisher agreed with the finding. "The court feels you have reached a fair and just verdict."

The insurance lawyers did not appeal, and Gandy received his money (less $22,391.98 that Carrier had paid for medical bills). Jones and Baldwin sounded satisfied, for seldom has a Texas jury given such a large verdict in a PI case. Nonetheless, Jones said he stood by what he said in his closing argument: that Gandy's loss entitled him to $2.5 million. "One way to stop unsafe machinery from going onto the market is to make it damnably expensive for manufacturers to produce it. American corporations understand the dollar sign. You give them a heavy enough whack, and they'll listen." But he did see one secondary benefit: Verson's press brakes now are equipped with fail-safe controls.

"There's another thing that makes me kinda' happy," Jones said. "The Gandys had their second kid a few weeks after we finished this lawsuit. They named him Franklin Scott."

Court Recess Two

The lawyer's downfall began with his fourth martini. The time was a spring noon in the early 1970s; the setting, the Oak Room of the Sheraton Cuyahoga Hotel in downtown Cleveland; his luncheon companion, a partner in a Cleveland law firm that specializes in representing insurance companies in personal injury cases. The lawyer—let's call him Wagon, which bears no relation to his real name—felt expansive. Here he was, only four years out of law school, and this very morning he had settled eleven cases with the insurance law firm. Eleven cases, $137,000 in checks, just like that, of which more than $45,000 would go into his own pocket, under a one-third contingency fee arrangement. Wagon impulsively told the insurance lawyer, "Come on, I'll buy you lunch. I owe you something for all that money."

The insurance lawyer, who will be called Centel, wasn't excited about spending another hour with Wagon. Although he had met Wagon only half a dozen times for informal discussions of cases, he found him brash and obnoxious and not totally trustworthy. Centel once left Wagon alone in his office a few moments and when he returned the younger lawyer was standing over his desk, eyes fixed on an open file. Embarrassed, Wagon picked up an ornate paperweight and said, "This is most unusual, I couldn't take my eyes off it . . ." Centel said nothing but thereafter he was careful not to leave Wagon in his office unattended. Finally, Centel didn't think Wagon to be all that good a lawyer. That very morning he had been willing to settle an auto crash case in which a woman had lost the use of a leg for considerably less than Centel *knew* his insurance client would have paid. But Wagon had seemed eager to settle all eleven cases as a package, and when Centel had halfheartedly offered $24,500 in the leg case, he had snapped at it. Centel thought to himself, *My God, this guy is willing to sell out a client just to save himself work*. He had been tempted, passingly, to signal that the case was worth more, but had stopped: the insurance company paid him to make the best settlements possible, and under the canons of ethics he had no obligation to hold Wagon's hand.

And now he was regretting his acceptance of Wagon's luncheon invitation. The man simply *would not shut up*. He downed two martinis and was signaling the waiter for a third when Centel insisted they order lunch. The arrival of food did not allay either Wagon's thirst or tongue. "You know," he insisted, "I learned how to do these personal injury cases a hell of a lot faster than I thought possible. Here I am, in my fourth year of practice, and I have work coming out of my ears, all I can handle. And I'll bet I'm making twice as much as anybody in my class, even the guys who went with the big downtown firms."

More gin, more talk. "What I really need is an associate to help me with some of the paperwork crap. I'm wasting too much time writing interrogatories. Hell, 95 percent of the time we never use them anyway; the cases are settled before anyone even thinks about a trial. Look at me: I've been in business four years, and I've gone to trial once, and we settled before I had even finished presenting my case. Why should I screw around with worthless paperwork?"

Yet more gin, yet more talk. "I'm amazed at how easy some of these cases come in. My first year I did a divorce for a nurse out at St. ——— Hospital, and while it was in progress her girl friend was hurt in a wreck. The nurse sent her over, and I managed to get her some money. You know, I'll bet those two broads have given me twenty cases in the last three years. They're right there on the emergency ward, and if somebody comes in hurt and says the word 'lawyer' they drop my card on them." Wagon paused and laughed across the table at Centel. "You have to pay those fancy country club dues to meet your clients; all I have to do is take a nurse to dinner every once in a while. And I get laid in the process."

Ignoring the steady drum of Centel's fingertips on the table, Wagon told the waiter, "No, no coffee for me. Hit me with one more of these things."

The fourth martini, Wagon sipping a bit more slowly now. "The real surprise—and I guess I know you well enough now to talk candidly—is how willing you insurance lawyers are to pay out money."

"Oh?" said Centel.

"Yeah. Like today. You could have shoved me on two or three of those cases, and I would have taken a lot less. I find the same thing all over town. Even the worst dog of a case is worth a couple of thousand. I've collected on crap that I almost turned down." Sip. "But I'm not complaining. This is none of my business, but I'll bet I gross more this year than many of the lawyers in your firm . . . Maybe even more than you." Sip. "So when these young guys come out of law school and ask me what sort of practice. . . ."

Wagon droned on, but Centel wasn't listening. *You little son of a bitch*, he said to himself, *I intend to give you a whack in the ass that you'll remember as long as you live.*

Wagon wanted a fifth martini but Centel insisted he had to get back to his office. "I'm just an insurance company drone," he said. "I can't take these long lunch hours like you hot-shot PI people can." Wagon laughed. "Oh, don't take me too seriously," he said, "I'm really a pretty nice guy." He did not understand why Centel insisted on paying his share of the luncheon check.

Back in his office Centel had a law clerk screen the files for cases the firm had pending with Wagon. He called friends in three other firms that did insurance work and spoke with them briefly, and they agreed to meet three days later for lunch at the Mid-Day Club. They did, and they talked for two hours, and they shook hands and went away.

Centel also called the administrator of St. ——— Hospital, who happened to be a social friend. The next morning a memo was distributed to all personnel at the hospital, "reminding" them of a strict policy against referring patients to lawyers under *any* circumstances, and warning that the penalty was immediate dismissal. Two young nurses on the emergency ward thought it odd that they were directed to sign an acknowledgment that they had read and understood the memorandum; other nurses were simply given a copy and did not have to sign anything.

Within a week Wagon noticed substantial changes in his practice. One morning's mail alone brought staggeringly intricate interrogatories in no less than seventeen cases, more than half of them supplemental to information Wagon's clients had already provided. Wagon blinked at some of the medical questions and realized he had not the slightest idea what the other side was asking about. Even more interrogatories in other cases arrived that afternoon, and the next day, and the next day.

Other things happened as well. On one day that same week Wagon received notices that opposing lawyers wanted depositions from his clients and witnesses in exactly twenty-one cases—all within a ten-day span. There were motions to strike his pleadings; there were motions to schedule pretrial conferences; there were motions to compel Wagon clients and attending physicians to produce medical and other records.

Wagon dealt with this deluge of paperwork as best he could—which he soon realized was not very well. During a rare lull outside a coffee shop one morning he told another lawyer what had happened and said, "It's as if every case in my office came to life at the same time. I feel like I'm caught in an artillery barrage. I can't stand it." The other lawyer clucked sympathetically and told Centel, the insurance attorney, of the conversation. Centel laughed and called his friends in the other firms.

Wagon selected six cases pending with one firm and requested a negotiation conference. "Sure," said the opposing lawyer, a senior partner, "come on over; you are a reasonable fellow, we've done business in the past, and I'm sure we can work out something."

A secretary escorted Wagon into the senior partner's office, and they shook hands, and the senior partner said, "Now I want you to meet Mr. Jones, one of our new associates. He's a good man, and he'll talk over these cases with you. Good bargaining, gentlemen."

A junior associate. Wagon felt vaguely uneasy, but he followed Jones down two bends of the corridor to a cramped, windowless office. "Let's take these one at a time," Jones said.

"Okay with you if we start with Molley?" He opened the file and began reading. "Give me just a minute to familiarize myself with some of the facts here . . ."

Fifteen minutes later he was still reading, and Wagon fretted. "Look," he said, "this is a simple intersection collision case, and there's no way your man is going to avoid liability. Our medical expenses and loss of earnings are all spelled out, so why don't we talk a dollar figure?"

"In a minute, in a minute," Jones said, and he read for a quarter of an hour more. He turned to Wagon. "Now, why don't you tell me what you think it's worth." "$4,700," Wagon said. Jones smiled. "I'm not saying we're going to settle, but even if we did, that's much too high." They sparred for twenty minutes, and Wagon finally said, "I don't like this, but I'll go for $3,800."

"Let me find out what my lead attorney thinks," Jones said, and stood up to leave. "You mean *you* can't decide?" Wagon asked, incredulously. "This will just take a minute, I'll be back," Jones said, and he was gone.

Wagon waited half an hour. He smoked three cigarettes. He went to the rest room. He fiddled with his files. Jones returned. "I'm sorry, but I don't think we can make an offer on this one. The thinking in the office is that we can win at trial."

Wagon's jaw dropped. "Oh, come on, don't give me that shit. You know you don't have one chance out of twenty. Why the hell do you want to tie us both up in court for a day on crap like this?" Jones replied, "That's the decision. We're not paying. Care to go on to the next one?"

Wagon glanced at his watch. They had spent almost two hours on a single case. Well . . . Jones pulled over another file. "Give me just a minute to familiarize myself with some of the facts here . . ."

Wagon had come to the office a few minutes after 9:00 A.M., and at 1:15 P.M., when he had to leave to attend depositions, he and Jones had gone through three of the six cases, without a single settlement being offered. "Shall we try again tomorrow?" Jones asked at the door. "Let me call you, I'm pretty busy these days," Wagon said.

Wagon's misery mounted as the weeks rolled on. The paper blitz continued. In two months he managed to wheedle one out-of-court settlement, and that from an Akron firm; Cleveland lawyers seemed unwilling to offer a dime in *any* case. His cash flow dwindled to the vanishing point. At court calendar calls Wagon knew what he would invariably hear from the opposing side: "Defense is ready to proceed to trial, Your Honor." Wagon's office day began at dawn and dragged past midnight. The first case in which he was forced to trial resulted in a $5,300 verdict for his client—but it consumed three days, which meant the office backlog grew even higher. *A year ago*, Wagon thought, *I would have settled that case easily for ten or twelve thou.*

Wagon found himself so inundated with work that he didn't have time to search out new business. Some days he couldn't return phone calls even from other lawyers. But when he called defense attorneys to try to discuss settlements he almost always heard a secretary say, "I'm sorry, Mr. ——— is tied up in conference, he'll call you back." But Mr. ——— never did. In frustration Wagon once asked a secretary to put him on hold; he would wait for the other attorney. She did. He waited fifty-five minutes until shame compelled him to hang up.

Wagon realized he hadn't received any new referrals from his nurse girl friends at St. ——— Hospital. He called Donna, who told him, "I don't think I'd better pass out any more of your cards. You see, this peculiar memorandum came down from the hospital administrator, and . . ." Wagon asked Donna out to dinner anyway; she went, but she wouldn't go home with him. "You see, I have this new boy friend, and . . ."

Almost fourteen months to the day, after his four-martini lunch, Wagon sold his case file to another personal injury firm and left Cleveland. The last anyone heard from him he was in California. His new occupation: internal claims adjuster for an insurance company. The office that bought Wagon's old cases settled the bulk of them within two months.

Centel, the lawyer who coordinated Wagon's downfall, was mildly embarrassed when he told me the details several years later. "This began as a situation when some of us tried to teach a grasping young bastard some needed lessons in law, ethics and good manners. He all but admitted to ambulance chasing in that luncheon conference, and he all but bragged about making us pay off in bad cases.

"The interesting feature is that when we subjected his cases to close scrutiny, just to slow him down a bit, we realized that most of what he had was in fact worthless trash. So we fought payment, legitimately and ethically. In retrospect, the one thing I regret is that we did not find a way to pay off promptly on the good cases he did have. We were within our rights to refuse settlement, and to put the cases to trial, but I'm afraid we did step on some innocent toes in the process.

"Did all this have any salutary effect? Oh, in the sense that we cut short the career of someone who should not have been practicing law, I suppose it was a success. But someone else will take his place, I know. Any business that produces as much money as PI law does will always have its marginal operators. But it was an inexpensive exercise. We used associates, who don't make that much, and it gave them experience in defending cases. And I suppose it also made us a little more careful in our screening process; we don't pass out thousand- and two-thousand dollar checks as readily these days.

"Another lesson, though, is that PI law—both the plaintiff and defense sides—depends upon the good faith and mutual respect of opposing lawyers. Let's face it; the insurance companies, if they simply declared they wouldn't pay a single claim without going to court, could so screw up the justice system in this country that it would come to a complete standstill. There are bastards in the insurance defense bar, I'm the first to admit that, but as a whole we're committed to playing square and making the system work.

"I still have one question in the back of my mind, though. Did that jerk Wagon ever realize what happened to him, and why?"

After several hours on the phone I managed to find Wagon, in a Los Angeles suburb. When I began telling him the nature of my inquiry he said he did not care to talk about anything that happened in his Cleveland law practice, and he hung up. I later wrote him a letter. He did not answer.

Chapter Three

"Let Us Do Your Thinking"

Not so many months ago a world-renowned singer finally found privacy—and much-desired anonymity—on a 3,000-acre farm in the foothills of the Blue Ridge Mountains near Charlottesville, Virginia. The man has been veritably a household word for a generation and a half of American youngsters, but people don't bother him around Charlottesville. One class, the mountain-oriented people, don't fuss over a man's bona fides as a matter of practice; if he seeks company, he's welcome, but it won't be forced upon him. A second class, remnants of Virginia's Bourbon society, socialize with their very own, a category that does not include people who sing for a living.

At any rate, the singer received a letter in the mail from New York one day that told of a serious tax problem. He consulted the yellow pages of the local Chesapeake & Potomac Telephone Company, and found a listing under "lawyers," and made a phone call, and went to town to talk with the attorney.

The tax problem, upon exploration, seemed to be as complex as it did serious, and the Charlottesville lawyer, after consultation with his conscience, told the singer, "This is really out of my league. I think you should go over to Washington and talk with a tax specialist there. I'll be happy to give you a reference."

The singer accepted the offer—the referred office was the firm of Covington and Burling—and drove away, and the Charlottesville lawyer hasn't seen him since—a matter of no little chagrin, because the singer has subsequently encountered some minor, and local, legal problems, and for advice he looked not to Charlottesville, but to Washington.

A lawyer in central Michigan earlier faced the same kind of problem. A former client, a local man, came to him with a complaint that smacked of medical malpractice. Although the lawyer had never handled a malpractice suit, the doctor's conduct seemed so bizarre that he thought liability could be readily established. Further, the consequences of the doctor's supposed conduct were so horrid that the lawyer saw the case as a once-in-a-career chance to earn a six-figure fee.

Despite nagging misgivings about his lack of experience with malpractice cases the lawyer took the suit. Several factors bolstered his confidence. He knew that insurance companies were increasingly chary of giving a jury a chance to rule on alleged malpractice wherein the doctor had left the plaintiff in pitiable physical condition. *Trial Magazine* and other journals regularly advertise texts that claim to give the lawyer the basic facts he needs to conduct almost any suit that arises in the fields of product liability, personal injury, or medical malpractice. Further, the lawyer said to himself, "If I win this case, I have the financial cushion I've always wanted."

Seventeen months later the lawyer realized that he was on the verge of disaster, both for himself and the client. Although he remained convinced the doctor was at fault, defense lawyers had so snarled the case that the attorney despaired of ever bringing it to trial. He spent his weekends at medical school libraries, studying literature pertaining to his case. He read the trial manuals he purchased through the Association of Trial Lawyers of America, the plaintiff lawyers' group. He even found a friendly local physician who (although he would not testify in court) gave him a short course in the medical procedure at issue. At one point the lawyer discussed the case in depth with a law school classmate at a bar gathering, and he said, "I feel as if I've been swimming in Lake Michigan for six hours, and I'm wearing out, and try as I can, I can't make my feet touch bottom."

Shortly thereafter the lawyer gave up. He made an urgent call to a malpractice specialist in Detroit, spent a day with him, and effectively signed over the case—and the bulk of his prospective fee.

The Detroit lawyer picks up the story: "This was the worst mess I've seen in twenty-one years of law. This local guy tried hard, but he was really out of his league. The defense did cute things to him that were unconscionable, but legal, because they knew they were playing with a patsy.

"The lawyer made any number of mistakes. He entirely missed joining* a physician involved in the case who was almost as important a figure as the other doctor. I worked my ass off, and I managed to salvage the case. But as I told this bird later, 'I'm tempted to slap your ass with a legal malpractice suit on behalf of your original client, because you screwed up this case so badly that you almost lost $300,000 for a person who had been grievously mistreated by a doctor.' "

American law is exploding. A century ago country lawyer Abraham Lincoln could thrust a law book or two into his saddle bags and travel the court circuit for weeks, his portable "library" sufficient support for any case that arose. Court fights essentially were over land and money, and a knowledge of basic contracts was enough to keep a lawyer in business. Although United States case law was slowly building, lawyers and courts still looked to the sparse English common law for precedents. Populist and frontier Americans operated under the notion that the less government interfered with man's activities, the better. They followed, more or less, the dictum once pronounced by Sam Houston, the hero of the Texas Revolution, "Never seek redress for a personal wrong in a court of law." Houston was scratching his head with a .44 caliber pistol as he spoke. His point was not lost on listeners.

Even through the first decades of this century a small-town lawyer could make do with a single shelf of law books—the statutes of his state, and perhaps the reported decisions of his state's appellate courts. What gaps appeared were filled by common sense, or imagination. In my early reportorial days I interviewed an octogenarian of the Dallas bar—his name has drifted far beyond the reach of my memory—who talked for hours about the way it was decades ago. "Lots of us operated on bluff," he said, "because the judges didn't know any more law

*Naming as a codefendant.

than we lawyers did. If I got into a tight spot, I'd just say, 'Your Honor, my authority on this point is what the Texas Supreme Court held in *Craig* versus *Walpole*.' The judge would nod wisely and rule for me, and the other lawyer might look a little put out at my erudition. 'Course, fact of the matter was that I'd pull the case out of midair, and I used *Craig* versus *Walpole* as my authority on everything from a hog theft case to a railroad collision. Handy case to have, even if it didn't exist."

Leonard Ring, the eminent Chicago personal injury specialist (and a former president of the Association of Trial Lawyers of America), recalls the "prediscovery era" in which opposing sides were not obligated to reveal in advance how they intended to prove their case.

"When I tried a personal injury case in those days—and I began practicing twenty-six years ago—I'd tell the client, 'Find any friends and relatives you can who aren't working, and bring them to court.' They'd come in with six or eight or even a dozen bodies, all of them sitting behind the plaintiff in the court. Sure enough, the other lawyer would spot them and come over and ask, 'Who are those people?'

"I'd say, 'They are with the plaintiff.'

" 'Are they witnesses?'

"I'd smile sweetly and say, 'You'll find out.'

"Another thing, I'd bring in a big old suitcase or briefcase, and put it conspicuously on the table, and rummage through it. It'd look like I had files on anything that could conceivably arise. All a front, of course: I'd simply bring along everything that happened to be on my desk, and the 'file' on the case at hand would be a sheet or two of paper.

"The other lawyer would look at those 'witnesses' and my 'files,' and he'd lean over and whisper to me, 'Why can't we talk about this case?' So we'd go out in the hall and settle. You'd come to court in the morning ready for trial; by lunchtime you'd be through.

"All this was permissible because the other side wasn't giving you anything, and you certainly weren't volunteering your case. This technique was especially helpful in intersection collisions, where you might have *really* found some witnesses through investigation. Make a guy think you're loaded for bear, and he won't take you head-on.

"You can't do that now, of course. Unless you are a lazy lawyer, at the very least you are going to send out interrogatories for the names of witnesses. Any names he doesn't give you, he can't use, so the idea of packing the courtroom with non-relevant people just doesn't work.

"Discovery eliminates the sort of trickery I resorted to as a youngster. I don't apologize for it. You worked by the seat of your pants. The rules were that you walked into court with a thin file, and it was up to the art of the advocate to take a few bare facts and win a lawsuit."

Such casual flummery no longer suffices. The law explosion is inundating American attorneys, partly at their initiative (for instance, the ingenious use of the doctrine of product liability to get at previously immune defendants); partly because of expanding government (at one time a "land lawyer" could survive if he knew how to write a deed and search a title; now he must know environmental law as well); partly because of the increasing proclivity of aggrieved citizens to take their case to court (a San Francisco secretary sued the local transit company a few years back, claiming that an accident had transformed her into an insatiable nymphomaniac. She won, and she collected). The resulting flow of paper is staggering, and is accumulating at a rate far beyond the reading capacity of any practicing lawyer. The librarian for a major Washington firm told me, "Stuff comes in here faster than I can catalogue it and put it on the shelves. How the dickens anyone is supposed to read it is beyond me." An out-of-town lawyer marveled at what he had seen at the Federal Power Commission (FPC) offices in Washington: "Each day, at ten in the morning and three in the afternoon, the FPC issues as many as thirty separate statements and opinions, some of them thirty to forty pages. Many of these rulings have the force of a statutory law or a court opinion. And this is just the FPC, a relatively small agency."

So how does a lawyer remain abreast of what is happening in his profession? A large firm can afford in-house experts on every subject. Covington and Burling, the Washington firm, has people on the premises who can give an hour briefing on the Colombian tax code, or Section 1013(b) of the McCarran-Ferguson Act* or a ruling of the Federal Communications Commission

*15 USC section 1013(b), 1970. The section exempted several business activities from the general immunity from antitrust liabilities granted the insurance industry in the original act.

published the previous afternoon—and most likely without resort to an outside law library. There are cliques of specialists who never venture outside their own highly inbred fields. Most of these specialists are candid about their capabilities. A Houston admiralty lawyer told me, "If you bust up your rental car on the way back to the airport, don't bother to call me. I wouldn't remember how to write the pleadings in a conventional PI case. But if you ever happen to run your tugboat into someone else's freighter, I'm in the phone book, and I'll give you a helluva' lawsuit."

But a vast number of American lawyers are neither specialists nor big-firm practitioners. They work by themselves or with two or three other attorneys. (The American Bar Association says that 75 percent of the lawyers in the United States are in firms of three or less attorneys.) Being human, they like to make money, and they do not like to appear ignorant when a potential client comes in with an exotic problem and enough cash to pay the fee. So how do these persons survive?

Fortunately for them, lawyers are extraordinarily loose-lipped with their trade secrets, which means there is an abundance of how-to-do-it (and how-I-did-it) literature in any law library. "Form books" give chapter and verse on how to prepare pleadings on any conceivable case, from a slip-and-fall accident in a supermarket to a bankruptcy or adoption. Such literature is especially copious in the personal injury field. Half a dozen or more commercial publishers offer what are tantamount to "prepackaged lawsuits"—forms for every phase of a case from the initial complaint through motions, interrogatories, pretrial briefs, elements of proof, the suggested form of questions for witnesses, the closing argument, the judge's charge to the jury.

One of the heftiest how-to-do-it books is a volume entitled *Bender's Automobile Interrogatories*, published by the Matthew Bender Company, which lists just about everything any lawyer would want to know about a car crash—519 separate questions, some with as many as 8 parts, covering 80 printed pages. Examples:

41. State:

    a. The name and address of each and every school you have ever attended.

b. The highest grade attained in each school.
c. The name and address of each and every teacher who has ever taught you.

42. Do you attend a church or Sunday school?
43. If you do, state:
    a. The name and address of the church or Sunday school.
    b. The name and address of each and every teacher who has taught Sunday school to you.

72. With reference to the trip you were taking at the time of the accident herein, state:
    a. Where it started.
    b. When it started.
    c. Where it was scheduled to end.
    d. When you were due to arrive at your intended destination.
    e. The stops which had been made prior to the collision.
    f. The stops which you intended making over the uncompleted part of your trip.
    g. The reason or reasons for the trip.

Other sections list basic interrogatories for bus and motorcycle accidents. The auto list is supplemented by questions for specific accident causes ranging from defective brakes to broken motor mounts. One frequent use of such forms—one unadvertised by the publisher—is to make life miserable for the opposing party. States a personal injury lawyer: "You'd be a fool to follow the forms exactly and not rely upon anything else. But they are a fast and inexpensive way to make a lot of work for the other side. A lawyer who says he has no intention of settling can change his mind in a hurry when seventy-five pages of interrogatories plop on his desk. That's a lot of work for him, man, and all you've done, basically, is pull out the form book and tell your secretary, 'Mary, run these through your typewriter.' "

But lawsuits are not won by paperwork alone. Hence the astute lawyer turns to professional meetings and publications to learn the trade tricks that give him the added courtroom edge. For the PI defense lawyer, the *Insurance Counsel Journal* is a veritable cornucopia of practical—and cold-bloodedly realistic—information. And defense lawyers consult this journal. In

Boston one afternoon I spent several fruitless hours trying to persuade a young insurance lawyer to discuss a case with me. Appeals had ended, and the case had received wide press attention; nonetheless, he refused to talk about any specifics. At one point I glanced over his desk and saw a bound volume of the *Insurance Counsel Journal*, and I noted the title and the date (July 1970) of the article to which it was opened. The lawyer had underlined several passages, and I said to myself, *Okay, fellow, maybe you won't talk, but at least I can go to the Library of Congress and see what you like to read during office hours.*

The article proved to be "Thoughts on Critiquing the Plaintiff's Medical Picture," by William R. Moeller, of Regnier, Moeller & Taylor, of Hartford, Connecticut, an insurance lawyer noted for his handling of medical witnesses. In this particular article Moeller emphasized restraint and common sense, urging that care be taken in making frontal attacks on medical reports when defending an accident case:

> If the plaintiff is a resident of a small community and has as his doctor the most highly respected physician in the locale, it would be foolhardy to request the plaintiff to come for an examination before the "big city specialist." The jury would at once "sense the insurance" and would be called upon to uphold their doctor against this kind of interloper from the rich outlands. Similarly, if the treating doctor is the head of the medical staff of the only hospital in a large area, no responsible doctor is going to jeopardize his future by questioning the conclusion of the chief of staff.

Moeller also warned of over-preparing a case. If the plaintiff lawyer has a good reputation, and if the medical examination he arranged seems "clean," demanding an independent defense exam "is surplusage and can be dangerous," Moeller suggests. If the defense exam supports the victim's case, the plaintiff lawyer is certain to put it into evidence—thus buttressing his claim at the expense of the insurance company. Comments Moeller: "Obviously, if the plaintiff has sustained an amputation, there is no need to have your doctor examine and further describe the stump."

Other Moeller tips:

—If the defense has a choice between using a general practitioner or a plastic surgeon as a witness, choose the former, for he is used to seeing scars as the unavoidable concomitant of accidents and surgery. "Besides, he talks about them in normal language. A two-inch scar in the hairline does not appear to him as a five-centimeter induration of the forehead."

—If the plaintiff is old, avoid taking his deposition for as long as possible—he might die. If he has not deposed, the other lawyer won't be able to emphasize his pain and suffering by reading the questions and answers to the jury.

(After reading Moeller's article I telephoned the Boston lawyer and asked if he had put it to practical use. "You are a damned snoop," he said, "and I don't think it's proper for you to look at what is on my desk." He hung up.)

Another source of coaching is the periodic workshops staged by the Practicing Law Institute, in New York. Lawyers listen to specialists over a two-day period, and the emphasis is on practical advice. The workshops are expensive, running upward to $350, but in the words of a Baltimore attorney, "If you want a cram course in a subject, and are willing to take the time to listen, you come away with a fast overview." Workshop proceedings are sold at from $20 to $40 per slim volume. And the emphasis is upon practicalities, not theory.

One such session, on personal injury damages, stressed stratagems for putting the jury into the most sympathetic frame of mind possible. John C. Shepherd, of Coburn, Croft, Shepherd & Herzog, a St. Louis PI firm, suggested how to use drama to keep the jurors' attention:

> If you know in advance you are going to have trouble bringing in, let us say, an old lady in a wheelchair, tell the jury about it in your opening statement. Say, "I expect to bring as a witness a lady who was on her porch and who saw this accident. She is an elderly woman and she is crippled. I hope she will be able to come to court. I am telling you that . . . if she testifies, she was sitting there and looking out across her yard and saw this accident."
>
> You build up a little drama at the outset. Will the witness be here? Won't she be? Let the jury think about the trouble you are having. Then when that door swings open and in comes your elderly, crippled witness, you have created a dramatic moment even before she starts to testify.[1]

For the working lawyer, the trouble with relying upon the do-it-yourself form books and the twice-annual seminars is that they are haphazard. According to a staff member at the Practicing Law Institute, "I'd be less than candid if I tried to claim that *every* lawyer benefits from attending one of our workshops. Certainly, they learn something. But they might go two or three years without putting it to use in their practice." For this reason, among others, American law is spawning truly revolutionary support organizations—quite literally, outside groups and specialists who help a specific lawyer prepare and try a specific case, for a fee.

I learned of these groups through the advertising columns of *Trial Magazine*. One two-page advertisement in particular stirred my interest. The left-hand page pictured the women's clothes area of a department store. The big-type caption read, "Find the Inherently Dangerous Instrument. And Win $100,000." The right-hand page carried a first-person account by a pseudonymous lawyer, "William Cabell Wynne," who outlined the case and the way he solved it.*

The client, a "Mrs. Orsini," had tripped on a coat hanger, suffering permanent back injuries. The lawyer could find no evidence of negligence by either the store or its employees. Customers occasionally dropped coat hangers, but clerks picked them up as fast as reasonably possible.

"So where was our case?" lawyer Wynne asked. "I called in The Research Group. We decided to waive the negligence suit and to proceed on grounds of strict product liability." Since the coat hanger was made of clear plastic, it was almost impossible to see on the floor. "We built our case on the 'invisibility' of the coat hanger and the foreseeable likelihood that it would fall to the floor." Wynne presented expert testimony that their transparency made the hangers defective and inherently dangerous, the legal criteria in a products liability case. He also argued that modern merchandising intentionally attracted shoppers' eyes away from the floor to display shelves. Wynne continued:

> The Research Group prepared a comprehensive trial brief which legally substantiated my factual conclusions. The Research

*An italicized line at the bottom of the ad read, "The facts as stated here are true. Names and places have been changed to conform with the [ABA] Code of Professional Responsibility. Documentation is available from The Research Group."

> Group brief established the applicable law of product liability and argued that liability did not depend on the sale of the product. Under the bystander theory, the manufacturer is liable even if the person injured had no intention of ever purchasing the product. The coat hanger was in the stream of commerce and was a part of the defendant's marketing scheme.

Wynne won $100,000 in the case, and he sang the praises of The Research Group for several paragraphs. He had used the group's services, in his words, "*in every significant case* I have had in the last three years [Wynne's italics]," and its briefs and memoranda were instrumental in recovering more than $1 million. Wynne continued:

> Investing in The Research Group's legal research and advocacy is also an investment in the growth of my own reputation in the legal community. The return on that investment has been invaluable to me.
>
> In 1974 I earned a net of $193,000. To achieve that income, I've developed a highly organized practice of law.
>
> The Research Group is part of my practice . . .

At the bottom of the ad was a photograph of a Monticello-esque two-story brick building with flowing white columns. The Research Group listed a home office address in Charlottesville, Virginia, just over the Blue Ridge from my home in Page County, and branch offices in Berkeley, Boston and Ann Arbor. I asked myself, *What in the dickens are these people doing? Is The Research Group some sort of superlaw firm?*

I wrote a letter to Charlottesville, and in due course I found myself one morning in an office on the second floor of the Monticello-esque building, with an earnest young man named Walter Morrison, TRG's president. During the small talk I noticed models of several futuristic houses tucked into odd corners. "Are you people into making courtroom exhibits as well?" I asked Morrison.

He smiled. "No," he said, "my wife and I just built a new house, and those are models of some of the possibilities we considered."

"You must be making a buck or two," I said.

"Oh," he replied, "we're doing all right. But let's do this from the beginning. I am a native Virginian, and I went to law school here in Charlottesville, at the University of Virginia. My first job was in Hartford, Connecticut, clerking within a twenty-five-lawyer firm.

"I worked directly under a senior partner, doing his paperwork, his research, and assisting him in general in both settlement negotiations and in court appearances. Immediately I recognized a striking imbalance. We'd be up against a single practitioner with no assistance whatsoever. Clearly it was a case of unequal advocacy. The sole lawyer could be the senior partner's equal, intellectually, but our productivity, power and resources far outstripped him. The thought came to me gradually that the need existed for an organization that could provide big-firm resources and support to the small firm or individual lawyer."

Morrison quit the Hartford firm and returned to Charlottesville. This was in 1969. He hired a single law student as his "staff" and rented a one-desk, one-phone office and began calling lawyers throughout Virginia, offering backup research work. "Law students had done this before on an ad hoc basis. A small-county lawyer with a problem would call the law school and ask for assistance. The problem was, students are on tight class schedules and they can't drop their work and devote full time to the lawyer's request, even if they are paid. Nor can the small-town lawyer afford to abandon his practice for a day or so and come to U-VA [the way it's said in Virginia] or the William and Mary Law School and do his own research. The man who leaves a one-man practice even for a day misses any potential client who walks in. Prospective clients don't like that, they'll go somewhere else."

Morrison's pitch was straight: give me a problem, see what I can do with it. The first one hundred calls produced five assignments, which in turn produced enough money to finance a direct-mail solicitation of most lawyers in Virginia.

Things snowballed. In two and a half years The Research Group balance sheet showed black ink. When Morrison and I talked in the fall of 1976 it was up to seventy-five full-time attorneys, some 150 law students and seventy-five-odd support persons, and two branch offices. The group boasts 13,000 clients during its six years.

Morrison's notion is that practicing lawyers can do a better job if they do not bog down in books, that the more library work they slough off on professional researchers, the more time they can devote to "creative advocacy" on behalf of clients.

"Our bread and butter is the ten-man firm, or less, principally the five-man firm, with a few large ones thrown in. We also help the legal departments of smaller corporations which have problems."

Morrison began piling paper on the coffee table for me to take with me. There was a nine-page pamphlet containing a topical index of the types of cases TRG has handled. "You'll see that we run all the way from A to Z—administrative law to zoning," he said. There were a number of "case histories" with identifying data removed. They ranged from a landfill case in New Jersey to stray cattle in Texas, and each concluded with a glowing comment from the attorney ("I liked the research; I was able to obtain a settlement because I had my guns loaded") and the fee (a high of $575.10, a low of $243.90). There was a fifty-five-page brief TRG had prepared for the Nevada firm of Laxalt, Berry & Allison (the state's Republican Senator, Paul Laxalt, is one of the name partners) in a sales tax case. A cover summary quoted Reese H. Taylor, the attorney in the case, "The brief you prepared for me was of the highest quality. It enabled me to argue much more effectively than the [state] deputy attorney general. My client was ecstatic that I saved him $90,000 in back taxes." TRG's fee for the brief was $1,267.14. There were handsome reprints of various TRG advertisements, including the one that had caught my eye in *Trial Magazine*.

A photocopy was attached to the ad: a page from the *ATLA Bulletin*, which reports on cases won (and occasionally lost) by PI lawyers around the country. I scanned an item that someone had marked:

> PLASTIC HANGERS—TRIP & FALL BY CUSTOMER IN DEPARTMENT STORE—STRICT LIABILITY. Zayre Department Store That Manufactured Clear Plastic Hangers to Display Its Merchandise Held Liable in Strict Products Liability for Back Injury to Customer Who Tripped & Fell on Hanger Lying in Aisle.

The item went on to give details of the case that had been described in the TRG ad, and thanked "ATLA member Elmer

Oberhellman, St. Louis, counsel for plaintiff," for supplying the story.

"Hey," I said to Morrison. "So Oberhellman is the lawyer in your ad, eh?"

"Right," said Morrison. "He's one of our most satisfied clients. He must be in touch with us two times monthly with some case or another. Everyone in the PI field will connect our ad with this ATLA item, so that's why I think it's okay to mention him by name."

TRG's main physical resources, the law books in which it does its research, belong to someone else—the libraries of the law schools adjacent to its offices. Why do the ruling authorities of the Harvard, UC-Berkeley, Michigan and Virginia law schools permit a private profit-making business to use their books? Morrison cites several reasons. TRG hires both graduates and students, a boon to placement and student-aid officers of the schools. Student researchers working for TRG in effect are in an intensive clinical program, an on-the-job training that law professors apparently feel adds to their education. And, finally, TRG gives the student workers a crash course in research techniques—one so respected that several schools have adapted TRG's book, *Basic Legal Research Techniques*,* for use in their courses.

Internally, TRG is organized along the lines of a major law firm, with divisions for such specialties as tax and commercial law, and with a partner–junior-partner–associate hierarchy, in function if not in title. Although students and young lawyers do the bulk of the library work, Morrison stresses that the work is coordinated by a senior attorney, who also reviews the final work product.

Ideally, TRG's work is a "starting point" for the lawyer, although reality indicates otherwise. For instance, the form that lawyers use to request briefs offers a choice: should it be typed on plain paper, or otherwise? Unmarked briefs, of course, can be shuffled before client or court as the attorney's own work—and they are, regularly. For this reason, many lawyers and big firms that use TRG are wary of publicity. The reason is obvious.

*A corporate effort, but with most of the organization and editorial work done by Neill H. Hollenshead, vice-president.

They hire out to conduct a citizen's lawsuit; they run to an outsider for assistance; they humph with contrived pride at the brief that is produced. An ignorant client tends to be a happy client—and, conceivably, a slightly bilked client as well.

"What do you charge for this service?" I asked Morrison. He replied, "$19.50 an hour."

I wrote the figure, and my pencil stopped, and I looked at him. "Did I just write down a typographical error?"

Morrison smiled a sort of indulgent smile, one that could have irritated me, for I don't like to be considered naive. His smile was legitimate, because the figure surprises many people. "Our hourly rate is lower than a plumber," he said.

Okay, how the devil do you charge such a low figure? Why, you can't get a letter typed at some of the big Washington firms for nineteen bucks and fifty cents.

"Volume. Methodology. We know the sources; we know how to get to them and to use them in a hurry. No big secret. If you haven't done a Supreme Court brief, it takes a lot longer than if you have done one hundred. Well, we have done our hundred.

"That we charge this amount and that we make a profit proves you can do it through good management and specialization. And our work is done professionally, without violating any canons or doing anything wild." Morrison's message, unstated, perhaps even unintended, is that lawyers charge too much.

A lawyer is under no obligation to tell his client that TRG or a similar group did his homework, and the American Bar Association estimates that U.S. attorneys average between $40 and $50 hourly for their services. How much of the difference between $19.50 and $40 is passed back to the client? "Frankly," said Morrison, "I don't know. But theoretically the client can receive double the amount of research time for the same price. But whether this happens—well, there's no way to know." *Juris Doctor*, the legal publication, commented in 1975, "Doubtless there are greedy—and lazy—attorneys who will retain private research firms to do the bleary-eyed dirty work in the stacks in order to keep their caseloads moving to the tune of a ringing cash register. But more selfless souls might consider passing on savings to clients—especially in view of the rising tide of anti-professional consumerism."[2]

The new-graduate glut that hit American law in the early

1970s, with three or more applicants for every job, coincided with TRG's rise, and hence Morrison asserted the group has no problem "being competitive in hiring. We go after the top graduates; we pay the same salaries as a good-sized law firm. We are comparable to a class firm." (Perhaps. But if any lawyers over age forty were in the TRG premises the day of my visit I did not see them.) TRG also contains lawyers who have tried other things and didn't like them. There is the graduate who goes to a big firm and spends two or three years filing papers and hustling from one court clerk's office to another—even doing chauffeur work for a partner's wife or going to an out-of-town trial with duties no more discernible than carrying another man's briefcase from the hotel to the courthouse and finding a safe place to hang his overcoat. There is the lawyer who really wants to be teaching law, but can't find a faculty position. There are the lawyers who don't like the hassles of private practice—the finding and feeding of clients, and the paper pushing endemic to real law.

Respectability and acceptance are ephemeral qualities, ones incapable of objective definition. Morrison feels one turning point came when the White House Task Force on Products Liability recruited TRG to write draft legislation on one of the major economic issues confronting modern America. Manufacturers claim they are being forced out of business because of the high cost of liability insurance. Consumer groups, abetted by the personal injury bar, are asserting that safe products, rather than insurance premiums, are the real issue. Money is rolling around with thundering sounds. The metals processing industry alone claims that $30 billion will be cleaved from the gross national product unless it wins relief. Morrison walks between these special interest groups with supreme detachment: "We received this contract because we are objective, and because we do not align ourselves with any group. And as long as I have a say, we'll stay that way."

In its early days TRG came under sharp criticism from some bar elements who didn't like the idea of an outside group doing lawyers' work. There were mutters about the "unauthorized practice of law," although Morrison felt the real opposition was from lawyers "who didn't like the idea of the opposition coming in with one of our thorough briefs, or who considered us as a competitor." So TRG solicited formal opinions from various bar groups and state supreme courts, all of which approved its service. No complaints have been heard in recent years, and TRG is a welcome exhibitor at bar conventions. Indeed, according to Morrison, TRG does much of its direct solicitation of business at these gatherings. (One way TRG skirts the issue of unauthorized practice of law is to serve attorneys only. A lay citizen who approaches TRG with a request is advised to work through a lawyer.)

"Candidly," said Morrison, "I think The Research Group and similar organizations can save the small firms.* There *must* be a way for them to get their hands on quality information."

We had talked for several hours, and at Morrison's suggestion I gathered up the several pounds of material he had accumulated for me and followed him around the corner. "I want you to meet some of the guys who really make The Research Group go," he said.

Three neat young men awaited me, and the thought crossed my mind, *This is comparable to the briefings the Pentagon used to give us journalists back in the Vietnam War days. Will Bob McNamara pop out with flip charts and a pointer?* I pushed away the beginnings of a smile and listened to Frank Orban, a vice-president, who is putting together an international division for TRG. The information will flow both ways: about U.S. law for foreign lawyers and businessmen, and about foreign law for U.S. attorneys and investors. Orban explained that international law is considerably more complex than domestic practice, partly because of inherent mechanical problems.

"A client's letter will arrive written, say, in French. We have people who can do the translation, but we must be very exact in how we reply: you've got to be accurate in both the legal and the linguistic points of view. The report also must carry with it copies of cases cited, for a law firm in Milan, Italy, isn't going to have the *Southwestern Reporter*** lying around the office.

*Groups patterned roughly along the same lines as TRG include the American Legal Research Corporation, Gainesville, Florida; Counsel's Aide, Inc., Chicago; and the Hastings Research Services, San Francisco. The latter is a nonprofit adjunct of the University of California's Hastings College of Law; earnings go into a scholarship fund.

**The periodic volume containing state court opinions in the Southwestern United States.

"Not so many years ago an 'international practice' in the United States traditionally meant tax law. Now other countries are developing antitrust and environmental law, and U.S. attorneys are having to learn about them, and do not have the necessary in-house expertise. Take a hypothetical case. A company in Kansas City has a problem in Austria, so it goes to its Kansas City law firm. The lawyers there, of course, don't know a thing about Austrian law, so they go to Covington and Burling in Washington or Shearman & Sterling in New York, which shuffles the problem to a European office, in Paris.

"We're getting closer, but no one in Paris knows Austrian law, so they call a Viennese firm that has someone who can speak English. Passing around this paper is expensive and confusing, and there's always the chance that the problem won't be defined succinctly by the time it gets to the lawyer who actually does the work."

TRG has foreign-born lawyers in Washington and Boston who handle assignments from U.S. firms, doing basic research at the Library of Congress's law division or Harvard. The problems can be devilishly complex, as if a mischievous law professor had set out to create a fact situation designed to reduce students to gibbering. An example:

A TRG client represents a manufacturer who supplied military goods to Israel that were used in the June 1967 war. The Israelis claimed the equipment was defective and caused injuries to soldiers in the Sinai campaign. In a preliminary report TRG concluded that in a suit brought against the manufacturer in a U.S. court, the judge would follow the law of the place where the accident occurred. A researcher easily supplied the statute of limitations (the lawyers' question suggested that the manufacturer hoped that the passage of time had put him out of reach of the Israelis).

But wait. The accident happened in the Sinai, land historically fought over by both Israel and Egypt. So which country's laws should apply? If Israel prevailed, were there any variations between civil law and that followed in occupied territories? Should the injured soldiers' claim be lodged against their own government? What effect should their compensation from the military have on their claim against the U.S. company? Could sabotage be proved, and if so, what would this fact do to the case?

Orban sat in his office and ticked off these questions with the manner of a man drafting plans for a maze. I had to wave my hand several times to slow him down; the flow of possibilities and contingencies was so fast, so complex, I could not get them onto paper. Orban laughed. "The lawyers in this case didn't have any inkling of the tiger pit they were walking through."* Orban gave a couple of other examples of foreign cases:

"In the past two weeks a client wanted to know all the laws in the world which limited liability for nuclear reactor accidents. We searched the laws of thirty countries, and we did it in seven days.

"Again, a major regional bank wanted to loan money in Latin America, and the general counsel asked about laws that would impact them. This was an open-ended query in which we had to devise the questions that should be answered. What a variety! Must banks register before lending in a country? And with what agency? What about taxes? What are the permissible rates of interest? Must the notary be in the country of the borrower? What about default of payment? We did this for fourteen Latin American countries."

James Arnold, another TRG vice-president, is responsible for attracting business ("Development, we call it!") and he tossed out some intriguing figures. TRG, he says, has serviced "one out of every five lawyers in Virginia," and some firms have asked for TRG's help more than one hundred times. Arnold told me a story intended to illustrate how useful TRG is to clients because it can move fast in an emergency.

An attorney called in a panic at ten o'clock one morning and said, "I have an important client coming in at two o'clock and I'm sorry to confess that I haven't done the work I should have done. Could you run down something on this problem and call me back by 1:30 and brief me so that I can talk intelligently with him?" "Done," Arnold said with a smile.

I felt uneasy. The situation Arnold had described to me smacked of a lawyer who was skittering very close to legal malpractice. Was TRG in fact nothing more than a respectable-

*Orban and others at TRG declined to discuss specifics of the case or to reveal the identity of the parties involved, on grounds of client confidentiality. I am sorry to say I cannot report the outcome, for I am truly curious myself.

appearing crutch for lawyers too lazy to do their own work? I began listening a bit more closely.

Arnold continued. The cases about which he—and TRG—have admittedly ambivalent feelings are those in which a litigious citizen is pressing a lawyer to find grounds to sue someone simply to work off frustrations. "There are certain factual situations in which a lawyer must be most creative to find grounds for suit or someone to sue," Arnold said archly. "A Massachusetts man read in his local newspaper that a highway would open on July first or some such date. So he went to the highway on the announced date, drove around the barricades, and went off an embankment and was injured. The highway wasn't finished, and the paper had not run a story about the delayed opening. He wanted to sue the newspaper. The attorney tried to dissuade him, but with no success. So he came to The Research Group for help in putting together a case so that he wouldn't look like a complete idiot. He didn't win, but he satisfied his client."

He satisfied his client. What more should be expected of a lawyer? I talked with the TRG people a bit longer, and came back over the mountain to my home, and I thought about what these young lawyers had told me. One rule I've long followed as a writer is that I do not accept self-endorsements at face value. If a lawyer—or anyone else—tells me what a splendid fellow he is, I like to talk with people with whom he has done business and ask for objective comments.

TRG received a mixed report card. "Damned good—and fast," said a Washington PI lawyer. "You want a brief on a particular point of law, they can supply it almost overnight, and in a form you can submit directly to court." A suburban Virginia lawyer was not as enthusiastic. "They tend to be so academic that they are useless, from a practical trial sense," she said. A Chicago lawyer wrote, "I used them once, when I was in a time bind. I got by okay, but I later learned that their brief had missed an Illinois case that was relevant to my suit. Fortunately, my opposition missed it, too. Yes, I'd use them again, but I'd check the end product more closely than I did previously."

Before I got around to writing about The Research Group, a quirk of circumstances made it possible for me to do my own private evaluation of the organization's effectiveness. I needed background information on three Federal judges, and time and other pressures made it inconvenient for me to do the research personally. *Aha!* I thought. *I'll give the assignment to TRG. Not only will I get my needed facts in a hurry, but this gives me the opportunity to double-check TRG.*

I found the brochure TRG circulates to potential clients—one of the innumerable pieces of paper pressed upon me by Morrison and Arnold—and called the Charlottesville office and told a functionary who I was and what I wanted. I did not mention my previous contacts with TRG's hierarchy, for I did not want any special treatment. So far as TRG staff was concerned, I wanted to be treated like a walk-in client.

Oops. A problem. "I'm sorry, sir, we don't do work for anyone other than a lawyer. Now if you have an attorney. . . ." I had forgotten the TRG policy about nonlawyer clients. No matter. In fact, sending a request in blind should insure that TRG would not give my query favored attention.

My query, ultimately submitted by a Washington lawyer friend, was threefold. I wanted the names and current addresses of clerks to three judges for a stated period in the early 1970s. I wanted copies of the judges' confirmation hearings before the Senate Judiciary Committee. And I wanted legal biographical material, including representative clients of their old law firms as listed by *Martindale-Hubbell*, the leading legal directory. My lawyer friend called back. "They're right on it," he said. "They said they'd have the information in less than a week."

Well, TRG flunked, and as I wrote Morrison in a moment of pique, "not with a D, but with an F." The researcher (I do not know the person, so I shall leave him nameless) drew a blank on two of the three questions, gave bad legal advice in the process and overlooked a rather basic research source. In order:

—In seeking the names of the past law clerks the researcher asked the judges, who (predictably) declined. An imaginative researcher—or even a raw cub reporter—would have immediately asked, "Where else could I obtain this information?" One source is obvious to anyone with a passing knowledge of the legal system: the Administrative Office of the U.S. Courts, which is just what its title implies. Obtaining the names of paid court employees requires nothing more than a phone call. I know, for I made the phone call, and I had the names within an hour.

—Similarly, when the researcher asked the National Archives for copies of the judges' confirmation hearings, he was told he needed permission from the Senate Judiciary Committee. He proceeded no further. I called the Committee directly and told a clerk the names of the hearings I needed, and I read them in the committee office within the week. These are transcripts of *public hearings*, assuredly not sensitive material in any sense of the word.

—The most disturbing paragraph of TRG's report was a suggestion that a "Freedom of Information Act proceeding might be of value" in gaining access to the transcripts. I doubt it, for the act does not cover congressional documents. As I asked Morrison in a letter, "How many more hours of paid 'research time' would TRG have expended before stumbling over this rather relevant fact?"

—TRG's billing listed 33.2 hours of "research, writing and editing" time. The report indicated that because of the researcher's "inability to inspect the transcripts of the committee's hearings a substantial amount of time was required to track down the pertinent bibliographical material, i.e., untold volumes of *Martindale-Hubbell* had to be examined." Oh, nonsense. While in the Washington area one afternoon soon after receiving the TRG report, I stopped in a suburban library, in Vienna, Virginia, walked over to the reference desk and looked through the current *Who's Who in America*. In eleven minutes flat, which included reshelving the two volumes, I had the basic data required to run down the *Martindale-Hubbell* material.

TRG's bill was $749.46—33.2 hours of "research, writing and editing," at $19.50 per hour, $647.50; typing and clerical, 1.9 hours at $4.00, $7.40 ; telephone tolls, $10.55; postage, $0.47; and "other (travel, lodging, meals, etc.)," $83.40.

TRG responded to my comments by vigorously defending its work. In the first place, it claimed to have told my lawyer friend that his requests were outside the normal scope of TRG's work. But according to TRG, he insisted that it proceed anyway, which it did "reluctantly." (My friend's recollection is somewhat different.) TRG did not ask the Senate Judiciary Committee for permission to examine the confirmation hearing transcripts because, in the researcher's words, "I would need [the lawyer's], permission to do so" and he "might not wish to divulge his reasons."

We settled for $212.14. So much for The Research Group.

I returned to the classified columns of *Trial Magazine*, a veritable bazaar of experts willing to do lawyers' homework and then testify for them at trial. "Medi-Legal Services evaluates malpractice; we provide the expert, any kind of expert," proclaimed an outfit in San Diego. "Our last case settled for $800,000. SERVING THE ENTIRE U.S." An engineer in Media, Pennsylvania, offered himself as a "consultant and expert witness" in airplane and helicopter crashes. Another, in Minneapolis, cited "35 years experience" in foods, beverages and confections. A Philadelphia "actuarial-economic consultant" asked in boldface type:

> WHAT DATA IS NEEDED TO DETERMINE
> THE VALUE OF A HOUSEWIFE'S SERVICES?
>
> Governmental and private research studies, combined with actual schedules of the weekly tasks that had been performed by the injured or deceased housewife. Call or write to discuss the problems in your current injury or death case. Services for plaintiff or defense counsel.*

Malpractice Research, Inc., which listed as its address a post office box in Herndon, Virginia, a Washington suburb, offered to review medical records "conscientiously and thoroughly" for $400, and return "unbiased opinions," and provide "medical witnesses . . . to assist with deposition and to testify in any court in the country." It was signed "Sincerely yours, H. Barry Jacobs, M.D."

H. Barry Jacobs. The name was vaguely familiar, and I searched my files. Yes. The *Washington Post*, April 5, 1976. Jacobs had become the first physician ever expelled from the Fairfax County, Virginia, Medical Society, on charges stemming from supposed overcharging of patients and advertising three

*Many of the ads said the experts would work for either side. But if any of the experts advertised in the insurance lawyer journals, I overlooked them.

medical clinics he operated. In pleading for leniency Jacobs told the society, "When I first went into practice I think I made a lot of mistakes. I was greedy, I was very depressed . . . and that's how I got into this clinic mess. . . . But I feel now that I'm under a microscope and I'm really afraid even to burp at a table for fear of being unethical." According to the *Post*, Jacobs became medical director of Malpractice Research shortly after his expulsion from the medical society. (He denied any earlier association with or knowledge of the group, even though his attorney and personal secretary were directors.)

I kept reading, and I kept returning to an advertisement from something called Medical-Legal Consulting Service, Inc. (M-LCS), of Chevy Chase, Maryland, a Washington suburb. M-LCS described itself as "the only full-time consulting firm dedicated to assisting attorneys in all jurisdictions with screening and preparing medico-legal cases. . . . Since 1969 our technical and medical staffs have pioneered significant advances in the medical field. Our full-time staff, the immediate availability of our medical experts, the world's most complete medical library,* and our accessibility to federal agencies have led to our clients' success in the following areas—medical malpractice, personal injury, cause-of-death in insurance claims, pharmaceutical claims in Food and Drug Administration disputes, product liability, environmental and criminal."

The bottom line of the ad contained three words: "Experience. Success. Integrity." I went to Chevy Chase.

Three days before he was to have been graduated from the University of Miami School of Medicine in 1965, Robert J. Militana received a summons to the dean's office. The message: do not bother to appear at graduation; you are not to receive a degree.

The news stunned Militana, who had passed his course work and done everything required for a degree. "I knew the reasons. As a student I was a consumer advocate. I didn't like the emphasis of pocketbook over patient. I didn't like the high attrition rate. Miami kicked out students right and left to keep down the

*True, but the cited library is not M-LCS's property. It is the National Library of Medicine, located in the National Institutes of Health complex just north of the M-LCS offices. It is a federal facility, and it is open to any interested citizen.

ranks of physicians. One third of the group which entered school with me did not become physicians, and these were guys who had been tops in their classes in undergraduate school. The American Medical Association decides how many people will become physicians, and the schools oblige."

Militana sued for his degree, but lost, a Florida state judge holding that since courts "are not learned in medical education," they should not interfere in school-student relations. ("Ridiculous reasoning," scoffs Militana. "By that criterion courts would never rule on any issue.") Militana kept trying. Through his father, an Annapolis graduate as well as a lawyer, he obtained an audience with the navy surgeon general and offered to become a career military physician, specializing in experimental pediatric surgery. "Both of us would have benefited. The armed services have a chronic problem in obtaining enough skilled doctors, because of the money problem. Money didn't especially interest me; I wanted to do surgery." Several days later the surgeon general passed more bad news to Militana: the AMA would not approve the arrangement. Sorry.

During the appeals and court fights Militana did further graduate work, in psychology, and finally ended up back in his native Washington, D.C., as chief of hematology for a medical laboratory. Having his career aborted in such peremptory fashion galled Militana—and indeed, denying Militana his M.D. must rank as one of organized medicine's more grievous and costly blunders, in view of the direction he took at this point. He says, "I wanted to be an advocate for better medicine, but I had no power base at all." Militana cast around for ideas on how to put his medical knowledge to good use.

"One area I hit upon was the need for communication between doctors and lawyers. The conspiracy of silence was rather heavy at this time, in the late 1960s. Plaintiff attorneys could not find fair and objective case evaluation when medical malpractice was suspected, much less doctors who were willing to testify at trial. There were a few courageous doctors, but the way the system worked, they compromised themselves. They would testify outside their fields of specialty simply because no one else was available, and therefore the defense denounced them as greedy and as 'guns for hire.' What the system needed was a source of dependable, objective, thorough evaluation of suspected malpractice cases, and equally competent trial evaluation. Let's be realistic. The insurance companies, with their vast resources and the formal cooperation of the medical profession, are uniquely equipped to defend such cases; a balancing force definitely was needed.

"Personally, providing such a service was obviously a way I could make a living, use my medical knowledge and also do something of social significance."

So Militana quit his job at the medical laboratory and began spreading the word to Washington area lawyers that he would discuss malpractice cases with them. "My 'office' was an efficiency apartment on Washington Circle. I spoke at seminars. I spent much time trying to persuade the giants in the personal injury field that I could help them. The first time I met Melvin Belli he said, 'What the hell is a medical-legal consultant?' Well, he learned, and he and other lawyers began using me." He formed his own company, Medical-Legal Consulting Service, Inc. Eventually he moved from the cramped downtown quarters to a modernistic office suite in Chevy Chase, on Connecticut Avenue just north of the District of Columbia. Militana is making his living—and a handsome one—at the expense of the profession that rejected him, and he seems to be enjoying every moment of it.

Militana doesn't work alone. The core of M-LCS is an informal pool of some two hundred physicians who help him evaluate prospective cases, and who testify in court if the need arises. During the past eight years Militana has developed a sophisticated screening system.

Most of the four-thousand-odd queries Militana and his firm handle each year begin with a phone call from an attorney who thinks he might have a malpractice case. "During the first five to ten minutes I can weed out the obvious non-cases," Militana said. "For instance, you might have a case where the patient suffered from metastatic cancer prior to the claimed act of negligence—say, from failure to diagnose the tumor. It's impossible to prove that malpractice was the proximate cause of death, since the cancer had probably already spread and doomed the patient. Most times you don't proceed past the telephone contact in such cases. The exception is where you can give the attorney a formal report ruling out malpractice, as a means of helping him cope with a disturbed family. An expert opinion often enables them to defuse the hostility they harbor against a physician who they suspected mistreated poor old Dad or Mom."

If the case sounds as if it has merit, Militana's next step is to review what he calls the "data sources." He says, "I ask the lawyer what is available in the way of medical records. I have him send me everything he has—legible copies of the doctor's office notes, the hospital reports, the material he has turned up during depositions and discovery."

Medical-Legal Consulting Service retains two physicians who work full time and eight others who are available from eight to thirty hours weekly. They do the next screen. "These are specialists who are able to act as generalists and take a broad look at a case. They can also call on the two hundred or so experts around the country who have agreed to review cases with us.

"One important point. We do work for defense attorneys as well as plaintiff attorneys, although the bulk is for the latter.* When a case goes out for review, the physician doesn't know whether we represent the doctor or the patient. That is essential, for the screening must be objective."

Militana's outside experts generally have an academic connection, and for a reason: "I want people who are so high up in their profession that no one except maybe a dean or a chancellor can bother them. My guidelines? Well, they must be board-certified in their specialty and also have a private practice in their specialty. They must be respected in their community. They must be willing to work in exchange for a fee that is about their costs, and nothing more. I'm not interested in making doctors rich, only in compensating them for their time." Another criterion is that the consultants be able to give a cram course to the trial attorney and to testify in language intelligible to the judge and a jury of laymen.

The work of the staff and the consultants is woven into a case report that lists areas of malpractice if they exist, and the additional information needed if the case is to be brought to trial. The bottom-line conclusion is whether the case has "merit"

*M-LCS advertises in *Trial Magazine*, the monthly magazine of the Association of Trial Lawyers of America, the leading plaintiff lawyers' group. It does not advertise in such defense-oriented publications as *Insurance Counsel Journal*. "The insurance companies know who we are, and where we are," Militana said.

—that is, if the facts warrant a lawsuit—or whether it should be dropped. M-LSC does not have the facilities to keep statistics on this point, but Militana estimates that about two thirds of the time he tells the lawyer he has no suit.

"Personal injury attorneys who work on a contingency fee basis want to know whether the case is meritorious, whether it's a winner or a loser, before they invest their time. If we do our job in a convincing way, they will not take a bad case. In turn, they convince the client no case exists." Similarly, an insurance company that seeks Militana's advice, and learns that its insured doctor has goofed, has strong incentive to bail out of the case and settle. "I like to use a military analogy. In history, the bloodiest battles are the ones that are close. Battles in which one side overwhelms the other are quicker and more decisive, and less blood is spilled. I find this true in the warfare of tort advocacy. We overprepare with superexperts, and we devastate the other side with evidence—and work."

"Well, once you say a case has merit, how often does the attorney win?" "On the plaintiff's side, 97 percent of the cases we termed meritorious. On the defense side, we've never lost."

If a case goes to trial, Militana holds the lawyer's hand veritably into the courtroom, if necessary; at the minimum, he or another consultant is only a phone call away. "Preparation is the key. The lawyer must be able to explain the pathogenesis of the injury to the jury. On the particular medical issue that is in question, he must be as knowledgeable as the doctor. He must have great versatility. Otherwise experts from the other side can hit him with information he knows nothing about. On one case—this is by no means typical, by the way—we spent a thousand hours preparing a lawyer for trial. But this was a case where the other side was holding back on information, which meant we had to work harder." (The $1,550,000 verdict was affirmed on appeal.)

"When you have a meritorious case, and the other side will not settle and chooses to go to trial, you *know* they are going to have to stretch the truth to win. You can prepare an attorney for the truth, but not for the absurd—for concepts that are not sound, or for events that did not occur. If the other side, through its 'experts,' starts to bombard you with preposterous issues, you must cope with them."

Militana cited an example. A sixteen-year-old boy died during dental surgery in a southern hospital. M-LCS reviewed the case, and concluded that improper ventilation during the anesthesia caused the death. The attorney sued both the hospital (and the nurse-anesthesiologist) and the dental surgeon. During discovery the attorney decided the dentist was not to blame, but kept him in the case anyway so as to have an ally in trying to prove liability on the part of the hospital.

The defense expert witness, a West Coast anesthesiologist, testified to a story that Militana dismissed as "absolutely outrageous." By his account, the dentist erred in using a waxy substance called "tiger balm" to coat a tooth socket during the surgery. The balm broke into small globules, which permeated the capillaries in the youth's jaw, formed into a large lump, and eventually lodged in his lung as an embolism, causing heart failure. "This is a pathogenesis that God has never even thought of," Militana exclaimed. "This defense witness admitted at trial his fee was $8,000, paid by the hospital's insurance company, which didn't help him with the jury." Primed by a Militana crash course, the lawyer destroyed the "expert" in short order; the jury brought in a verdict for $560,000.

Militana is not a universally popular man, and his Medical-Legal Consulting Service has come under attack from a broad range of interests—including, peculiarly, many plaintiff trial lawyers. Organized medicine, predictably, views him with the same disdain a surgeon would hold for a rusty scalpel; medical journals regularly swipe at M-LCS as a sophisticated form of ambulance chasing, or worse. So, too, the insurance companies, who see M-LCS as the harbinger of bad tidings for their profit-loss sheets.

The major substantive criticism of Militana is his acceptance of cases upon a contingency basis. If the client wins, M-LCS takes 5 to 10 percent of the gross. This is in addition to the 30 to 40 percent typically charged by the PI lawyer, and does not include court costs and fees for expert witnesses assembled by Militana. Hence an injured person conceivably could collect less than half of the amount awarded him by a jury or through negotiation. ("Putting an expert witness on a contingency basis would be highly improper, for he would lose his objectivity," says Militana. "I find the experts for the lawyer and work closely with them. But their bills go directly to the lawyer, and they are paid their fee—generally an hourly rate—regardless of the outcome of the case.")

Militana's billing practices came to public view in a malpractice case in which a federal district judge in Washington asked some hard questions about lawyers' use of outside consultants who in effect "package" cases. If a lawyer is not capable of handling an intricate case without outside assistance, is the client obligated to "pay for his education"? What are the ethics of a consultant's entering a suit on a contingency fee basis? At what point do attorney, consultant and expert witness fees become so high that they are unconscionable?

The case revolved around the birth of Sabrina Pluvinage, on October 22, 1970, at Sibley Hospital in Washington.[3] Both parents were French. The father, Pierre, worked as a chef; the mother, Simone, was a secretary at the French Embassy. The delivery, which took almost eight hours, was difficult, and Sabrina emerged from it with a condition known as Erb's palsy, which caused partial paralysis of her left arm and shoulder. Erb's palsy is often associated with the method by which a child is delivered.

The Pluvinages contacted Washington attorney Leslie Scherr and asked him about filing a suit against the obstetrician and the hospital. They had one talk, then Scherr asked them to bring Sabrina back to his office so Militana could observe her and determine whether she in fact had Erb's palsy. Mrs. Pluvinage would not let Militana physically examine the child "because she had seen many doctors before," but Militana did watch her crawl around the floor for approximately twenty minutes. He agreed she had Erb's palsy. Scherr agreed to take the case for a contingency fee of 30 percent of the amount recovered, plus expenses. He asked $150 as an advance against expenses, and he told the Pluvinages they owed Militana $500 for his observation of Sabrina and his efforts in attempting to obtain her medical reports. (In his account, Militana estimated he spent twenty hours evaluating the case and doing research on Erb's palsy.)

Almost two years passed, with both sides taking depositions and gathering evidence. Scherr made little headway. He claimed he could find no expert witnesses to testify for the Pluvinages, and when the defense talked in general terms of settling the case for $10,000 or $15,000, he urged that the parents accept because of "the questions of negligence and the difficulty in its proof." The Pluvinages refused, whereupon Scherr brought another attorney, Leonard Keilp, a youngish malpractice specialist, into the case to help him.

Keilp's entrance is significant because it is tantamount to an acknowledgment by Scherr that he could not handle the case on his own. Scherr admitted in a subsequent affidavit that he was in a bind: "As the scheduled trial date approached, I realized that I had been unable to obtain satisfactory expert medical witnesses on the issues of liability and causality." Keilp, the record suggests, could do no better. So the two lawyers—whose very acceptance of the case implied they claimed to be capable of prosecuting it—had to seek even further help at the expense of their client.

Scherr and Keilp told the Pluvinages that they wished to retain Militana, claiming he could find the expert witnesses needed.

Here memories of key events begin to differ. By Militana's account—supported by the two lawyers—he offered to work for $100 an hour, with $5,000 paid in advance. Simone Pluvinage said she heard no such offer. She gave this account of how she came to retain Militana:

> Mr. Scherr and Mr. Keilp had a contract which they . . . presented to us and asked us to sign. At that time the contract was in blank form and nothing had been written in the blanks. Mr. Keilp and Mr. Scherr told us that we would have to sign this quickly in order to get Mr. Militana to perform his services because Mr. Militana would be able to get expert witnesses who would testify favorably for us.
>
> I did not want to sign the contract because I believed the costs were very high and because I was not sure of the effect of signing such a contract. I told Mr. Scherr and Mr. Keilp that I would like to take the contract and get it translated into French, my native language and that of my husband.
>
> I remember that we were informed again that if we did not sign the contract and do so quickly, it was possible that our case would not do very well. Mr. Keilp told us that the fee would be ten percent, although he did not write it in until after my husband had signed.
>
> My husband was upset because there was no real choice and he

believed that if the doctor who had performed the delivery had been wrong that we should go to court and if there was no other way but to sign the contract, as we were told by Mr. Scherr and Mr. Keilp, then he agreed to do so.

My husband then signed the contract and Mr. Keilp wrote in ten percent and passed the contract to me to sign. Thereafter, I attempted to translate to my husband, who speaks very little English, the contents of the contract. . . . Finally, I signed the contract.

I would like to state that I have always been unclear of how much money would be paid to the experts and how much to Mr. Militana. At the time I signed the contract I believed that the experts and doctors would be paid from the Medical-Legal Consulting Service's ten percent. If I had known that Mr. Militana would have the right to get ten percent, and that the doctor and experts would be paid by us separately, and not out of Mr. Militana's fee, I would not have signed the contract. . . .

Washington attorney Jay T. French, retained later by the Pluvinages to overturn the M-LCS agreement, commented tartly in court papers: "Mr. Scherr and Mr. Keilp offer no explanation of why they waited until three weeks before trial to disclose to the parents that expert witnesses must be found. Such a delay resulted in pressure upon the parents to accept the M-LCS contract . . . In fact, no serious effort to obtain expert witnesses had been made during the period of nearly two years" after the Pluvinages had retained Scherr.

The Pluvinages say they asked for, but did not receive, a copy of the contract with Militana—a claim denied by the lawyers. At trial, attorneys Scherr and Keilp pressed their malpractice claim on two grounds: that the obstetrician applied excessive pressure to Sabrina's head and neck during the delivery, and that he was negligent in not anticipating a difficult birth and preparing Mrs. Pluvinage for a cesarean. Militana supplied an obstetrician and a gynecologist to talk about medical aspects of the case, and an economist to testify about the Pluvinages' financial losses. U.S. District Judge Howard Corcoran permitted Militana to sit at the counsel table (although he was to indicate later he did not know the consultant's exact role in the case). There was no visible sign of strain between the Pluvinages and their lawyers.

The first trial resulted in a mistrial. The second time around, in

August 1973, a jury returned a verdict of $75,000 for the child and $20,000 for the family. The apparently grateful Pluvinages wrote thank-you notes to the lawyers and Militana, and hosted them at a dinner party at their home. Then, trouble.

By the Pluvinages' account, several days after the trial Scherr and Keilp asked them to sign papers for distribution of Sabrina's share of the award. Because she was a minor, Judge Corcoran's approval was needed for payment of legal and witness fees. To their dismay, these fees ate up almost half the award. Under their contingency contract, the attorneys asked $25,000. Another $9,500 was for Militana. One medical witness was to receive $2,000; another, $900; another, $150. The economist, Richard J. Lurito, was to get $1,000. All told, the fees came to $36,050.

The papers submitted to Corcoran contained some peculiar features. For one thing, Militana's contingency arrangement was not mentioned. His fee was computed on the basis of 127 hours at $75 per hour, a total of $9,525. As another attorney involved in the case commented later, it was "an unlikely coincidence" that the time claimed "equals the ten percent contingency fee in the case by a margin of error of one third of an hour, or $25."*

The Pluvinages protested that the fees seemed "very expensive." The attorneys reassured them: they would have the chance to protest to Judge Corcoran if they thought the fees too high. A few days later the Pluvinages accompanied the lawyers to court and waited in an anteroom while they conferred with Judge Corcoran. As Mrs. Pluvinage later said:

> Later, Mr. Scherr and Mr. Keilp returned and I asked if we were now going to see the judge. Mr. Scherr told us that we did not have to see the judge because he and Mr. Keilp were representing us and that it was not necessary for us to see the judge.
>
> Then, Mr. Scherr said to me, "Anyhow, Mr. Militana's fees have been approved." I said then, "Why is it that we did not get to see the judge?" Mr. Scherr said, "You know that we are representing you and you don't have to see the judge. We are talking in your behalf."

*Militana submitted a single bill to support his claims on both the child's and the parents' awards—$9,500, or 10 percent of $95,000.

Scherr did say that Judge Corcoran was going to "chop off" some of the $2,000 fee requested for one of the physician witnesses Militana supplied.

Judge Corcoran, in fact, intended to do even more. When he saw the amount specified for Militana, according to a court source, "he went right through the roof of his chambers." Corcoran told Keilp and Scherr he had thought Militana was "associated with trial counsel" and did not realize he was an "independent contractor." He ordered that Keilp and Scherr pay Militana's fee out of their own share of the award, the Pluvinages' contract with Militana notwithstanding. Corcoran also addressed strong language toward the two lawyers:

> The court is of the opinion that an attorney who holds himself out as capable of trying a malpractice case should be sufficiently versed in the medical aspects of that case to be able to handle it by himself; and if he is not so capable, then he should absorb the costs of any education necessary to render him capable.

The attorneys' fees combined with Militana's charges were "unconscionable and exorbitant," Corcoran held. In informal comments Corcoran was said to be even more tart. "If a lawyer can't handle a case he should either refuse it or go back to law school," he said. "How the hell can he justify making a client pay for his on-the-job training?"

The case fell into total disarray at this point. There were several complications. Judge Corcoran put the $75,000 due Sabrina into the court fund pending the outcome of appeals, and his order meant that Keilp and Scherr could not touch it. The $20,000 due the parents, however, was in the form of a check to both the Pluvinages and the lawyers. The parents refused to sign an endorsement so it could be cashed, saying they feared the lawyers could pay Militana's total claimed fee of $9,500 from it. So Keilp and Scherr sued the family in state court in Maryland (their residence) for full payment. This action brought Corcoran off his bench with a judicial roar. He accused the lawyers of trying to bypass his court and suggested ("in pretty strong language," in the words of a lawyer involved in the case) that Keilp and Scherr drop the state suit forthwith. They did, and turned the $20,000 over to Corcoran's court. Judge Corcoran added to the legal snarl by asking the D.C. bar's committees on legal ethics and the unauthorized practice of law to rule on the "appropriateness of the fees" which Militana was attempting to charge, and whether his consulting service was tantamount to a legal practice.

Corcoran's order threw Washington personal injury lawyers into a tizzy, and they swiftly rallied behind Militana. When Militana petitioned the court to withdraw the order, a dozen PI lawyers filed affidavits saying, in essence, that it was "established community practice" for the client to bear the cost of expert witnesses.

In the opinion of a lawyer involved in the latter stages of the case, the bulk of these affidavits did not address the chief point of contention: "The question, in a broad sense, was whether it is proper for an attorney to take a case on a contingency fee basis, then to tell the plaintiff that in order to win, he must retain a consultant to supply the expertise. By accepting a case, and saying nothing to the contrary, an attorney holds himself out as being capable of handling the case." This lawyer surveyed by telephone several of the PI attorneys who filed the supporting affidavits and asked if they "really understood what was at stake in this case." He continued, "They didn't. It's a little game lawyers play—you scratch my back with your affidavit, and someday I can scratch yours. Sure, the plaintiff pays for the expert witnesses. But a consultant on a contingency fee is an entirely different matter. And the affidavits avoided this point."

Militana's lawyer, Richard S. Paulson,* a PI specialist since 1959, complained of the complexity of malpractice cases—the intricate factual situation, the difficulty in locating medical witnesses, the time-consuming nature of pretrial work. "In my judgment," swore Paulson, "an attorney who represents a plaintiff in a potential medical malpractice case runs the risk of

*A close professional friend of Militana. Paulson once handled a malpractice case in which two outside physicians, in his words, said "categorically that we did not have a meritorious case and it should be abandoned." The insurance company made no settlement offers. Militana worked a full year, researching medical literature and analyzing depositions, and he sat at Paulson's elbow during trial, offering suggestions. The jury award was $630,705—at the time the highest ever sustained by the D.C. Court of Appeals. (Later Militana participated in another D.C. malpractice case where the award was $1.5 million.)

being charged with professional negligence if he does not make use of the best technical assistance available in preparing and presenting his case." If the lawyer "absorbs the cost of this technical assistance as a part of his case expense or overhead generally, then as a matter of pure business economics the attorney must necessarily adjust his fee accordingly in order to afford this unusual overhead expense and the cost thereof would be passed along to the client in a different form."

Keilp, in his affidavit, noted that the parents indicated before trial they would be happy with $60,000; that the insurance lawyers evaluated the case at $15,000 to $20,000 (although they made no specific settlement offer); and that Militana was "extremely instrumental" in obtaining the $95,000 jury verdict. In fact, Keilp said, Militana was so effective that the jury ruled for the plaintiff on the key issues of liability and causality (that is, that the doctor's conduct caused Sabrina's condition) "within an hour after beginning deliberations." And Keilp also tried to refute Judge Corcoran's assertion that lawyers should not accept complex cases they cannot handle on their own:

> . . . Counsel, despite holding himself as being capable of trying malpractice cases, could not obtain, without consultation, the necessary medical knowledge to try this or any specialized case; that counsel would have to be the equivalent of an expert in all fields of medical specialty in order to attempt the same without the services of a consultant and other expert witnesses. . . .

By Keilp's definition, a malpractice attorney asserts only that he has a "certain basic knowledge of the human body and its function," and such related fields as biology and physiology, among others, sufficient to allow him to be "generally conversant" with the subject matter; and that this knowledge permits him to talk knowingly with experts such as Militana, who in turn "effectively fit the adduced facts into a trial plan understandable to a lay jury."

When Corcoran referred the Militana matter to the D.C. bar committees, he implicitly agreed to follow their findings. And this he did, albeit unhappily: one committee said that Militana's operation was not an "unauthorized practice of law"; the other said his contingency fee was not unacceptable so long as the client understood it. The American Bar Association's Standing Committee on Ethics and Professional Responsibility, in response to a query by the District of Columbia bar groups, gave a conditional approval to Militana's arrangement:*

> Nothing in the Code of Professional Responsibility proscribes a lawyer from recommending that a client contract with a lay person on a contingent fee basis so long as: (1) the lay person or agency is not to engage in the unauthorized practice of law; (2) the lawyer does not share legal fees with the lay person, or agency; (3) the contingent fee is not payable for the testimony of the lay person or agency . . .
>
> However, a lawyer who recommends such an arrangement to a client must at all times retain full control of the litigation which has been entrusted to him by the client, and may not abdicate to another his ultimate professional responsibility for evaluating the course to be followed. . . . [4]

Facing this bar opposition, Corcoran partially backed away. He refused to permit Militana to collect the full 10 percent, and he pressured the lawyers to reach a compromise. They ultimately did, although Militana refused to either accept or reject it. In essence, the deal gave Militana $6,750, rather than his expected $9,500. Keilp and Scherr reduced their fee by $1,250 each. The end result was to give Sabrina and her family $5,200 more.

With Corcoran's feelings as hot as they were, why was not the Pluvinage case pressed to final resolution before an appellate court? The proliferation of consulting services parallel to that offered by Militana, and the mixed feelings they evoke among lawyers and judges, demanded that a standard be defined.

When I spoke to various attorneys involved in the Pluvinage case, some three years had lapsed. Although feelings remained high, none of the lawyers who opposed Militana would speak for attribution. One spoke bitterly of "fancy-dan negligence lawyers"; another matched Judge Corcoran's tartness in discussing

*As is customary in advisory opinions, the ABA committee did not use actual names. However, the facts cited in the opinion letter (Informal Opinion 1375, August 10, 1976) parallel those of the Militana-Pluvinage case. Further, Fred Grabowsky, counsel for the D.C. bar, volunteered a copy of the opinion when I inquired whether the ABA had spoken on the issue.

Militana's fee system. Yet pragmatism ultimately ruled: a protracted conflict over the questioned $9,500 would consume, in legal fees, far more than that amount. So why not a compromise?

Which is, in essence, the story of American law.

Court Recess Three

The PI lawyer and I had dawdled over lunch and coffee for more than two hours in a Philadelphia luncheon club, talking about such things as no-fault and medical malpractice. He had told me about the six-figure verdicts he had won, and some that he had lost, and he related his how-I-won anecdotes with professional relish. Then he fell silent, as if it was really time for him to get back to the office, and I began gathering my pencils and note pad. He gestured for me to stay where I was.

"The general public has very little contact with the sort of thing we've been discussing," he said. "How many people do you know who've ever been hurt badly enough to try to collect a hundred thousand dollars? One? Maybe two?

"Okay, let's talk about the more relevant kinds of PI cases. As a trial advocate you deal with a series of cubbyholes that are seemingly impossible to match up—the cubbyhole of human nature, the cubbyhole of common sense, the cubbyhole of the law. Your job is to try to make these cubbyholes coincide.

"Now you can dress up this statement with any fancy language you wish, but it means perjury and subornation of perjury, and therefore if you cite me by name in your book I'm going to deny I ever saw you, and sue your pants off. But in a trial neither side is prepared to state its case candidly. It is a tribute to the jury system that citizens, after hearing the classic, stereotyped presentations, return fair verdicts 99 percent of the time.

"A good example is the intersection collision, where one driver runs a red light and plows broadside into another. The defense lawyer is eventually going to ask when the injured driver first saw the other car. 'I never saw him until he hit me.' That's the honest answer most of the time. But, say it, and the case is over. Under the doctrine of contributory negligence, both the drivers share blame in such a case, so no one collects—even though the blame might be split ninety-five to five. A handful of states now have *comparative* negligence, but in most jurisdictions, if you are to blame at all, you are barred from recovery.

"So what does the PI lawyer do? When you come into his office, he is going to give a little lecture which usually begins with the words, 'You know you are right in this case, otherwise you wouldn't be here.' He will then explain just what I told you. My job, as a PI lawyer, is to take the facts you give me and articulate them to your best advantage.

"After the lecture the client, if he is bright enough, will say, 'I did see the other car, which seemed to be stopping for the light. I then looked to the right to see if other cars were coming. I caught sight of the first car out of the corner of my eye, just before he hit me, but I could not avoid the accident.'

"The jury gives you the verdict, which you deserved. Justice was done by plugging your cases into the magic cubbyhole the law demands.

"Take a city freeway. To avoid being negligent at fifty miles an hour you must stay a football field's length behind the nearest car, even during rush hour. Try that out on the Schuylkill Expressway some afternoon and see how long you last. The cops would run you in. The law does not take into account a sudden stop by the preceding car.

"The defense gambit in any auto case is to try to show contributory fault on the part of the plaintiff, to find some way to suggest that he was careless. Listen to this:

" 'How fast were you driving?'
" 'Thirty miles an hour.'
" 'Were you looking at your speedometer?'
" 'Certainly. That's how I know how fast I was driving.'
" 'Oh! So you did take your eye off the road!'

"You get to a products liability case, and the defense will try to show that the plaintiff is clumsy and not very bright:

"'Don't you know that a rotary lawn mower can kick up a stone?'
"'Then why did you permit your teenaged son to use the mower?'

"'Were you not aware that certain fabrics ignite when put into proximity to fire?'
"'Then why did you permit your little girl to stand near the stove in her nightie?'"

We ordered more coffee. The lawyer asked, "Does all this sound rather cynical to you?" Yes, I replied, it did. "Well, if distortion gives you good results, it's no longer distortion—it's trial tactics." He reassured himself that he was not talking for attribution, and he continued.
"The classic case for coaching is what we call the 'fall-down case.' You have the supermarket, with the freshly mopped floor or the aisle covered with produce. Along comes Mrs. Smith, who falls on her ass and breaks her hip. Now in Pennsylvania an airtight defense under contributory negligence can be built with one question: 'Did you look before you walked?' If she says no, good-bye, her case is over.
"Now this is ridiculous, for the *leitmotiv* of a supermarket is to attract the customer's attention with bright displays and piles of fancy foods. If the manager is put on the stand and testifies honestly, he'll say just that. Hell, if customers walked around with their heads down, it would be catastrophic to the national economy. But the law says this must be done, otherwise you bust your ass at your own expense. So again you resort to coaching to fit the facts to the cubbyhole. An intelligent client, once he hears your lecture, can come up with any number of answers:

"'I stepped around a crate on the floor and fell on the first step before I had a chance to see what was before me.'
"'A lady friend called to me just about that time, and I looked at her.'
"'The shopping cart blocked my view.'
"'I was carrying a shopping bag, and doing my best to see where I was going.'
"'The sun blinded me.'

* * *

"Those are good for inside stores. On sidewalk cases, the best friend the PI lawyer can have is the bark of a dog or the honk of a car horn—your client looks up, and falls, and collects.

"These aren't the kinds of things you learn in law school; you pick them up in practice. I once helped run an advocacy clinic at the University of Pennsylvania Law School, and we told the students the no-no questions that you shouldn't ask. They ate it up; one said to me, 'Man, this is *reality*!'

"Well, it is, but I don't like the fudging. I'd like a system of justice where you could lay out the facts and let common sense prevail—and not some doctrines the insurance industry managed to wheedle through the Pennsylvania legislature and the Pennsylvania Supreme Court. This would mean an effective end to lawyering, I suppose, but more and more I feel like a coach, not a trial lawyer."

We left the club and walked down Chestnut Street in the direction of the lawyer's office. We shook hands at Sixteenth Street and I started to step off the curb. A taxi honked at me. "Remember," the lawyer called to me, "you looked both ways, and you made sure the light was in your favor. Understand?"

Yes, I did.

Chapter Four

The Watchdog of Wall Street

. . . Just as a fine, natural football player needs coaching in the fundamentals and schooling in the wiles of the sport, so, too, it takes a corporation lawyer with a heart for the game to organize a great stock swindle or income tax dodge and drill the financiers in all the precise details of their play.

Otherwise, in their natural enthusiasm to rush in and grab everything that happens not to be nailed down and guarded with shotguns they would soon be caught offside and penalized, and some of the noted financiers who are now immortalized as alltime all-American larcenists never would have risen beyond the level of the petty thief or short-change man.[1]

—Newspaper columnist Westbrook Pegler
January 1923.

Stanley Sporkin, the government lawyer whom Wall Street considers to be a seven-letter cuss word, was messily consuming a pastrami sandwich and griping because whoever went out for lunch forgot the potato chips. He waved at the confusion of papers on his desk. I thought of two comparable past spectacles: the aftermath of a Cub Scout paper drive, and the debris left when a tornado went through a stationery store in East Texas.

"This mess," Sporkin said, "this is what drives men to pastrami sandwiches. And ulcers. I make you a bet. Before I finish my Coca-Cola, we're going to be interrupted."

We sat in a fourth-floor office on the corner of the Securities and Exchange Commission Building in Washington, in the enforcement division, which Sporkin heads. Securities lawyers consider this suite to be something of a Star Chamber, and they speak of it in the same words Dante used to describe Purgatory. One story told about Sporkin in the New York law palaces has a distinctly apocryphal ring; however, since it was printed in that august forum, the *Los Angeles Times*, I shall repeat it anyway.

A few years back Sporkin summoned a platoon of corporate executives to the SEC for questioning about some misdeed or another. He took the ranking man into his office and left the others in an anteroom. Sporkin's questioning was tough, as it tends to be, and the executive suddenly gasped, grabbed for his chest, and pitched face forward to the floor, victim of an apparent heart seizure.

Medics arrived and hauled the man out on a stretcher, oxygen mask clamped to his face.

Sporkin supposedly stood in the door until the stretcher vanished, then motioned to another executive in the anteroom: "You're next," he said, jerking his thumb towards his office.*[2]

So there the ogre sat, a rumpled guy in his early forties, as scruffy as a West Philadelphia police lieutenant. "The nation's top securities cop," an admiring Ralph Nader once called Sporkin. "A despicable, power-hungry bureaucrat who can't make it as a lawyer, and who wants to recast the securities bar in his own peculiar mold," a Wall Street lawyer had told me only a few days before. A man President Carter seriously considered for the post of FBI director. Only one of the 27,000 lawyers who work for the federal government, and assuredly one of the more effective and, therefore, controversial.

Stan Sporkin. His branch of the SEC toppled C. Arnholt Smith, the multimillionaire California banker (and chum of Richard Nixon) whose city once named him Mr. San Diego. Sporkin's office forced dozens of blue-chip corporations to admit—through angrily clenched teeth—that they paid off foreign and domestic politicians.** His crusade wrenched Investors Overseas Services, the big offshore mutual fund, from the hands of Robert Vesco and drove the rogue to refuge in Costa Rica.

*Asked about the story's veracity, Sporkin shrugs and grins.

**As of summer 1977, more than three hundred companies had disclosed to the SEC more than $400 million in payments from secret slush funds to politicians and agents of other countries in return for business favors, and the scandal had by no means ended.

Stan Sporkin. In civil law suits he accused accountants and lawyers of being equally culpable, with their clients, in stock rip-offs. This is not entirely new: professionals are not immune from the securities laws, and the SEC has slapped a few of them in the past years—mostly, however, outright con men who actively shaped crooked deals. Sporkin gave two new dimensions to SEC enforcement: first, he held that if a lawyer or accountant signed a registration statement, he assumed responsibility for its accuracy, even if the client had misled him; in Sporkin's view, a lawyer hired out as an independent professional, not as a rubber stamp. Second, in enforcing this doctrine Sporkin struck at the upper echelons, dragging into securities "fraud" suits such accounting firms as Arthur Andersen & Company, and Peat, Marwick, Mitchell & Company, and the Wall Street law firm of White & Case. To call these offices prestigious and respected—both by peers and clients—is not hyperbole. And here came Stan Sporkin, taking them into court with the same flourish the SEC used to save for boiler-room operators and mail-order uranium-stock salesmen.

"So let's talk," I said to Sporkin. "You're in a rather responsible job; lots of people like you; others don't. How did you get here, and how do you go about your business?"

Sporkin finished a mouthful of pastrami, remembered something, excused himself, pushed a button on his phone, said to his secretary outside, "Tell them anytime," and hung up. Then he told a bit about himself: a native of Philadelphia, where his father, Maurice O. Sporkin, is a judge of Common Pleas Court; training as an accountant; Yale Law School; three years' clerking in federal courts in Delaware; a year of private practice in Washington. "I found it hard to do meaningless things, to get a client past the line of legality and have one leg dangling over it just for a competitive edge."

So in 1961 he joined SEC "as a foot soldier," a member of a task force charged with finding ways of tightening enforcement of the securities laws. Booming mutual funds, glamor stocks and national prosperity had made the stock market a con man's paradise in preceding years, and Sporkin learned about Wall Street from the seamy side up. The report concluded that "inept, ignorant or rapacious" broker-dealers and salesmen often preyed upon "the naïve, the unsophisticated and those with slender resources." It recommended dozens of changes in rules for the stock industry, including tighter disciplinary controls over brokers.[3]

But the report shied away from any discussion of securities lawyers. "Their abuses tend to be subtle," Sporkin says. "What we had in '61 and '62 were a lot of out-front bad guys who were a hell of a lot more immediately dangerous than the lawyers." When the study ended in 1963 Sporkin went into the SEC's enforcement division, hoping to use his dual talents as accountant and lawyer. "With my background I was able to take a deal apart, to see it both from the financial and legal standpoints. I marveled at some of the perpetual-motion machine stuff that speculators used to try to run through."

In Sporkin's words, as he worked his way through the trenches from foot-soldier rank, "I saw more and more cases where lawyers and accountants were culpable, along with their clients. These people simply had to be held responsible." So when he became enforcement division chief, he and subordinates hit upon what he calls the "access point strategy." He reasoned this way. Although there are some 15,000 brokers in the country, 100 to 200 of them do 95 percent of the total business, and use the same group of lawyers and accountants. "A crooked deal, a shady deal, a bad deal, call it what you like, it isn't a deal unless it has access to the marketplace, and this access can be provided only by the professionals. We can't watch 15,000 brokers, but we sure the hell can watch the people they use. Cut it down that way, you have a smaller universe to police.

"We started by saying, in effect, 'You people, you lawyers and you accountants, you are going to be held responsible when you put your name on paper that comes to this commission for filing.' Now right away this doubles or triples your enforcement staff, because they must take measures so they are not unwitting participants in a bad deal. I take great pride in this concept, to rely upon the private sector to do the overall job of keeping the market in line. We stand by and pick out isolated cases and make sure that no one gets out of line."

The predicted interruption. Three staff lawyers, in shirt sleeves, trooped into the room to report near settlement of a case.

Sporkin: "What's the holdup?"

One of the lawyers named an accountant in the SEC hierarchy. "He's not sure he can live with it from his standpoint. We think he's silly, that we've got the best we can without going to trial. The defendant wants to settle, and I think he's given quite a bit."

Sporkin to his secretary: "Get me [the accountant] on the phone." As he waited he found a stray chunk of pastrami, and ate it, and wadded up the paper and put it into the Coke cup, and dropped it into the trash basket, and brushed crumbs off his desk. He saw me watching him. "Just once before I leave Washington," he said, "just once, I want to eat lunch at the Sans Souci. Just once."

Sporkin into the telephone: "Hey, you're being unreasonable. We're on the same side, remember? Can't we wrap this up today? I'm satisfied, my men are satisfied, why can't you be satisfied?"

Pause. "Yeah, yeah, I know, I know. But is that really realistic?"

Pause. "I see your point, you make a good point. But if we go for it, the whole thing blows up, and we start negotiating again. They want out; our people are satisfied; why do you want to be such a schmuck?" (He winked across the room at me.)

Smile. "Okay, thanks. I really think you're doing the right thing, and I appreciate you going along with me. I owe you one, hey?" He hung up.

To the trio of lawyers: "He'll sign. Now get over to him in a hurry before he changes his mind." The lawyers left, and Sporkin sighed, "Jeez," he said, "you have to negotiate with your own people to win a case. Sometimes the other side is easy by comparison. You know what I mean?"

Well, perhaps, for surely "the other side"—securities lawyers—has never considered Sporkin's division easy competition. The SEC goes into combat with psychological and other practical advantages that enable it to generate a "climate of fear," in the opinion of Kenneth J. Bialkin, a partner in the Wall Street firm of Willkie, Farr & Gallagher.*[4] An ABA committee a few years back said many lawyers were afraid to assert clients'

*The Willkie in the firm's name was the Republican presidential nominee in 1940.

positions "with full vigor" because "the possibility of overzealous action by the staff has been . . . a fact of life throughout the commission's history."

Much of the staff's inherent advantage lies in the broad language of the Securities and Exchange Act, which applies the word "fraud" to any violation, however trivial or unintentional. Unlike other areas of law, a securities "fraud" does not necessarily mean an intentional criminal act. Nonetheless, when the enforcement division starts a proceeding, it does so with a press release announcing that the SEC is bringing charges of "fraud" against some supposed offender. The next day's financial page headline reads, SEC CHARGES LAW FIRM WITH SECURITIES FRAUD, to be scanned by laymen with no appreciation for the semantic niceties. Securities lawyers have fought this procedure tooth and nail, and unsuccessfully; as recently as 1974 a federal appeals court ruled that in the securities field, "negligence means fraud."

The result is that when the enforcement division decides to go after someone, it wields a nail-studded public-relations club—a fact not unknown to the intended target. So attorneys make a pragmatic decision: they settle with the SEC and minimize the publicity. Milton Freeman, of Arnold & Porter in Washington, laments the ethical strains put upon a lawyer in such a situation. "I do not tell the client to bail out [and take a consent decree]. I tell the client the facts, and he makes the decision." Freeman cited an instance where he was convinced—and told the client—that the SEC had "absolutely no case whatsoever," even though the enforcement staff acted as if it had treed another Ponzi. He quotes the client as replying, "Settle with them. I don't want to see my name in the papers." "It's your money," Freeman responded. But even a surrender can be expensive, for taking a non-contested consent decree to court for a judge's pro forma approval requires much negotiation with the staff. "Right away there's a $50,000 'penalty' in legal fees," Freeman says.

Accepting a consent decree, however, involves more than loss of money (in legal fees) and professional pride—even if the outcome involves no more than what Bialkin has called "a promise not to do it again."[5] A consent decree can cause a party problems in obtaining a new or renewed license from a regulatory agency, or in purchasing a bank or other federally regulated institution. It invites civil liability suits from persons who claim they were harmed. Law and accounting firms are subject to contempt proceedings if future clients violate the securities laws.

Given these drawbacks, Los Angeles attorney Robert S. Warren, of Gibson, Dunn & Crutcher, suggests that a consent decree should not be accepted lightly. He told a bar meeting about a multidefendant case which the SEC "apparently considered important," because eight government attorneys handled it:

> We were sitting in front of the judge, some 25 of us lawyers, and we had been involved in this case for a year, and I don't know whether the judge was kidding or not, but I couldn't take a risk. The judge said to the SEC trial counsel, "Mr. So and So, what are you here for?"
>
> The SEC attorney said, "An injunction, Your Honor."
>
> The Judge: "Under what statute?"
>
> The SEC attorney went back to his seat and scurried around until he could tell the statute that he wanted the injunction under.
>
> The Judge: "And what do you want enjoined?"
>
> SEC attorney: "I want to enjoin the defendants from violating the securities laws."
>
> The Judge: "Is that all?"
>
> SEC attorney: "Yes."
>
> The Judge: "Well, why are we here? The defendants will surely consent to that."
>
> You have never seen 25 defense lawyers that looked like that before in your life. And I raced to the podium and fortunately had a laundry list of disqualifications stemming from imposition of an injunction, and was able to use them at that time to demonstrate, if the court was serious, why the defendants were spending all this time and trouble in litigating the matter.[6]

Securities specialists such as Kenneth Bialkin think that Sporkin takes an unrealistically narrow view of the lawyer's role in the industry. He and colleagues agree that any lawyer who becomes aware of outright fraud is obligated to resign and make a public disclosure of the facts. "Usually, however, the lawyer is not confronted with a misrepresentation or omission which is part of a patently fraudulent scheme," Bialkin told a bar group in 1975. "Finer, more subtle and difficult questions confuse the issue. The historical and socially desirable nature of the lawyer's relation to his client requires, it seems to me, that the lawyer not be placed in an agonizing role. His emphasis should not be on law enforcement as such; it must be on the protection of his client's rights subject to ethical considerations." Bialkin feels that if a particular course of conduct "is at least arguably legal, lawyers should not be disturbed from advising a client to the full extent of what the law might permit." Bialkin even has a little speech for clients in such a situation: "I don't think this is clearly illegal. I can't tell you it is illegal. You may have the right to do it, but the precedents are unclear. If you do it, you are acting in good faith. You may be found to have violated the law, but I can't tell you at this time that the law has reached the point when your conduct is clearly illegal." If the client turns out to be wrong, Bialkin continues, he can be sued, enjoined, even indicted. "That is *his* choice to make."[7]

Another factor disturbing securities lawyers is that "full disclosure" can unfairly harm a party who has no direct responsibility for the questioned actions. James Purcell, of the New York firm of Paul, Weiss, Rifkind, Wharton & Garrison, gave this example to a meeting of a business group: the events, he said, were real, although the actual facts are fuzzed somewhat.

In July 1972 the XYZ Construction Company bought a New Jersey corporation named the ABC Paving Company. Fourteen months later, XYZ discovered that some years earlier, ABC and other New Jersey contractors had conspired to rig bidding on construction contracts, in violation of antitrust laws. The conspiracy ended about a year and a half before XYZ and ABC merged.

During a routine audit XYZ's outside accounting firm asked XYZ lawyers for a "description and evaluation of any litigation, impending litigation, claims and contingent liabilities." The auditor's report would become a public document at the SEC.

XYZ's dilemma: under law, it had succeeded to all the liabilities of its merger partner. If the former conspiracy became known before the statute of limitations lapsed, XYZ was potentially liable for treble damages in any private antitrust suit brought by anyone injured by the bid rigging.

If XYZ lawyers did not respond to the request, the refusal would be noted in the auditor's report—a Klaxon horn that would bring in the SEC. But, according to Purcell, "if they [the lawyers] respond fully and truthfully . . . the report, when circulated, will virtually shout, 'Sue me, sue me!' to those aggrieved by the old conspiracy."

Purcell surveyed a number of accountants and lawyers and asked what they would do in such a situation. "I drew from them a variety of answers, all of which, when stripped of their polite, protective verbiage, boiled down to one single piece of advice, 'Lie.' "[8]

I listened to Bialkin and his friends, and I read their bar journal articles and the proceedings of their ABA groups and the court decisions they cited. Their complaints about the SEC contained the unmistakable sound of true, heartfelt outrage; right or wrong, these people felt they (and their clients) were being persecuted, and they did not like it. But let me be honest: my quotient of sympathy is limited, and of all the classes of persecuted persons in the world upon whom I intend to expend it, Wall Street and its functionaries are far down the list, alongside the telephone company and fast-food restaurateurs.

But a curious thing kept recurring as I talked with Bialkin, Milton Freeman of Arnold & Porter, and other lawyers: each would relate his own horror story of the SEC and then say, "You really should talk with Monroe Freedman, the dean of Hofstra University Law School, on Long Island."

I knew Freedman. Formerly a professor at the George Washington University Law Center in Washington, and head of a neighborhood poverty law clinic, he is a pillar of the American Civil Liberties Union in the District of Columbia and a bitingly articulate critic of establishment lawyers. Freedman is a casual friend, and as I once said to him, "Monroe, had you come from the South, you would have made a damned fine Populist." Never had I detected any pro–Wall-Street sentiments in him. When I telephoned him I told him at the outset that securities lawyers had been slandering him.

"How?" he asked. "What are they saying about me?"

"That you are their friend, and that you've been taking a stick to Stanley Sporkin and the SEC on their behalf."

Freedman laughed, and a few days later we ate shad roe at Jean-Pierre's in Washington, and over coffee he gave me a sheaf of photocopies of things he had been writing and saying about securities lawyers and the SEC. "As a civil libertarian," he said, "I'll defend anybody who is being kicked around."

"Even Wall Street lawyers?"

"Yes, even Wall Street lawyers." He showed me a quotation from the *Harvard Civil Rights/Civil Liberties Law Review:* "It has become both professionally and legally dangerous to be a lawyer representing the poor, minorities, and the politically unpopular."

I read the sentence, and I looked back at Freedman. "So what?"

"I'll add another category," Freedman said. "The attorneys who represent the securities industry. These lawyers are no special friends of mine, but right now I'd say they have about the same degree of rights as Rap Brown would receive in Alabama.

"I've heard Sporkin's argument—that he makes lawyers part of his enforcement apparatus because the SEC doesn't have manpower or money. Isn't that what cops always say when they start fudging with the Constitution?" Freedman related some specific instances told to him by securities attorneys:

—SEC staff members commonly tell witnesses not to discuss their testimony with counsel for the other side. "In at least one case," Freedman has written, "an attorney was threatened with being prosecuted for obstruction of justice simply for making efforts to interview a government witness." Such conduct by a prosecutor would be grounds for bar disciplinary action, Freedman notes.*[9]

—Persons are subpoenaed without being told they are targets of an investigation and at times are led to believe otherwise. This gives investigators a chance to interrogate the intended defendants without their being on guard and to trap them into making damaging admissions.

—A lawyer who asks time to prepare a defense or who invokes the attorney-client privilege in refusing to reveal information may be asked rhetorically, "Are you saying your client won't cooperate?" Freedman writes, "In one case, when the attorney indicated that the client intended to invoke his constitutional privilege against self-incrimination, he was advised by the

*The ABA publication *Standards Relating to the Prosecution* states, "A prosecutor should not obstruct communication between prospective witnesses and defense counsel. It is unprofessional conduct to advise any person to decline to give information to the defense."

SEC staff member, 'That's the best way to guarantee an indictment.' "

—Attorneys have appeared before the commission on behalf of a client without being told that they themselves are the subject of investigation.

—The SEC has told lawyers that an entire law firm may be disbarred or suspended for a violation by one firm member—"a sanction that is particularly vicious in view of the fact that disbarment or suspension may result from simple negligence without any showing of improper intent."[10]

—And the worst threat of all: Freedman cites the lawyer whose defense of a client was too vigorous for the SEC's liking. An SEC staff member pointedly advised the lawyer he should "take a look at the *National Student Marketing* complaint." The lawyer needed no further explanation. The words "National Student Marketing" were akin to inviting a condemned man to inspect a collection of hangman's nooses.

Let us give credit for outright audacity: National Student Marketing (NSM) was one of the most successful business scams of the 1960s, one skilled enough to hoodwink such sophisticated investors as Morgan Guaranty Trust Company of New York, Dreyfus Overseas Fund, First Milwaukee Company, the Mellon people in Pittsburgh, Hartford Fire Insurance Company, Cornell University, Harvard University, the Wilmington Trust Company. Each of these bought NSM as an investment; each ended with a handful of sand and a mouthful of ashes.

National Student Marketing was the creation of Cortes Wesley Randell, a hulking young Washingtonian who could sell himself, and his ideas, better than he could more material objects—a distinction investors did not understand until too late.[11] As a University of Virginia undergraduate Randell wrote a thesis, "How to Start a Small Business," and he did just that a few years later while working as a salesman for ITT. He assembled a book on summer jobs for college students, huckstered it via gaudy posters advertising "high-paying, fun-filled positions" on four Wisconsin campuses and received so many orders the first week he quit ITT and went into business for himself.

Randell put together what he called a "network of campus

representatives" to distribute samples, do market research and peddle fad items—in essence, a link between business and all those well-heeled college kids who supposedly bought stereos and sports cars and scuba-diving gear. Randell sold business on the idea that "the Youth Market" existed, and that money jingled in its pockets, and that he was an entrepreneur who could reach it. Posters. Ballpoint pens. Advertising space on book covers. Travel. Cigarettes. Room-sized refrigerators for dormitories. If a company offered any service or product with the remotest chance of appeal to a student, Randell either signed it on as a client—or bought the company and tucked it into one of the fastest-growing conglomerates of the 1960s.

Only a handful of insiders realized the NSM operation was a sham—that the computer job service did not match employer and graduate; that students ignored NSM's blizzard of coupon offers; that as an advertising medium, book covers ranked right alongside airsickness bags.

Nonetheless, the acquisitions enabled NSM "sales" to grow from a few hundred thousand dollars in 1966 to almost $100 million in 1968.[12] The stock, issued at $6, zoomed to a high of $143 during the same period. And in acquiring other companies Randell often used NSM stock instead of cash—a tender eagerly accepted by executives of companies who wanted some of Randell's fast, easy money. In the words of one of his former executives, "Randell's earnings prophecies were self-fulfilling. By announcing phenomenal earnings projections [that is, guesses] he got a phenomenal valuation of NSM stock, which then allowed him to buy enough earnings to meet his projections. Then, to keep the momentum high, as all glamor stocks must, he would make another round of phenomenal projections."

Although Randell continued to fool supposedly brilliant investors, by late 1968 only the most imaginative of figure juggling enabled NSM to maintain its go-go image. On August 31, the end of the fiscal year, the books showed an operating loss of more than $220,000. This would never do. So NSM had its field salesmen write memos describing what it called "contracts in progress," few of them in signed form, which were then infused into the NSM books. By December 1968, when NSM filed its annual report with the SEC, the $220,000 loss had been converted into a before-tax earnings of $699,116, compared with $168,616 the previous fiscal year.

The "contracts in progress" passed under the supposedly sharp eyes of NSM's accountant, the firm of Peat, Marwick, Mitchell & Company. Why did not the firm's auditors confirm these "contracts"? The two men directly responsible for the NSM account, Anthony Natelli and Joseph Scansaroli, told the SEC later that Randell and other officers warned that the clients might "back off," that is, decline to fulfill the contracts, if they were questioned. Hence the auditors accepted NSM's word that the "contracts" were valid. (The voluminous NSM record is silent on why supposed clients would shy away if approached.)

By early 1969, many of the "contracts in progress" had turned out to be as ephemeral as a salesman's expense account. An NSM internal auditor advised Randell to face reality, to stop "adding insult to injury," to clear the bogus sales off the books and "stop deferring our problem." Randell did no such thing. The crisis, if anything, only whetted his imagination.

Andrew Tobias,* who joined NSM after a college career as a business whizbang, told of finding Randell laboring with a secretary late one evening, trying to retype a letter. NSM had been negotiating with the Pontiac division of General Motors for a million-dollar contract, and NSM needed a confirmation letter to file along with financial statements. Randell complained to Tobias that a "ridiculous typographical error had been made by the Pontiac executive's secretary. She had hit a *t* where she should have instead hit a *w*. Instead of a sentence reading, 'We are no*w* planning to spend umpty-ump dollars with your programs' (or words to that effect), we had a sentence reading, 'We are no*t* planning to spend. . . .' " Randell told Tobias the Pontiac executive had been reached by phone, had apologized for the error and had promised to send another letter. Told that would take too long in view of the deadline for the financial statement, he "had asked us to retype it for him." Tobias stepped into the breach and tapped out the letter.

*Now a writer, Tobias escaped from NSM with both integrity and sense of humor intact, and wrote an account of his adventure that is at once hilarious and terrifying, *The Funny Money Game*, Playboy Press: 1971.

The result of this "forgery," as the SEC said later, was to inflate NSM's earnings the first six months of 1969 by $500,000.

The few outsiders who managed close glimpses at the way Randell ran his company quickly became disillusioned with him—not because of any firm evidence of chicanery, but because of NSM's sloppy management and lack of control. Consider Covington and Burling, generally regarded as the premier Washington law firm. The firm began representing NSM in 1967, with partner James McKay assigned prime responsibility. Covington and Burling helped NSM with several acquisitions and did the routine legal work essential to any corporation. In April 1968, when NSM decided to market its shares on the American Stock Exchange rather than over-the-counter, Covington and Burling lawyers obtained SEC approval for the registration.

But there were constant problems. Cort Randell insisted on making decisions on legal matters, despite constant admonitions by Covington and Burling: "If a legal problem arises, or anything that even smells like a legal problem, let us handle it; that's why you hired us." Randell also played loose with the truth. One episode that got back to the firm involved Randell's telling another company that Covington and Burling had given him a legal opinion stating it was illegally infringing upon NSM affairs. "National Student had been advised exactly the opposite," said Cyrus V. Smith, Jr., a partner specializing in securities matters.

In another instance, NSM got into a dispute over fees with a dating service it had acquired—the service thought it was to receive $1.25 per contact; NSM wanted to pay only $0.75. The disagreement was not resolved when Covington and Burling filed NSM's registration statement with the SEC, and the firm was much surprised—and irritated—to hear of it later via an SEC staff inquiry. Covington and Burling felt the dispute was important enough to warrant mention in the registration statement, a document which by law must cite any legal problems a corporation faces.

But the crowning insult—and the law firm called it just that, an insult—came in June 1968, some two months after NSM went public. One morning the mails produced a lawsuit by a New York firm with a name similar to that of NSM, charging NSM with various unfair trading practices and infringements upon its own business. Attached to the complaint was a letter, dated before the effective date of the SEC filing, threatening litigation if NSM did not change its practices. Randell had never mentioned the threatened litigation to anyone at Covington and Burling. The omission caused the firm much professional discomfort. Withholding information from the SEC, even if unwittingly, is serious business. But in the words of Cyrus Smith, the firm was even more "embarrassed" because it had told Arthur Andersen & Company and Auchincloss, Redpath & Parker, then NSM's accountant and investment banker, respectively, that no litigation was pending.

Various Covington and Burling men talked among themselves and decided they had had it with Cort Randell. As one of them later told an outside lawyer, Randell and coterie were "mavericks" in the business world, men so unsophisticated that they were essentially beyond control. So McKay and Smith, the partners directly concerned with NSM, summoned Randell to a meeting at the Covington and Burling offices just across LaFayette Park from the White House.

Smith showed Randell the court papers filed by the New York competitor, and handed him the warning letter that had been sent to NSM, but never given to the firm. Yes, Randell said, he had received the letter. And did Covington and Burling know what he thought of it?

"No," Smith and McKay said, "what do you think of it?"

Randell silently folded the letter into a paper airplane and with a flick of his wrist sailed it across the room.

Smith and McKay sat in stunned anger. *This little creep, do we have to endure such arrogance on the part of any client?*

Randell apparently realized the airplane stunt wasn't all that funny. He apologized for not telling Covington and Burling about the threatened suit, saying it was an "innocent mistake." He wanted the firm to continue representing his company. McKay and Smith heard him out, then politely but firmly said the association was at an end. The firm would continue the work in progress, but Randell should seek new counsel.

Covington and Burling lawyers are gentlemen. They fight hard in court and before the regulatory agencies, and they can be abrasive. But they carry the composure that accompanies class and money. The firm is so large, so institutionalized, that the loss of a single client is a triviality. Nonetheless, when Cort Randell left the offices that summer afternoon, he carried the distinct impression that his former attorneys considered him something of an ass.

The scene now shifts to Wall Street, and the offices of White & Case, where Lawrence B. Morris was spending an unhappy summer. A member of the firm since 1948, and known as one of the better securities lawyers in town, Morris didn't like the way the firm was run. Older partners such as Orison Marsden, the former president of the American Bar Association, kept an iron rein on younger people. Morris and contemporaries, men in their forties, felt partners past age sixty-five should have no say in firm management. But Morris was losing: the office elders were polite, but insistent: they had the wisdom and maturity needed for the perpetuation of such an august firm. If any upstart wished to call them senile, why, let him step forward and say so, and *we'll see about that.*

Morris, an outspoken and somewhat bluff man, but nonetheless a cautious rebel, fretted and went about his business, one part of which consisted of listening to an exciting overture from an associate with news about a prospective new client, National Student Marketing Corporation. The intelligence that NSM wanted a new lawyer—a New York firm—came from an executive in the investment house of E.F. Hutton & Company. The executive "believed he had come on a client that was extremely exciting, new and important . . . a very exciting piece of new business," according to Morris. Morris also felt that the man had his own motives in pushing NSM so avidly: "Everybody had [an] ambition to gain a partnership at Hutton." The man's story was that Cort Randell wished to leave Covington and Burling because NSM was moving its headquarters to New York. For convenience, NSM wanted New York lawyers, accountants and investment bankers.

So Morris met with Randell. By his later testimony, he told the young tycoon that Covington and Burling could handle his affairs from Washington as easily as could a New York firm, that a move of corporate offices did not necessitate a change of law firms. But Randell told Morris the differences were deeper than geography. As Morris related in a deposition:

> [Randell] indicated that because of the age differential with the people with whom he was dealing, there had been differences between his approach and the approach of the [Covington and Burling] attorneys to a very dynamic, new, and let's call it explosive market, that Covington and Burling and [NSM officers] did not necessarily view things in the same light that he did. I got the distinct impression that there were personal conflicts between Randell and his nature and his personality and the particular individuals at Covington and Burling and the nature of their personalities.

Randell did tell Morris the paper airplane story, saying it "really upset terribly a senior member of that firm." Morris agreed he might have been a bit irked, too.

Morris mostly listened during this first meeting, for the brash Randell was not the sort of client who usually sought out White & Case. Morris had spent his career dealing with "old and postured" corporations such as Seagram's, Federal Paper Board, Detroit Edison, Lincoln National Life Insurance Company, and Heublein. Also, "we weren't client stealers," Morris said. Case & White lawyers were "trained . . . not to go after other people's clients without discussing that with whoever had been the other attorney, and I followed that practice." Finally, Morris wished to know more about the circumstances of the split.

But Morris ran into a veritable blank wall when he made inquiries at Covington and Burling. One "very good friend," a college classmate, would say only that Randell was a client "you would have to control, have to try to train." But the partner directly responsible for National Student Marketing, James McKay, barely gave Morris the time of day. According to Morris, McKay said the NSM affair was a "touchy matter within the firm," and that Covington and Burling intended to say nothing of substance to the "outside world." Although McKay would say nothing specific, Morris got the impression that a senior partner had been "insulted" and that there was a "very very deep personality conflict."

Morris was not easily dissuaded. In fact, he said, he pushed McKay so hard for information that he felt compelled to apologize after the conversation. But Morris did satisfy himself on what he considered to be important points. According to Morris, McKay said there were no questions about Randell as to "truthfulness, broad crookedness or anything else."

But Morris' curiosity still was not satisfied. When he pressed Randell to explain why National Student Marketing was leaving Arthur Andersen & Company for another accounting firm, Peat, Marwick, Mitchell & Company, Randell sloughed him off with a vague statement about the "books being in a mess." With two decades of securities experience Morris knew Andersen's reputation, so he was suspicious. He called Ronald Garwych, the Andersen executive in charge of the account. (Randell had already rather presumptuously asked Garwych to back his bogus story. Garwych had refused, for Covington and Burling had told him why the firm had quit the NSM account. The firm apparently did this for professional penance, since it had earlier given Arthur Andersen false information based upon Randell's misrepresentations.)

Garwych, however, told none of this to Morris. All he said was that "in the best mutual interest of both parties it was decided to terminate the relationship."* Morris pleaded. But Garwych was adamant: Arthur Andersen would not discuss specifics.

When the conversation ended, Garwych felt that Morris was ready to wash his hands of Randell. In a "strictly confidential" memorandum written for the Andersen files, Garwych opined: "Before he [Morris] closed, he commented that he would probably decide to terminate his firm's association with NSM and mentioned advising [E.F.] Hutton & Company, investment underwriters, that they should do the same."**

Morris, however, said that Garwych misinterpreted "hard questions" for a decision. "If I ever had the assumption or ever been led to believe that I wasn't dealing with an honest and truthful man," he said, "I think this thing would have been very

*This phraseology, by coincidence, came from Arnold & Porter, Arthur Andersen's counsel at the time. Arnold & Porter later represented White & Case. Arnold & Porter, according to Garwych, cautioned that Andersen had no direct firsthand knowledge of "any action [by NSM] that we could term to be misleading, a lie"; hence, the firm should speak obliquely when asked about the termination.

**Actually, Morris said later, White & Case had not formally accepted NSM as a client at the time he spoke with Garwych.

early terminated. If the answers had been of a nature from a firm of the quality of Covington and Burling that would have triggered a red flag, I would have stopped."

But Morris did take the relatively rare precaution of discussing NSM with the White & Case management committee at a meeting in early September 1968. White & Case has no formal procedure for screening new clients. The question of representing an individual or a corporation is left to the partner or associate who makes the initial contact. So, too, is the decision on whether to discuss new clients with the management committee, which meets weekly, or at a partnership meeting. For example, Morris noted, "If I was doing a seventeenth offer of Detroit Edison bonds, I wouldn't bring that to the firm." There are also established firm policies, such as refusing to represent the raider in a tender offer. "We normally represent the established client, the one who is defending," Morris said.

Morris summarized what little information he had unearthed about National Student Marketing. He described Randell and associates as "young and brash" men who would require some supervision. He said that when he asked a Covington partner point-blank whether "these fellows were crooks" he was "assured that there was no question of their integrity." He did not tell the committee—because he did not know—that Covington had broken with NSM because of Randell's lies and evasions.

Morris' story did not disturb the White & Case hierarchy. Indeed, one senior partner, Haliburton Fales, said the paper airplane episode "just tickles my funny bone," the Covington and Burling office being a "rather formal place." So without formal vote, the management committee accepted National Student Marketing as a client.

Marion Jay Epley III—"Jay" Epley, his friends called him—stepped into the epicenter of this swirl of funny money in mid-1969. The year had been a good one for Epley. A few months after his thirty-fourth birthday, on July 1, he became a White & Case partner, meaning he would earn at least $100,000 annually for the rest of his professional life, and in all probability considerably more. Lawyers around Wall Street spoke of the boyish-faced Epley as one of the brightest securities men of his generation. The partnership carried special significance to Jay

Epley: he had established a career and a name in his own right, and no longer was he obscured by the commanding shadow of his father, the board chairman of Texaco. "I finally felt," Epley told me a few years later, "that I was my own man, and I had done it on my own." A charming wife. Two attractive children. Money. Professional reputation. Some mornings when Jay Epley got out of bed he felt so good he wanted to throw out his arms and shout with pure joy.

Among the clients for whom Epley assumed responsibility was National Student Marketing, which came to the firm at approximately the same time he was made a partner. Epley had introductory chats with Cort Randell and other NSM officers, and he reviewed the financial statements they had used in the past. What the books did not show—and what Epley therefore did not discover—was that National Student Marketing's financial situation was grave.

During the fiscal year ending August 31, 1969, the company had operating losses of $1.5 million to $2 million. But an escape loophole remained. If NSM could acquire other companies, profitable ones, their earnings could be used to offset its own losses. Thus NSM could show Cort Randell's promised profit—as measured by acceptable accounting practices, if not by the realities by which most citizens do their business.

No one outside NSM knew the crisis facing the company. The same week glum accountants told the NSM finance committee that the company needed acquisitions to "offset present losses," Randell was telling the New York Society of Security Analysts that NSM would earn around $3.5 million—half from its own operations, half from acquisitions then under way. This statement was a lie. And had the lie been known to the investment community, NSM stock would have tumbled, bringing down Randell's artfully contrived paper empire.

So NSM sought takeover targets with an urgency born of desperation. One especially tempting possibility was Interstate National Corporation, a Chicago-based company which marketed a number of specialized insurance lines. One subsidiary sold accident and health insurance to students, an enterprise that dovetailed neatly with NSM's main market. More importantly, Interstate's 1969 earnings of $1.5 million would give NSM a substantial boost towards the $3.5 million profit Randell was predicting (or, perhaps more accurately, for which Randell was *praying*).

An indication of Randell's desperation is the terms he offered Interstate owners. Interstate stock sold for about $14.50 over-the-counter on June 10, 1969, the day the serious merger talks began. Randell guaranteed Interstate $30.00 per share, in NSM stock—a bonus of slightly more than 100 percent, based on the market price (and more than 400 percent, measured from Interstate's book value of $7.17 per share). The $30.00 per share represented almost fifty-eight times Interstate's earnings per share for the year ended December 31, 1968.

To be sure, the deal contained risks. After the merger the book value represented by each former Interstate share would drop to $2.95. Despite NSM's meteoric rise, the company paid no dividends and did not intend to do so in the foreseeable future; investors bought NSM for its speculative value, not in anticipation of a quarterly check.

These factors were known to Interstate management and owners. But they did *not* know that Randell had lied about NSM's earnings, and that the stock they were to receive in exchange for their profitable company was in fact nigh worthless, were NSM's true condition known.

But Randell talked persuasively. "Look," he in effect told the key Interstate owners, "you are getting to be old men, and there's really not much market for insurance stocks. Come in with us, and you can unload the NSM stock almost as soon as you receive it and carry off a bundle of cash."

Interstate believed Randell, and both parties announced an agreement in principle on June 11.

Then came the legal carpentry, to be performed by White & Case for NSM, and Lord, Bissell & Brook, a Chicago law firm, for Interstate. Bulky though it may be, the documentation for a corporate merger is largely boiler plate—ponderously dull representations that the subject corporations are indeed duly organized, and that their shareholders authorized the merger. Such humdrum scutwork has bored many generations of apprentice Wall Street lawyers, and Jay Epley, understandably, put the Interstate details into the hands of young associates. "There are variations from deal to deal, of course," a Wall Street lawyer once told me, "but generally anyone who paid attention during the securities law course in law school should be able to muddle through a merger. You pull out the file on a similar deal someone else in the office handled last year, and you adapt the papers. The format seldom varies."

In the Interstate merger, however, problems arose immediately. The first draft of the merger agreement, prepared by a White & Case associate, called upon Interstate to provide a comfort letter from its accountant declaring that its financial statements were accurate. The draft placed no such requirement on NSM. Max E.Meyer and Louis Schauer, of Lord, Bissell & Brook, protested, and NSM agreed to submit a parallel comfort letter through Peat, Marwick.

But the revised merger agreement had a more significant omission. Interstate directors met at the Chicago Racquet Club on August 12 for what was expected to be pro forma approval of the deal. The space set aside for NSM's financial statements for the period ending May 31, 1969, contained only blank pages. Some directors wanted to proceed anyway, trusting Randell's previous assurances about NSM's conditions. But director Robert P. Tate, the board chairman, absolutely refused. Angry words were exchanged. Someone finally telephoned attorney Meyer, who sided with Tate: hold off until NSM produces the figures, he said.

Much scurrying ensued, with Randell flying to Chicago to meet with the Interstate directors, and using his private plane to ferry two Peat, Marwick accountants from Washington to New York, where they worked all night at a printing plant putting the financial data into the agreement. The record suggests that at least a glimmer of suspicion crossed the minds of attorney Meyer and chairman Tate, for they cross-examined NSM officers thoroughly about the company's financing and accounting practices. (NSM vice-president James Joy complained to another Interstate director later that Meyer appeared to be hostile and that he asked "a lot of questions." Joy said, "What is he trying to do?") But none of the NSM people would admit any financial problems, and their answers apparently satisfied Meyer and Tate. The agreement was signed on August 15. Shareholders of both corporations approved the merger at separate meetings in October (NSM voted at the same time to acquire six smaller companies as well, through stock swaps).

Epley played a minimal role in these deals, even though he supervised the younger associates who did the paperwork. According to his time records, from July through October 31 he charged 22 percent of his billable time to NSM, 7 percent of it concerning the Interstate merger. But as a law firm, White & Case was heavily involved in the acquisitions, through preparations of proxy forms and other documents attesting that NSM was financially sound.

In a corporate merger the final step is for the two parties to sit at opposite sides of a conference table and to sign, more or less simultaneously, the myriad documents involved in a corporate marriage. This ceremony—a "closing," in Wall Street parlance—is a minuet of paperwork, befitting a Latin American bureaucracy or a Central European passport control point, mind-numbing to the lay clients who sign what is pushed before them, but essential in establishing the intellectual and technical superiority of the securities lawyer. In our instance, a dress rehearsal preceded the performance. On October 30 two White & Case associates met with Schauer of Lord, Bissell & Brook, to review the documents that were to be exchanged the next day. Several documents were missing, among them the required comfort letter from Peat, Marwick attesting to the truth of NSM's financial statements. Schauer was to say later—and White & Case was to deny—that he asked about the letter, only to be told, first, it would be at hand later that day; then, later, that it would not be delivered until October 31, the actual closing date.

The missing letter apparently caused no alarm. Only a day earlier NSM vice-president Joy had told an Interstate executive that NSM's earnings for the fiscal year were "on target." Joy, however, did mention that in an effort to make NSM's books as "clean" as possible, Peat, Marwick was proposing some changes that might affect reported earnings for the nine months ending May 1969. But no one at White & Case heard of these possible "adjustments."

In any event, a full cast assembled at the White & Case offices the morning of October 31—Epley and a phalanx of associates; top management of NSM and Interstate; Lord, Bissell & Brook lawyers from Chicago. The comfort letter was still missing, a matter of no concern for the moment because of a last-minute crisis that threatened to scuttle the entire deal.

Briefly: under the agreement, Interstate principals intended to market immediately 26 percent of the NSM stock they received in the merger. Cameron C. Brown, Interstate president, arranged with White, Weld & Company, a Wall Street brokerage house, to handle the sales at $49.50 per share. But late in the morning White, Weld, passed along upsetting news. The Interstate shares Brown and others were to trade for NSM stock had been acquired via another merger, with the stipulation they were for investment purposes. White, Weld's lawyer, Thomas O'Boyle, of Shearman & Sterling, advised that under securities law, only about 6 percent of Brown's stock could be sold immediately, rather than his anticipated 25 percent. Thus Brown could realize only about $530,000 cash, rather than the $2,000,000 he anticipated.*

Brown, understandably, was miffed, and said, in effect, the hell with it, the deal is off. His attitude alarmed Epley and James Joy, and especially the latter, who knew the Interstate acquisition was vital if NSM was not to collapse. But Brown made some phone calls to Chicago, to shareholders whose stock was similarly restricted, and found them willing to proceed, even if keenly disappointed.

This round of calls ended around 12:30 P.M., and everyone left for a lunch at a nearby private dining club. That the parties ate together is virtually the last pertinent fact on which memories agree for the rest of the day. First, the SEC's version.

Shortly before noon on closing day Anthony Natelli, the Peat, Marwick partner in charge of the Washington office, called Thomas L. Holton, an officer in New York. He told Holton that it had "just been discovered" that NSM's prior statement about its income for the quarter ending May 31 was wrong. If corrected, the statement would show a "slight loss" rather than the claimed $700,000 profit. NSM had been told this change must be revealed in the comfort letter.

According to Holton, he called Epley sometime between noon and 1:00 P.M. and told him he was "concerned" about the merg-

*As a lay student of lawyers, I was amazed that a multimillion-dollar merger proceeded as far as it did without its high-priced legal counsel's noting—and correcting—such basics as the legality of Interstate principals' marketing their NSM stock immediately. One is also permitted to wonder why White & Case permitted Peat, Marwick to dally until veritably the twelth hour before producing the required comfort letter.

er's proceeding without shareholders' being told of the corrected nine-month financial figures. Epley was said to have replied that Interstate lawyers and management knew of the adjustments, and agreed there were "no serious legal problems involved" in going ahead.

The SEC, in polite but intelligible legalese, charged later that Epley lied to Holton on two key points. According to what Interstate lawyers Meyer and Schauer said during depositions, neither Epley nor anyone else from White & Case ever told them or other Interstate principals that the nine-month figures might be changed. Further, they denied agreeing with Epley that the adjustments posed no legal problems. Interstate lawyers and executives alike avowed they knew nothing of any proposed adjustments, regardless of what Epley claimed.

The parties also differed on the timing of the calls between various parties. Holton's recollection—one relied upon by the SEC in its action against White & Case—is that the first Epley-Holton conversation ended no later than 1:00 P.M. This Epley flatly denied; by his account, he first learned of Peat, Marwick's intention to issue a "revised" comfort letter around 2:00 P.M., after the group luncheon adjourned.

Holton's version—again, the one adopted by the SEC—is that he was so alarmed by his conversations with Natelli and Epley that he called the Peat, Marwick house counsel, Victor Earle, and asked what he should do. (Holton timed this call at approximately 1:00 P.M.) Earle saw the problem immediately. He told Holton to talk with partners of both White & Case and Lord, Bissell & Brook and "obtain their opinions that no significant legal problems would be involved" if the closing proceeded regardless of the misstatement of earnings in the NSM proxy statement.

According to Holton, he reached Epley shortly after 2:00 P.M., when the luncheon adjourned. He asked for the opinion requested by Earle. Epley replied that neither White & Case nor Lord, Bissell & Brook would do so. Epley also said that both White & Case and Lord, Bissell & Brook were aware there could be "serious legal implications in completing the closing" in view of NSM's financial misstatements, but that both counsel were willing to proceed.

Epley flatly denied saying any such thing. By his account, he first heard of the missing comfort letter upon returning from the luncheon around 2:00 P.M. He telephoned Natelli, who said the letter would be dictated over the phone from Washington to Epley's secretary. Epley's understanding was that a signed copy of the letter would later be delivered to White & Case.

The letter, dictated to Epley's secretary between 2:00 and 2:30 P.M., made a shambles of NSM's nine-month financial statement. It cited three "significant adjustments" which should be made retroactive to May 31, 1969—writing off $300,000 in uncollectable accounts; listing various program costs of $500,000; and changing $84,000 in various acquisition expenses from one account to another. The changes were highly technical, and their details incomprehensible to anyone outside the accounting profession. Nonetheless, they had the effect of cleaving $884,000 from NSM's claimed profits, causing an operating loss for the period of approximately $80,000.

Epley immediately smelled trouble. Since the merger agreement provided that the comfort letter had to be "satisfactory to Interstate," he felt Interstate could walk away from the deal. He showed the letter to John Davies, NSM's house counsel, and one of the men supposedly quipped to the other, "This will blow the deal." (Epley denied that any such comment was made.) Epley made copies of the letter, went to the conference room and distributed them to NSM and Interstate principals. Then he went back to his office and sat down with Davies, fingers figuratively crossed.

Holton, meanwhile, had talked again with Earle, his lawyer, and told of Epley's refusal to give an opinion that there were no significant "legal impediments" to completing the merger. In that case, Earle replied, Peat, Marwick should add another paragraph stating that if the adjustments listed elsewhere in the comfort letter had been made as of May 31, NSM "would have shown a net loss of approximately $80,000." The new paragraph also said that were it not for acquisitions such as Interstate, NSM would have about broken even for the full year.

Shortly after 3:00 P.M. Epley spoke with Natelli and heard the new paragraph. Natelli's testimony depicted Epley as a most angry lawyer. According to Natelli, Epley said the paragraph was "gratuitous" and merely summarized information already in the letter. Epley said that "any child could do the arithmetic and figure out the results" that the paragraph reflected. Epley said he and others were "trying to close a $40,000,000 deal" and that the new paragraph "would make the closing more complicated." Epley would not accept Natelli's opinion that the paragraph was needed and demanded that he check with a superior. Natelli agreed to do so; first, however, he dictated the new paragraph to Epley's secretary.

Epley and Davies, however, did not pass news of this new development along to the Interstate and NSM principals still meeting in the White & Case conference room. Epley's position was that he was still uncertain as to the final form of the letter. Around 3:30 P.M. Epley spoke by phone with Holton, who was insistent that the paragraph be included. Epley argued. He pressed Holton to explain "what new information" the paragraph added to the letter. And he also pointed out that since Peat, Marwick had helped prepare the May 31 financial statements, the firm "now appeared to be challenging the accuracy of its own work."

Delivery of the first form of the comfort letter alarmed the Interstate officers who popped acrimonious questions to Randell and Joy. The ever-optimistic Randell continued to insist that NSM was sound, and that the earnings projections of $0.75 to $0.80 a share would be met. Randell called the comfort letter "ancient history" and said nothing in it surprised him—that NSM, as a growing company, was an entirely different corporation in October than it had been in May.

Epley took little part in these first talks, for he was busy with the call from Peat, Marwick during which he learned of yet another change in the comfort letter. He felt at the time, he said later, that Interstate had to make a "business decision" on whether to proceed. He knew, as did the Interstate lawyers, that the merger agreement gave directors of either company the right to waive "any of the conditions" for the merger. Further, Interstate was represented at the meeting not only by its board chairman (Tate), its president and chief executive officer (Brown) and its general counsel (William J. Bach) but also by a majority of the directors and four of five members of the executive committee.

The Interstate people, after listening to Randell, talked privately. Their depositions indicate they wrestled with several varieties of fears. One was economic—a threat to the windfall stock profits each could earn in the deal. Interstate stock had risen from $15 a share when the merger was announced in June to more than $34 a share on October 31. During the same period NSM stock went to $54 a share, substantially higher than the $45 guaranteed price in the merger agreement. Calling off or postponing the merger could cost Interstate shareholders what the directors considered "a very favorable deal for them."

Further, the Interstate officials knew that the office in Washington where the merger documents were to be filed closed at 4:00 P.M.* It was already past 3:00 P.M., so they had to decide, and fast. Investors knew the closing was scheduled for that day. If for any reason it was postponed, the directors feared an "adverse market reaction" would tumble the price of Interstate stock. If this happened, the directors faced lawsuits from investors who had bought stock after announcement of the merger or held it in anticipation of the merger. The Interstate directors could be charged with unwisely aborting a favorable merger, especially if National Student Marketing's year-end earnings matched Randell's predictions.

All in all, a complicated situation, and in the end the Interstate directors decided to proceed because of the advantages from a "practical and business point of view." They so informed the NSM people, at around 3:30 P.M.

The rest of the process was mechanical. Signatures went onto the papers. A White & Case associate, executing a prearranged plan, stepped into a phone booth in the conference room and called an executive in the New York office of the U.S. Corporation Company, a firm which assists lawyers in corporate matters. This executive, in turn, telephoned his company's Washington office, in the National Press Building, and directed a messenger to take the necessary papers to the office of the Recorder of Deeds, some ten city blocks away. The merger documents were time-stamped 3:46 P.M.

Epley, it will be remembered, was still haggling with Holton of Peat, Marwick over the necessity of the additional paragraph in

*Formally, at the Corporation Division of the Office of the Recorder of Deeds in the District of Columbia, where NSM was incorporated. Filing articles of merger is the final technical step required to consummate a merger.

the comfort letter. When he finally put down the phone and returned to the conference room—at a time variously estimated at 3:35 to 3:45 P.M.—some of the Interstate representatives had their coats on and suitcases in hand, ready to go to LaGuardia Airport for their return to Chicago. The closing, someone told Epley, had been consummated.

Epley said nothing about the intense debate of the last hour with NSM's accountants. As summarized in a pretrial brief by his lawyers, Arnold & Porter:

> Prior to the departure of the Interstate group, Mr. Epley did not discuss with them the telephone conversations he had had with Messrs. Natelli and Holton about the possible addition of a paragraph to the comfort letter. Despite specific inquiries from Mr. Epley, neither Mr. Natelli nor Mr. Holton had explained . . . what the proposed additional paragraph would add . . . beyond a simple arithmetical computation. Mr. Holton had advised Mr. Epley that he intended to discuss with [Peat, Marwick's] counsel whether to add the paragraph, and Mr. Epley understood that the decision as to its inclusion was still under consideration by [Peat, Marwick].

As Epley said later, since the deal had been closed, apparently to Interstate's satisfaction, and with Interstate's full knowledge of the basic comfort letter, he was obligated to say nothing. So he remained silent.

Thus the act that made Jay Epley the central figure of the most celebrated case ever on the obligation of a securities lawyer.

The SEC was to maintain later that Epley should have told Interstate about the disputed additional paragraph, even though Peat, Marwick was still considering its exact language, and even though the merger was completed. By remaining silent, the SEC charged, Epley stepped outside the securities laws.

Holton and Earle, meanwhile, apparently realized that Epley intended to ignore their demand for the extra paragraph. Their next move strongly suggests that the accountants wanted to build a "paper record" to protect themselves in the event the deal turned out poorly. So they drafted yet another paragraph for the comfort letter which read as follows: "In view of the above mentioned facts, we believe the companies should consider submitting corrected interim unaudited financial information to the shareholders prior to proceeding with the closing."

The Interstate directors, in fact, had considered just such a move and decided against it because they did not have enough time before the deadline for the merger lapsed.

Holton telephoned Epley about 4:30 P.M. and read him the new paragraph and told him it would be in the final version of the comfort letter, which was to be delivered shortly. Holton said Epley told him, "Well, that's very interesting, but the deal is closed and if you or your counsel would like to tell us how to reverse the merger, I would like to hear it." Epley called the paragraph "pointless" and noted that the Interstate group had already left the White & Case offices. Holton said he intended to mail copies of the letter to both the companies and their individual directors.

Davies, the NSM house counsel, heard this conversation, and when it ended he and Epley discussed whether NSM was required to make a public announcement of the comfort letter, either via a press release or a letter to shareholders. Davies noted that announcement of the final year-end figures was imminent—within a week or ten days—and they met Randell's projection of $0.75 to $0.80 per share.

The situation worried Epley because a few years earlier he had worked on a markedly parallel case. Responding to widespread market rumors, Texas Gulf Sulphur issued a pessimistic press statement about a mining venture in Canada. The stock price plummeted. Within the week, however, management announced discovery of a lode of copper, zinc and silver with an estimated value of $2 billion. The stock price rebounded. The result was a flood of lawsuits by former Texas Gulf Sulphur shareholders who had sold on the basis of the negative report. Epley told Davies that if NSM made an immediate announcement of adjustments appearing to wipe out its nine-month earnings, and followed it shortly with an announcement of substantial year-end earnings, its stock might follow the dip-rebound pattern of Texas Gulf Sulphur. Anyone who sold NSM stock at reduced prices following the first announcement might sue management for issuing a negative report when the company knew it had in fact earned healthy profits.

Conversely, Epley said, if NSM remained silent, and its year-end earnings were not as good as anticipated, causing a stock decline, management could be sued by shareholders who had held or bought stock after receipt of the comfort letter. They could claim that their loss resulted from NSM's failure to announce the bad financial news.

Epley and Davies discussed the relative risks. White & Case, Epley said, would not advise NSM whether one course of action was safer than another; the law was "totally unclear." According to Davies, Epley said he felt no obligation to Interstate shareholders, past or present, because they were represented by sophisticated management and competent counsel who were "big boys." (Epley denied making this remark.) In a file memorandum written a few days later, Epley said:

> The possible exposure of NSM and its officers by reason of a non-disclosure of the interim adjustments was discussed in detail with Mr. Davies and I told him that we were not in a position to give an opinion that no liability exists. I believe that he thoroughly understood the situation and the determination to make no release was based upon consideration of other than legal factors.

Epley's implication seems clear: releasing the adverse earnings report would hurt NSM stock.

In due course Peat, Marwick sent the final version of the comfort letter—bad financial news and all—to principals of both corporations. Schauer, the Interstate lawyer, was not happy. In a phone conversation with Epley on November 4 he sarcastically told the White & Case lawyer it "would have been nice" if someone had told Interstate the final comfort letter would read as it did. Epley repeated that the differences between the various forms of the letter were not material, and that the deal was closed before he received the final version.

The major Interstate stockholders certainly did not complain. Between the merger date of October 31 and the end of November they sold NSM shares totalling $2,945,250. For Interstate president Brown, his $500,000 represented a 100 percent windfall profit.

In subsequent weeks Epley and other White & Case lawyers helped National Student Marketing prepare several routine filings with the SEC. None mentioned the disputed comfort letter. And during November, National Student Marketing bought out three other small companies—two school and charter bus operations, and a class ring manufacturer—without a candid disclosure of the Peat, Marwick findings. The SEC claimed later, among other things, that Epley and Davies told one or more of these merger partners that half of NSM's 1969 earnings would come from the parent company, as distinguished from the acquired companies—a statement the SEC said that Epley, White & Case, and other principals knew to be "materially false and misleading."

One of these closings was stormy. Norman D. Finkel, Chicago lawyer for Ritzenthaler Bus Lines, Inc., and some related companies, noticed early on that NSM's financial statements were not complete. Specifically, he wanted a copy of the proxy statement NSM had used in acquiring Interstate, the Illinois insurance complex. According to Finkel, Epley put him off, saying that much of the information was confidential, and that since NSM's stock was publicly traded, the "market price . . . readily indicated the attitude of the financial world towards NSM." (At one stage, Finkel said, someone in either NSM or White & Case told his client he was "being an obstructionist in this matter." The client wanted the deal so badly, Finkel said, that he was told, in Finkel's words, "I shouldn't give anyone a hard time.")

According to the SEC, Epley later did produce the documents—but for the bus company president, not for Finkel. Angered, Finkel bearded Epley, who pleaded "inadvertence." The deal went through, and someone opened a bottle of champagne, and everyone drank a toast to the merger. This was in November. By January, NSM stock was dropping so rapidly that Finkel's client was "rather upset," in the lawyer's words. Finkel resisted the opportunity to say, "I told you so."

Concurrent with the acquisitions, NSM tried to slough off money-losing subsidiaries whose red ink could not be concealed. In one instance, this required backdating sales papers to make it appear the transactions had occurred in the 1969 fiscal year. The company was Compujob, started in 1968 by two college students who sold lists of computer-selected résumés of students to prospective employers. Their total investment was $1,200. NSM bought Compujob; it lost $127,000 in 1969. On October 23, 1969—almost two months after NSM's fiscal year ended—NSM decided to dump Compujob via papers dated August 27. The details are complicated, and involved shares in such NSM subsidiaries as a Delaware corporation formed to develop resort condominiums in the Virgin Islands, but the net result was that the juggling enabled NSM to cut a $127,000 loss from its books—posthumously, if you will. A similar deal cast off a Canadian subsidiary with losses of around $254,000.

Again, a problem for Epley and White & Case. During the Interstate closing, White & Case—under Epley's direction—had prepared papers stating, among other things, that NSM owned Compujob and the Canadian company. These were dated October 31. However, on November 20, almost a month later, White & Case issued another opinion letter approving the backdating of both sales to August 29—thereby cutting NSM's 1969 losses by more than $400,000.

As the SEC said, Epley and his law firm "knew or should have known" that the November 20 opinion letter was "materially false or misleading," and that both sales were bogus.

Cortes Randell had built an empire of paper and promises. White & Case, wittingly or unwittingly, helped keep it erect from mid-summer 1969 through December. Then, on December 22, 1969, Alan Abelson, columnist for the financial weekly *Barron's*, picked through NSM's annual report and cried, in effect, "Bah, humbug." Instead of a profit, Abelson said, NSM actually lost $600,000 during fiscal 1969. He criticized NSM's accountants, but not White & Case.

NSM stock fell 20 points the next day. It did not rise again, ever. And the Securities and Exchange Commission suddenly was very interested in NSM's books.

White & Case's first reaction, oddly, was an intense intra-office debate on whether to advise National Student Marketing to sue *Barron's* and Abelson for a variety of libel known under New York law as "corporate defamation." Vernon Munroe, Jr., the partner in charge of White & Case's corporate department, seemed particularly displeased. Peat, Marwick had adhered to standards of the accounting profession; why, then, should NSM be criticized?

Meetings lasted throughout the day. At their end, Munroe gave Epley a backhanded endorsement. His actions during the October 31 closing with Interstate were correct, although Munroe did state it "might have been better" had Epley instructed NSM to issue a press release.

Epley did not recognize it at the time, but Munroe's statement was an omen: White & Case was capable of second-guessing.

A final item of business rounded out the year: White & Case billed National Student Marketing $325,000 for six months' work.

On January 2, 1970, the SEC moved. Staff attorneys asked Epley for a variety of information, including copies of Randell's speeches and press releases, and explanations of certain financial statements. The SEC was particularly curious about the large year-end adjustment of earnings. Could not some of these changes have been foreseen earlier—say, after the May 31 quarter? Asked this question directly at a meeting on January 19, Jay Epley gave the SEC a copy of the much-disputed comfort letter.

The SEC did not realize the significance of the letter at the time. As a staff attorney later said, "We knew by this point National Student Marketing was in a mess. Their books looked as if they were written in double-talk. Of course now, in fairness, some of this could be laid to the fact that they had made lots of acquisitions, and many sets of financial figures had to be meshed together. But the overall picture was of a company in very very bad trouble. We were also on the spot at the commission. If NSM went under, many investors would be hurt, and they'd ask, 'Where the hell was the SEC when I was being swindled?' "

With the SEC now looking over its shoulder, NSM no longer could use its "creative accounting" techniques to show profits. The company's fall was swift. In February 1970 NSM reported it anticipated a loss of between $1.2 and $1.7 million for the quarter ended November 30, instead of a predicted profit. A few days later NSM reported first-quarter losses for the new year of $859,889.

But Cort Randell wouldn't give up. He continued making optimistic speeches about NSM's future, despite entreaties by other company officers that he accept reality and keep his mouth shut. Exasperated, the officers consulted Epley, who in turn talked with ranking partners at White & Case. If Randell was harming the company, the partners told Epley, he should be forced out. Epley and other lawyers started drafting documents for the NSM board to use in dismissing Randell. They were not needed. Confronted by directors the night of February 19, the one-time boy wonder of finance quit his $100 million empire. NSM stock plunged, plunged, plunged, finally selling for $1.

Now it was the SEC's turn. For two years staff attorneys and accountants burrowed through NSM's books and interviewed officers, lawyers and accountants. Finally, on February 3, 1972, the SEC filed a civil complaint that, in the words of legal journalist Paul Hoffman, "echoed like an anarchist's bomb blast through the canyons of the financial district."[13] The complaint, filed in federal court in Washington, named not only NSM and its ranking officers as defendants, but also outside lawyers and accountants—Jay Epley; Max E. Meyer and Louis F. Schauer of Lord, Bissell & Brook; and Anthony M. Natelli and Joseph Scansaroli of Peat, Marwick. The law firms of White & Case and Lord, Bissell & Brook were accused as well.

The principal count against Epley involved what the SEC called his "fraudulent responsibility" for the much-disputed comfort letter that was used, first, in NSM's acquisition of the Interstate insurance companies, and later in its acquisition of the bus lines and the school jewelry firm. He was also accused of giving NSM "false and misleading opinions" in the backdated sales of the computer-job and Canadian subsidiaries, and of misleading Peat, Marwick about what use was made of the comfort letter. "As a lawyer," the SEC said, "Epley should have fully appreciated the seriousness of his conduct and the fraudulent conduct he was facilitating." White & Case was charged with responsibility for all of Epley's actions.

Specifically, the SEC said Epley should have attempted to show the final version of the comfort letter to Interstate representatives, even though the acquisition was completed before he received it. The SEC said that Epley and the Lord, Bissell & Brook lawyers should have refused to issue an opinion after the merger, attesting to its legality, and that they should have insisted that the new earnings figures be disclosed to shareholders. If either NSM or Interstate refused to do so, the lawyers should have resigned and notified both the SEC and the Interstate shareholders of the "misleading nature of the . . . financial statements."

The SEC asked the court to enjoin Epley and the other defendants from further violations of the securities laws—the commissions's usual weapon in civil cases. But the SEC knew this would be no pro forma case, for its suit struck at the very heart of how the securities bar did its business.*

Jay Epley was in Detroit consulting a client when his office called with news of the civil complaint. Stunned, he finished his work, then telephoned his father. "I didn't want him to learn of this second hand," he said. "I felt in turmoil." Back in New York the next day, he went to the White & Case offices and dictated a letter of resignation and hand carried it to the firm's senior partner, Orison Marsden. "I didn't think I had done anything wrong, and I thought that I had explained all of my actions to the SEC's satisfaction. Nonetheless, the 'fraud' headlines were in the newspapers, along with the White & Case name. In the three quarters of a century of the firm's existence not a single lawyer—partner or associate—had even been subjected to a disciplinary action, and that's a very long time. Rightly or wrongly, my actions had caused the firm problems, and the only honorable course I saw was to resign and clear my name."

Epley handed the letter to Marsden and explained his reasoning as the older man read it. Then Marsden wadded the letter into a tight ball and tossed it into the trash basket. "Nonsense, young man," he said. "You are our partner, and you did not violate any laws. We are behind you all the way." In Chicago, the elders of Lord, Bissell & Brook made a similar decision.

One frequent complaint of corporate executives is that the big New York and Washington firms "overlitigate" cases, that is, spend so much time on nit-picking details that the client is stuck with an unnecessarily astronomical bill. One critic, Lester Pollack, chairman of the finance committee of CNA Financial Corporation, of Chicago, once charged that lawyers suffered from

*The SEC probe also resulted in criminal charges. Cort Randell pleaded guilty to four counts of fraud and conspiracy and served time in prison. John G. Davies, NSM director and house counsel, pleaded guilty to violating securities laws and was disbarred. Anthony M. Natelli, Peat, Marwick vice-president in charge of the Washington office, was convicted by a jury of uttering false and misleading statements. His colleague, Joseph Scansaroli, was also found guilty, but an appeals court reversed the conviction.

"messiah" complexes and likened them to "Roman gladiators" who wanted to fight every dispute in court at great length—and at great expense. Sounding much like a man who had signed big checks for legal fees, Pollack predicted to a bar group in 1977 that if litigation and legal fees kept increasing, "businessmen, through their associations, will seek legislation or regulation" to control them.[14] But White & Case's defense demonstrated the effort a law firm felt to be required when its own interests were involved: White & Case spared neither money nor effort.

Its own considerable in-house talents notwithstanding, White & Case's first step was to retain the Washington firm of Arnold & Porter, which knows the twisted byways of the capital at least as well—and perhaps better—than any other law office in town. Arnold & Porter reputedly had enjoyed special status at the SEC. Abe Fortas, a founding partner of the firm who resigned when he went onto the U.S. Supreme Court, boasted to clients and other friends that he was responsible for the appointment of at least one previous SEC chairman, Manuel F. Cohen.* A current senior partner, Milton Freeman, was an SEC attorney and assistant solicitor from 1934 to 1946. And it was Freeman whom I sought out when I began looking into the White & Case affair.

The Arnold & Porter offices are in an elegant red-brick townhouse just below Dupont Circle in Northwest Washington. There is usually a limousine in the curved driveway, and a chauffeur idling away the time with a chamois skin or a newspaper; secretaries and messengers bustle in and out, bound for the firm's overflow offices in nearby buildings. I found Freeman to be a bouncy fellow in his sixties, resplendent in a gold shirt, pink tie, and pink-and-white checkered socks. The White & Case suit was in its final pretrial stages, and Freeman sat on a couch and waved his hand at a four-foot shelf crammed with depositions which he and colleagues had taken around the country.

"This case is a legal absurdity," Freeman said, "a ridiculous

*Fortas made this assertion, among other places, in a conversation with financier Louis Wolfson in 1970, nine months after disclosure of a $20,000 payment by Wolfson to Fortas resulted in his resignation from the court. Fortas' former law firm was representing Wolfson in an SEC investigation, and Wolfson apparently expected the justice to intervene, saying, "I thought you told me you were responsible for his [Cohen's] appointment." "I was," replied Fortas, according to a recording Wolfson made of the meeting. But he said he declined to contact Cohen because "it would have been like lighting a fuse on our own dynamite." Bob Woodward published an account of the transcript in the *Washington Post*, January 23, 1977.

waste of everyone's time and energy. In February 1972 the SEC asks for an injunction against something that happened in October 1969; the trial won't come until 1977; and the lawyers' meters have been running all the while.

"The SEC's position is that White & Case 'conspired' with National Student Marketing to conceal the accountants' letter, and that the Chicago law firm 'conspired' with someone or another to keep it secret so its principals could make money on the stock.

"Absolutely absurd! What's in it for the law firms? They are on a retainer; they are paid whether or not the deal goes through; there's no profit for them to get involved in a crooked deal. One client means so much to White & Case that they risk seventy-five years of reputation on one measly little acquisition? I repeat, ABSURD!"

Freeman then talked about the SEC's investigative procedures and reforms that have been suggested by him and other critics. One key change would permit potential defendants to present their case before the full commission prior to the filing of civil or criminal charges. The present system is for the staff to present evidence and to ask the commission to authorize action. Such a reform was recommended a few years ago, in fact, by a committee formed at the commission's own request. The so-called Wells Committee was composed of John A. Wells, senior partner of what is now the New York firm of Rogers & Wells, and two former SEC chairman, Manuel F. Cohen and Ralph Demmler. "The staff fought this proposal like a tiger," Freeman said. He mimicked the staff's attitude, waving his arms and rolling his eyes and putting his voice into a shrill key: " 'That's impractical. That makes us try the cases twice.' " Freeman calmed and shook his head. "Nonsense," he repeated.

"So what happens in this case? The SEC gives two prestigious firms a real Pearl Harbor—the first time in forty years that law firms are named in a suit—and they know nothing about it until they are in the newspapers.

"It's an awesome thing when the federal government takes after someone. Think about it: 'The United States of America versus Milt Freeman, or the United States of America versus Joe Goulden.' How'd you like to see that caption on a piece of paper?"

I agreed I might become very nervous. I thanked Freeman, and I left and rode across town to inspect the force and majesty of the United States government.

All I knew about the SEC's handling of the NSM case was that it was in the hands of a staff lawyer named Richard Patterson, who told me by phone I was welcome to read any of the files he had that were in the public domain, either as court or commission exhibits.

The SEC is an agency that discourages citizens from wandering in from the streets and making themselves at home. As Ted Sonde, Sporkin's deputy, told me earlier, "Reporters would come up here, leave their coats in the pressroom and wander around in their shirt sleeves, looking like anybody else on the staff. Anyone who can read can always find interesting documents lying around on desks. So if we appear unfriendly, there's a reason." Thus I stopped at a reception desk and telephoned Patterson, who said, "Someone will come out and get you."

Enter a blond, lank young man in blue jeans and a denim shirt. "Back here," he said, motioning to me, "we have to ride the elevator down."

Small talk. "Are you working with Mr. Patterson on White & Case?"

The guy looked at me, and after some consideration he gave me a bemused smile. "I *am* Richard Patterson," he said, "and one reason I work at the SEC instead of White & Case, or the like, is that I can wear what I want to wear to the office."

We stepped out into an unfinished basement and walked down a narrow corridor and around two or three corners, past chain-wire doors to various supply rooms and stopped in front of a greenish-metal door. Inside, a young lady named Sally Hamrick, a paralegal working under Patterson, busily tried to make order of files that poked from drawers, covered desk tops, spilled over into neat stacks on the floor. "Hi," she said, waving, "welcome to the command post. Or the bunker. Or the dungeon. For goodness' sake don't knock over anything. We're organized, but the organization is in delicate balance."

Patterson gave me a stack of depositions that were in the public record, and I went upstairs to a public room to read through the first of 25,000-odd pages of testimony and pleadings.

The pretrial briefs—the documents the various parties had

filed with the court as a preview of the evidence they intended to prove at trial—contained an interesting point. Lord, Bissell & Brook, a codefendant along with White & Case, was striking out on its own course. Its brief adopted many of the SEC pleadings as its own—insofar as they pertained to White & Case. The brief claimed that Lord, Bissell & Brook lawyers—and the firm's client, Interstate—had been misled by White & Case, and specifically by Jay Epley. The Lord, Bissell & Brook brief, in sum, was tantamount to being a supplemental brief for the government. Lord, Bissell & Brook defended its own actions, quite understandably. But one could search the bulky document in vain for any supporting words for White & Case.

As I sipped a bitter cup of SEC cafeteria coffee and read the briefs and depositions, my mind kept returning to that basement room. I thought, okay, so that's the power of the United States government—a lawyer and a clerk, both in their twenties, stuck away out of sight in the basement of a government office building. And I remembered an estimate that a New York lawyer had given me several days earlier: "The way I figure it, White & Case has laid out $4,000,000 in fees already, based upon the motions they've filed and argued, and the volume of the depositions. This might sound trite, but they are playing for keeps."

With the principals and their lawyers under a court-imposed gag rule—the voluble Milt Freeman had commented more on SEC procedures than specifics of the National Student Marketing case—I made what I could of the masses of paper accumulated by both sides, and tried to be properly respectful of their opposing positions.

Yet an anomaly worried me. Law is a pragmatic profession, and I had heard attorney after attorney speak of foolish clients who wanted to fritter away money on meaningless causes. Did White & Case really wish to spend a decade and $6 million—money from its partners' pockets, mind you—to fend off a court order which much of Wall Street would accept as meaningless? Did White & Case really believe that one alleged misdeed, committed during the hurried confusion of a closing, would offset whatever reputation it had acquired in seventy-five years? Freeman had told me, "It's a matter of pride and honor. They did nothing wrong, and they don't like being called 'crooks' in public papers." But I expected this of Freeman, who seemed to be rehearsing a jury speech.

I wanted to talk to Jay Epley, the lawyer with the most to lose from the case. His SEC deposition told me little: Born in New Orleans February 8, 1937. A graduate of Princeton, class of 1958, and of its Woodrow Wilson School of Public and International Affairs. Next, Harvard Law School, graduating in 1961, and joining White & Case the same year with the intention of specializing in corporate law. This wouldn't suffice. I confess to an inability to get the feel of a man from the questions and answers of a deposition or from the inane generalities people use in talking about one another.

Epley, however, is a lawyer who plays by the rules. His situation was serious and inquiries to his office for an interview—even one with National Student Marketing strictly off-limits—were gently but flatly turned aside. Then, by happenstance, I met a man who happened to know Epley, a publicist who had worked with White & Case on securities deals over the past decades.

"Look," I pleaded, "all I want is to find out how the man smells. I'm writing a chapter on a case that is rather central to Epley's professional career. Christ, I think it's rather important that I know what he looks like in the flesh and what he sounds like."

The man was dubious. "I did the same thing some months back for a guy from the *Wall Street Journal*, and he crucified Jay. How do I know I'm not buying him more trouble?"

We talked some more, both that evening and by long-distance telephone, and in due course I met Epley and his friend at the Palm, the restaurant on the East Side of Manhattan that serves a steak better than one can buy even in Fort Worth or Kansas City.

Epley was just coming off his fortieth birthday, but in the dim light, sipping a glass of white wine, he looked a decade younger—fraternity-rush openness in a pin-striped suit. We kept away from National Student Marketing, save by indirection. Epley's chief concern was the impact of the case on his law firm, his family and his father. "Dad started as a lawyer with Texaco in

Louisiana, where I was born. Then he went up through the ranks in the legal department and eventually became president. He always felt himself to be a lawyer, not a corporate executive, and that is one reason this case is so important to me. I don't want any Marion Jay Epley, be he the second or the third, to go down in the legal history books as someone found guilty in a stock case. That's the discouraging factor: I'm not the only one on trial. What I did brings my law firm into court, and my father, by indirection."

We talked about the logistics of his case, which was to go to trial in the summer of 1977, and which was expected to last several months. Epley intended to bring his family to Washington and rent an apartment for the duration, and I gave him a discouraging prognosis about summertime comforts in the capital.

Epley's friend wondered about press coverage. I had been a newspaperman, he noted. What interest would the *Wall Street Journal* and the *New York Times* have in the case? I guessed: opening-day stories, a periodic recap, perhaps weekly, as the trial progressed; then a verdict story. "Hmmmm," said Epley's friend.

Late in the evening Epley talked about his law firm. "White & Case is where I chose to come after Harvard, and where I was fortunate enough to be accepted. White & Case is the only professional life I have ever known. Why is White & Case spending the kind of time and money that it is on this case? I won't get into figures [I had told him of the trade talk about the supposed $6,000,000 price tag], but, yes, the amount is substantial."

Epley stopped talking for a moment, and his eyes seemed to focus elsewhere in the room, as if he wanted to withdraw himself and think about what he wanted to say next.

"I'll go even further than calling White & Case my profession. Being a partner in White & Case is much more than being a member of a law firm. The day I tried to resign, and Mr. Marsden told me not to be ridiculous, I knew I was accepted.

"No, White & Case is my home, and the people there are my family."

I gave Epley my Virginia address and telephone number, and we made a vague agreement to do something social when he came to Washington for the trial. Then we shook hands and walked our separate ways on Second Avenue.

* * *

The dinner meeting was on Wednesday evening, April 27, 1977. Exactly a week later, on Wednesday morning, May 4, as I ate breakfast at my home with the *Washington Post*, I saw a two-paragraph item at the bottom of the financial page:

> White & Case, a major New York law firm, agreed to settle an SEC suit growing out of litigation involving a client, National Student Marketing Corp.
>
> Under the settlement, Marion J. Epley III, the White & Case partner who handled the National Student Marketing account, was barred from practice before the SEC for six months and the firm agreed to certain SEC dictated procedures in dealing with securities accounts.

I arose with such a start that a cup of hot tea spilled into my lap, to the distress to both me and my cat, Bernie, who was occupying her personal breakfast perch. What the devil! A week ago Jay Epley is defiant, ready for trial, and there are no audible sounds of surrender anywhere around White & Case.

The telephone. "Epley got his legs cut off," one man was saying. "White & Case had a partners' meeting within the last week and decided it wanted out of the case, to make the best deal possible. The cost was one thing; the publicity was another. These people didn't want to be in the newspapers all summer."

Epley wasn't receiving calls. When I finally obtained the formal court order, I realized why, for he had taken the heavy hit in the settlement. Epley is a securities lawyer, which means that he does things for corporations that have business with the SEC. In the court order he "agreed that he will not engage in the practice of law before the [SEC] or advise clients with respect to filing or other matters involving securities registered under the Federal Securities Laws for a period of 180 calendar days."

Epley, of course, neither admitted nor denied the allegations made against him; he simply gave up a substantial part of his livelihood for six months.

I read further. There was the standard promise by White & Case that it would not violate the securities laws in the future. White & Case also neither admitted nor denied doing so in the past. (This language sounds like what you read in the italic type in the front pages of a Harold Robbins novel, that "any resemblance of the characters portrayed herein to any living character is strictly coincidental.") But the SEC did extract some concessions from White & Case:

—If a prospective client appeared on the firm's doorstep, and said its last group of lawyers had terminated the association, White & Case would ask the client to release the former lawyers from the obligation of confidentiality. White & Case would then ask the other firm why it had broken with the client. "Appropriate documentation" as to the reasons would be put into the firm files and made available to any lawyer working with the client. This wording moves in side steps. It does not require White & Case to reject bad actors. But it does mean that any adverse information about a client's dealings with former attorneys does go onto paper, and thereby into theoretical reach of the SEC. A similar rule would be applied to clients who had changed accounting firms within the past two years.

—Another agreement tightened the conditions under which a White & Case client could ask the other party in a deal to waive disclosure of financial or other information. This agreement stemmed directly from the confusion surrounding the Interstate insurance acquisition. To recapitulate briefly, NSM's accounting firm, Peat, Marwick, insisted that new financial data should be given all parties to the merger, including stockholders, even though the Interstate directors and officers were willing to proceed with the merger. They did merge, and Epley, on behalf of White & Case, signed an opinion letter stating the merger complied with all relevant laws. Under the court order, Epley (or any other White & Case lawyer) would have to obtain the concurrence of two other partners in the firm before delivering such an opinion.

—If any White & Case lawyer felt a client was playing loose with the truth and not making full disclosure to the SEC or the public, the lawyer would advise the client to comply with the law. If he did not, the lawyer would consult at least two other partners on "the need for the firm to withdraw from employment or take other appropriate action"—i.e., complain to the SEC.

* * *

The agreement (there were other, more technical paragraphs) amounted to a rare surrender of internal autonomy by an American law firm. A federal agency was telling lawyers how to conduct their profession.*

Why the turnabout? Why did White & Case go from a posture of defiance to conciliation? I turned again to the telephone, and the following is what I found.

Attorneys for White & Case—both in the firm itself, and those from Arnold & Porter, the outside counsel—showed signs of nervousness in early spring. After the pretrial briefs were filed the SEC trial staff had a series of meetings with White & Case counsel during which they spelled out the government's case in minute detail, covering not only the briefs but the essence of what witnesses would say. In the words of one SEC lawyer, "they began to see our case in a way they had not appreciated before."

Other factors were at work. One was the attitude of Lord, Bissell & Brook noted above, an effective casting off of White & Case as a codefendant. To observers the Chicago lawyers seemed bent upon preserving themselves; they claimed to be victims of, rather than conspirators with, White & Case, and would so argue in court.

Another factor of immeasurable weight was the attitude of the judge who was to try the case, Barrington Parker, of the U.S. district court in Washington. Parker repeatedly ruled against White & Case on pretrial motions. In one key ruling which enhanced the government's case, he permitted the SEC to amend its original complaint to include three additional matters: Epley's alleged misconduct in the bus and jewelry company purchases, his reputed concealment of the nature of the "sale" of a NSM subsidiary, and threats he supposedly made to Peat, Marwick auditors the night before the company's annual meeting in

*Lawyers at White & Case and in other securities firms laughed at the settlement as "achieving meaningless concessions." According to one White & Case partner, "What the dickens? We were already checking out clients who had left other law firms—look at all the work Larry Morris did with Covington and Burling, when NSM severed relations there." One person claimed—but the SEC would not confirm—that an unwritten part of the settlement was that White & Case would gloat publicly about its "victory." But I did hear some most unhappy off-the-record comments from SEC lawyers after the settlement was announced.

late December 1969. At another point, Parker refused White & Case's request for more time to file documents—even though the SEC had not opposed the extension.

Another action by Parker in an unrelated case caught the eyes of the SEC lawyers—and presumably those of the White & Case team. In the spring Parker was on a three-judge panel that heard a disciplinary action against two Washington lawyers accused of making a single false statement in an appeal in a criminal case. The panel suspended the lawyers from practice for eighteen months, an action many D.C. lawyers felt to be severe. In the words of an SEC staff member, "the only interpretation could be that Judge Parker would not look kindly at a lawyer accused of violating the law."

The SEC also had testimony from two Peat, Marwick executives—Anthony Natelli and Thomas Holton—that ran directly contrary to what Epley had said on deposition. Unfortunately for Epley, one key point they made was supported not only by their testimony, but by documentary evidence from the White & Case office. Epley insisted he had spoken to the two accountants only twice each the hectic afternoon of October 31, 1968. Natelli, however, remembered no less than six conversations, and Holton, four, or a total of ten. This figure was reflected in W&C phone billings and also in Epley's secretary's records. The point seems trivial—but Epley could be shown "not to be telling the truth, or forgetting what actually happened, in any event," on an issue where the documentary evidence showed him to be wrong. In a trial, such a discrepancy could weigh heavily against Epley.

From the SEC's viewpoint, the impetus for settlement seemed to come from a White & Case partner named Edward C. Schmults, who had left the firm to serve as general counsel of the Treasury Department during the Nixon-Ford administrations, then returned to his old firm in a senior capacity. Haliburton Fales, another senior partner, also favored settlement. "They realized," the SEC man said, "that Judge Parker wouldn't permit them to delay, to bury the government under paper. They began to realize they had a lot of uphill fighting to win this one."

But feelings were unanimous on neither side. On any given day the SEC was split four ways, in varying combinations of Stanley Sporkin, his deputy Theodore Sonde, and the trial lawyers, Richard Patterson and Bobby Lawyer. At least twice the negotiations ceased, the SEC being unwilling to give White & Case any further concessions.

The White & Case team—the firm's own members, and those from Arnold & Porter—had their disagreements as well. According to SEC lawyers, Milton Freeman flatly opposed settlement; he had a case he thought he could win at trial ("After all," he told one SEC officer, "I had both the facts and the law on my side"). But in private talks with White & Case principals, Freeman was giving diametrically opposite advice: settle; take what you can get and stay out of court. So, too, did Abe Krash and Dan Reznick, the Arnold & Porter lawyers who would have done the actual courtroom work.

The turnabout from supreme confidence to settlement did not sit well with some persons at White & Case. "Freeman and Arnold & Porter talked tough three or four years, then they folded. They panicked; they practically went into a catatonic trance as the trial date approached," one White & Case partner said. "They were saying to us, 'You've got to settle at any cost.' Much of the problem was Freeman. He is an appeals and office lawyer; he decided he couldn't win at trial, and he chickened out." White & Case people also detected no great eagerness on the part of Krash for trial.

"Some people at the office [White & Case] wanted to step in and do it [try the case] ourselves," the lawyer continued. But Schmults said no, White & Case should make the best deal possible and bury the proceedings as quietly and painlessly as possible.

Toward the end of April—the same days in which I heard Jay Epley avow that White & Case, which he regarded as a "family," would stand by him—the settlement talks suddenly became serious. A meeting was convened of the firm's fifty odd partners, and they heard a long exposition by Schmults. Epley, because of his dual position as partner and named-defendant, absented himself from the meeting. Whether a formal vote was taken could not be established with certainty; regardless, the outcome was definitive: the consensus was that a settlement should be accepted.

By the account of persons who talked with him during this period, Epley was most unhappy with the decision. He had been through months of hell, he remained convinced he had done no wrong, and he wanted his day in court. Indeed, had he remained obstinate, he could have insisted on going to trial, and White & Case would have had little choice but to stay in the case, lest it be put in the position of publicly abandoning a partner. And for several days at least one SEC lawyer thought that Epley would abort settlement; he remembers a late-night phone call from him with an urgent request for the whereabouts of Stan Sporkin, who was out of town on commission business.

In the end Epley bit the bullet and swallowed his personal objections—the loyal partner accepting the majority judgment of his professional associates; the son accepting the decision of his familial ruling circle.

Months later I spoke with Epley again. After pleasantries I asked, "What happened?"

A long silence. "Look," he said, "this is a sensitive subject, and you know it. What say we just let it slide?" I couldn't argue.*

*Judge Barrington Parker completed testimony in the Lord, Bissell & Brooks part of the case in the summer of 1977 but by April 1978 still had not decided whether the Chicago firm was guilty of the offenses charged by the SEC. The consent decree has no discernible effect upon White & Case; in the words of one man there, "We keep growing at the same percentage rate every year."

Court Recess Four

In the privacy of their lodge meetings, lawyers speak candidly of the emotional techniques they use to sway juries to their side. Consider a 1970 workshop sponsored by the Practicing Law Institute in New York on personal injury damages. The affair drew both defense and plaintiff lawyers, who shared some of their trade tricks.

Jacob Fuchsberg, then a Manhattan negligence lawyer (and now judge on the New York Court of Appeals, the highest state tribunal), suggested dramatizing the death of a litigant as the last part of the plaintiff's presentation. His recommended technique was to offer, "in slow, solemn, studied manner, a series of documents, certified and unquestionably admissible, the first of which may be the decedent's birth or baptismal certificate; the second his certification of graduation from school; the third may be his honorable discharge from the army . . . then the wife's birth certificate, their marriage certificate, the birth certificate of each child, and, finally, decedent's certificate of death."

Fuchsberg said, "You can get a quick glimpse of the high spots of a man's life in telescopic form. . . . It is the living human being who first evokes the warm, sensitive feelings that make you understand the meaning of the loss of a life."

From the defense side, Illinois insurance lawyer Philip R. Corboy counseled how to handle cases involving an injured child. The defense begins with an obvious handicap, for jurors are going to take emotional sides with a pitiable child. The defense,

Corboy said, "must anticipate that the plaintiff lawyer will depict the child as a potential president had he not been hurt." So what does the defense do? Corboy gave the seminar a mock jury speech:

"Ladies and gentlemen, we fully appreciate that serious injuries do not keep all people from attaining great heights. There was a president whose name you all know who reached a very great height, even though he was in a wheelchair.

"Beethoven, as you know, was deaf, and he wrote great music. Napoleon had epilepsy. That, too, was a brain injury, the same as this little child has, sitting here before you.

"But if any of these men were a plaintiff in a lawsuit, the court would tell you that the loss of future earnings is something you have to take into consideration in granting money."

Corboy conceded that such a speech is a "last-resort" tactic, that injured-child cases should be settled before trial if at all possible. "There are enough bad lawsuits on file without looking for more," he said.[1]

Chapter Five

Telex versus IBM: The Rumble of Millions

One winter noon in 1972 William Norris, the blunt-speaking president of Control Data Corporation (CDC), a computer firm in Minneapolis, wandered over to his office window. A functionary stood beside him, and they watched a line of black Cadillac limousines proceeding up the street.

"Wow," said the aide, "what a funeral."

"*Harrrrr!*" snorted Norris, whose CDC was in the midst of a protracted antitrust suit with International Business Machines Corporation (IBM). "That's no funeral procession. That's the IBM legal department returning from lunch."

As it turned out, the caravan in fact was a funeral cortege, but Norris' point was well made, nonetheless. IBM is perhaps the best thing that has happened to America's legal profession since the invention of the courthouse. For almost a decade now IBM has been under a legal assault unparalleled in U.S. business history. By one computation, in late 1976 IBM faced potential liabilities of more than $4 billion in antitrust suits brought by would-be competitors who complained that the giant had bullied them out of the market.[1] Even more ominous, the Justice Department's antitrust division was striking at IBM's very existence with a suit intended at cleaving the company into five pieces. The business and popular press brimmed with articles with such titles as "IBM Versus Everybody," "The Endless Trial of IBM," "IBM's Travails in Lilliput," "IBM on Trial" and "How Companies Make a Career of Suing IBM." "IBM has as many lawyers as salesmen these days,'' Joseph Millimet, one of IBM's attorney-adversaries, quipped in 1975 as he pressed a $255 million suit for Sanders Associates, a New Hampshire computer firm.[2]

All this turmoil, of course, means tremendous sums of money for lawyers on both sides. How much money, total? Any dollar figure must be based upon informed estimate, rather than hard fact, because neither IBM nor the companies suing it is obliged to publicize how much they pay their lawyers. My own estimate, after many months of sniffing around the IBM litigation and talking with the lawyers involved, is that the legal bills for the government and private antitrust litigation will be more than half a billion dollars before the cases are resolved. The fragments of information about legal fees that have drifted into the public domain share one quality: the figures are large, be they in dollar amounts or in body counts of lawyers. Some examples:

—In 1955 IBM retained only nine in-house lawyers in its domestic and corporate headquarters. In March 1975, according to vice-president and general counsel Nicholas deB. Katzenbach, the domestic staff was up to 105 full-time attorneys, including 31 at the executive offices in Armonk, New York. There are another 96 attorneys on IBM's foreign staff. Katzenbach did not discuss salaries, but a survey by Daniel J. White and Associates, a Chicago consulting firm, showed that lawyers for top New York corporations could count on starting pay of $22,000 annually, and $35,000 after six years.[3]

—This doesn't even begin the count, however. The New York superfirm of Cravath, Swaine & Moore, which is IBM's chief outside counsel in the antitrust cases, has upwards of 50 lawyers working full-time on IBM on any given day. Many of these attorneys, assuredly, are young associates who do the scutwork inherent in any big lawsuit—researching legal points, drafting pro forma motions, filing papers, taking depositions from second-rung witnesses. But the greenest lawyer on the premises is paid at least $21,000 a year, and third- and fourth-year men are past the $30,000 mark. And there are some heavyweights who are paid the top-dollar salaries to be expected in a firm such as Cravath, Swaine & Moore. Thomas Barr, for instance, the lead counsel, simply shrugs and smiles when asked if $200,000 a year is a close guess at his annual income. "Ask IRS or my wife," he says. David Boies, another of the nine partners working full-time on IBM matters, couldn't be more than some pocket change behind Barr. A former associate in the firm, after some jottings on the back of an envelope at lunch one day, told me, "Partners' salaries are something that aren't discussed at the lower levels of the firm, but based on what I pick up, IBM is paying well more than a million dollars a year for *partners alone.* Now that doesn't count the associates."

—Expenses other than salary push the costs even higher. Cravath, Swaine & Moore, for instance, has opened two branch offices exclusively for IBM matters: one is near the United States Courthouse on Foley Square in New York, where the government case went on trial in 1974; another is hard by the IBM headquarters in Armonk, a pleasant Westchester County community near the Rockefellers' famed Pocantico Hills estate. The Foley Square office is open twenty-four hours daily during the week, and the lights seldom go out on weekends either. Each Thursday evening, when U.S. District Court Judge David Edelstein recesses the trial for the weekend, a flotilla of limousines ferries Cravath, Swaine & Moore lawyers to Armonk, where they live in six rented houses and spend the weekend poring over the six billion-odd pieces of paper accumulated in the case. One of the firm's wags has been heard to jest, "Before this trial ends, we'll have spent $50,000 on parkway tolls and probably another $100,000 for coffee and midnight sandwiches."

—Control Data Corporation, which settled its suit against IBM on highly favorable terms, collected $15 million cash from IBM for legal expenses. CDC employed 10 lawyers full-time, and another 20 part-time, plus a paralegal staff of about 120 persons to screen an estimated 120 million documents in IBM files. "IBM employed about five times as many," Hugh P. Donahue, assistant to CDC Chairman Norris, told a Senate subcommittee later.[4] If Donahue's estimate is accurate, and no one from IBM has denied it, legal costs for this single case—which ended short of the courtroom—were in the neighborhood of $90 million.

—Legal costs for the private antitrust suits are as large a

drain. During the discovery phase of a suit brought by California Computer Products, Inc. (CalComp), IBM moved an 18-member team into its adversary's offices in Anaheim, California—along with a water cooler, a coffee machine, microfilm readers and a Xerox copier. The team, which included about half a dozen lawyers, camped in Anaheim for about five months. Another 15 IBM people descended on offices of Memorex Corporation.

Enough. The point has been made. The IBM cases are serious, and litigation expensive. And aside from generating a flow of dollars that is delighting lawyers all over America, the cases are important because they put the courts face to face with the timeless American dilemma of whether concentration of economic power is necessarily bad, and whether a corporation can be excused for occasional roughneck behavior toward smaller companies simply because it produces efficient products.

I vowed when I began this book that I would keep away from the IBM litigation, for two reasons. First of all I wrote at length about *U.S.* v. *IBM* in an earlier book and documented how IBM's lawyers developed dilatory tactics into a fine art, to the ongoing distress of opposing counsel and trial judges alike.* Indeed, at one point Cravath, Swaine & Moore did the legal equivalent of thumbing its nose at District Judge Edelstein by withholding documents he had ordered IBM to submit to government attorneys. Edelstein, normally the most phlegmatic of men, was so enraged at this conduct that he fined IBM $150,000 a day for contempt of court until the papers were produced. (The firm went all the way to the Supreme Court, which said Edelstein was right, and you best do what he says.) At any rate, what purpose could I serve by re-treading familiar ground?

The second reason is that I do not understand computers, and never will, and do not feel intellectually inferior to those persons who do. During a visit to a computer firm in 1976 an engineer escorted me around the manufacturing facility, and for an hour he explained exactly what the people were making and what the machinery did when finished. The engineer was a very literate, articulate chap, and he spoke in complete sentences, and after each phase of the tour he politely asked, "Do you have any questions?" I decided to shake my head and remain silent. For

***The Benchwarmers*. Weybright & Talley, 1974.

purposes of my comprehension, the engineer could have been explaining the conjugation of Turkish verbs or the physiology of the water flea. I am baffled enough trying to write intelligibly about lawyers. Leave computers to other souls, I said to myself.

Then, in mid-summer 1976, I began receiving phone calls and letters from executives at Telex Corporation, one of the early litigants against IBM. These people urged that I look into the case, but I resisted, because I knew it had been resolved in IBM's favor almost a year earlier (even though Telex at one point had IBM on the ropes with a $352.9 million antitrust judgment, largest in U.S. judicial history). But the calls continued, and eventually someone even said, "Roger Wheeler, our board chairman, is excited that someone get into this story. In fact, he is willing to send his privately owned jet to Virginia to bring you down here to Tulsa if you'll listen to us."

My ears perked up, for corporate jets are not dangled in front of my eyes many days. I fantasized the impact upon my reputation in Page County, Virginia—on the west slope of the Blue Ridge Mountains, a good place for serious business with a typewriter—if a sleek silver craft touched down at the Luray Airport early one morning and soared away with a single passenger—me. But reason prevailed, and I brushed away the fantasy and declined the jet.

Then a Telex official dangled bait even more tempting than a private jet. Scandal. "I don't want to get into this over the telephone," he said, "but some funny things happened at the Supreme Court level in this case. We aren't exactly sure what, but we wish you would listen to us."

So I went to Tulsa. I'm still not sure of the depth of scandal, even though some mighty suspicious things happened at the Supreme Court in the case's final stages. But *Telex* v. *IBM* provides drama of another sort through intimate glimpses into a high-stakes lawsuit—how it is conceived, prosecuted, defended, and, finally, settled out of court. Telex's agony at watching a $350 million verdict melt to naught is one factor. More intense suffering was endured by the blue-serge-suited lawyer who won the case at the trial level, and at one point stood to collect a contingency fee of more than $50 million, highest ever for a lawyer. And what does a corporation chairman do when a lawsuit that he initiated suddenly is transformed into a Frankenstein monster that threatens the destruction of his company? *Telex* v. *IBM*, in sum, was not a run-of-the-courts lawsuit.

But let us take the story in sequence, beginning with the day I met Roger Wheeler in his office in a low-slung building on the south outskirts of Tulsa. Wheeler is a bustling, compact man in his early fifties; two or three heavy briefcases stand alongside his desk, and he occasionally brushes his hands over his tight curls as if to sweep away the pressures of running a half dozen high-dollar enterprises simultaneously. A New Englander by birth, an engineer by training (at Rice Institute in Houston), Wheeler is now a financier by choice, after making a minor fortune in the magnesium business. Telex, despite its size ($106,243,000 in revenues in fiscal 1976), is a sideline for Wheeler. "For the time and energy I've invested," he said, "Telex is a net loss for me. There's no way to compete on a head-to-head basis with IBM. It would be great to be the best company to compete, successfully, but a lot of pioneers come out with arrows in their butts—'an empty bowl and an unmarked grave.' That's the fate of people who get out front." He proceeded to give me some background on why he even tried.

"After Rice I started out in the oil business, shifted over to magnesium, and by the 1960s was the principal shareholder of Standard Magnesium & Chemical Company, here in Tulsa. Dow, our principal competitor, held an acknowledged monopoly in the industry, and it was doing business under a consent decree that said, in effect, its officers could be held in contempt of court if there were any violations and sent to jail.

"The Justice Department would call every few years and ask if Dow was doing anything wrong. Dow ran the kind of monopoly that didn't bother me, as a competitor. Dow held the umbrella up there and kept the price right. Dow gave us technical advice when we got into problems. They were a benevolent monopolist."

Wheeler sold out to Kaiser Aluminum in 1964, acquiring stock valued at between $8 and $9 million, depending upon which day you read the ticker. He took an executive make-work position and soon found the most demanding challenge he faced daily was jogging up a seaside mountain near his San Francisco home. "I got bored. The atmosphere at Kaiser was competitive, but in a game I didn't wish to play. With all my stock, what did I have to gain?"

Casting around for something to do, he noticed Telex, whose then chairman, M. E. Morrow, was convinced the company "could be competitive with IBM." Telex had begun life as a hearing aid company and prided itself for having produced the first commercial wire and tape recorders, in the late 1940s. In the next two decades it developed and marketed a host of electronic and recording devices for home and commercial users, ranging from earphones to oscillographs and galvanometers. In the 1960s it began inching into the computer business.

Here, let us pause for some technical background. The core of the data processing industry is the computer itself, the "central processing unit," or CPU in industry jargon. These are IBM territory. Other companies make CPUs, but year in and year out IBM has managed to keep competitors on the further fringes of the market. Even the giant RCA could not crack IBM's preeminence in CPU marketing, despite an investment of $480 million.

Telex's intended share of the market involved so-called peripheral devices which help the CPU do its work. The peripherals store information; they are the conduits through which problems are fed into the computer; they are the printers which spew out answers at up to 2,000 lines per minute. Peripheral equipment is an important market, accounting for 50 to 75 percent of the total price of an electronic data processing system. IBM's revenues from peripherals in 1970 were $1.1 billion, about one third its total income. For our purposes—and that of Telex—the important point is that the peripheral devices must be "plug compatible" with IBM computers, that is, designed so that they can be readily interconnected.

Telex's serious entry into the peripheral market came at the behest of a customer, the Du Pont Corporation, which was upset at the tape drive rentals being charged by IBM. In 1966 Du Pont asked competitive bids, and Telex won, undercutting IBM's price substantially.

This development came about a year after Telex President Steve Jatras had asked Wheeler to consider investing in the company, which was sorely in need of capital and go-get-'em management. Wheeler did a quick study and concluded that IBM's monopolistic umbrella provided much the same price-stabilizing function for the computer industry as Dow had for magnesium. "I said to myself, 'Oh, boy, here's another opportunity to make a million. Here's a bird's nest on the ground.'" Wheeler assumed that IBM was so strong it wouldn't worry about puny "competitors" who scrounged for crumbs under the table. The computer industry was growing so fast that Wheeler felt IBM had all the business it could handle.* "They had 95 percent of the market. By logic, they would not cut prices to get the remaining 5 percent. Man, was I wrong. I didn't know there was such a thing as a bad monopoly."

Another factor that Wheeler did not foresee was that companies other than his Telex would make a strong bid for the peripheral market; by 1970, in fact, about one hundred other firms were in the field, some of them nothing more than a couple of engineers in a cinder-block building, looking for a better mousetrap, but collectively a force large enough to attract IBM's attention. IBM saw ominous omens. In January 1970, for instance, the U.S. Office of Management and Budget, which has broad powers over federal executive agencies, told them to consider using non-IBM gear—a direct threat to a major IBM market.** A research paper from the knowledgeable Wall Street firm of Loeb, Rhoades & Company summed up the situation that was being created: "There is a rule of thumb that a 10 percent penetration into IBM's installed market position is the level of irritation that causes IBM to react competitively. . . . When IBM does decide to move in response to inroads by independents it is analogous to a card game in which IBM is the dealer and knows all the cards before they are dealt."

So IBM moved. It created a task force to "recommend plans and product strategies to impede the growth of IBM's plug compatible competition."[6] The first move was to make meaningless changes in its own disk drive boxes, and market them as "new" at reduced prices. (A federal judge later called the word "new" a subterfuge used by IBM "for the purpose of avoiding a general

*Total revenues in the data processing industry were $48 million in 1952; by 1970, they had soared to $10.2 billion.

**The House Government Operations Committee was to report in 1976 that Federal expenditures for automated data processing were $1.5 billion a year—"approximately four percent of the entire federal budget."[5]

price reduction'' on equipment already being used by other customers.) The intention was to force Telex and another peripheral manufacturer, Memorex Corporation, to cut their prices.

IBM's own documents show the corporation wanted blood. At internal meetings, financial analysts discussed the effect the price reductions would have on the ''viability'' of Telex and Memorex—a polite way of talking about running other people out of business. The conclusion was that the cuts would have ''a very serious impact.''

One year of the price war shook Telex, but didn't destroy it, so IBM got even tougher. At a meeting of top IBM management in April 1971 the company's chief executive officer, Thomas J. Watson, Jr., demanded a ''clear understanding that the company swallow whatever financial pills [are] required now and get ready for the future . . . irrespective of financial considerations of one or two years.'' Watson stressed the need for IBM ''to make the hard decisions today so that the same problems don't have to be faced again and again down the road.'' In other words, accept the short-term losses caused by price cutting, in the knowledge that when the carnage is over, IBM would have no competition.

IBM launched a new wave of what a court was to call ''drastic . . . price cuts'' for peripheral gear, ranging up to 50 percent. ''When you boil it down,'' Roger Wheeler said, ''they actually made money by 'cutting' prices. First, they cut prices. They altered service contracts and gave discounts for long-term leases, a lot of little gimmicks resulting in an effective price reduction of 50 percent. Then they raised their prices on the main frames [the computers, available only through IBM] to offset the cuts. It was selective. They cut in areas where there was competition, they raised in areas where they had the monopoly.

''IBM, by their own documents, was ready to lose $400 million in one year, with the knowledge that once we were smashed, they could gain $1.2 billion over the next three or four years.''

IBM also shifted into what it called ''fixed-term plans'' (FTP leases), which locked customers into long-term contracts in return for substantial discounts. To Telex, the reason was obvious: the long-range commitments meant that customers no longer could price shop. If Telex produced a peripheral item at a price lower than IBM's, the customer might have to wait three years before he could lease it, for breaking the IBM contract cost him not only the discount but carried substantial cancellation penalties as well.

In retrospect Wheeler says he was surprised at the vehemence of IBM's reaction: "I talked earlier about the benefits of being in an industry with a 'benevolent monopolist.' Well, IBM was no such thing. I had bought a share of a riled-up bear. I couldn't believe what was happening."

Yet Wheeler didn't worry, at first anyway. At one point his holdings of Telex stock soared to $42 million—on paper—and he kept buying more. Why, in the name of common sense, did he not recognize that anyone who walks around tweaking the noses of monsters is apt to be stomped? "Price cuts don't catch up with you overnight when you have equipment out on a lease basis. I felt Telex could offer a better machine—and in fact, we did, and at a better price. The problem was that it was very costly to develop the more sophisticated equipment, much more so than to improve upon the stuff that has been out in the market for eleven years.

"When they [IBM] gave us the first whack, we built a better mousetrap. The second time, it was tougher. The third time, it was so costly, so time-consuming, that it was impossible. Your reaction time [for building competitive equipment] slows down from six months to two years."

Investment analysts lost confidence in Telex long before Wheeler did.[7] While waiting for an interview at the Telex offices one morning, I sat down with a cup of coffee and a six-inch-thick sheaf of copies of advisory sheets, newsletters and market analyses from assorted brokerage houses. They dated to 1970, and as I skimmed them I could imagine the gloom they engendered among financial officers at Telex, which as a thinly capitalized company is highly vulnerable to the fickle market. F. F. Smithers & Company: "near to intermediate term performance of Telex . . . could be unrewarding for most investors." Goldman, Sachs & Company: IBM's long-term lease plan should siphon away so much Telex business as "to preclude a positive investment attitude." Francis I. duPont & Company, Inc.: IBM's move "will place a negative sentiment over the entire peripheral group. . . . We are therefore deleting Telex from our [recommended] list." Merrill Lynch, Pierce, Fenner & Smith, Inc.: "We prefer to exchange [Telex] for higher quality issues and issues with less competitive uncertainties." A photocopy of a Reuters dispatch dated January 5, 1971, summarized Telex's plight:

> Telex Corporation, a favorite trading vehicle through the 1970 doldrums, took it on the chin in the first trading day of the New Year.
>
> It lost 1⅛ to 15½ yesterday at the head of the active list and analysts who had been hot on the Tulsa-based computer peripheral equipment firm generally bemoaned their selection.
>
> The analysts admit that where they went wrong was in judging giant IBM's role in the computer peripheral field. . . .

Telex's financial statements tell the same story—that is, one of woe, and bad woe. In 1967, the first year it received significant computer business, Telex had total revenues of $34 million and a net profit of $1.2 million. By 1971 Wheeler had built business up to $81 million annually, $58 million of it on computer gear, which earned a profit of $5.5 million. In 1973, with IBM's counteroffensive in full drive, Telex lost $13.3 million (on sales of $68.1 million); the next year, it had revenues of $89.7 million and losses of $32.2 million.

From the beginning Telex recognized the antitrust implications of what IBM was doing. President Jatras contacted Nick Katzenbach, the IBM general counsel, and politely warned him that, in Telex's opinion, IBM was "violating antitrust laws." According to Wheeler, "Katzenbach was a bit humble. He would see what could be done." Apparently, nothing, for IBM continued price cutting.

Wheeler says he did not want to resort to a lawsuit, even when his top management people said IBM had stepped outside the law. "We were in a highly competitive situation. We needed time and our total energies to get out of the trap. We couldn't do two things at once—run a lawsuit and run a business. Secondly, I didn't want the publicity. I was shocked at the headlines that eventually ran: TELEX SUES IBM."

According to Wheeler, both Jatras and another top Telex executive, Richard Martin, kept saying, "Let's sue the bastards."

"I replied, 'This is a battle you can't win.' At one point Martin threatened to resign. I needed him. He helped build Telex. With my key executives demanding that I sue, I felt I had to go with it."

Wheeler and I had been together less than an hour when he made this statement. I knew little about him. Yet even the most casual exposure to the man made plain that he runs Telex—that a slightly raised voice to his secretary will bring any resident executive into his office at a brisk trot; that he has the authority to dispatch his jet to the Blue Ridge Mountains to fetch a recalcitrant journalist. So I put my eyebrows into the raised position as Wheeler continued. Wheeler, to put it most simply, did not impress me as the sort of man who could be pressured into doing *anything*. He continued:

"Another squeeze came from my lawyer. He was writing letters for several months about how we should sue IBM, and how we had a 'cinch case.' I was concerned that if we got into such a lawsuit, IBM had the best lawyers in the country, while we had a local yokel."

"Local yokel?" I asked.

"Yeah," Roger Wheeler replied. "Floyd Walker."

Well, Roger Wheeler might be right in one respect, because Cravath, Swaine & Moore would never have hired Floyd Walker. He is distinctively an Oklahoma lawyer, a man who started his career with a congeries of personal and academic handicaps that would deny him entry into any of the supposedly "class" firms of Wall Street or Washington, but one who was to taste the sweetest of victories: a *trial victory* over the New York hotshots who had exchanged sotto voce wisecracks about his southwestern drawl, and who had acted as if they expected to find Indians war dancing around Tulsa.

Bob Foresman, business editor of the *Tulsa Tribune*, wrote after the Telex-IBM trial that Walker didn't exactly "have life served up to him on a silver platter."[8] Foresman understates; there was no platter whatsoever. Walker was born in 1920 in the Oklahoma crossroads hamlet of Kiefer and two years later his father, an oil field roughneck, died. His mother did the best she could to raise Walker and a sister. In 1937, when the Dust Bowl gripped Oklahoma with grim, gut-wrenching poverty, things got so tough for the Walkers that Floyd dropped out of high school and spent a year with the New Deal's Civilian Conservation Corps, working at camps in Oklahoma and Wyoming. What Walker earned, he sent home to support his mother and sister, and eventually he was able to return and finish high school. He went on to Tulsa, the mecca for boys who wanted to break away from small-town poverty, and he worked in an ice cream plant, and eventually he got a job as a letter carrier.

Seldom did Walker have money for any pleasures more fancy than a chicken-fried steak dinner and a movie on Saturday night, but he tried. He saved, and he managed a year at a now-defunct junior college in suburban Sapulpa. But for the three years ending in 1942, when he enlisted in the Army Air Corps, Walker in his more somber moments thought he would spend the rest of his life with a mailman's leather bag strapped over his shoulder.

"When I got into the service I became good friends with a fellow cadet who had been to the University of Chicago Law School. His brother, a Chicago lawyer, came down for a visit, and we spent the weekend in Amarillo, Texas, near our training camp. The brother picked up all the tabs, and I was quite impressed. I'd never seen anyone with that kind of money before, and I felt lawyers had a pretty good life."

Walker became a bombardier on a B-24 and flew many missions over Germany. Then, on a bombing run over Berlin his craft sustained such damage that the pilot had to land in Sweden. The crew sat out the rest of the war in internment.

After V-J Day, Walker returned to his old mailman's job, but with a different goal: he was to become a lawyer. Five nights weekly, from 6:00 to 10:00 P.M., Walker attended classes at Tulsa University Law School. Times were rough, financially and personally: he had a wife and three children to support, and Walker sometimes wondered if it was really worth all the effort.

Then he would think of that heavy mailbag, of the drudgery of walking dusty residential streets, of wanting a cold glass of water at midday, of trying to make friends with unruly dogs. Walker would shake his head and dive back into the law books, regardless of the lateness of the hour or the tiredness of his eyes. "Mail carrying is a good job and I respect people who make a living with their hands. But it's hard work, and I didn't want to lug that sack around for forty-two years, the time I'd need to retire. God, the thought repelled me!''

Walker finished law school in 1949, graduating second in his class, and joined an insurance company as a claims adjuster—one of the lower rungs of law—where he supervised investigation and litigation of casualty claims. Such is the route followed by countless young lawyers who lack the social or personal connections to join a name firm; ''night school lawyers'' must shift for themselves.

Things came slowly for Walker. He worked for the insurance company for four years, drawing a salary and doing things that were anathema to a man from an impoverished background: arguing down a claim by $50 or $100 here, finding a fine-print loophole there that denied any recovery whatsoever to an injured person. In 1953 Walker went on his own, taking the walk-in cases that support fledgling lawyers. He settled auto accident cases. He intervened in landlord-tenant disputes. He wrote some wills. He did some divorce work. He made a living.

His first case of any note involved a Tulsa schoolgirl who had suffered an injured eye during an eraser fight between six boys in her class. Walker sued the boys' parents, and the case went to the U.S. Supreme Court, which upheld the jury verdict of $31,000. ''This case got considerable publicity in Tulsa, and I suppose this is what got me started,'' Walker said. Other good cases followed. Walker won a $600,000 judgment for a man who had lost the use of both arms and legs in a truck accident—largest ever in Tulsa courts at the time. Walker took on a locally celebrated oil fund swindle in which investors claimed they had been cheated. The Oklahoma Supreme Court had ruled against them previously. Before the case ended, evidence developed that three of the justices had accepted bribes. Walker's client won.

Among his sometime clients was Roger Wheeler, whose business activities had spawned any number of suits over contracts and stock options. Walker won some; Walker lost some. Then, in the early 1970s, Walker and Wheeler began talking about supposed antitrust violations by IBM.

Walker studied a ''white paper'' on IBM's predatory practices, prepared by Telex president S. J. Jatras, and he reviewed what Control Data Corporation and other litigants were doing in their suits. On September 10, 1971, Walker wrote Jatras that in his "considered opinion . . . IBM is vulnerable to private prosecution for federal antitrust law violations," if what Jatras had alleged was true. In an accompanying twenty-nine page personal-and-confidential memorandum Walker told how he would proceed. He would keep the case "as small and simple as possible" by charging IBM not with monopolizing the entire computer industry, but only the market for "those items of peripheral equipment for computer systems manufactured by Telex." Walker warned that the task would not be easy:

> No doubt an extreme burden will be placed on Telex if it elects to prosecute an antitrust suit against IBM. Nevertheless, if the individuals and companies affected do not intend to make a mockery of antitrust laws, and if antitrust laws are to be vigorously enforced so that free competition can be preserved, Telex and other companies similarly situated have an obligation to assume the burden unless it is to their economic advantage to ignore the violation.

Nothing happened immediately, although Walker continued to urge that Telex sue. In another letter to Jatras, this one on December 7, he noted that Telex "probably has an obligation to itself and to its stockholders" to sue. This letter raised a red flag in the Telex offices. If management did not sue, would not it (and the directors) be liable to a stockholder suit for failure to protect shareholders' interests? Walker also wrote that he thought Telex could prove damages of $9 million to $12 million—which would be trebled if it won the suit. He urged that "proceedings be commenced as soon as possible," and offered to work full-time on the case beginning in January 1972.

By Wheeler's account, Walker's letter dashed any remaining reservations he had about suing IBM, so he said, "Go ahead, let's see what happens." Walker's confidence that he could win was demonstrated by his willingness to enter into a protracted complicated lawsuit on a contingency basis: if Telex prevailed, he would be paid; if Telex lost, he would not. On January 21, 1972, Walker and Wheeler signed a two-page single-spaced contract which spelled out the terms under which the lawyer would work. The salient paragraph read as follows:

It is agreed and understood that WALKER's sole and only compensation for the legal services thus performed is to be contingent (without retainer) upon the successful termination by settlement or judgment of said litigation. It is understood and agreed that out of any recovery by way of settlement or judgment TELEX shall first be reimbursed all of its out-of-pocket expenses, and, after such reimbursement WALKER shall be paid at the rate of One Hundred Thousand Dollars ($100,000.00) per year (or a pro rata portion for part of a year) for his time expended since date of filing of suit. That after deduction from the gross recovery of TELEX's expenses and such payment to WALKER then WALKER shall be entitled to receive an additional contingent fee upon the balance of the amount recovered in accordance with the following percentage of each of the following respective increments of such balance:

First $25 million	5.0%
$25 million to $50 million	7.5%
$50 million to $75 million	10.0%
$75 million to $100 million	12.5%
$100 million to $125 million	15.0%
$125 million to $150 million	17.5%
All over $150 million	20.0%

In what later proved to be a hotly disputed paragraph, Telex reserved the right to drop the suit "at any point or time." If this happened, "Walker would lose the right to any attorney's fees. A withdrawal as used herein means a termination of the litigation under such conditions or circumstances *that Telex receives nothing of value because of such termination.*" (Emphasis added) Telex also reserved the right to settle without Walker's consent, "subject only to the right of Walker to be compensated" under terms of the contingency schedule.

So much for the money arrangments. Because of Telex's pressing money problems Wheeler wanted the suit pushed to trial as rapidly as possible—no minor goal, in view of the success of IBM's slow-walk tactics in the other suits. Walker started with a singular advantage. Control Data Corporation's suit against IBM had already been under way for almost four years, and much of the material found by CDC lawyers during discovery was available to him.* Walker was quite happy to expedite

*Among these papers were the IBM management review minutes quoted earlier in this chapter.

the suit. As he told me, "My approach was the rifle, not the shotgun. We would not play IBM's game and get bogged down in the paper chase. I've been the only lawyer suing IBM not to fall into that trap. IBM would like to contest you on what I call 'the whole spectrum of the universe.' I aimed at three specific IBM practices involving four or five products that Telex made. The rest of IBM's product line I ignored.

"I deliberately limited my discovery in order to get to trial within a reasonable time. I asked about specific products and practices within a given time frame. I interviewed former IBM employees who had planned or implemented specific projects, but in the end three people gave me most of the input. Through them I was able to identify, with some particularity, the documents I needed. Still, I ended up with one hundred fifty rolls of microfilm, which means a heck of a lot of documents.

"The game IBM plays is to overwhelm you. We wouldn't be trapped. We made few objections to their requests for discovery. It would take longer to object than it would to comply. If they wanted to take five depositions simultaneously, we let them have them; we just hired more lawyers.

"They [the IBM defense] didn't think I could put it together in so short a time. Frankly, they thought I would fall on my face."

The available evidence suggests that Cravath, Swaine & Moore also considered Walker a "local yokel," especially when he hurried along the pretrial business. The firm may be faulted for overpreparing a lawsuit; no criticisms have to be heard about the firm's going into court with any blank spots in a case. During casual conversation one day an opposing lawyer asked Walker what background he had in antitrust law. Walker thought awhile and answered, "I once filed an antitrust counterclaim while defending a trades secret case. That's the only one I can think of offhand." The lawyer couldn't believe it: a rank neophyte opposing the classiest antitrust specialists in the country.

The opposition should have taken the trouble to look around Walker's office. One wall features a membership certificate in the American College of Trial Lawyers, a trade group so prestigious that it includes only one percent of the lawyer population in the United States. (Walker is but one of thirty members in Oklahoma, a fact he mentions casually, but with obvious pride.) Walker says, "I can try a suit as well as anybody if given the time to learn the facts. The facts are going to be strange when you start, but you can learn. A lawyer doesn't need to know the detailed technology.

"For instance, one of the first personal injury cases I ever tried involved brain damage and post-traumatic epilepsy. I studied, and I knew as much about the subject as you could learn from books, and I handled the case, and I won. I didn't retain the knowledge, and you wouldn't want me to treat you, but I had the background when I needed it."

Although he had done previous work for both Wheeler and Telex, Walker claimed no special expertise about the computer industry, so he worked. He spent three months winding down his law practice, then in December 1971 began devoting his full time to Telex. As Walker stated later in court papers, "Thereafter I usually worked 7 days a week, and many weeks I worked as many as 85 hours. During the 93 weeks from September 1971 to June 20, 1973 [when the trial ended], I averaged working 67 hours per week and devoted 6,231 hours to the case." Two other members of his firm worked full-time on Telex as well. Walker immersed himself in the computer industry—its technology, its economics, its marketing patterns. He "inspected, read and evaluated hundreds of thousands of pages" of IBM and Telex documents. He personally took the depositions of twenty-five IBM executive, technical and engineering officials, and supervised the preparation of seventy-five more. He interviewed all witnesses who appeared for Telex, and many more who didn't. "It was," Walker said later, "a rather busy period in my life."

And IBM did what it could to make Walker's life even busier. Depositions that should have taken two or three days (in Walker's opinion) dragged a week or more, with IBM witnesses seemingly unable to remember anything beyond their names and titles.[9] *I do not remember. I do not understand the question. Please repeat the question.* Each time Walker took depositions he steeled himself to cope with what he called "the worst memories, or else the worst liars, in Western civilization." One classic example can be found in the transcript of his interrogation of an IBM financial analyst named Ander Torgerson, who had done studies of such companies as Memorex. In the industry—and indeed, in countless thousands of IBM financial and technical documents—Memorex and others are commonly known as plug compatible manufacturers, or PCMs. The initials are as widely known in the industry as the letters "FBI" are to the general public. Torgerson, however, pleaded the next best thing to the Fifth Amendment, to Walker's frustration:

WALKER: In connection with performing your duties at IBM, have you had occasion to use or hear the term "PCM," or "plug compatible manufacturer," used in any way?

TORGERSON: I don't understand the question.

WALKER: In performing your duties at IBM, have you ever used the term "PCM" in referring to anything?

TORGERSON: I don't understand the question.

WALKER: Do you have a recollection, Mr. Torgerson, in your duties there at IBM ever using the phrase "plug compatible competition"?

TORGERSON: I don't understand the question.

WALKER: Can you tell me what it is you don't understand about the question so that I might better express myself?

COOPER (an IBM lawyer): Well, Mr. Walker—

WALKER: Now—

COOPER: We are here to answer the questions, not to ask them.

WALKER: This is a question .

WALKER: Will you tell me, Mr. Torgerson, what it was about the last question that I asked you that you did not understand?

COOPER: Let me state again that we are trying to answer the questions, not help you ask them. If Mr. Torgerson can't answer that question, if you can give him an example of what it is you don't understand in the question, all right this time, but there seems to be a problem in asking the questions. Go ahead.

TORGERSON: He is asking me within my duties have I ever used the terms. What is meant by "duties"?

WALKER: Mr. Torgerson, do you have any recollection in performing any work for the IBM Company ever using the phrase "plug compatible competition"?

TORGERSON: I don't recall.

WALKER: During the period of time that you have been employed by IBM since 1968, up to the present time, and whether it was then while you were performing work or not, have you ever heard the term "plug compatible competition" used?

TORGERSON: I don't recall.

Walker finally gave up and tried to quiz Torgerson about a most complicated IBM marketing scheme that went under the code name "Mallard"—or decoy duck. Briefly, IBM did some minor tinkering with a disk drive unit and then sold it as a "new" item, at a price lower than comparable gear offered by Telex and Memorex. (By terming the Mallard new, as noted previously, IBM avoided cutting prices on equipment already in use by customers.) Again, Torgerson evaded direct answers time and again.

WALKER: Are you familiar with the name "Mallard"?
TORGERSON: Yes.
WALKER: Where did you hear the term "Mallard"?
TORGERSON: It's a kind of a duck.
WALKER: In connection with the performing of any duty at IBM, have you ever heard, seen, written or used the term "Mallard"?
TORGERSON: I don't understand the question.
WALKER: Would you read the question to him? [Pending question read.]
TORGERSON: I don't understand the question.
WALKER: In connection with any work that you have ever performed at IBM, have you ever seen, used or heard or read the term "Mallard"?
TORGERSON: Would you read the question back? [Pending question read.]
TORGERSON: Yes.

For IBM's lawyers, the dilatory tactics in depositions were part of a day's work—a common strategy when defending antitrust actions by an impecunious opponent. For Telex, however, the delays were deadly serious. Telex's money was rapidly running out; at one point its executives wondered whether the company would survive long enough to press the suit to trial. "We used to joke about 'collecting from IBM posthumously,'" one of these men said much later. Further, Telex is a company whose engineering and management staff is vastly outnumbered by IBM. So IBM lawyers kept key Telex employees in deposition sessions for seemingly endless days. In the opinion of one outside observer, IBM was trying to "run [Telex] into the ground." Walker protested, and vehemently. He argued to IBM lawyers during one deposition:

> . . . we take the position that IBM is unnecessarily delaying and prolonging trial preparing by . . . forcing us to go back to the

Court on each individual witness to secure an order for the witness to answer questions involving matters that we have waived by the production of documents months and months ago, and something that has already been determined by the Court.

I feel that it's just a means by which they prolong and unnecessarily delay trial preparation in this case.

IBM's lawyers had other weapons as well. Walker attempted to use a host of former IBM employees as witnesses; some of them, in fact, voluntarily came forth and offered to testify. But he ran headlong into what he was to call, in a brief, "an apparent concerted plan of tampering with witnesses":

. . . In August of 1972 Telex filed its tentative witness list containing names of witnesses which might be used at the trial of this action. Included therein were certain designated independent witnesses who were to testify based upon their extensive research and knowledge concerning financial information about IBM and Telex.

After making the names of these witnesses known to IBM, there transpired a series of incidents so strange and coincidental, forming almost a pattern, as to cause Telex to inquire if there has not been a concerted effort on the part of IBM, its agents and attorneys, to impede the progress of pre-trial preparation by inducing and persuading witnesses not to testify. Telex believes that these witnesses have been induced to refuse to testify by pressures brought against them by IBM, its agents and attorneys, and that these matters should be called to the attention of the Court.

As this brief is being written Telex has just been advised that John Schmidt in the data processing department of the Midwest Stock Exchange Service Corp., who was listed as a prospective witness in the Telex final witness list, has been contacted by a sales representative of IBM and after such contact Mr. Schmidt now states he does not want to be a witness at trial even though he had previously indicated his complete co-operation.

The foregoing demonstrates a remarkable pattern of witness behaviour: a pattern that could not be formed without outside contact and interference. Telex inquired of IBM: Have witnesses and their employers been contacted and advised, suggested or in any manner urged not to testify? It should be emphasized that at one point prior to filing the final witness list, all these witnesses have indicated a willingness to testify and were actively cooperating in the taking of their depositions. Suddenly, after filing the final witness list, and without warning they have declined to testify. The importance of these witnesses cannot be overestimated. Of the ten (10) witnesses (outside of Telex employees and agents) designated to testify in person, four (4) have suddenly indicated an unwillingness to testify. Of the seven (7) designated to testify by deposition, three (3) have now declined. It is inconceivable that IBM had nothing to do with this new development.

IBM reached out after other potential witnesses as well. An analyst for White, Weld and Company, a stock brokerage firm, was on Telex's final witness list. According to an affidavit filed later in court, an IBM lawyer came to him, asked what he would say on the stand, and told him he did not have to be a witness unless he wished. Before the man could decide, White, Weld management told him the firm's policy was not to take sides in litigation. Walker suspected, but could never definitely prove, that IBM approached White, Weld and asked them to call off the witness. Tom Barr denied any wrongdoing: he said that IBM had only used the resources of law available under rules of civil procedure. Judge A. Sherman Christensen* agreed that IBM acted within the bounds of the law, but he commented tartly that the pressures directed against the witnesses did "chill their availability."

"IBM spent money like it came from a Monopoly game," said Jack Bailey, the Telex general counsel. "At one point they wanted a deposition from someone in Corpus Christi, Texas. IBM not only flew down a lawyer but also a clerk to wait around until the reporter transcribed the proceedings so they could fly the transcript right back to New York. The thing only took thirty minutes, and it was never used in trial. But it meant I had to squander a day in Corpus Christi."

As the trial date neared, IBM suddenly hit Telex with what both Walker and company officers considered to be a diversionary tactic—a counterclaim alleging that Telex had stolen IBM trade secrets. Walker said, "The counterclaim is a typical defense tactic in antitrust, for it gives the court a choice. Many a judge is known as 'half-a-loaf,' which means he'll do something for both sides. I saw the counterclaim as an attempt to divert me

*Judge Christensen, who usually sat in Salt Lake City, heard the case by special assignment.

from the main case, so I kept away from it as much as I could, and turned the defense over to another lawyer. I kept an eye on it, of course, but I stuck with the meat of the suit.

"IBM wasn't ready to go to trial, and under the court rules Judge Christensen would have given us an extension to prepare a defense. So the decision was whether to ask for the time. We [the lawyers] wanted it. But Telex management—and I mean Wheeler—said a six-month delay would bankrupt Telex; they were on the ropes. I asked Telex outright whether it [the counterclaim] could be substantiated, and I was told no.

"When IBM saw that their delaying strategy would not work, they changed. They accelerated, trying to put the trial on faster than I could get ready." So, many nights Walker worked in his office until four or five in the morning, napped on the couch an hour or so, shaved in the washroom, changed shirts, drank a cup of drugstore coffee and went back to the documents. "Work never was a stranger to me, even when I was a kid. What the dickens—I kept that kind of schedule to get through law school."

And, suddenly, the time had come for trial. IBM arrived in force and in style: an order went to the local Avis office for thirty-five comfortable sedans, and IBM took short-term leases on thirty-five apartment suites in the Center Plaza Apartments in downtown Tulsa. Jack Bailey tried to count the IBM lawyers but gave up; three years later he could only guess. "There were fifty lawyers around, more or less, some IBM in-house, some from the Cravath firm, some from the Oklahoma law firm IBM hired. Lots of days we felt damned lonely."

Almost half a year earlier IBM had set up a computer-controlled information retrieval system in the Tulsa law firm of Rucker, Tabor, McBride & Hopkins, its local counsel. Every bit of paper gathered in the case—document searches, pleadings and depositions—were put on microfiche, indexed and fed into the system. When the trial began, IBM ordered that rush copies of the proceedings be delivered twice daily. This information was also put into the computer, providing an instant cross-check on whether the testimony jibed with what was on record elsewhere.

Supporting the lawyer task force was a backup team of IBM specialists in every area touched by the trial—financial, marketing, engineering. Tom Barr stood at the head of an army numbering more than three hundred persons, and a Cravath, Swaine & Moore lawyer was assigned responsibility for each major area at issue. After court adjourned each day Barr convened a meeting in his hotel suite to review what had been said that day, to preview what the following day's testimony might bring and to decide upon strategy. Seldom did these sessions break up before midnight. IBM even brought in press agents to answer media questions on the staggeringly technical testimony that came out in the trial.

To local observers, Barr's armada resembled a legal doomsday machine, a phalanx that would simply roll over Walker. But one Tulsa lawyer pointed out a defect to Rex Malik, a British journalist who monitored the trial: "The method . . . never gives Barr a chance to be really on top of his material. It may be pleasing to the ego to command those troops, but command is a distraction. There is still nothing like steeping yourself in a case and using the very limitations of the human intellect to concentrate your attention and energies."[10]

Floyd Walker, meanwhile, worked essentially from one file—the information he had crammed into his head.

IBM's preoccupation with documents and organization provided an ironic backdrop for the way Walker presented his case. Quite literally, he beat IBM with its own papers and people. Maxwell M. Blecher, of Los Angeles, considered by many in his profession to be the best plaintiff antitrust lawyer in the country, once wrote that "aside from the Supreme Court, for which the plaintiff's bar must constantly thank Heaven, the single most important fact of antitrust life is the tendency of corporate executives . . . to record their misdeeds. This tendency probably results from the fact that only by a recordation and reporting process to their superiors can these misdeeds be rewarded."[11]

Using documents turned up in his own discovery and that of Control Data Corporation, Walker put together a paper record of how IBM tried to destroy the plug compatible manufacturers. He produced minutes of meetings of IBM's top management team (formally, the management review committee) and the exhortation by Thomas Watson, Jr., that IBM should "make the hard decisions today" on dealing with competitors, even at the cost of lost profits for several years. One item was particularly telling. It was intended to forecast the impact upon the PCMs of the new long-term lease program:

> Corporate Revenues Lower.
> —No Funds for MFG, ENG. [manufacturing, engineering]
> —Dying Company!

In other internal documents IBM executives spoke casually of "price control" and "price leadership." One such paper was written by H. F. Faw, IBM director of business practices, for the guidance of Cravath, Swaine & Moore lawyers preparing IBM's defense against the government's antitrust suit. Faw noted that the Justice Department's complaint specifically covered "varying profit margins" on IBM products. He continued, " . . . An intensive investigation of this issue would reveal the extent of our price control and its supporting practices. Such a revelation would not be helpful to our monopoly defense."

Other documents told of the immense profitability enjoyed by IBM and its competitors. One item, a control storage unit, carried a profit of 40.8 percent of the sales price; a disk drive, 41.4 percent if sold, 32.1 percent if leased. IBM papers estimated that because of these vast markups, the independent manufacturers could cut their prices below those of IBM, yet still earn profits of 25 to 30 percent.

On another key point, the papers indicated that IBM was aware of the antitrust implications of such actions as the fixed term lease plan (FTP). Lawyers warned against the size of price reductions proposed for long-term lessees, and forced management to scale them down. The same papers also forecast that the long-term leases would siphon hundreds of millions of dollars of revenues from competitors—just as Telex alleged in its suit. (An IBM market report put into the trial record boasted that the independents lost 48 percent of their business within four and one-half months of the fixed-term lease announcement.)

But were these pricing stratagems the normal writhings of a capitalistic enterprise under pressure—after all, under our system a man is entitled to make a dollar—or were they deliberate attempts to destroy competitors? Here the documentary evidence contained a glaring gap. IBM's management review committee, according to its cursory minutes, approved many of the actions discussed and recommended at the staff level. Seldom, however, did the *reason* for the decision appear in the record.

Hence Walker turned to live witnesses to connect the papers to reality. One of these people, Burton H.,* had worked for IBM for four years as a financial analyst in the data processing division. One assignment had been to assess the "viability" of Telex and Memorex as competitors in the computer accessory field. He said the studies were to be used to "put the screws to competition . . . to contain them," and to "become familiar with their financial alternatives." The implication was clear: IBM knew its price juggling could wound its competitors.

Tom Barr went for Burton H.'s throat in a cross-examination that demonstrated the depth of Cravath's preparation for the trial. Barr waved the letter of resignation H. had given IBM in January 1972 in which he said he was leaving to "become the President of the First National Bank of Joplin, Missouri."

"Are the facts in this letter true?" Barr demanded.

"No," H. replied.

"This is a deliberate misstatement?" Barr asked.

"Yes," H. said.

H. said he actually left IBM to become a computer industry securities analyst for a Wall Street broker. He had feared his move to the brokerage house was a "breach of confidence," so he made up the bank story. H. also admitted using a false name when he telephoned an IBM employee for information on the company.

Then Barr hit H. even harder. He asked a series of questions trying to prove that H. had bought stock personally, then recommended it to large institutional investors in the expectation that their purchases would drive up the price. This practice, called "scalping," is forbidden by the Securities and Exchange Commission. Barr even produced a supposedly forged letter which authorized H. to buy and sell stocks on behalf of a distant relative.

Walker's heated objections of "irrelevancy" succeeded in stopping Barr's questions, and so Barr never resolved the question of whether H. in fact was guilty of scalping. Judge Christensen agreed with Walker that allegations of criminal conduct

*Because IBM tried to discredit Burton H. through unproven allegations of criminal conduct I am not using his full name.

were outside the scope of the trial. But as one Telex lawyer said later, "The background that Barr had on this witness was chilling. When IBM produces copies of a letter written by a widow lady that was in our witness files, you begin to credit Barr with omnipotence."

Barr's trump card—one unrecognized at the time by Telex, and perhaps by the confident IBM as well—was the trade secrets counterclaim. Floyd Walker certainly thought little of it; he even stayed away from the courtroom during the counterclaim testimony, entrusting the defense to another lawyer so he could prepare for rebuttal testimony on the antitrust phase of the case.

IBM, to the contrary, pressed the counterclaim to the hilt, with voluminous testimony from employees who said Telex tried to lure them—and their knowledge—away. Engineer Richard Moore, who worked on IBM's monolithic memory project, testified Telex offered him a $250,000 bonus if he could develop a copy of IBM's latest memory product within a year. Moore said that Wheeler twice offered him "the Roger Wheeler bonus"—$15,000—if he would "take the job on the spot." The deal fell through, Moore said, when he refused to provide technical information which he considered confidential to IBM. Another witness, engineer Richard Wilmer, said Telex offered him two $100,000 bonuses if he could duplicate an IBM system and have fifty-one units installed within twenty-eight months. Wilmer said he told Telex president Stephen Jatras he felt the machine could be improved. "They didn't see the significance of a redesign. They didn't want it. They wanted one like IBM's," he said. He refused. Barr also presented testimony that IBM secret codes appeared in various Telex documents examined during discovery.

By the time testimony ended in late May 1973 Telex and IBM each had put 23 witnesses on the stand. The record contained 7,358 exhibits, 242 charts and 51 depositions, and the lawyers sat back to await Judge Christensen's decision.* Walker was confident. Before the trial he had talked with lawyers who had tried cases before Christensen and studied his opinions. "I read him as a liberally oriented individual with respect to enforcement of

*The bulky record contained so much inside information on IBM that the Computer Industry Association, an anti-IBM trade group, copied the entire 22,829 pages—which made a stack just short of 10 feet high—and sold three dozen sets for $5,075 each.

antitrust laws. I couldn't tell whether he was liberal or conservative as to relief [i.e., money judgments] because none of his previous cases had been all that big. His top had been around $2,000,000. But I thought he would react to figures, and be inclined to go high if he heard no amount less than $100 million during the trial." The IBM lawyers laughed at Walker. Even if Telex won, they said, Christensen would "choke" and give no more than $5 million or $8 million. Telex officials didn't expect much money either. In the office pool, Serge Novovich, an engineer-lawyer, guessed $300 million; the next high number was $80 million. ("I thought Serge was drunk, and he doesn't even drink," quipped Jack Bailey.)

Not until September 17 did Judge Christensen say he was ready to announce his decision. Lawyers, reporters and financial analysts overflowed the courtroom, and there was a bustle of excitement as an aide passed around copies of a 222-page opinion.

Telex won the day. Christensen found that IBM clearly had violated Section 2 of the Clayton Act by attempting to "destroy its plug-compatible-peripheral competition by predatory pricing actions and by market strategy bearing no relationship to technological skill, industry, appropriate foresight, or customer benefit." IBM's pricing changes were directed "not at competition in an appropriate competitive sense, but at competitors and their viability as such."

IBM, he said, took advantage of the arcane technology of the computer world and adopted anticompetitive techniques so "sophisticated and subtle" that only a computer expert could see them for what they were. Because such a velvet-glove approach is so hard to discern, he wrote, it may be even more dangerous "than the naked aggressions of yesterday's industrial powers." And Christensen did not accept IBM's protestations that IBM higher-ups were ignorant about the plots to destroy Telex. "Most of the studies," he wrote, "were made by highly trained and qualified IBM personnel acting within an organization justly noted for its perception and responsiveness. There is considerable direct evidence on vital points to indicate the top management did in fact subscribe to the anti-competitive views of lower echelons."

So what should be IBM's punishment? Judge Christensen

computed Telex's actual damage at $117.5 million: $70 million for loss of market share; $39 million for lost rental profits, and $8.5 million for lost profits from sales. Under the antitrust laws, damages are trebled, so the penalty amounted to $352.5 million, plus attorneys' fees and costs.

A reporter watched Tom Barr as he scanned the key passages. Barr "paled and strode from the room without comment," he wrote.[12]

The night of the victory someone had five-by-seven-foot blowups made of the *Tulsa Tribune*'s afternoon banner headline (TELEX AWARDED $352 MILLION) and posted them on either side of the front door of Roger Wheeler's house. Virtually everyone in Telex gathered there for steak and champagne, and there was whooping and hollering far into the night.

Among the happier celebrants was Floyd Walker, the erstwhile Tulsa mailman. God, but the sweat and the agony of the CCC camp, of the mail route, of the night school law course—suddenly, all was worth it. Floyd Walker had *made it*. Figures danced through Walker's head as he sipped champagne and felt hearty congratulatory handslaps pound his shoulders. *Atta-boy Floyd, wow, you beat their ass off! Old Barr, he ain't drinking champagne tonight; he sipping ulcer medicine.* Has ever in the history of our Republic there come a moment when an individual citizen enjoyed the task of applying a sliding percentage scale to $352.5 million, with himself as the beneficiary? The figures jumped around Walker's head. The zeros seemed to march in lockstep. There were variables. Interest would run on the award until it was paid, at the rate of almost $100,000 a day, of which $20,000 would go to Walker. *$20,000 a day.* More money than his daddy had seen in maybe five years. Walker surrendered to mathematics. Floyd Walker was going to receive from $50 million to $60 million for his fee in a single case. He and Roger Wheeler could let the accountants run down the odd dollars. Walker is a collected man. But this night he smiled and took another glass of champagne. Hot damn. Floyd Walker had made it.

The news stories—but not the headlines—did mention a second phase of Judge Christensen's order. He also ruled that Telex had stolen IBM trade secrets, and that IBM was entitled to damages of $21.9 million. But what the hell? Telex could pay this sum out of the interest that IBM would build up during the appeals. Telex had won, and Telex was drinking champagne.

The Telex celebration was on September 17, 1973, but after the champagne bubbles drifted away, Roger Wheeler felt uneasy. Telex was months away from collecting any money, and Wheeler could not be certain his victory would survive the appellate courts. Telex was heavily indebted to the banks, and the continuing heavy losses ($13.3 million in the fiscal year ending March 31, 1973) made it unlikely the loans could be repaid from revenues. Many experts with whom Wheeler talked made glum predictions.

Maxwell Blecher, the Los Angeles antitrust lawyer, told Wheeler of an airline case where he proved damages of $15 million—yet prayed for a verdict of only $5 million because he (and the judge) knew the defendant airline would be ruined if he won the larger amount, and that the $15 million would not be sustained on appeal. (He received $7 million, the verdict was upheld, and the airline survived.)

Blecher told this story to Wheeler as they walked into a luncheon club, and the lawyer rubbed his hand over his belly. "Their guts," Blecher said, "their [the appellate judges] guts won't let them do it." Blecher said that if Wheeler saw the chance to settle the case, he should grab it.

Floyd Walker, too, thought of settlement, and for somewhat the same reasons (although he was convinced he had built a case that would not be overturned on appeal, if the law, and not external factors, guided the judges). Walker knew that IBM did not want Christensen's adverse findings on its business practices to become a final verdict, so he telephoned Tom Barr and said, in effect, "If you are going to do anything [about settlement] now is the time to do it." Barr sounded agreeable, and he and Walker decided to talk to their respective clients.

Wheeler was already a step ahead of his lawyer. On his own initiative he called IBM president Frank T. Cary and put the question directly, "Would you like to settle this lawsuit?" Cary said he would talk about "anything, any time, any place." But they decided to cut the lawyers out of the negotiations and handle it themselves.

Walker did not like this development. "I had never seen this procedure work, not having lawyers around when you are discussing big legal matters. The clients do not have an understanding of their legal positions, and the ramifications of decisions."

Walker briefed Wheeler before the meeting, but memories differ on who said what. According to Wheeler, "Walker told me, 'Don't take a dime less than $350 million. The foreign claim is even more valuable than what we won in the domestic case, and giving that up is enough.' "* Walker denies saying any such thing. "I told Roger, 'The place to start is the $350 million judgment you already have. Use the foreign claim as a bargaining chip.' I didn't want Wheeler to give away the store."

Wheeler and Walker do agree on one point. Telex wanted a substantial amount of money to settle, for it needed it. Taxes would take one bite from the settlement. So would repaying the bank loans. So would Walker's contingency fee. By the time all these obligations were deducted, by Wheeler's computations, the $350 million "was actually $10 to $15 million clear." Walker said, "Telex needed at least $160 million. Roger wanted to walk away whole and clean. Based on my talks with Barr and Nick Katzenbach, I felt the suit could have been settled for $75 million to $100 million."

In any event, as Wheeler tells the subsequent story, "I got in my airplane, and Cary got in his airplane, and we met in a motel across from the St. Louis airport." The choice of a discreet site was deliberate, for neither party wished to cause any further stock market blips. IBM and Telex remained silent, and Wheeler and Cary and their entourages remained as inconspicuous as possible.

Wheeler began the meeting by stating, "We can't take anything less than the $350 million."

No way, Cary replied, in effect.

Wheeler pressed on. IBM could "dress up" the settlement in any manner it wished to make the company look good. He mentioned that Telex was liable for Walker's contingency fee, a factor that must be considered in any settlement.

"You are about three times the amount I had in mind," Cary said. He did not spell out numbers, but he hinted at $100 million.

*Telex's complaint charged IBM with foreign antitrust violations as well, but both parties agreed to try the domestic case first and hold the foreign claim in abeyance.

Nothing was resolved. The executives left the motel suite only with the vague agreement, "Let's talk again—sometime."

In hindsight, Wheeler's asking for the full $350 million—even if he thought (as he claimed) he acted on the advice of his lawyer—was a grievous tactical blunder. Given the warnings by Max Blecher and others that the circuit court was unlikely to give Telex the full $350 million, why did not Wheeler give himself more bargaining room?

Wheeler does not mope about what proved to be a sour decision. "Things were happening pretty fast," he said. "I had to go with Floyd Walker. Floyd felt, in the first place, that we could get a momentary recovery, when the rest of us were thinking mainly in terms of injunctive relief. Walker wanted to sue when a lot of people here were saying just the opposite. It was Walker's show. It seemed to make sense at the time."

Then, an omen of disaster for Telex.

On October 9, less than a month after his $352 million decision, Judge Christensen responded to an IBM motion for a new trial by stating he had made a "substantial" error in computing damages, and would issue a new judgment. Tom Barr chortled. "'Easy come, easy go'—that's your headline, boys," he shouted to reporters as he left court. Barr's exuberance was short-lived. A month later Judge Christensen cut Telex's award to $259.5 million, but left intact the core of his decision that IBM had broken the antitrust laws. Telex breathed somewhat easier, and the squads of lawyers marched away to the Tenth Circuit Court of Appeals, the intermediate appellate layer between the trial court and the U.S. Supreme Court.

During the thirteen-month wait for a decision Roger Wheeler often found himself wrestling with an unexpected emotion: doubts about whether Telex *should* win a victory of the magnitude decreed by Judge Christensen. Wheeler's feelings were complex. He agreed with Christensen's legal and factual findings that IBM deliberately inflicted grave damage on his company. But after the euphoria of victory, he watched IBM stock slump by almost 10 percent—from 272 to 246—causing investors a paper loss of $5.5 billion, and touching off a prolonged stock market dive. "I am a capitalist, and I have investments in the market myself," Wheeler said. "The Wall Street analysts were yelling that our suit was responsible for the crash. I said to myself, 'If the alternative is creating a major depression, I'd rather let Telex go down the tube.'" Christensen's decision was a moral and (for the moment, anyway) monetary victory, and even if Telex never collected a dime, its effort "did bring about competition—which is what this country is all about." Nonetheless, Wheeler fretted as he knocked a golf ball around Southern Hills Country Club, and wished the court would end the suspense.

January 24, 1975, was a Friday, and Wheeler spent the first part of the afternoon at a meeting in a luncheon club in the Fourth National Bank Building in downtown Tulsa, a few flights above Floyd Walker's office. Around four o'clock the clerk of the Tenth Circuit Court telephoned Walker from Denver: a decision in *Telex* v. *IBM* would be announced in about half an hour, when all the stock markets had closed. Could he be available to hear a précis? Walker could, and he located Wheeler and asked him to come down. They made small talk for half an hour, then the phone rang again.

Jack Bailey, the Telex house counsel, had spent most of Friday on Wall Street, heading a delegation that had argued with the New York Stock Exchange that the firm should not be delisted on the big board, even though its annual revenues had slipped below the required minimum. En route back to Tulsa the Telex jet stopped at Louisville for refueling. A man in the party phoned his wife to report an approximate arrival time. "Have you heard the news?" she asked. He hadn't. He did. "There was an awful quiet on the plane for the rest of the flight," Bailey said.

What the executives and lawyers heard was the worst possible news for Telex: the three-judge court had thrown out the damage award against IBM, saying it had not violated the antitrust laws, but held that Telex must pay IBM $18.5 million in the trade secrets case. "Christ, I couldn't believe it," Wheeler said. "I was sick. I came back to the plant in a daze, listening to the news over and over again on the car radio. It was like hearing your own death knell." At the Telex offices secretaries and executives alike stood around crying.

The three judges disagreed with almost everything Christensen had said about IBM.* IBM's actions against its competitors

*The opinion was unsigned, and its literary style indicates more than one person had a hand in the writing.

"constituted valid competitive practices and were neither predatory nor otherwise violative of the antitrust acts," they wrote. That was one ground for reversal. On another point (one watched even closer by other companies suing IBM) the appeals judges held that Christensen had erred on the "threshold issue" of defining the "market" IBM was accused of monopolizing.

This is complicated. Section 2 of the Sherman Antitrust Act provides that "Every person who shall monopolize . . . *any part of the trade or commerce among the several states* . . . shall be deemed guilty of a misdemeanor." (Emphasis added.) But how should the "relevant market"—the legal term—be defined? For purposes of crystallizing its suit—Walker's "rifle shot" approach versus the shotgun—Telex had defined the relevant market as that portion of the computer industry serviced by the manufacturers of equipment plug-compatible with IBM. But the circuit court disagreed. It harked back to a 1950s case in which the Du Pont Corporation was held not guilty of monopolizing the cellophane industry because there were other flexible wrapping materials available to the public that were "reasonably interchangeable" and thus easily substituted for cellophane. The same situation prevailed in the computer industry, the circuit court held, so the relevant market should be defined as consisting of *all* peripheral products, not just those compatible only with IBM.

By broadening the definition of "relevant market," the decision vastly increased the number of firms that could be said to be "competing" with IBM. Consequently, its share of the market diminished from Telex's claimed 70-plus percent to around 35 percent. By what stretch of the imagination, the court asked, could IBM be termed a monopoly?

Oddly, the court's definition varied from the way IBM *itself* viewed the PCMs. Scores of its own internal documents made clear that IBM considered the IBM-compatible PCMs a definable market. But as one industry observer noted, the court "skipped over" these documents. The appeals court's discussion of the trial record was markedly cursory at some points (and shorter as well, only 98 pages versus 222 for Judge Christensen).

No matter, Telex had lost, and the atmosphere became grim in Tulsa. Should the circuit court's opinion be upheld by the Supreme Court, Telex would be driven into bankruptcy. Telex owed $100 million, almost $30 million of which was in arrears. Telex was so broke, in fact, that it had to get court permission to waive posting of a bond while appealing the trades secret judgment: it did not have funds to pay a premium to a bonding company.

Wheeler gave the case one last try. He hired Moses Lasky, a prominent San Francisco appeals lawyer, to write briefs for the Supreme Court. Lasky's services are not bought cheaply. His contract called for a retainer of $25,000. If the court refused to hear Telex's appeal [by denying a writ of *certiorari*] that was to be his entire fee. If *certiorari* was granted, Lasky would be paid $15,000 to argue for reversal. If he succeeded in obtaining a new trial or a reinstatement of Christensen's verdict, he would receive 5 percent of the first $100 million recovered, with a maximum of $5 million. As one Telex official said, "With the Lasky contract, we rapidly approached the point where the lawyers would get all the money, even if we won."

Next, Telex tried to persuade the Justice Department's antitrust division to file an *amicus curiae* brief on its behalf. Telex reasoned that since the government's antitrust suit paralled its own in many respects, Justice would be helping itself by helping Telex. Jack Bailey said, "The story we got was that lower-level guys in Justice favored the *amicus*. But they kept citing a 'policy' that if the U.S. government was involved in a similar case, the Department would not file an *amicus*. The Justice Department never came out and said flat no; they just never did anything."

The government's attitude disturbed Bailey: could it be that the Justice Department shied away from joining the suit because it smelled a certain loss for Telex? "We were going up before the 'new Nixon court,' and I thought about it a lot—especially late at night—and decided our chances were maybe 5 percent. Lots of things were happening. Justice [William O.] Douglas should be a Telex vote, but he was in and out of the hospital. I felt the tilt was heavily against us."

Litigants apply for a writ of *certiorari* through the medium of written briefs, without oral arguments, and by late spring the paperwork was done. As the summer progressed the strain began to twang Roger Wheeler's nerves. His group of bankers, led by

Continental Illinois Banking & Trust Company, made nervous noises about the status of their loans: as one Telex official said, "They knew that if we didn't get *cert*, all they'd receive in repayment would be a bankrupt computer company—less, of course, the $20-odd million we'd be paying to IBM."

According to Walker, who by this time was on the brink of estrangement from his client, Wheeler became downright frantic. "Wheeler was not listening to the lawyers most intimately involved in the case—Moses Lasky and me. He would talk to lawyers literally on the street corner and ask what they thought the Supreme Court would do. He would call up prominent lawyers he didn't even know and ask the same question."

Wheeler indeed was in a bind, and a paradoxical one at that. Telex's business was beginning to pick up again, now that key executives could devote their time to the computer business, rather than the lawsuit. But the IBM threat was omnipresent. Bailey explained: "Lessees of computer equipment want to be sure you are around to deliver the service which is a part of any contract. We were in the black, but barely, and it seemed to us that if we could get rid of the IBM case we could survive, even if in a small way." In mid-summer the Securities and Exchange Commission forced Telex to circulate an auditor's advisory opinion stating that the company could not survive if it were forced to pay the IBM claim. Telex stock, for purposes of trading, was worthless.

So what should Wheeler do—pray that the Supreme Court would come to his rescue, or scramble for shelter? He began putting out feelers. With Telex board approval, in early September 1975 he wrote IBM, asking that negotiations for an out-of-court settlement resume. Two days later, on September 12, IBM president Cary called Wheeler and asked, "What do you have in mind?"

"We'll take $15 million," Wheeler replied.

Cary is too polite a man to laugh in someone's face, so he continued the conversation. "Under no circumstances will we give Telex any money. Our thinking is that you should pay IBM $3 million."

Wheeler would not agree, but he and Cary did decide to let their lawyers meet and see what formula, if any, could be found.

So Wheeler began to prepare for the worst. He and Bailey met with Royce H. Savage, formerly a United States district judge in Tulsa, who subsequently resigned the bench to become general counsel of Gulf Oil Corporation. Now in quasi-retirement, Savage maintains an office in Tulsa. The gloom the afternoon of the Telex meeting was accentuated by the presence of another Tulsa lawyer, James Ellison, of Boone, Ellison & Smith, who could be likened to a legal undertaker: his speciality is corporate reorganization and bankruptcy.

"For about an hour and a half," according to Bailey, "we talked about what was to happen to us. We were staring at a Chapter X or a Chapter XI [the portions of the federal statutes pertaining to corporate reorganization under the aegis of a U.S. district judge]. In my language, we were talking about reorganization. In layman's language, we were talking about bankruptcy. The string had about run out."

What should be done? Judge Savage listened and picked at Wheeler and Bailey until he had the facts in hand, then made a suggestion. Cary, the IBM president, was in Italy, but he had told Wheeler that Nick Katzenbach had full authority to negotiate if Telex wanted to enter into open-ended, nothing-promised settlement talks. "I know Katzenbach," Savage said, "maybe I can call him and get something started." He did, finally reaching Katzenbach early on Tuesday, September 30. Katzenbach agreed to come to Tulsa the next day.

Now entered the new element of time pressures. On September 29 the Supreme Court had reconvened after the summer recess, and the justices commenced conferences on pending cases—presumably including *Telex* v. *IBM.* The consensus among lawyers on both sides was that the Supreme Court would rule on the appeal early in its term, and the first decisions were to be announced on Monday, October 6. IBM was emphatic: any deal negotiated would have to be final before the court ruled, otherwise, forget it.

Formidable legal and financial talent gathered in Judge Savage's office the morning of October 1: Katzenbach, formerly lawyer for the entire United States. Paul W. Knaplund, who good-naturedly bore the title of "IBM vice-president for lawsuits." John Hunt, of Cravath, Swaine & Moore. (Tom Barr by now was again working eighteen hours daily in his role as field marshal, this time in the New York trial of the government's antitrust suit.) Truman B. Rucker, of Ruker, Tabor, McBride & Hopkins, IBM's Tulsa counsel. For Telex there were Wheeler, Bailey, Judge Savage and Jim Ellison.

Katzenbach opened by repeating the demand Cary had made earlier. IBM held the higher hand, and IBM wanted Telex to know it. IBM wanted money, either in cash or in the form of long-term notes to be paid from earnings. He mentioned $15 million as a "talking figure," although the Telex contingent felt they detected flexibility on the amount.

Telex would not bite. Bailey said, "I told Katzenbach that no employee of Telex had any interest in working for IBM, which we would be doing if we made a profit only to pay them." Bailey said Telex might consider a "wash" in which both sides dropped their claims and called the match a draw, with no money exchanging hands.

The adversaries separated periodically to discuss strategy, and eventually the IBM representatives moved several blocks to Rucker's office so they would have readier access to telephones. There were calls to lawyers working for IBM in Washington; there were calls to IBM headquarters in Armonk; there were endless huddles.

Around noon something happened that unsettled Wheeler and Bailey.

According to Bailey, Hunt left the room a few minutes, then returned to report that "they had been informed the Supreme Court had decided the case the previous day" in conference. The list of decisions would be prepared for the printer on Thursday, for issuance on Monday when the court sat in formal session. Once the list was composed, "it would be in concrete." So if Telex and IBM settled and wished to have the case withdrawn, the court must be notified by no later than noon on Thursday.* Musing over this announcement later, Bailey would remark that the IBM lawyers suddenly "exuded great confidence." His impression at the time was that IBM knew how the court was to rule.

In subsequent court papers IBM lawyers told the mechanics of their contacts with the Supreme Court, but denied any

*The justices reach their decisions in executive conference sessions. Four affirmative votes are required to grant a writ of *certiorari*, and the "order" simply states "granted" or "denied." There is no explanatory opinion.

advance knowledge of the justices' decision. By IBM's account, during the October 1 negotiations Paul M. Dodyk, a Cravath partner who is one of Barr's chief lieutenants, contacted Michael Rodak, the clerk of the Supreme Court. Dodyk told Rodak a settlement was likely, and he asked "whether the court required notice of any disposition of the litigation by a certain time and, if so, what that time was." Rodak was quoted as replying that Telex's petition was on the list for the justices' conference that week; that in "normal course" the decision would be published the following Monday, October 6; that to keep the decision off the list, the clerk's office should be notified by Thursday, October 2. "The substance of the anticipated order was not disclosed to counsel," IBM lawyer Truman Rucker said in court pleadings.

The talks continued (Katzenbach so certain of success that late Wednesday he left Tulsa for Washington, to pursue other IBM business) and on Thursday IBM made an offer that Telex considered acceptable. Both sides would drop monetary claims, and in effect wipe the slate clean. Realistically, Telex could have expected little better, so Wheeler accepted. But much detail work remained, and neither side felt a final package could be devised by the Supreme Court's noon deadline. So more calls were made, this time to James Campbell, a partner in the Washington superfirm of Wilmer, Cutler & Pickering, which is Cravath, Swaine & Moore's correspondent firm. (The firm's ranking partner, Lloyd Cutler, once worked at Cravath, Swaine & Moore. The tie between the offices is so close that at one time they shared the same phone and address listing in the Washington telephone directory.) Campbell made some calls on his own and reported back that clerk Rodak said the "absolute deadline" was midday on Friday.

Things became frenzied. Bailey of Telex and Hunt of Cravath set about writing the settlement document, necessarily complex because both sides wanted language that would inter the suit for good. In post-midnight calls Wheeler alerted his Washington lawyer, Gilbert Cuneo, to be ready to file the necessary withdrawal papers with the Supreme Court on Friday.

All this was being done, of course, without the participation of Wheeler's outside lawyers, Floyd Walker and Moses Lasky. When Walker learned what was happening he reacted bitterly, telling Wheeler he should stay with the suit to conclusion, rather than bail out. Wheeler retorted that all Walker wanted was his $50 million, that he had to think of the survival of Telex. Walker laughed bitterly in recounting the conversation: "Roger twisted the factual situation to suit whatever his purpose was at the moment. He urged the contingency contract to give me the greater incentive to do the best thing for Telex. Then he used the contract's existence so he could say my financial interest meant my advice was no longer objective." Walker would not discuss details, even a year later, but he made plain to Wheeler during talks that week that as Telex's attorney-of-record he did not like what was going on. Neither did Moses Lasky, the Supreme Court counsel.

IBM knew Walker and Lasky were mad, so Rucker demanded that Wheeler personally indemnify IBM against any claims they might make later for legal fees. Wheeler agreed.

Jack Bailey picked up IBM's draft of the agreement from Rucker and Hunt about one o'clock Friday morning and took it to the Telex office for study by Wheeler, Telex president S. J. Jatras and financial vice-president William F. Styler. The legal portions they approved almost at once, Bailey saying he was "surprised at how closely they met Telex's wishes." The accompanying press release was another matter, for it used such terms as "theft of valuable trade secrets" which Telex thought unnecessarily direct: if the suit was to be buried, could not the services be conducted with dignified language? "IBM wanted complete control of the press release," Bailey said. "I know why. Regardless of the language in the formal papers, what the press writes would come from the press releases. So we didn't want to be butchered there." In the end, both sides decided to issue their own releases, after mutual approval.

At two o'clock in the afternoon signatures finally went on the paper—Wheeler signing for Telex, Paul Knaplund for IBM. "The typist was already working on the list to go to the Supreme Court printer when the word was flashed," Bailey said. "The case was over."

But was it over? When Roger Wheeler finally lured me to Tulsa, he told me that quite a few things still mystified him about *Telex* v. *IBM*, and he gave me his theories, and he listed some concrete leads for me to pursue. Wheeler did not think the U.S.

courts had given him a fair shake. Wheeler is no populist—the man has made several fortunes in rugged industries—and I think that had we talked several days more, we would have found areas of considerable philosophical disagreement. But we did reach common ground on one core issue: that everyone who goes to court is entitled to a tolerably fair proceeding.

So he talked about Wall Street's reaction to the original Telex victory, and how the analysts and brokerage houses had thought their private corner of the world was coming to an end. Because of Telex's problems and the resultant financial pressures, Wheeler is not as favorably disposed toward banks as he once was, and he wondered, in our conversation, whether Wall Street's influence, in ways both subtle and direct, prompted the circuit court to decide his case on grounds totally unrelated to antitrust law. In a word: did the court believe a decision adverse to IBM would jolt the stock market into another sharp crash? Did the judges not wish to assume such a responsibility?

"The hoariest of political sayings," I told Wheeler, "is that the Supreme Court follows the election results."

He nodded, and he added, "In this case, the circuit court followed the stock market tables."

One of the leads Wheeler gave took me to the office of Gilbert Cuneo, the Washington lawyer for Telex Corporation. Cuneo is one of those quiet, effective birds you occasionally still find in the much-glamorized world of Washington law: a guy whose name seldom gets into the papers, but who has been around town for thirty-odd years, which means he began during the Truman administration, and who sits in a subdued whole-floor suite at 17th and K streets and represents affluent corporations and earns his six figures annually.

Gil Cuneo had been sick earlier in the year and spent some time at the Mayo Clinic, and he received me from a wheelchair.* We chatted awhile, exploring one another through small talk. Then Cuneo called in his secretary and said, "Get me a copy of my report to Roger Wheeler. It's you know where."

The secretary returned with a key and unlocked one drawer of Cuneo's desk, and took out another key and in turn unlocked

*Cuneo died in April 1978.

another drawer, and rummaged through a file. My curiosity must have been obvious, for Cuneo smiled and explained. "This is not the sort of paper you want to leave around an open file. In fact, I was uneasy about whether I should even discuss it with the partners here who were not involved."

I read the letter, and I realized why Cuneo kept it locked in a private file, for it dealt with a suspected leak from the Supreme Court and Cuneo's efforts to find whether in fact one had occurred. The point was important: had IBM known in advance that Telex's writ of *certiorari* had been granted, an act that would have opened the door for restoration of its mammoth damage award, IBM certainly would have had incentive to rush along a predecision settlement. Similarly, had Telex been tipped in advance and known it would have another day in court, Wheeler would not have been under such intense pressure to abandon the lawsuit. I read Cuneo's letter again, and we talked about his role in the case.

By irony, Cuneo's involvement began with a request from Wheeler that *he*, on behalf of Telex, try to find out whether the Supreme Court was going to grant *certiorari*—the same sort of insider information that was to so disturb Telex. Cuneo said he doubted it, but that he would try. He did, without any success, and so reported in late-night phone calls to Wheeler and to Moses Lasky.

These calls were on Thursday and early Friday. Wheeler by dawn Friday had decided to settle, and so the machinery was put into motion. And right away, two suspicious happenings.

One of Cuneo's partners called the Supreme Court to ask a procedural question about withdrawing Telex's petition for *certiorari*. A member of the Supreme Court staff asked who the petitioner would be. "I'm sorry," the partner replied, "I cannot advise you on that point." Whereupon, according to the partner, the staff member "volunteered" that it "must be *Telex* v. *IBM* since that case was up for settlement." The comment surprised the partner, but he said nothing further, and the functionary gave him the information requested.

Later, during a visit to the court, Cuneo by chance overheard a conversation between the staff member and one of the many lawyers IBM had working on the case. The staff member said to the lawyer, "How can you say that to me in light of all I have done for you this past week?" The lawyer appeared flustered, Cuneo said, and told the staff member, "This is Mr. Cuneo, counsel for Telex." In turn, the staff member "appeared to get somewhat flustered and left the room without saying anything more."

Cuneo said nothing about the episode but it nagged him, to such an extent, in fact, that later, in his words, "my conscience began to bother me that I should have notified my client" about what happened. He was in the process of writing a report to Wheeler when he received a call from A. G. W. (Jack) Biddle, president of the Computer Industry Association—a trade group consisting of almost every company in the business save IBM. A West Point graduate, and a long-time management consultant, Jack Biddle is a vociferous foe of monopolistic power in general and of IBM in particular, so much so that IBM lawyers dragged the association into the government's antitrust case and obtained a court order permitting them to examine its files to determine, among other things, the sort of adverse information Biddle was leaking to the news media, and whether opposing lawyers were using Biddle as a public relations conduit to circumvent gag orders that prevented counsel from commenting on various cases. (If IBM found any evidence to support either thesis, nothing was ever said publicly.) Biddle's opinion of IBM was capsulized in a speech he gave to a computer industry group in the spring of 1976: "What has gone wrong with our country and our system of legal justice that permits the giant corporations to stand all-powerful and above the law? Is it that they simply have the financial resources to retain so many hired guns that the sheriff doesn't stand a chance? . . . I don't know. I do know that, as a full-time observer of what is going on in the various litigations against IBM, what I see stinks to high heaven. The pattern of behavior that I see may be perfectly legal, in the lawyer's view, but I think . . . that it is a pattern of behavior that is morally wrong, if not totally unethical. . . ."[13]

In the conversation Biddle told Cuneo that he, too, had heard reports of a leak, but that his search for evidence had been fruitless. Biddle's statement was truthful, so far as it went, but it was not totally inclusive either. In a later interview Biddle elaborated somewhat.*

Two young Washington lawyers, law school classmates both in their first year of practice, met and got into a what's-been-happening conversation. "I'm in computers," one of them said. "Hey," replied his friend, "I'm doing antitrust work with [and he named a government agency] and something interesting happened the other day. The fellow who has the desk next to me is a friend of a clerk of Justice ———. He said he had just prepared a 'summary reversal of a major case that would interest you [meaning the agency where the man worked.]' " The government lawyer thought about the "major cases" then pending in the antitrust field, and he immediately focused on *Telex* v. *IBM*. "It will come down Monday, watch for it," the clerk supposedly said.

The gist of the second-hand conversation was passed along to Biddle several months after the settlement. "I'm convinced that the story is true, but how do you use it without ruining the career of the young lawyer involved? Any clerk who leaked Supreme Court business and was found out would be professionally disgraced. But if he was dropping things like that into a social conversation, it's not unlikely that word would get back to someone interested in the Telex case. Like a lawyer for IBM."

In trying to run down this and other leads, however, Cuneo found himself in a series of blind alleys. He sought out the lawyer who had told Biddle the story about the law clerk's comment. But the lawyer flatly refused to identify the persons involved. Nor would Biddle give any further assistance. The Computer Industry Association, Cuneo wrote Wheeler, "did not want to talk without some assurance that they would benefit from any aid which they might give us." Cuneo's primary aim was to help Telex, so he could make no such promise. He talked with a number of former clerks, who said "almost without exception" that "leaks are very possible in the handling of the votes by the justices." The news did not surprise Cuneo. "Many

*I am not using names of the persons involved, in the following paragraphs, for two reasons. First, they either denied or refused to discuss the episodes related. Second, braggadocio is endemic among many of us, be we writers or young lawyers. Thus, can a casual remark to a friend be considered puffery or hard evidence? I give the lawyer concerned the benefit of the doubt, and therefore he remains anonymous.

people are involved in the reporting of decisions, other than the justices and their clerks. There's a mechanical process involving typists and proofreaders and the printers themselves. I've heard stories of contractors wining and dining the lower-level people when a big decision is expected, trying to wheedle out advance information. No place in Washington is leak-proof." But try as he could, Cuneo could find no hard evidence of a leak in *Telex* v. *IBM*.

So ultimately Cuneo reached a dilemma, in the truest sense of the word. As counsel for Telex he suspected, but had no means of proving, that something was amiss in the handling of the case—that IBM, either by design or by accident, had learned how the court was going to rule. Hence Cuneo owed an obligation to his client to press the matter as far as he could; after all, one of the stakes was the possible reinstatement of an award of a quarter of a billion dollars. Yet Cuneo concurrently felt a professional stricture. The Supreme Court is an institution that save for the Fortas imbroglio has been virtually immune from the scandals that periodically sweep the Congress and White House. Would not the mere act of raising charges about a leak damage the court, especially in the post-Watergate period when the public had come to expect the worst of its public officials? Pragmatism was another element. Chief Justice Warren Burger is renowned among lawyers for his ego and the aura of regality he has brought to the court, from antique furnishings to a bench design that supposedly "enhanced the dignity" of the justices. Burger is not a man a lawyer offends lightly, particularly when his clients have frequent business before the Supreme Court. (Indeed, the day the Telex-IBM case was to be announced, Cuneo had another decision come down deciding a $200 million defense contract dispute between two defense firms; he lost.)

In the end Cuneo decided to take a middle road that would satisfy his client's rights and also avoid unnecessarily smudging the court's reputation. On April 15, 1976, he and a senior partner, Ashley Sellers, visited Mark Cannon, Justice Burger's administrative assistant. During a seventy-five-minute conversation he spelled out the story of the negotiations, the various incidents that aroused his suspicions and the inconclusive nature of his inquiries.

"What we intended to do," Cuneo told me later, "was to file

an action asking that the court appoint a special master to investigate the facts of the case. We would accuse no one of a breach of ethics; we would simply state the allegations that we had heard and that we had not been able to pursue because of the reluctance of the lawyers involved to speak with us.'' Cannon did not object; he did suggest that Cuneo ''be sure to check the rules of the court so that we file our action properly.''

Then Cuneo made Cannon a proposition: if he were told authoritatively that the court had voted not to grant *certiorari*, there obviously would be no need to proceed with the case, for Telex could not gain anything.

''He did not blink an eye when I put the statement to him,'' Cuneo said. ''I reaffirmed to him that we did not wish to embarrass or hurt anyone by what we might do and, therefore, if our case was hopeless we would not wish to bring an action or expose the names of any one. Mr. Cannon said he understood that.''

Cuneo and Cannon also discussed where in the court the action should be filed, Cuneo noting that he did not think the Clerk's office to be appropriate, if, in his words, ''we were to identify anyone there as a possible source of the leak.'' Cannon said he would see what Justice Burger had to say on the point.

Cuneo will not discuss specifics of what happened subsequently, on the grounds that conversations between a practicing lawyer and two Supreme Court justices are so extraordinary that the jurists deserve some confidentiality. He did, however, give a verbal report to Wheeler, his client, as follows: within the week Cuneo was called back to the court and met with Justice Burger and Justice William Brennan, the most senior member. They told Cuneo they had inspected the file—not wishing to trust their memories on such an important issue—and that Telex in fact had been denied *certiorari*. Cuneo thanked them, said they could forget about any suit and left the court.

Well, was Cuneo in fact satisfied with the outcome of the affair? He gave me a long, carefully qualified answer to the effect that based on the information he was able to obtain he could not prove there was a leak.

I tried again. What did he *think*? Again, a hedged response, this time that he had been ''unable to establish without a doubt'' that a leak had not occurred.

We talked on about other matters—about Washington lawyers we knew; about Roger Wheeler's unlikely hobby (for a corporate executive) of trail-riding overpowered motorcycles; about the intricacies of representing companies that get crosswise with the Defense Department and the big military contractors on multimillion-dollar weapons-systems deals. I knew Cuneo had another appointment at four o'clock, so I began gathering my pens and notebooks a few minutes before the hour. I sensed he had something else on his mind, and he finally said it just before I walked to the door:

"I would still," he said, "like to get into this case again with the power to subpoena the necessary witnesses, and to put them under oath, and to ask some rather obvious questions."

What do you think you would find?

"I don't know. But as a lawyer, I'd feel a lot better, even if things didn't turn out the way I thought they might at one time."

So there the IBM-Telex matter rests, two Supreme Court justices affirming that Telex lost the case, and that reopening it made neither economic nor legal sense. Cuneo and Wheeler accept their statement that the court denied *certiorari*. Why, then, the continuing suspicions? If IBM had known in advance that the court had ruled against Telex, its attorneys could have broken off the negotiations and waited for a ruling that would have driven Telex into swift bankruptcy. Lawsuits had preoccupied IBM for almost a decade, and the opportunity for a final, crushing victory over the most public of its adversaries surely would have had sobering impact upon the other litigants: when one sues IBM, is bankruptcy the consequence of failure?

But a person on the periphery of the case offered a scenario—and he stressed it was purely hypothetical—that could explain IBM's settling out of court, even though its lawyers knew they were about to win a favorable Supreme Court decision. He elaborated: "IBM management is sophisticated enough to realize the public relations consequences of totally destroying Telex, which is what would have happened had Telex stuck with the suit and lost.

"The death of Telex would confirm what IBM critics have been saying: that it is a 'monster corporation' capable of smashing anyone who gets in its way. Suppose you are Frank Cary or Nick Katzenbach, and you've had a close call on losing a $250 million lawsuit but have managed to pull it out at the last minute. It makes about as much sense for IBM to take $20 million or so off Telex as it does for Willie Sutton to steal a school kid's lunch money. IBM takes its win and goes on to other things. Telex 'survives,' and the fact that it exists helps keep up the fiction that there is 'competition to IBM.'

"All of this is rank speculation, of course, but it could offer an explanation as to why IBM settled even though it benefited from the leak.

"But we'll never know, will we? Maybe Katzenbach will write his memoirs when he is an old man . . ."

One messy aftermath of the suit remained. Not until I was in Tulsa and had talked with the Telex people, did I realize that they and Floyd Walker had split and were clawing at one another's eyes in an Oklahoma state court. Jack Bailey said many nasty things about Walker and gave me a thick file on the lawsuit. His basic accusation was that Walker had lured Telex into filing a can't-win suit that had almost ruined the company and then had had the chutzpah to insist on an umpteen-million-dollar fee.

Lawsuits that come after the main event do not usually excite me. Most deserve the same attention one would give to second-division baseball teams playing a night game in October. Yet as I listened to Bailey cuss out Walker, one thought kept drifting through my head: Walker at one point had stood to collect a fee of anywhere from $35 million to $60 million, an extraordinary event in the life of any man, be he a Tulsa lawyer or a Wall Street tycoon. Even the old robber baron E. H. Harriman would have harrumphed appreciatively at the size of such a pile of money. Most of us live in a financial milieu where any sum over five digits takes on the aura of a lottery player's fantasy. *Telex* v. *IBM* had brought this onetime postman with a night-school degree to the brink of wealth, and then the appeals court had grabbed his collar and tugged him away, leaving him to quibble with his former client over relative pocket change. I had to inspect Walker, because I was curious as to how he was weathering such a reversal of fortunes.

I expected Floyd Walker to be in a foul mood, even though a year had lapsed. Walker had tasted glory. *Fortune* magazine had run his picture under the headline "Floyd, the Giant Killer." No, Walker had told *Fortune* during those splendid happy months, if and when he collected his millions he did not intend to change his style of life. "I'll practice law as I have in the past," he said. "Not a bad practice," commented *Fortune*, which respects money.[14] Other Tulsa lawyers nodded approvingly as Walker spent scores of thousands of dollars on a fancy new lake house outside town.

When I got to Walker's office suite high in the Fourth National Bank Building I looked at him closely for signs of psychic distress. But whatever pain he had, if any, was shielded behind an open, weathered face and a broad welcoming smile.

No, no, Walker said, after the initial disappointment he had accepted the loss of the fee as "just one of those things—lawyers learn to win; lawyers learn to lose. So you don't get excited when one slips away from you."

Oh, sure, there were some material losses. Walker had wanted to establish an endowment for his law school at the University of Tulsa. Walker had wanted to create trust funds for his children. He had wanted, in his words, to "give my family some of the nicer things we've never been able to afford." He had anticipated "working a heck of a lot less and devoting much of my time to managing money." But Walker dismissed this array of dashed hopes with a wave of his arms and talked about his suit against Telex.[15]

Walker based his claim on two assertions. First, he claimed that his contingency fee contract should be applied to the $22.2 million trade secrets judgment in favor of IBM that was voided by the out-of-court settlement.* Walker asserted that the settlement gave Telex a "settlement" of that amount and that under the contingency contract, he was entitled to a fee of $1,395,424. As an alternative, Walker asked compensation on a *quantum meruit* basis, that is, for the worth of his services, which he put at $2.5 million.

Telex, of course, considered Walker's claims absolutely daft. "A contingency contract is a gamble," Jack Bailey said. "Walker could have signed on for a flat fee, but he chose the other

*The judgment was $18.5 million at the circuit court level. Interest pushed it to $22.2 million—on paper, anyway—by the time Walker filed his suit.

route. Now he's trying to change the rules.'' In formal court pleadings Telex said the trades secret counterclaim was ''fiction'' because no money existed to pay it, regardless of what the courts had ordered. So how could Walker claim a percentage of nothing?

Telex was so outraged by Walker's suit, in fact, that it fired back a salvo of its own, charging in a counterclaim that he had bungled the suit by not paying enough attention to the trades secret counterclaim. It also charged that Walker had falsely represented himself as a skilled antitrust attorney when in fact ''he had only very limited experience in such fields of law.'' Telex demanded that Walker pay $938,676 that it had spent in litigating the suit.*

After listening to Walker for an hour or so, I decided that he suffered from hurt pride as much as from the loss of the bonanza fee. He berated Roger Wheeler for shunning his advice. He called Wheeler a ''pest'' who had kept interfering in the case, and said he was happy that he had been able to persuade Wheeler to take a month-long cruise during the actual trial: ''otherwise he'd have had his finger in everything.'' He said that Telex's decision to settle was ''insane'' and ''absolutely stupid.''

As I rose to leave, Walker walked over to the window and looked out across downtown Tulsa. It was late in the afternoon, and people were hurrying across the street, dodging buses and cars, and the Oklahoma sun put a golden cast on the tops of lower office buildings. Walker turned back to me.

''You know,'' he said, ''the Telex case was a creative piece of work. When you do something different and then see it go away, you are disappointed. Sure, I did some daydreaming about what it would be like to be a wealthy man. But . . .''

Walker let the thought trail away. But I understood him. We shook hands, and I left.

*At the trial level, Walker and Lasky each received more than $1,000,000 on their claims, Walker from a state court trial jury, Lasky from a federal district judge in San Francisco. As of the spring of 1978 Telex continued vigorous opposition to both suits in the appellate courts.

Court Recess Five

Bruce Littlejohn, a judge in South Carolina since 1949, once heard a case involving a man who claimed injuries suffered in a fall made him impotent. A urologist called as a witness so testified.

So the insurance lawyer, Mortimer Weinberg, Sr., balding and in his sixties, set out to determine just how serious the impotency was. According to Judge Littlejohn, the sequence went as follows:

WEINBERG: Doctor, just tell the jury, if you will, about how often does a man have sexual relations anyhow.

DOCTOR: Well, Mr. Weinberg, that's a question that is pretty difficult to answer. I don't know that I could give you an answer with any real accuracy.

WEINBERG: But even so, Doctor, you have come here as an expert. Certainly you can give this jury some idea about a thing like this. It may be important in the trial of this case.

DOCTOR: Well, Mr. Weinberg, it just depends on so many things that it makes the question very difficult to answer.

Weinberg and the doctor sparred through several more questions, the physician saying the frequency depended upon such variable factors at the man's health and, the "inclination of his partner, among other things." But Weinberg pressed on.

WEINBERG: Certainly you can give us some idea. Just take an ordinary man and give us an estimate, if you can't testify with any accuracy.

DOCTOR: Mr. Weinberg, for example, take a man between twenty and thirty years of age—for him it might be a number of times; take a man between thirty and forty, it would be a different number, a smaller number, if you please; and between forty and fifty the number would change again, still a little smaller.

And between fifty and sixty, the number would get even smaller. And then, Mr. Weinberg [and the doctor wearily waved his hands] it just dwindles out.

WEINBERG: Doctor, you have broken my heart.[1]

Chapter Six

Turning the Tables: Legal Malpractice

Silvio Sciutto admired the famous lawyer on Montgomery Street, Mister Belli, whose name suggested he also must be Italian.[1] He saw Mister Belli on television, and his wife Jean would sometimes read to him an item about the famous Mister Belli from the *San Francisco Chronicle*, in the column written by Herbert Caen. Silvio Sciutto himself had come to the San Francisco area from Italy as a boy of seventeen, and although he had earned a comfortable living for Jean and their two sons as a mattress salesman, much of the Old Country remained with him. Sciutto, for instance, had never completely mastered the writing and speaking of English. But this was no handicap, for he could rely upon Jean to open and read and answer the mail and to handle many other of the family affairs.

But now came a family affair with which Silvio Sciutto must involve himself personally. The doctors had hurt his Jean. In 1966, when she had gone to the doctor with one problem, they had put her into the hospital, and examined her, and said she had a cancer, and removed her entire left breast.

This worried both Sciuttos. Did not cancer return to harm women, and especially breast cancer? Silvio tossed in the bed at night and hoped that his Jean would not be pained again. Cancer was a word that seldom, if ever, passed between them. But the possibility of a recurrence was omnipresent.

The consolation was Doctor Patrick Flynn, an Irishman with a frizzly brown beard, an unconventional man, to be sure, with an accent of his own and a relaxed manner unlike that of many of the American doctors. Jean Sciutto visited Dr. Flynn almost monthly, chiefly to look for any sign of further cancer.

One June night in 1968, two years after the first operation, Jean Sciutto came home from her sewing club and complained that her right breast was "swollen and itchy." Silvio insisted that she see Dr. Flynn the next day. She did, and within twenty-four hours she was on the operating table again, for removal of the other breast—this one containing a fist-sized cancer.

There was more. The doctors feared the dread cancer might have spread, and so they prescribed radiation therapy—essentially, that Jean lie on a table while X-ray beams were directed at her body.

The treatments did not go well. After fifteen or so of them she complained of sickness and of congestion in her lungs. Other doctors got involved. One of them said her lungs had been burned by the radiotherapy. Although no one said so outright, Silvio Sciutto could listen between the lines: his beloved Jean was dying. She had been under the care of many doctors, and someone had made a mistake, and now someone must be punished.

Silvio Sciutto wanted help. He thought of Mr. Belli, whom he knew "in the TV and the newspapers and so on, so forth." In family discussions, he said, "We felt that the damage was done, a terrible one, and so we went to see the best, at least one of the best."

Melvin M. Belli. The "King of Torts," as he is known to both friend and enemy, is not a difficult man to find in San Francisco. The King's court is in a sandblasted red-brick townhouse on Montgomery Street, the city's financial district, a onetime bistro faced with yards of twisting black wrought iron, story-high blue-tinted windows and flower boxes alive with pink ivy geraniums and Virginia creeper. Almost, but not quite, hidden by the greenery is a shingle bearing the words MELVIN M. BELLI LAWYER.

Three or four times daily the Grayline Tour buses ease to the curb opposite The Belli Building, as Belli has rechristened his working quarters. Off clamber the tourists, Instamatic cameras at the ready, and the guide bellows, "This is the office, ladies and gentlemen, of America's foremost personal injury lawyer . . ."

That Belli is. Belli revolutionized—yea, *made*—personal injury law in the postwar years by putting the question directly to the collective public conscience, "If a person is maimed through the careless action of another person, is he not entitled to be made whole again, financially at least?"

Belli brought "demonstrative evidence" into the civil courtroom. Don't *talk about* an injury; *show* the injury. Did your client lose a leg? Wrap the artificial limb in butcher paper and leave it on the counsel table during testimony, a silent horror for the jurors to contemplate. Then, during your closing argument, unwrap the device and pass it to the jurors so that they can decide whether leather and steel can substitute for flesh and bone.

Many days Belli is visible through a ground-floor window—talking on the telephone, dictating a letter, even taking a deposition from a witness in one of the hundreds of cases that come through his office each year. Belli chose the street-level office "so I could see passersby, so they could look at me," he recounted in one of his eight books.[2] The view is impressive, both of the lawyer and of his trappings: Belli, in his late sixties, with striking gray hair offset by black horn-rimmed glasses; the office, floor-to-ceiling mahogany bookcases, four sparkling chandeliers, a massive wooden bar, bric-a-brac and souvenirs that would take four pages to catalogue. Belli likes being on quasi-public display, and he gives San Francisco an occasional special treat.

Like the time he impishly displayed a garish red, white and blue poster proclaiming FUCK COMMUNISM in his window, to the delight of late afternoon crowds. A cop finally came in and said, in effect, "Hey, Mr. Belli, a joke is a joke, okay, but is that really appropriate for public display?"

The way Belli has told the story, he huffed himself up in mock indignation and demanded, "Officer, are you *for* Communism?" The poor patrolman retreated.

Belli's animosity toward the insurance companies and the medical profession is reciprocated, and one lawyer in the personal injury field (a man who is friendly toward the San Franciscan) commented, "The hatreds being what they are, I'm surprised that Mel's enemies haven't encouraged more malpractice cases against him. When you have a high-volume operation, with a lot of lawyers on your premises you can't watch that closely, mistakes inevitably happen. I think it is a tribute to the quality of Mel's work that he hasn't been sued more than he has.'' In at least one previous instance a court did return a malpractice verdict against Belli.

The case came via referral from another law firm, and the statute of limitations had almost run. The client, an elderly man, suffered from diabetes. The doctor, knowing this, nonetheless did surgery on a foot callus. Diabetics have difficulty recovering from surgical and other wounds, and gangrene often develops. In this case, other operations became necessary, and the man ultimately lost his leg. The lawyer assigned to the case by Belli's office could not find medical witnesses, and after one continuance the judge dismissed the case. Whereupon the old man hired another law firm which sued Belli for malpractice. This time a medical witness did appear, and he said he would have testified in any ''justiciable'' medical malpractice case. The court returned a verdict of $33,000 against Belli, who commented:

> I have adequate insurance, of course, but this is a case probably of first impression since it was proved in this case (1) that I was *negligent* (!) in not being able to get a doctor; (2) that it is ''*easy*'' to get a doctor to testify, they all do so ''*willingly*''(!) whenever called upon; (3) if I had been able to get a doctor, I could have won the first case.
>
> I guess I've tried more malpractice cases and got more adequate awards in this field than any lawyer in the United States. If there is anyone who knows you can't get a doctor it is I, yet the trial judge announced that such a practice did not and could not exist![3]

TV shows. Magazine interviews. Speeches to legal groups, especially the Association of Trial Lawyers of America of which he is the ongoing guru. Even an appearance in an advertisement for Scotch whiskey.* As a personal injury lawyer Belli works in

*An affair that cost Belli a thirty-day suspension by the California State Bar on grounds of unethical advertisement for himself, contrary to bar rules. The bar recommended a one-year suspension; the California Supreme Court reduced the penalty to thirty days. Belli sued the bar for $3,000,000 but a federal judge dismissed his suit, saying the bar was just doing its job in policing the conduct of lawyers.[4]

what long was an underdog's role, and by promoting himself he concurrently promoted the notion that a citizen with a grievance against a powerful entity—be it corporation, medical doctor, or insurance company—can find someone willing to stand up for him in court.

So it was to Melvin Belli that Silvio Sciutto turned for help. One reason, as he told another lawyer later, was that he thought that Belli—given his name—was a fellow Italian-American.

Belli is not. Belli's ancestry is Swiss, an irrelevancy, but a distinction that Sciutto never understood—even after he had turned against the Belli firm, and sued it and its partners and two of its associates, and collected a $200,000 judgment for an offense that lawyers seldom speak about in mixed circles: legal malpractice. In fact, long after the suit was ended, when Sciutto was talking with someone about the case, he said, "You know, all through this whole thing, I never even see the Mr. Belli. I want him as my lawyer; I only see his other people; but when I go to court and get my money much of it comes from a man I never know in person. This law, it is a funny thing."

That lawyers such as Mel Belli are feeling the sting of malpractice suits is a matter of no small irony. Lawyers taught the public to demand expertise from physicians, accountants, architects and other professionals. If a surgeon took out a gallbladder instead of an appendix, an architect's building collapsed, or the IRS examiner didn't accept the accountant's figure, the lawyer was quick to urge the unhappy citizen, "Let's take him to court." Now the lawyers are plagued by a monster of their own making. Bar trade journals speak of a "legal malpractice crisis" in the same alarmed tone physicians use in lamenting the rise of medical malpractice cases. *The Barrister*, organ of the Young Lawyers Section of the American Bar Association, even suggests that legal malpractice "may be an even greater crisis than that faced by the medical and other professions."[5]

Belli is such an individualist—*sui generis*, if you will—that nothing concerning him or his practice can be called typical of trends elsewhere in the legal profession. But the Sciutto case is significant because it points up a reason that legal malpractice is scaring American lawyers silly. No attorney, regardless of skill or reputation, is immune to suit if a client thinks he botched a case. Belli himself has written, "If lawyers are to urge that doctors take their place with other defendants, shorn both of legal and practical immunity, then we too must recognize the malpractice suit against other professional classes of people, and certainly, lawyers." Malpractice is not restricted to what Chesterfield Smith, the onetime president of the American Bar Association, called a "fringe of incompetents in the profession." Disgruntled clients are going after bar association moguls, after Washington superfirms, even after judges for alleged misdeeds in private practice. A sampling:

—Twice in two years a federal court in Philadelphia found Common Pleas Court Judge Charles A. Lord liable for mishandling of personal injury cases while in private practice. The gist of each of the client's claims was that Lord had neglected to file proper court papers on time. One award, in 1974, was for $260,000; the other, in early 1976, was for $122,000.*

—In California, the president of the Sacramento Valley Bar Association, Jerome R. Lewis, was slapped with a $100,000 judgment for failure to research adequately an issue in a divorce action. As a result of Lewis' negligence, the wife did not claim a share of her husband's retirement benefits and settled for a rather paltry monthly payment. The California Supreme Court, in upholding the trial jury's verdict, broadened drastically the standards of conduct to be expected of a lawyer (as shall be elaborated below). In one biting comment the court conceded that a lawyer is entitled to choose among various alternative strategies, but added, "There is nothing strategic or tactical about ignorance . . ."[7]

—Frequently stung themselves in malpractice suits, physicians are now turning tables on the lawyers. In a rash of cases in the mid-1970s, doctors collected damages from attorneys for bringing allegedly frivolous medical malpractice actions. One such suit was brought by Dr. John Sullivan, an orthopedic sur-

*Judge Lord did not appear in court to contest the second claim but tried to file papers later. The trial judge, Daniel H. Huyett III, refused to consider Lord's papers, saying, "Especially in view of the sorry history of this action, we feel that any claim the defendant has to our consideration and possible acceptance of his lately raised contentions is far outweighed by our duty to protect the plaintiff from unfair surprise and prejudice. . . ."[6]

geon in Vero Beach, Florida. A patient claimed that when Sullivan set his broken arm, the steel rod implanted in the limb to help it heal was an inch too short. Sullivan insisted he had not been negligent, even though his insurance company wanted to settle. The day before trial, the patient's lawyer, Otis Parker, dropped the suit. Whereupon Sullivan sued the patient and Parker for malicious legal prosecution. A jury awarded Sullivan $175,000 damages.[8]

—In the late 1960s a fisheries company hired the prestigious Washington firm of Steptoe & Johnson to draft a supposedly routine contract for a vessel that would fish Latin American waters. Venezuelan authorities seized the boat on grounds that its American registration was illegal. The owners sued Steptoe & Johnson for negligence, and the law firm pleaded that the statute of limitations had lapsed. But the U.S. Court of Appeals of the District of Columbia ruled that the statute began to run at the time of the seizure—when Steptoe & Johnson's alleged negligence was discovered—rather than on the date the firm had drafted the contract. The case was eventually settled.[9]

In sum, legal malpractice cases are no longer the exclusive concern of the fringe operators who work at the outer ethical limits of their profession—the drunks, the stupid, the ambulance chasers, the outright thieves who pilfer money from their clients. Malpractice can touch any lawyer in the profession—even a Melvin M. Belli.

Silvio and Jean Sciutto had never heard of legal malpractice the December day in 1968 when they entered Melvin Belli's baroque townhouse office at 722 Montgomery Street and told the receptionist, "Hey, we'd like to see Mr. Belli, please." As Silvio told a Belli lawyer later during depositions, "My purpose was to come because I knew that was a wonderful firm, known the world over, and I had some damage done—at least I thought I had—to my wife, and I felt I wanted to come to see your people."

Mel Belli, unsurprisingly, does not interview walk-in clients. Indeed, at times they seem to irritate him. After one grueling day he walked into his reception room "to find it full of the lame, the halt and the blind," all awaiting the magical services of Melvin

Belli. "I had had it. I slipped into the john, lathered up a bucket of soap suds, smeared them all over my face, and came out on all fours, growling, "Hooo! Heee! Haaaa! Hey!" The receptionist yelled "Mad dog! Mad dog!" One woman looked up and nodded in seeming approval. The other clients continued sitting with heads down, absorbed by their own problems.[10]

No such exhibition greeted the Sciuttos. The receptionist shunted them off to a junior associate, Frederick A. Cone, who took their story. The couple complained mainly about the radiologist who had been treating Mrs. Sciutto. Her lungs had been burned and she felt some doctor should be sued. As Silvio put it later, "They give her the X-ray treatment. After about fourteen, fifteen, or whatever it was, they stopped. The woman, she started temperature. The burning, the radiation, the burning and everything." Silvio was to assert later he also complained that his wife's internist, Dr. Flynn, the Irishman, was negligent in not detecting the second breast cancer at an earlier stage. During two years of visits, Mrs. Sciutto said, Flynn never examined her breast. Cone and other lawyers in the Belli firm denied this claim; their story, essentially, was that the Sciuttos' demand was to sue about the radiation treatment. In any event, Cone said he would have to review the medical file before deciding whether the firm would take the case—standard procedure in a possible malpractice action—and he would talk with the couple later. Mrs. Sciutto signed a pro forma release authorizing the firm to obtain the records. By Silvio's recollection, Cone said "It's a good case and . . . no doubt it's worth some money."

The Sciuttos never saw Cone again. When they called the Belli firm later to check on progress of the case, they were referred to another associate, David Kogus. Cone's involvement, fleeting though it was, was costly: it brought him into Silvio's subsequent malpractice suit as a named defendant.

Kogus did not control the case much longer. In the late spring the file passed to a more senior lawyer, Seymour Ellison, a name partner in Belli's firm.* Kogus did conduct another interview with the couple, and he did a major part of the work in drafting the formal complaint which they filed on May 19, 1969. The

*The firm's name has gone through several mutations, which is not unusual for large offices. At the time the Sciuttos did business with the firm—and sued it—the name was Belli, Ashe, Ellison, Choulos & Lieff.

named defendants were St. Joseph's Hospital, where Mrs. Sciutto had received her post-surgery radiation therapy; the doctor who had performed both breast removals; and the radiologist who did the radiation therapy. The complaint also named a "John Doe" defendant, a procedure that enables a plaintiff lawyer to bring in other parties if he finds they contributed to the medical malpractice. Sciutto claimed that Kogus insisted the "John Doe" citation covered Flynn, although the actual pleading did not mention him or any alleged negligence in overlooking Mrs. Sciutto's second cancer. Sciutto consistently maintained he thought the suit named Flynn as a defendant, because of what he had told the lawyers. But he conceded he had never read the complaint, citing his problems with English.

According to Sciutto's testimony later, he heard things at the Belli office on various visits that alternately encouraged and bothered him. Kogus, he said, told him the case should be worth $150,000. "Coming from a firm like Belli, I know that more or less they know what they're saying," Sciutto said, "and I took it for granted that that was, more or less, the case." But then there was a comment he remembered Ellison making one day as an interview ended: "By the way, I must tell you that I do know Dr. Flynn. And he has testified with us different times. But that, I'll assure you, won't have any bearing on the case." As Sciutto told Ellison during a deposition:

> That I remember, because it was quite a sting that I got. I already sick about the case. There wasn't too good news, and then when you said that, that sort of . . . shook me up.
>
> But, of course, I just let it go. I didn't say nothing. I figure, well, who knows, we might not have a case. Who am I to judge, you know what I mean? You are a lawyer, so—let it go at that. But you told me that, I'm sure of that.

Ellison denied saying any such thing, and Flynn said he had only the vaguest recollection of the lawyer: "I was giving expert testimony . . . and he was either on my side or the other side, I don't remember which." (Nothing developed during the trial which substantiated any suggestion of a special relationship between Ellison and Flynn.)

Kogus' confidence in the suit he had helped prepare did not last long. On July 14, 1969—a bare two months after its filing—

Kogus wrote Ellison a memo recommending that the firm withdraw, presumably because he saw no legal liability on the part of the doctor, radiologist, or St. Joseph's Hospital.

And, indeed, Ellison told the Sciuttos in 1971, three years after their first contact, that he was skeptical about winning a recovery. X-ray cases are difficult to prove, he said, and the Sciuttos did not "have a strong case." Jean Sciutto left the office crying.

The next time Silvio Sciutto saw Ellison was by accident. Mrs. Sciutto was in Marin General Hospital, north of San Francisco, for continuing treatment of her lungs, and Ellison brought his daughter into the emergency room with a broken arm. The men met; they discussed the case; Ellison was discouraging. He even offered to take Sciutto to lunch with a doctor and another lawyer to discuss why the case was weak and why X-ray injuries "happen quite often," in Sciutto's words. Sciutto, angered, refused; shortly thereafter, Ellison sent him forms withdrawing the Belli firm from the case.

So far as Sciutto could remember, he never once saw the famed Mr. Belli, whose reputation had drawn him to 722 Montgomery Street in the first place. But a quirk of malpractice law is that every partner in a firm is equally responsible for an error committed by another. Hence Mel Belli was a legal equal of lawyers Cone, Kogus and Ellison.

Silvio Sciutto now was livid. Life was slipping away from his Jean, and her pain increased daily. *The doctors*, he would say to himself, *those damned doctors*. He went lawyer shopping. *Would someone else sue these damned doctors—not for me, but for my wife*?

Any number of lawyers listened to Sciutto, but then he would come to the part where he said, "Mr. Belli's office, they had this case for two years, and they said no medical malpractice existed. Now they are wrong, and I want you to take this case and . . ."

Sciutto seldom got any further. The reaction, in so many words, was, "Mel Belli's office turned loose of the case? Forget it, fella'; if the recognized wizards don't see an action, it doesn't exist. Let's not waste our time, okay?"

Sciutto plodded from office to office—pleading, crying, raging, taunting. When someone finally read the Belli firm's suit to him and explained that Dr. Flynn was not named a defendant, he became even angrier.

Sciutto finally persuaded a young lawyer named Lawrence Handleman to take the case. Although Handleman had minimal experience in medical malpractice, he did several things the Belli firm had not accomplished. He obtained the daily radiation records of the radiologist, and he found a radiation therapy expert, Dr. Lawrence Margolis, of the University of California at San Francisco, who would testify that the treatment given Mrs. Sciutto was bad. He also joined Dr. Flynn as a defendant.

There were problems. Mrs. Sciutto was near death, and although he asked for an expedited trial, Handleman was not sure the woman would live long enough to have her day in court, much less enjoy any benefits from a favorable verdict. Also, in a personal injury case, including medical malpractice, death cuts off damages for pain and suffering.

So Handleman struck what he considered the best deal possible. A month before the trial was to begin, he negotiated a settlement of $25,000 from the surgeon's insurance company and $14,250 from Dr. Flynn's. In return for the latter, Sciutto waived any future right to sue Flynn for wrongful death. In Handleman's opinion, a wrongful death action was worth $50,000 to $100,000. But he was in a bind. The Belli firm's original complaint did not state any cause of action against Dr. Flynn for failure to diagnose cancer during the period before June 1, 1968. Thus if Handleman had amended the complaint, Dr. Flynn would have escaped under the statute of limitations, or the trial would have been further delayed, and at a time when Mrs. Sciutto was on the brink of death. As Handleman put it, his intention was to "get what I could for a dying woman."

The settlement did not assuage Silvio Sciutto's grief. He continued to care for Jean. He took the settlement money, and he packed her into his automobile, and he drove her to a clinic in Tijuana, Mexico, which used the controversial drug Laetrile, an extract from apricot pits, to treat cancer. Nothing helped her. She died on October 31, 1972.

Silvio Sciutto grieved deeply. Almost every day he went to the cemetery and sat by his wife's grave and, in the words of a man who knew him later, "he talked with Jean. He asked her questions; he heard answers." Now Silvio added the Belli lawyers to his list of villains. He decided to sue Melvin Belli.

Easier decided than done. Once again Sciutto made the rounds of law offices, pleading for someone to listen to his story. Lawyer after lawyer turned him away, most often before he got beyond the first few sentences. A nut, and a broke one at that: the $39,250 settlement money was gone, paid over to the "cancer clinic" in Mexico, and any action would have to be on a contingency fee basis. In the words of a lawyer involved in the case later, "No lawyer wanted to sue Mel Belli. They did not like the repercussions. They worried about collecting, because the Belli firm was going through some 'reorganization.'* Also, the case would be complicated and hard fought. The Belli firm gives you a lawsuit." A further obstacle was the fact that Sciutto had already collected $39,250. Would not a jury dismiss any additional suit as evidence of greed?

One lawyer who heard Sciutto practiced in Marin County, the suburb across the bay to the north of San Francisco. In Long Beach, in Southern California, a few days later, he glanced across the courthouse coffee shop and saw Robert Aitken and Anthony J. Murray chatting together. Aitken, a compact, intense attorney in his mid-forties, practices with the firm of Ball, Hunt, Hart, Brown & Baerwitz. As a trial office, one of the best in California, the firm defies capsulization. My first encounter, earlier this decade, was with the lead partner, Joseph Ball, via a letter of introduction from Carey McWilliams, long the editor of *The Nation*, and before that a California lawyer himself. Ball gave no inkling of his politics that day because he was too busy advising me not to write critically of federal district judges in his state. The next time I saw Ball's name it was as counsel for Herbert Kalmbach, the personal attorney to Richard M. Nixon who was disgraced in the Watergate scandal. Murray, a slim brown-haired man in his late thirties, had worked with the Ball office before becoming a partner in the firm of Hitt & Murray.

Listening to the Marin County lawyer talk about the potential malpractice case against the Belli firm, Murray and Aitken felt surges of excitement. Consider Aitken, who at first glance seems

*Concurrently with the Sciutto suit, the Belli office had a major shaking out of partners and associates, for reasons that are heated but obscure and not germane to our story.

archetypical of the conservative office lawyer. Such is not the case. One of Aitken's hobbies is mountain climbing in the Sierras, a high-risk sport regardless of the season. On one winter trip, with snow and an ice storm, Aitken got into a situation which he was not sure he would survive. Suing Melvin Belli's firm would be the legal equivalent of climbing across a face of glare ice in a gale. So Aitken felt doubly comfortable knowing that old-friend Murray, a most skilled trial lawyer, would be sharing the trial burden.

Murray and Aitken discussed the pros and cons. The trial would be 450 miles away, which meant considerable, and expensive, travel during the preparatory stages. Winning would mean, in effect, trying and winning *two* cases—first, proving malpractice on the part of Dr. Flynn for not finding the second breast cancer; and second, proving malpractice by the Belli firm for not proceeding against him. The legal malpractice phase would be especially difficult. Lawyers work in a world of highly subjective decisions. As professionals, they are paid to exercise judgment. Thus, how can it be proved that they erred? Should a baseball star such as Pete Rose be chastised for swinging at a 3–0 pitch that he thought he could knock into the stands? Should conductor Eugene Ormandy be faulted for adding two violins to the string section of the Philadelphia Orchestra? The Belli firm built its reputation—and its fortune—through unorthodox legal tactics. Would it be possible to persuade a jury that even the "King of Torts" could hire lawyers who made errors?

"We knew it would mean a lot of work, money and harassment, but it sounded exciting," Aitken recollected. "One of us finally said, 'I'll do it if you will do it.'" They shook hands across the table and went to work.

Aitken and Murray filed suit in March 1973, naming as defendants the Belli firm and the three lawyers who worked on the case: Ellison, Cone and Kogus. In December the firm moved to dismiss the case, but the judge said no, it must go to trial. And battle was joined.

"At this point Ellison was the big target because he had done most of the work on the case," Aitken said. "So we got hit with a broadside of interrogatories, more than a thousand of them, with a twenty-day limit.

"Now in such a situation you normally ask for an extension,

and the other side grants it. Lawyers know what is possible, and what is not. But the Belli firm objected to an extension, so we didn't get one. They also served notices of deposition, to be taken in San Francisco. They made plain they were out to make everything as miserable and inconvenient as possible. They set the tempo of the case right there, and we knew we were in for the fight of our lives.

"Remember, we were at a tremendous logistical disadvantage. Every time anything happened, one of us had to fly round-trip from Long Beach to San Francisco.* Costs mounted and mounted. We were dipping into our own pockets as we took the depositions."

During one round of depositions Ellison and Murray got into a raised-voice exchange over accusations that Murray was coaching Sciutto in answering questions:

ELLISON. You are in San Francisco, not Los Angeles, and here the witness testifies, not the lawyers.

MURRAY. You mean up here you don't have the witnesses explain their answers like we do down in Los Angeles?

CONE. Gentlemen, gentlemen.

ELLISON. We let the witness answer the question as best he can.

Legal malpractice makes strange bedfellows. In some of Belli's most celebrated cases the defense lawyer was from the large (seventy-five-plus attorneys) San Francisco firm of Bronson, Bronson & McKinnon, which specializes in insurance defense work. The Belli firm's malpractice policy with St. Paul Insurance Company provided $100,000 coverage per partner. Facing a potential $300,000 liability, St. Paul dispatched Bronson, Bronson & McKinnon to defend its interests. "They offered nothing in settlement and let us know they'd take us to trial," Aitken said.

Legal malpractice must be proved through expert witnesses, that is, other lawyers who will get on the stand and specify exactly what errors were made. In searching for such experts Ait-

*One has to strain to summon any sympathy for Aitken and Murray's logistical plight. Everyone involved in the case except for them lived in the San Francisco area, and they recognized the travel required when they accepted the case.

ken and Murray encountered the same "conspiracy of silence" that lawyers so stridently decry among medical doctors. According to Aitken, "We could get lawyers from Southern California; that was no problem. But there is a good deal of regional animosity between Northern and Southern California, and we didn't want the defense to be able to say, 'Who are these Los Angeles lawyers to come up here and tell us that San Francisco attorneys don't know how to try a lawsuit?'

"So we shopped all over San Francisco. We must have talked to forty or fifty attorneys, either by phone or in person. With a few we got as far as lunch. We would lay out the case, and the lawyer would look at us in horror. 'These people are not practicing law properly,' they would say.

"We would ask the golden question: 'Will you testify to that effect?'

"There would be a long pause, then a shake of the head, negative. 'I know someone in the firm.' 'I am going on vacation.' 'My partners wouldn't let me.' We heard this same stuff over and over again."

Through perseverance Aitken and Murray finally found their first lawyer witness, Dick Bridgeman, who practices in Oakland. He was unequivocal once he heard their presentation: "Hell, yes, I'll testify. I feel it is my duty and moral obligation as a lawyer." Bridgeman was doubly useful because he specialized in plaintiff work, hence he could not be attacked as an "insurance company flunky" motivated by animosity towards San Francisco's leading personal injury firm.

Aitken and Murray wanted an insurance defense attorney as well to testify that the Belli firm's conduct looked bad from both sides of the courtroom. Pat Burdick, of a San Francisco defense firm, agreed to testify for them. More typical, however, was the insurance defense lawyer whose firm had several cases pending with Belli's office. A friend asked, "If you testify against Belli and Ellison, won't you sour settlement of these suits? Aren't you buying yourself a piece of somebody else's trouble by getting involved?" The lawyer, after consideration, decided not to testify for Murray and Aitken.

With two Northern Californians in hand Aitken and Murray felt confident enough to use one Southern Californian, an Orange County lawyer, Jack Trotter, as their third witness.

Next they searched for medical witnesses. "Initially we had the same kind of crisis," Aitken said, "We could get any number of Los Angeles doctors, and indeed one of them educated us on the medical aspects of the case. But we needed some Northern California doctors as well, and we made absolutely no headway at all.

"Then a lawyer friend of ours who practices in San Francisco passed us through to a physician in Marin County. We talked over dinner, and he listened to us, and he said, 'Obviously, this is medical malpractice.' Well, would you testify? 'No, I won't, but I promise you I'll get someone who will.'

"He lived up to his promise, too. He got us Dr. Laurens White, a professor and tumor specialist at the University of California in San Francisco. We spent an entire Sunday going over the medical records with Dr. White, and he readily agreed to testify. He also mentioned a doctor named Jesse Steinfeld, who was chief of the department of medicine at the Veterans Administration Hospital in Long Beach.

"White's referral was good news for another reason. Dr. Steinfeld had been surgeon general of the United States. Now that is the sort of witness you like to put on the stand. We shipped the records over to Dr. Steinfeld, and he went through them and showed us where Flynn had gone wrong. He told us, 'I'm leaving California shortly to become dean of the Medical College of Virginia, in Richmond, but when you are ready for me I'll fly back and testify.'

"Then another good break. We still needed an internist to help build the case against Dr. Flynn. One night we had dinner with Dr. White on top of the Bank of America Building in downtown San Francisco, and around eleven o'clock I said, 'Laury, do you know of an internist who'd be willing to testify?'

"White thought a moment and mentioned Dr. Richard Bohannon, who was on the tumor board at the Children's Hospital in San Francisco. 'You might want to use him,' White said. 'Among other things he's president-elect of the local unit of the American Cancer Society.'

"So we finally had our witnesses, and good ones."

Aitken and Murray rented an apartment in San Francisco for six weeks, and showed up for trial in March 1976 "expecting an onslaught from the Belli office," in Aitken's words. To their surprise, however, the only medical witnesses there for the defense were the doctor defendants in the original malpractice case. The defense lawyers told the trial judge they estimated the case would last only five days (it stretched over six weeks). Murray and Aitken routinely inquired of Edward Bronson, Jr., the chief defense lawyer, whether any settlement was possible. Nothing resulted. According to Aitken, "He evidently had a problem getting any authority to settle from the defendants because of the deductible insurance policy they had."

To prove the medical malpractice phase of their case, Aitken and Murray had to destroy Flynn. And this Murray did. The bearded Irishman was a disaster as a witness. His testimony was vague and often contradictory.

Indeed, he admitted under questioning, he had missed finding even the first cancer. Mrs. Sciutto had complained to him of vaginal bleeding in July 1966, and he admitted her to St. Joseph's Hospital. A medical student found the breast tumor during a routine admission examination, and her left breast was removed.

His office notes pertaining to Mrs. Sciutto were cryptic. He saw the woman twenty-two times between January 1967 and May 1968, but not once did his notes mention that he examined her remaining breast—even though he knew full well she had had a mastectomy. He insisted from the witness stand he had examined her right breast but could not fix any dates, saying only that he "must have" or "probably" conducted the examination. Flynn said that during his training in Dublin and London he was not instructed to write extensive notes. "Here in America," he commented somewhat ruefully, "doctors are trained to write notes because of the danger of lawsuits." British medicine is cheaper, he said, "because there is less need for secretaries."

The defense sought to prove that the second breast cancer was a "very fast-growing" metastasis of the first tumor, and that Mrs. Sciutto had slight chance of surviving more than five years even had it been detected earlier. But the plaintiff expert witnesses testified the second tumor was a new one and could have been found six months earlier, had the attending physician been attentive.

The most effective witness, in terms of dramatic impact upon judge and jury, proved to be Dr. Steinfeld, the former surgeon general; one juror who had dozed intermittently sat up wide-eyed and attentive when Steinfeld mentioned his former position. Bronson, on cross-examination, walked carefully. At one point he did try to portray Steinfeld as a paper-shuffling administrator, not an active physician. "When was the last time you actually sat down with a patient?" he asked Steinfeld.

Steinfeld rubbed his hand over his chin for a moment. "Let's see, this is Friday, and yesterday I flew here for the trial. Oh, I'd say Wednesday morning about ten o'clock." Steinfeld went on to say that one reason he had obtained a staff position at the Mayo Clinic was to "get closer to patients," and that he had treated thousands of cancer sufferers while there. He also mentioned that he had issued the order that a warning be put on cigarette packages that "smoking may be injurious to your health."*

Pat Burdick, the insurance lawyer turned plaintiff's witness, was perhaps most damaging to the Belli firm. He was astounded that Ellison had sued the surgeon who performed the mastectomy and overlooked Flynn, her longtime internist. Ellison's position was that Sciutto's first complaint had been of the bad radiotherapy treatments. But when the firm accepted the case, the history mentioned that she had had surgery for a breast tumor in 1966 and that she had seen the internist, Flynn, from 1966 to 1968. "The lawyers should have picked up on that," Burdick said.

Aitken elaborated later. "In an auto accident case, the facts are generally pretty clear on how you were hurt and by whom. Medical malpractice is considerably more sophisticated. You must sort out the doctors and find the person responsible. The attorney is supposed to take a detailed statement and get *all* medical records and pass them to a reviewing physician, who says you either have a case or do not.

"They [the Belli firm] did not do this. They signed up the case and focused on radiotherapy. They did not get Flynn's records, even to find the woman's ongoing condition, until after the statute of limitations had run.

"Then they made the second mistake of telling Sciutto he had no case, and put it in writing. What they should have done was

*The trial judge, Vincent J. Campilongo, had a vast collection of pipes in his chambers. During a recess after Steinfeld's testimony he declared he was so impressed by the testimony that he would never smoke again.

to tell Sciutto, in person, that *they* did not think he had a case, and suggested that he see another attorney if he wished. It's most unusual to tell a client to withdraw a case."

For trial purposes, Murray had the withdrawal letter blown up to poster size and displayed it before the jury—an effective use of the "demonstrative evidence" technique perfected by Melvin Belli. Murray also brought into court an exact-size plastic replica of the breast tumor and handed it to a witness along with a pair of calipers and asked him to measure it. Nine by eleven centimeters. Several jurors gaped at the model in seeming amazement, as if they were asking themselves, "How could a doctor overlook something *that* big?"

Ellison, in his defense, said he had in fact obtained Dr. Flynn's records, in late 1970, but decided they did not support a malpractice case. He also contended that the Sciuttos had never told him to sue Flynn, that their main target was the radiologist.

But the lawyer witnesses mustered by Aitken and Murray, all of whom qualified as "experts" in medical malpractice, testified that a specialist has a duty to ascertain all the facts, to be diligent in seeking out records and expert witnesses and to recommend suit when warranted. Failure to do these things, the experts said, would be "below the standard of good legal practice."

For its defense the Belli firm put on five lawyers who testified, in sum, that Ellison did not proximately cause any harm to the Sciuttos because their medical malpractice case had little or no merit. But under Murray's cross-examination one of the lawyer-witnesses said he would not have written the letter recommending that the family drop the case.

The jury debated four and a half hours. At one time, foreman Peter Wolf reported later, one faction wanted to grant Sciutto \$600,000; other jurors voted for \$100,000.[11] Eventually, they compromised: \$200,000 against the Belli firm, and Belli, Ellison and former or present partners Lou Ashe, Vasilios Choulos and Robert Lieff. The jury absolved Cone and Kogus—the associates who originally interviewed the Sciuttos—of any responsibility.

Although Ellison and the other Belli lawyers continued to assert they had done nothing wrong, they did not appeal. One dissuading factor was Murray's announcement that if they did so, he would ask the appeals court to overturn Judge Campilongo's ruling that the trial jury could not consider granting punitive damages (the $200,000 verdict was held to be the actual damages suffered by the Sciuttos). "They didn't want to risk losing any more money," Aitken deduced. "So they paid off."

Belli fumed against the judgment. He told a San Francisco reporter, "It was a very bad verdict because we had a case where we couldn't get any doctors to testify for us. They [the plaintiff] had the former surgeon general of the U.S. and the head of the cancer society. It was a conspiracy. I'm against every doctor now."

Aitken, for his part, had the professional's satisfaction of winning a tough and ticklish lawsuit. "To me the fact that the defendants happened to be lawyers was secondary. Our system works on the philosophy that if you make a mistake and injure someone else, you should be held accountable. I don't intend to make a career of suing other lawyers [although publicity from *Sciutto* v. *Belli* brought prospective clients scurrying to his office] but I do say this: I'll look at legal malpractice suits the way I look at any other potential case. If the facts justify suing, and I think it's a case our firm would like to handle, I'll take another lawyer to court without a second thought."

But for Aitken and Murray, the most satisfying moment came after the trial. "Silvio and his family invited us to their home for a huge Italian dinner. Silvio had gone to North Beach, San Francisco's Italian section, where he had once worked as a baker and ordered a huge congratulatory cake. After profusely thanking us for our help and recounting their problems in achieving a just conclusion, they lifted their wine glasses with tears in their eyes in a salute to their gallant Jean."

Historically, malpractice wasn't much of a problem for lawyers, even though cases arose in America as far back as 1796. The bulk of the cases that did occur involved such clerical-type errors as failing to file court papers on time, garbling the language of a document or overlooking encumbrances on a deed to real estate. The error literally spoke for itself, and wronged clients occasionally did recover. But more subtle errors were difficult to challenge, for the courts effectively built a protective barrier around the profession. One frequently cited opinion written in 1872 held that "A lawyer must exercise such skill, prudence and diligence as *lawyers of ordinary skill and capacity* [emphasis added] commonly possess and exercise."[12] But what was a lawyer of "ordinary" skill? The question—as was perhaps the intention, of the judiciary—was unanswerable. Lawyers certainly would not testify against their brethren.

Indeed, one of the leading standard desk books for lawyers—*American Jury Trials*, a multi-volume compendium published by the Matthew Bender Company—suggests subtly but unmistakably that a lawyer who takes a malpractice case against another attorney is close to being a damned fool. The section on professional negligence, authored by Sterling Hutcheson and C. M. Monroe,* of the San Diego firm of Gray, Cary, Ames & Frye, comments rather sniffily:

> *Many mature lawyers* [italics added throughout] refuse to appear, under any circumstances, as plaintiff's counsel in an action against another lawyer for damages for professional negligence. They know that such suits may *disturb the amicable relations they enjoy with other members of the bar* and thus impede the disposition of other claims in which they are involved. And they are fully aware that a client who is willing to sue a lawyer for those services he is dissatisfied with may have no hesitancy about suing the latter's successor.

Hutcheson and Monroe do concede that clients can have legitimate claims against attorneys and that it "would be unjust" for them not to have competent representation. But they urge caution at every turn, "No lawyer wishes to be in the position of commencing an action for professional negligence and then having to admit that the suit is not justified." If the case looks meritorious, try for an out-of-court settlement if possible, for the benefit of both parties. An irate client, "especially if he is talkative," can ruin a lawyer's reputation, particularly if he is new to the bar. A defendant-attorney, conversely, is almost certain to refuse settlement once a suit is filed and he feels the sting of bad publicity.

If a case does manage to slip through to trial, Hutcheson and Monroe urge that the defense keep laymen out of the proceedings, and for very pragmatic reasons: "Too frequently one or more of the jurors will have had an experience that has preju-

*Monroe, a former judge of California Superior Court, is now deceased.

diced him against lawyers. Proof that the defendant was unsuccessful in his representation of the plaintiff client might well be sufficient to convince such jurors of the defendant's negligence." Further, *American Jury Trials* would prefer that a judge decide any "close question of fact as to whether the attorney's conduct was reasonably proper and whether he used reasonable skill and diligence."[13]

Until the recent revolution in legal malpractice law, even if an upset client managed to breach the conspiracy of silence, he found equally formidable roadblocks between him and justice. Courts generally applied the same statute of limitations to legal malpractice as they did to any contracts case, meaning one to four years, depending upon the state. Further, if a lawyer's negligence injured a person other than his client, the courts refused to hold him liable, under the doctrine known as "privity of contract." These are intricate points, but important ones. A person who buys a house normally has no reason to inspect his title until he is ready to sell, years after the purchase date. Consider a hypothetical situation. Lawyer A handles the sale of B's house to C in 1961, providing, among other documents, a certificate asserting that the title to the house is clear. A decade later, C wants to sell the house to D. Another lawyer checks the title and finds that an old creditor of B still holds a valid lien on the house, one overlooked by lawyer A during the first sale. If the sale is to be consummated, C must clear the title by paying off the note. C has no legal recourse against the original lawyer for two reasons: the statute of limitations has lapsed long before his discovery of the error, and he and the lawyer had no direct contractual relationship.

Another factor that protected erring lawyers from the courts was the bar's insistence that it policed itself and that self-discipline corrected any mistakes made within the profession. The prevalent notion for decades was that malpractice problems "should be resolved administratively by the bar, leaving only the most flagrant cases to the courts." What a fallacy! By any objective measure, including that made by the bar itself, attorney discipline is a farce—"a scandalous situation," in the words of a study committee commissioned by the American Bar Association and chaired by no less a legal establishmentarian than Tom C. Clark, the former Supreme Court justice. The report of the Clark Committee,* issued in 1970, found that lawyers' attitudes toward discipline ranged from "apathy to outright hostility." It cited enough sins by lawyers to discourage anyone who read the report from *ever* crossing the threshold of a law office. It listed a congeries of disgraces found almost everywhere it looked around the country. Disbarred attorneys moving to other states and hanging out a new shingle.** Bar groups refusing to move against members convicted of bribery, income tax evasion, theft of clients' funds and other crimes. Failure of lawyers to report ethical and criminal wrongdoing by other attorneys. Prominent firms and individuals with a *de facto* immunity from discipline, especially in smaller towns where they dominated the local bar association. Indeed, one wonders after skimming the Clark Committee's report whether any problem should be entrusted to a lawyer, for the tales of wrongdoing are numerous, and they are varied. The committee quoted an officer of a state bar association disciplinary group:

> In my own town, I learned quite by accident in a restaurant that about six weeks ago a lawyer was removed as executor of an estate because it had been found by the probate court that he had come up short and that he had misused funds, that he even compromised claims by the estate against other clients of his, at prices that were unfair to the estate. Various other allegations of wrongdoing were found to be warranted and on the basis of these findings he was removed. No report of this was made to the local grievance committe. No report was made to the state bar association . . . although there were no less than six lawyers involved in that case who represented various heirs, at whose insistence this other lawyer was removed as executor. Nobody reported it. Why?
>
> [In another instance] another member of the disciplinary agency . . . ran across a case just a couple of weeks ago where a lawyer had embezzled funds from no less than five different clients over a period of time, and one lawyer knew all about it but didn't say a word and sat on the information for a matter of years.

*Formally, the American Bar Association Special Committee on Evaluation of Disciplinary Enforcement.

**This particular dodge, while still possible, is now difficult. The ABA office in Chicago maintains a computerized listing of all disciplinary actions, and state bars are supposed to check names against it before admitting applicants to practice. So far as the ABA knows, no disbarred lawyer has slipped past the screen.

According to this bar officer, even judges rarely acted when they learned of lawyer misconduct. Contempt-of-court proceedings usually "involve such things as impertinence to the court. They ordinarily do not involve things that we consider breach of duty to a client."

The committee quoted another bar ethics committee official as saying, "A good and decent profession has a headache that cries out for fast relief. We have been put on notice repeatedly. We will compound our own cure or someone will mix up a dose which will curl our hair."

The man understated. The substitute for self-discipline—legal malpractice suits—is not curling the bar's hair, it is causing the hair to drop out by the handful. And the moving forces, notably in California, are lawyers who are willing to take other attorneys to court in malpractice cases, and judges who no longer permit the legal profession to hide behind self-constructed shields.

The most important malpractice attorney in the country, in terms of persuading the courts to write ground rules that give the layman a chance of winning a case against a lawyer, is Edward Freidberg.[14] A fortyish Californian who in relaxed moments has the flip demeanor of a seashore condominium salesman, Freidberg goes after erring professionals with ferret intensity, be they physician or attorney. Freidberg first gained national note for his pursuit of Dr. John G. Nork, a Sacramento surgeon with a somewhat shaky scalpel who cowed (and sometimes charmed) his patients into unnecessary high-risk back surgery. Nork worked with all the finesse of a palsied butcher, and he maimed dozens of persons during the 1960s.

But he was a gregarious fellow popular with patients and fellow physicians alike, and the latter tended to overlook the occasional little mistakes—such as accidentally breaking a woman's spinal column while trying to repair a defective disk, or yanking nerve fibers from another woman's neck.

Behind Nork's confident façade, however, was a harried man who gulped amphetamines before donning his surgical jacket (as much as eight times the prescribed daily dosage) and who did the unnecessary cutting because he was strapped for money.

The first time Freidberg tried to sue Nork for malpractice, in 1963, a reviewing physician looked at the records and said,

"There's no case, Ed, leave him alone." Six years later Freidberg learned the reviewing physician was a close friend and sometime associate of Nork. He was not as careless again. When other Nork cases surfaced, Freidberg searched until he found more than three dozen persons maimed by the surgeon. To prep for the trial Freidberg put on a surgeon's robes himself and, with the guidance of a physician, personally performed a laminectomy* on a cadaver one night in the morgue of an out-of-town hospital. Freidberg's massive evidence so appalled the trial judge, B. Abbott Goldberg, of California Superior Court, that he called Nork "an ogre, a monster feeding on human flesh . . . [who] for nine years made a practice of performing unnecessary surgery, and performing it badly, simply to line his pockets." He awarded Freidberg's client a record $3.7 million, $500,000 of it against the hospital where Nork practiced, the remainder against the physician. By late 1976 Freidberg had socked Nork (or, more specifically, Nork's insurance carriers) for some $13 million in judgments, with another $8 million of claims still to be heard in court.

Nork's performance spoke for itself. So, too, did that of physicians who saw his mistakes and said nothing. "Apparently butchery is commonplace enough that it doesn't bother other doctors," Freidberg said. But Freidberg is no hypocrite: during his own fifteen years of practice he has seen equal incompetence—and coverups—by fellow lawyers. "If you gave me dictatorial powers here in Sacramento, I'd cut off 10 to 15 percent of the lawyers tomorrow on grounds of incompetence. And these are just the ones I know. I'm constantly amazed at the shoddy practices."

Freidberg's first lawyer target was a big one—none other than the president of the Sacramento Valley Bar Association, Jerome R. Lewis. Socially prominent, if somewhat stuffy, Lewis handled most of the upper-crust divorces in Sacramento and had a thriving general practice. He was popular with other lawyers as well. But in 1969 a woman sat in Freidberg's office and told him an incredible story about Lewis' conduct.

In January 1967 Clarence D. Smith retired from the California National Guard with the rank of general, after twenty-one years

*The surgical procedure for repairing a faulty spinal disk; the bulk of the malpractice claims against Nork stemmed from this type of operation.

of service as full-time administrator and staff officer. A month later his wife of twenty-four years decided to sue for divorce, and she hired Lewis to represent her. The couple had few assets: $1,800 equity in a house, some furniture, shares of stock worth $2,800, and two automobiles on which money was owed. During the discussion, however, Mrs. Smith raised a question with Lewis. Her husband was to receive $796 monthly in state retirement; seventeen years later, when he reached age sixty, he would be eligible for an additional federal pension based upon his participation in the reserve program. Could not these benefits be considered community property, and could she not share in them?

No, no, counseled Lewis, those belonged to the general alone. A preliminary decree listed only the physical assets as community property, and the court awarded Mrs. Smith $400 monthly in alimony and child support. The decree became final in February 1968.

Women talk about divorce settlements, and the clucking tongues in Mrs. Smith's circle told her, in effect, "Dearie, you received some bad advice. Now my ex-husband draws such and such dollars in retirement, and when I got *my* divorce, the judge said it was community property, and therefore I get. . . ."

She told her problem to another lawyer one evening at a cocktail party, and he said, "You are absolutely right." This conversation sent Mrs. Smith steaming back to Lewis. "Hey," she said, "I told you so about this community property thing, why didn't you listen?" Threatened with a suit, Lewis did some more research and agreed she might have a point.

In July 1968, five months after the Smiths' divorce became final, Lewis asked the court to amend its decree and award her more money, saying that because of his "mistake, inadvertence and excusable neglect" he did not list the retirement benefits among the Smiths' community property.* The divorce judge dismissed the appeal as untimely.

*The California Supreme Court held later that these words, "although manifestly a confession of error," should not be held against Lewis, for they were legal boilerplate made only to request the amended judgment. "In short, an attorney should be able to admit a mistake without subjecting himself to a malpractice suit," the court said. But evidence in the case other than Lewis' admission supported a malpractice finding, the court held.

Mrs. Smith began making the rounds of Sacramento law offices, trying to find someone to sue Lewis for his negligence. Several attorneys seemed sympathetic and suggested she indeed had a case. But sue Lewis? Take the president of the bar association to court? "Look, lady, I have to live in this town . . ."

Mrs. Smith finally found her way to Freidberg's office. The thought of suing a bar bigwig gave no pause whatsoever to Freidberg, a relative outsider—born in San Francisco, he had come to Sacramento only eight years previously, after graduating from Boalt Hall Law School. "As a lawyer," Freidberg told me, "I take cases as they walk in the door. Whether I accept a case is not determined by the profession of the defendant. If he happens to be a lawyer, this makes no difference to me."

Although Freidberg does little domestic relations work, a few minutes' research in the major legal reference works convinced him that Lewis had goofed. The California courts had consistently held that state retirement benefits, when partially financed by an employee contribution, were community property. The *California Family Lawyer*, which domestic relations attorneys read about as closely as brokers do the stock market reports, had said flatly as far back as 1962, "Of increasing importance is the fact that pension or retirement benefits are community property, even though they are not paid or payable until after termination of the marriage by death or divorce." There *was* a question about federal pensions; however the $796 that General Smith already received came directly from the state of California, and his federal stipend was not to begin until 1983.

But could Freidberg find concrete proof that Lewis knew the law? He dispatched a research clerk to files of the local legal newspaper, which publishes a listing of all cases filed and the names of the lawyers involved. The clerk picked out Lewis' divorce cases over the past ten years, and then went through court records. The results warranted the work, for the clerk found numerous cases in which Lewis had listed military retirement benefits as community property. Lewis had done so in 1965 for a National Guard reservist's wife. He had done so in 1967 for the husband in a divorce action. And he had done so for an Army colonel. But Freidberg found an astounding anomaly amidst these cases. In a 1965 divorce action Lewis had apparently insisted to a wife that she had no community interest in a pension. She had argued to the contrary and finally written the state retirement system, posing the question directly, and brought Lewis letters stating that she indeed had an interest in the pension benefits. Nonetheless Lewis had continued to insist the benefits were not community property and the woman had finally acquiesced.

Freidberg states, "This sort of research can be done in lawyer malpractice cases because much of what they do is a matter of public record. The raw material is there if you want to spend the time and the money to dig it out.* Doing such an extensive cross-check on physicians is impossible, of course, because of the confidentiality of their records."

According to Freidberg, Lewis took the suit lightly. "He thought it was harassment. He never really prepared a defense at the trial level. I devastated him during deposition. He seemed to have no idea of what the law was concerning community property, even though he specialized in family law. He made wrong statements. The fact is, he never believed he could lose the case, because he was a lawyer, and he was prominent. He never talked settlement, and he never prepared."

Freidberg prepared his case not once, but twice. Originally, several Sacramento lawyers had agreed to testify that Lewis had committed malpractice. Just before the trial, however, they called Freidberg with varying, embarrassed excuses as to why it would be impossible for them to appear. So Freidberg hurriedly recruited lawyer witnesses from San Francisco.

The trial lasted twelve days, and the jury deliberated only thirty minutes before sending word to the judge it had reached a verdict. As the jurors filed into the courtroom one of Lewis' lawyers beamed at Freidberg: "We won; how could they have reached both liability and damages in half an hour?"

The verdict: $100,000 for Mrs. Smith.

And Freidberg wasn't surprised at all. "A lawyer doesn't stand much of a chance in a malpractice case if you make inferences against his competence or integrity. Jurors do not identify with lawyers."

*Freidberg does not hesitate to invest money in a case that he senses will be a winner. To prepare for the key malpractice case against Dr. Nork, he spent $175,000 in research and staff work.

On appeal Lewis argued that the community property laws are so tangled that even well-informed lawyers can differ on their interpretation.* Under California law, he maintained, an attorney cannot be held liable for error in such a situation.

The California Supreme Court roundly disagreed, in a five-to-one decision written by Justice Stanley Mosk. Had Lewis "conducted minimal research into either hornbook or case law, he would have discovered with modest effort" that General Smith's state retirement benefits were likely to be treated as community property. The court cited many of its own opinions to this effect, as well as standard legal reference works. And the court listed four specific criteria by which a lawyer's professional performance should be judged:

—He is expected to "possess knowledge of those plain and elementary principles of law which are commonly known by well-informed attorneys."

—If there are gaps in his knowledge, he must "discover those additional rules of law which, although not commonly known, may readily be found by standard research techniques."

—Even if the law in a specific area is unsettled, the lawyer is obligated to "undertake reasonable research in an effort to ascertain relevant legal principles."

—Once this is done, the lawyer must "make an informed decision as to a course of conduct based upon an intelligent assessment of the problem."

Justice Mosk's opinion asserted that Lewis flunked all four points. Rather than doing his necessary book work, Mosk wrote, Lewis "rendered erroneous advice contrary to the best interests of his client without the guidance through research of readily available authority."

Freidberg's victory over Lewis did not make him a popular figure with California lawyers, each of whom realized, "Now it's easier for *me* to be sued, and lose!" Nor did his snappy re-

*Lewis' lawyers in the action were the Sacramento firm of Bullen, McKone & McKinley, through George W. Bullen; and attorneys Robert A. Seligson of San Francisco and Stephen J. Gray of Sacramento.

marks to press interviewers who came around after his landmark case. "I'm really anxious to start going after lawyers," he told *Juris Doctor*, a legal publication. "Lawyers," he told Roger Rapoport of *New Times*, "are worse than doctors." Speaking at a cocktail party of the San Francisco Trial Lawyers Association, he said, "You've got to clean up your act or expect to get sued." Journalist Robert Kroll wrote that the audience responded with "catcalls, cursings and cowardly insults." (Kroll also noted that some of the hostility seemed motivated by Freidberg's "slightly too serious" attitude and a "great deal of professional jealousy" at his fees in the Nork cases, which trade talk put at $3 to $4 million.) And someone grumbled to *Time* that Freidberg was "just a wise guy looking for trouble."

All of which, of course, serves solely to whet Freidberg's appetite for battle. "I'm not a bar politician," he told me. "I don't care what other lawyers think about me. In fact, if I was too popular, I wouldn't be doing my job properly." So Freidberg ignores the cold stares and the snooty remarks: his aim, when I talked with him in early 1977, was to push the boundaries of professional malpractice even further, by making attorneys liable for punitive damages in instances where they harm a client through deliberate action, rather than negligence.

The first such case, appropriately, came against his old adversary Jerome Lewis.[15] The client in this instance was a Greek-American woman, Mrs. Lili Kromidellis, who was the chief beneficiary of her uncle's estate. She hired Lewis as her lawyer. Somehow Lewis also ended up representing the executors of the estate, and a special administrator. The dual representation did not come to Mrs. Kromidellis' attention until Lewis had persuaded her to settle the estate on terms which she decided were grossly unfavorable. In essence (this is complicated) she lost 45 percent of the estate to the uncle's disinherited son and to a woman who once lived with the uncle and cared for him. She fired Lewis, and when he threatened to sue for payment of his bill, another lawyer referred her to Freidberg, who after reading the file gleefully took the case. He wrote Lewis a letter saying, in effect, "What you have done is improper." Whereupon Lewis replied, "Go to hell." Freidberg said, "This was right after the Smith case, when I had beaten Lewis in court, and he was feeling rather feisty. So he sued my client—his former client—for a

$3,000 fee. I crossed-claimed for fraud, and we won $25,000 in compensatory damages and $35,000 in punitive damages. Brother Lewis was not happy."

As a private attorney Ed Freidberg does not come equipped with white horse and lance. Unless he is granted membership on a bar ethics committee or is a firsthand witness to legal chicanery, an individual lawyer cannot pin on a policeman's badge and patrol the behavior of his colleagues. But malpractice suits, when they bring recompense for punitive as well as actual damages, bear the sting of punishment. In another case, this one outside Sacramento, a lawyer kept a client's money after a divorce settlement. The amount involved was relatively small and when Freidberg wrote the lawyer a stiff letter on the woman's behalf he paid it over promptly. "In actual damages, we suffered only $32 loss, the amount of interest for the time he illegally held her money." But Freidberg sued anyway, asking for punitive damages. "I am convinced that had not the woman hired another lawyer, the guy would still be sitting on her money. Lawyers shouldn't do such things."

The case wasn't easy, even after Freidberg got it to court. For one thing, the judge (Freidberg discovered belatedly) was a former law partner of some of the attorneys involved, and they still owed him $25,000 for his share of the partnership. Further, the judge's wife, under her maiden name, had a role in the case, another relationship of which Freidberg was unaware. "I didn't find out these things until pretty far along, and I was pretty sore. The judge was doing some odd things for the defense without giving me any say. For instance, he would set a hearing, and then cancel it the night before, without giving me any notice or reasons. I demanded that he get out of the case. He refused." Freidberg won anyway, the jury giving him punitive damages of $32,000.*

What galls Freidberg is that regardless of the malpractice—even in instances involving possible criminal activity—the California State Bar is laggard in going after erring lawyers. "The state bar is good when it comes to drunks, pillheads, the easy

*The defense later moved for a reduction, arguing there was a "remarkable disparity" between the actual and punitive damages. The judge was ready to agree and reduce the award to $16,000, when Freidberg quietly pointed out that the statutory period for asking reconsideration had passed before the defense had moved for a reduction. "They paid off; there was no appeal," Freidberg said.

cases. They don't have the time nor the money to get into more sophisticated things."

But Freidberg does have a long-range confidence. Tort litigation eventually had a salutary effect on manufacturers and physicians, if only to kick their insurance rates to a level where they either took greater care or lost coverage. "When the insurance companies cut out the bad apples, they stopped practicing." Also, tort litigation alerts enforcement agencies to derelictions within a given profession—although, as Freidberg tartly notes, "A man can be convicted of converting a client's funds, and still remain a lawyer, provided he is prominent enough in the bar."

As we talked Freidberg spewed out yarn after yarn of lawyer derelictions—including even a case where a woman client offered her own attorney $2,000 under the table if he would quit his stalling and finish her case. Then Freidberg surprised me.

"I've been guilty of malpractice myself," he volunteered.

Oh? Tell me more.

"Sure. There have been situations where I missed filing pleadings on time or let a statutory period lapse. The only way to handle it, in my opinion, is to admit error to the client and to your insurance carrier.

"In one of these cases, fortunately, the other side had screwed up as well, and I saved the case, which was lousy to begin with. But I sent the client to another lawyer, so she would be fully advised of her rights, and I paid her out of my own pocket. The way I see it, any lawyer can make an honest mistake. What's worst is the lawyer who makes a mistake, and hides it, and lies to the client. This sort of lawyer, my friend, does not command any sympathy from Edward Freidberg."

But the evasive lawyer, for years, did command the sympathy of the courts, which gave him privileges not afforded other professionals. But the special protections are falling, lawyer anger notwithstanding. In another of its landmark decisions, this one handed down in 1971, the California Supreme Court drastically revised the statute of limitations as it pertains to legal malpractice. As the court noted, "An immunity from the statute of limitations for practitioners at the bar not enjoyed by other professions is itself suspicious, but when conferred by former practitioners who now sit upon the bench, it is doubly suspicious."[16]

The case involved a wrongful death action against San Bernardino County, California, by the family of a man named Neel. The family retained a lawyer named Delaney to press the claim. Without informing the family, Delaney in turn brought in the Los Angeles personal injury firm of Magana, Olney, Levy, Cathcart & Gelfand. Suit was filed in May 1962. But none of the lawyers ever got around to serving a summons on any county officials, and three years later, in December 1965, the court dismissed the case.*

But Delaney said nothing to the family, who during 1966 and 1967 thought the suit was still pending. When someone would call to check its progress, Delaney answered with double-talk. During depositions he admitted he was "dodging" having to explain how his negligence had caused the suit to be dismissed. Finally, the family went to another lawyer, who in December 1967 found the truth: the suit was no more.

Robert S. Scuderi, of the Los Angeles firm of Wagner & Scuderi, sued both Delaney and the Magana firm for the Neel family. Both defendants tried to hide behind the statute of limitations. Any error for which they could be sued, they maintained, occurred on May 25, 1965, the last day on which they could have served summonses in the original action, and the two-year statute began running as of that date. Hence by December 1967 they were months beyond the reach of any malpractice suit. Judge Robert W. Kenny, who heard the case in Superior Court, agreed and ruled for the lawyers, saying he was bound by past decisions of the Supreme Court.

But just how definitive were these past decisions on limitations? Justice Matthew Tobriner, one of the more brilliant state jurists in the nation, delved into the judicial history of the statute of limitations pertaining to legal malpractice and came upon a most peculiar situation. The lead case, *Hays* v. *Ewing*, decided in 1886, involved a lawyer's negligence in pressing a collection

*After a 1961 court ruling against a public hospital, the California legislature temporarily suspended actions against public entities. Delaney and the Magana firm suggested they thought this act prevented them from issuing a summons to the county-defendant, despite a 1962 decision to the contrary by the court.

suit. The question was whether the statute should begin running at the time the lawyer erred, or when the court dismissed the suit, or when a higher court affirmed the dismissal. The state supreme court accepted the middle date—that is, the time when the client actually realized he had been damaged. But when the opinion was published by the West Publishing Company, the quasi-official reporting service that compiles judicial decisions throughout the country, it had acquired a headnote summarizing the holding as follows: "A cause of action against an attorney for neglect of duty in the management of an action is barred at the expiration of two years after the neglect occurred."

Almost a century later Justice Tobriner read the headnote and the text of the opinion, and as he later wrote:

> We search[ed] in vain within the body of the opinion or within the facts of the case for any justification for this publisher's note.
>
> Yet this unwarranted headnote generated the peculiar rule that only in legal malpractice cases does the statute of limitations begin to run before damage and before discovery.

The California courts continued what Tobriner called a "doleful reiteration" of the rule that never was for decades. Other professionals, however, did not enjoy sanctity. A tougher rule, holding that the statute did not commence running until a client *discovered* he had been damaged, was applied, at various times, to an accountant, a stockbroker, a title company, an escrow holder and an insurance agent. "In each of these cases," Tobriner noted, "the defendant had argued that the rule of the legal malpractice cases should apply to bar the action, and in each case the courts rejected that plea." Lawyers take care of their own—a favoritism for which Tobriner could find no justification. Hence he led the California Supreme Court full circle on the issue, in an opinion that stressed the "special relationship" between the professional person and the client:

> . . . [T]he special obligation of the professional is exemplified by his duty not merely to perform his work with ordinary care but to use the skill, prudence, and diligence commonly exercised by practitioners of his profession. If he further specialized within the profession, he must meet the standards of knowledge and skill of such specialists.

Corollary to this expertise is the inability of the layman to detect its misapplication; the client may not recognize the negligence of the professional when he sees it. He cannot be expected to know the relative medical merits of alternative anesthetics, nor the various legal exceptions to the hearsay rule. If he must ascertain malpractice at the moment of its incidence, the client must hire a second professional to observe the work of the first, an expensive and impractical duplication, clearly destructive of the confidential relationship between the practitioner and his client.

In the second place, not only may the client fail to recognize negligence when he sees it, but often he will lack any opportunity to see it. The doctor operates on an unconscious patient; although the attorney, the accountant and the stockbroker serve the conscious client, much of their work must be performed out of the client's view.

In the legal field, the injury may lie concealed within the obtuse terminology of a will or contract; in the medical field the injury may lie hidden within the patient's body; in the accounting field, the injury may lie buried in the figures of the ledger.

Tobriner recognized that the ruling would "impose an increased burden upon the legal profession," for an attorney's error might not be discovered for years, "and the extension of liability into the future poses a disturbing prospect." But when a lawyer cites the statute of limitations to stop a client from suing, he wrote, "the resulting ban of the action not only starkly works an injustice upon the client but partially impugns the very integrity of the legal profession." He concluded:

Today . . . is no time to perpetuate an anachronistic interpretation of the statute of limitations that permits the attorney to escape obligations which other professionals must bear.

The legal calling can ill afford the preservation of a privileged protection against responsibility, a privilege born of error, subject to almost universal condemnation, and, in present-day society, anomalous.

Court Recess Six

The secretary had come in half an hour earlier and asked, "Is that all? I think I'll be moving on now." The lawyer waved her a farewell, and a bit later his partner appeared in the doorway and they spoke in monosyllabic grunts about someone they would be seeing the next morning. My host loosened his tie and threw his coat on the couch, and he went into the storeroom in search of a piece of paper he wanted to show me that would illustrate a point. He returned with the paper and two cold cans of Budweiser, and we popped the tops, and he sank into his chair with some body language that I had come to recognize during months of lawyer interviewing. The formal stuff was over. He had told me some case histories about his representation of athletes, being modest enough to avoid entanglement with bar strictures on self-praise, and hinting all the while that some *real* stories existed that he'd like to tell me. Okay, the promise was made: no attribution, no names.

"Any relation 'sports law' has to the rest of law is coincidental. Start with the clients, the basic thing. Kids don't understand the difference between an agent and a lawyer, and they're out for the bigger buck, and the sharpies are always there to help them along.

"It's fundamental in law that you cannot solicit business. Well, in this particular phase of 'law,' the solicitation is fantastic. You do it, or you don't survive—which is one reason I'm getting out of it. It's rotten.

"Take the coach at one of these small schools that turn out guys good enough to make the pros on a regular basis. The place is isolated, and the kids are probably a little bit ignorant and frightened at being away from home. The coach is all things to them—father, big brother, banker, friend. The kid needs money to take his girl friend to a movie or to send his momma a present, the coach drops it on him. He even lets the kid use his car. It's inevitable that he develops a special relationship with the athlete.

"So this kid is in the seven-foot range, and he can make a basketball do anything he wants it to, and he is going to go pro for six figures his first year, provided he plays it right. The sports lawyers, the active ones, they run as effective a scouting system as any pro teams. And the coach knows that if he helps the right lawyer, the chicken feed he's spent on the star can be exchanged for a many-thousand-dollar fee.

"The coach is vulnerable. His jerkwater state college pays him $15,000, maybe $20,000 at the most. So he winds up driving a pretty new car that sells for what he makes in a year. Did the lawyer pay him off? Who can prove it?*

"Some lawyers, I'll admit, find more subtle ways to get around the ethical canons." He named a prominent sports attorney from the East who seems to know quite a few basketball players and who "won't solicit directly himself; he hires a nonlawyer to act as a runner and do his legwork. He's the guy who visits the campuses and hangs around the dressing rooms at the big tournaments and makes the pitches at the stars. 'Hey, come on, sign with my guy, ———, we'll make some money for you.'"

I suggested that if a personal injury lawyer used such techniques, the bar association would pounce upon him with cries of "ambulance-chaser" and drive him from the profession.

"Nobody polices this area [sports] because so few people are

*Section 6(e) of the constitution of the National Collegiate Athletic Association reads as follows: "Staff members of the athletic department of a member institution shall not represent, directly or indirectly, a student-athlete in the marketing of his athletic ability or reputation to a professional sports team or professional sports organization, and shall not receive compensation or gratuities of any kind, directly or indirectly, for such services." This rule has been in effect since January 8, 1975. "So what?" my lawyer friend asked after reading the rule to me. "The Ten Commandments date back a bit longer, and they have about as much validity when one of these coaches smells a fast buck."

involved in it. What do the big establishment bar guys care about a few basketball players?

"I once had a line on a football player at Penn State. A mutual friend suggested I talk with him, and he told the player I was coming. The player was noncommittal, but said, come ahead. I did it by the book. I talked with Joe Paterno, the coach, and got permission to see the kid once the season ended—the NCAA says if a player signs with an agent or lawyer before his season is over, he is ineligible to play anymore. Well, I got to State College [Pennsylvania] the middle of January, a few days after the Penn State season ended, and this kid and everyone else had already made up their minds. And from what I heard, they'd done so long, long before the season ended.

"Players can be a pain in the ass to represent. They are of questionable maturity. They're a pampered class. They are used to having their asses kissed. They are put on a pedestal in Little League and from then on they're told how great they are. So when they hit the pros they are at their peak, and they smell money. They see O. J. Simpson selling American Express on TV, and Joe Namath wearing panty hose, and they say, 'Hey, man, get me some of that.' The unscrupulous agents and lawyers—the sharks—they'll make the promises. They never say that for every O. J. Simpson there are a thousand jocks who never see a dime for commercial endorsements.

"The bad lawyer gets the kid a contract, takes his fee from the front money and cuts him loose. Say the kid gets a $400,000 long-term contract, which isn't unusual for a star in pro basketball. He is to pay the lawyer 10 percent. There is $50,000 front money as a cash bonus, the rest is to be paid out over four years. The lawyer takes his $40,000 cut out of the $50,000, and maybe he isn't careful to insure that the contract guarantees compensation even if the kid is hurt in his first season and can't play anymore. Well, in one instance I know about this actually happened—all the kid ever saw was about $50,000, and the lawyer took between $35,000 and $40,000 as a one-time fee. It's legal, I suppose, but it's damned well unconscionable, I don't care what the contract said.

"Another type of agent-lawyer can be just as harmful in the long range. These are the guys who provide 'full service representation.' They receive the athlete's checks; they pay his bills;

they invest for him; they do his taxes, they send him a nice monthly printout showing what came in and where it went. So what does it cost? Up to 15 or 25 percent of the athlete's net income, which is a hell of a lot for paying somebody's Exxon charge bill and mailing him an allowance check every month.

"I have a different philosophy. I give the athlete only as much guidance as he really needs, and I tell him at the start, 'Start preparing to leave pro athletics the day you enter.' Most of these guys enter the real world at age thirty, when they retire or are cut. Think of the reentry problems! Few have any salable skill other than a sport. Oh, while they are active they might stand around a car agency or a pizza place for promotion, but people forget in a hurry when you are a has-been and somebody else is wearing your old number.

"I think it's ridiculous for a twenty-one-year-old kid to have thirteen phones in a three-room apartment or to ride around town in a Rolls-Royce. I tell him at an early stage that he's got to stand on his own two feet. Maybe that's why I don't get any more clients than I do."

Chapter Seven

Discovery: "A Painful Alternative to Torture"

The senior partner drank too much, especially late at night, during the strains of a trial, and it fell the lot of the associate, a younger lawyer, to sit and listen to his stories and to fill his glass every half hour ("Easy on that water, boy, we don't want to mess up good scotch, do we?") and eventually to guide him gently toward the bed, loosen his belt, remove his shoes, pull the blanket over his neck, and turn out the light and lock the door.

The senior partner, to his credit, did his work before assaulting the scotch bottle. He specialized in personal injury defense, working for the insurance titans who are happy to collect premiums from the citizenry but who resist giving back any of the money when a policyholder injures someone or is hurt himself; after all, as the senior partner once said in a hotel room in central Kansas, "Boy, we've got an obligation to the shareholders and the directors; some people think an insurance company is a big ol' welfare tit that they can suck on all they want. Well, it ain't!"

So the senior partner would go over the day's testimony with the associate, and perhaps interview the next day's witnesses, and ponder what the Other Side—usually "those damned Jew-boy-lawyers from St. Louis" or their generic equivalent—might be plotting. Then he would delve into his suitcase for a bottle of Dewar's White Label, and the associate knew it was time to fetch ice cubes and settle back and listen to stories.

The senior partner fancied himself a teacher; each anecdote, however bawdy its core, however biting toward a judge or a fellow lawyer, however cynical its depiction of the legal system, supposedly carried a lesson. Some of the stratagems seemed legitimate enough given the rough-and-tumble realities of personal injury law. Suppose the plaintiff imported an out-of-state expert witness (because no local physician would testify in a medical malpractice suit). "You rear back and you ask him, 'Well, Dr. Klein, you get around the country quite a bit don't you, testifying as much as you do for these plaintiff lawyers?' The other side, they'll holler and object, but you've put the mark on him—he is a *pro-fesh-on-al* witness, and you say it just like that, loud and slow, when you get to your closing argument." The senior partner would snort, as if enjoying a private, pleasing memory about the rout of *some damned Dr. Klein* and wave his glass for a refill.

One anecdote especially remained with the associate. When he told it to me he did not try to recreate the senior partner's distinctive dialect, but the story ran roughly as follows:

A Midwestern company, manufacturer of a widely used farm implement, brought a new model onto the market. Within weeks the company realized it had created a monster. Because of a design defect the machine was ripping off fingers and arms all through the farm belt. The company immediately alerted its insurance carrier to expect lawsuits. The insurance company, in turn, ran to the senior partner's law firm and said, "We stand to lose many hundreds of thousands of dollars; what can you do?"

The senior partner (or so he told the associate) went to the manufacturer's home office and reviewed engineering data on the implement. Two of the tests, when subjected to hindsight, foretold the very problem that was maiming farmhands in seven states. These will never do, the senior partner said. Are any other copies around? He and an executive rummaged through files all one weekend and satisfied themselves they had all copies.

Then the senior partner called in the director of testing, a man only six years shy of retirement. How horrible it would be, the senior partner said, if these lawsuits drove your company into bankruptcy and you were unable to collect your pension. They talked about the avaricious city lawyers who soon would be descending upon the company and demanding private documents. Now, would you like an outsider to read the personal letters you might send your wife from time to time, or listen to the private conversations you have? The city lawyers, he said, would be demanding that he betray his employer. Did not decency demand that he remain silent? Can you really remember everything you have done the last five years, testing this new machine? Aren't you proud of it? Would you like to get on the stand and admit that you made a mistake? And that pension—I realize you are an older fella and that you probably couldn't land anywhere else if this company happened to go bust. . . .

The associate remembers the senior partner's summation: "I caught that scared old pecker on three counts: fear of losing his money, fear of being called a fool, fear of going against his very own. When these hotshot lawyers got around to discovery they couldn't find paper-one on the machine, and the testing man played so damned dumb that they thought he was senile and gave up. Course now, we paid out some money—fair amounts, I assure you—but if I hadn't done that little bit of groundwork it would have been maybe ten times worse.

"You remember this, boy: Discovery is only as good as what a lawyer leaves around to be discovered, and I don't see nuthin' in the law book that says you got to go out and find a piece of rope for somebody who wants to hang you."

This chapter is not nice reading, for it concerns instances in which a linchpin of capitalism, the auto industry, performed its own, more sophisticated versions of the legal sleight-of-hand so charmingly described by the drunken insurance lawyer. The younger lawyer—the associate—related the story to me during a moment of moral introspection as he tried to explain why he left the legal profession for the ministry. "In my new field," he said, "there is a distinct advantage. Mary Magdalene reformed. I wish I could say the same about some of my former colleagues."

Law, as practiced in America, is based upon root assumptions that lawyers often recite, but which they accept at their own risk. One of these assumptions is that the other side plays straight, that a lawyer's word should be accepted at face value. An example: Sheldon Miller, a very aggressive personal injury lawyer in Detroit, is cordially detested by insurance defense lawyers because he has nerves like . . . well, they were described in the Prologue when he refused a $153,000 settlement offer during trial and won a jury award of more than $1,000,000—the sort of gamble that ages men rapidly. In any event, during a conversation on legal gamesmanship, Miller told me, "Look, we knock one another's brains out in court, but we remain friends and we don't lie to one another. Suppose you have a hearing set, and the other guy wants an adjournment for a few days. He calls you rather than the judge, and you agree. He doesn't show in court. If you're dirty, you could move for a default judgment. A half-million-dollar default can ride on a lawyer's honor. So you play it straight. Similarly, you can enjoy a lunch with a defense lawyer and be the best of buddies. But put on your brass jockstrap when you go back to court, because he'll be trying to kick your balls off."

A rough situation. What is the dividing line between tough lawyering and legal roughnecking? Where does strategy end, and chicanery begin? As is true with so many of us, lawyers suffer from an incipient paranoia, a belief that the Other Side is stomping around in hobnailed boots. When I began asking for stories about unseemly courtroom tactics, my files rapidly filled with stories both amusing and horrible. (One laughs at the lawyer who sets his pocket alarm watch to disrupt his opponent's closing argument to the jury; the other attorney, presumably, does not find the episode so funny.)

But can isolated trivialities be considered indicative of the way lawyers do their everyday work? During less somber journalistic days I took advantage of misintroductions to pose, fleetingly, as such luminaries as Joe Dealey, publisher of the *Dallas Morning News* and Captain Joe Golden, chief of the homicide division of the Philadelphia police department.* Nonetheless I do not consider the transient, *ad hoc* disguises indicative of the way I normally go about my business.

Isolated incidents are one matter. An ongoing course of conduct is another. Which brings us again to the auto industry.

For purposes both of convenience and justice, the courts

*In the first guise I gave an outrageous interview to a Boston newspaperman. Conscience prevailed before he got it into print, and I telephoned him and revealed the truth. He was not amused. Unfamiliarity with the statute of limitations in the Pennsylvania criminal code suggests that I say nothing further about my tenure as a police captain.

over the past three decades have laid down rather specific rules for a legal process known as "discovery."*

As the U.S. Supreme Court said in the leading case defining discovery, "Mutual knowledge of all relevant facts gathered by both parties is essential to proper litigation. . . . [P]ublic policy supports reasonable and necessary inquiries. . . ."[2] In the practical sense, discovery means that both sides are entitled to know the factual underpinnings of the other party's case. If a plaintiff claims he is suffering from permanently disabling injuries, the defense can go into his medical records, interview his physician, even have its own doctor examine him. Conversely, the plaintiff's lawyer can inspect the manufacturing and test records of whatever equipment caused the injury, be it automobile, motorboat, or home exerciser. The aim of discovery is to eliminate the "sporting theory" of justice and to give litigants access to facts that opponents otherwise could hide away in their files.

Discovery is also a process acutely subject to abuse. A lawyer can flood his adversary with trivial questions or provide answers so evasive as to be nonsensical. Joseph L. Alioto, a leading antitrust lawyer in San Francisco (and a onetime mayor of that city), tells of an instance where defense lawyers evaded an order to file certain information in a central depository for study by all parties involved in a complex multistate suit. The judge demanded an explanation. "The excuse by one defendant was that other financial details from which the study might be reconstructed were in fact produced," Alioto said. "This would be tantamount to saying that an order to produce a copy of *Hamlet* could be satisfied by filing an unabridged dictionary with the court." Through any number of stratagems a lawyer can drag out the discovery process for such a long time that his opponent is driven into bankruptcy or gives up in disgust. In the tactful phraseology of *American Jury Trials*, a leading legal hornbook, discovery can be used for "harrying or harassing an adversary." But on a case-by-case basis, the worst abusers of discovery have been the auto manufacturers, and for a direct economic reason. If a certain type of vehicle is proved to be inherently defective,

*The English invented discovery while casting around for a substitute for torture for parties unwilling to reveal facts at issue in a lawsuit. Their idea was a good one; but the way it is carried out causes the litigants less torment only in the sense that their agony is mental, not physical.[1]

the manufacturer risks suits by scores of thousands of purchasers. Chief Judge William H. Becker, of the United States District Court in western Missouri, frustrated by Volkswagen legal tactics in a products liability case, dryly noted that auto companies defendant in such situations "have been unusually evasive and loath to make discovery."[3] Judge Becker, in fact, was so piqued with VW's lawyers that he used the judiciary's ultimate weapon against dilatory litigants: He entered a default judgment for the plaintiff on the issue of liability, leaving the jury only to compute the damages. But default judgments, because they are a courtroom version of a forfeit, in which one team is not permitted even to take the field, much less to defend itself, are rarely imposed. "The normal course of events," says an Atlanta lawyer who has tried dozens of auto liability cases, "is for the defense to stall until the judge is on the brink of apoplexy, and then to yield an inch. The judge often is so relieved at even that iota of progress that he takes off the pressure. So you go through the whole rigamarole again.

"Discovery against an auto company? I'd rather be marooned on a desert island with a 300-pound woman with bad breath.

"Which company is the worst? Friend, it doesn't make a damn. The 'worst' is whomever I happen to be trying against at the time you ask the question. Just look around you and read some of the cases. You'll find out for yourself."

That I did, over a period of some two years, and the episodes speak for themselves.

Volkswagen: "Not to my knowledge."

A foreign corporation doing business in America goes into a lawsuit with an U.S. citizen with several distinct advantages. Records and witnesses are thousands of miles away, meaning they are damnably expensive for the opposing lawyer to obtain. There is a language problem, one that not even the most skilled interpreter can overcome. "In cross-examination," says a New York attorney, "you learn to listen for nuances of phraseology, for areas of uncertainty. There's no way you can do a first-rate cross if you don't speak the other guy's language." A no-nonsense judge, however, can minimize language difficulties. In

1974 a Georgia woman sued Kawasaki Heavy Industries, Ltd., a Japanese manufacturer of a popular motorcycle, for damages allegedly resulting from a faulty design. Her lawyer, Alfred B. Adams, III, of the Atlanta firm of Greene, Buckley, DeRieux & Jones, requested Kawasaki to produce documents on the cycle's manufacturing specifications. The defense complied—with reams of papers written in Japanese. Adams complained, and Chief U.S. District Judge Newell Edenfield ordered Kawasaki to pay translation costs. Companies that do business in the United States, he said, should realize they occasionally will be sued, and that American courts, "by and large conduct their proceedings in English."[4]

The chief lawyer for the Volkswagen enterprises in the United States* is Ian Ceresney, of the New York firm of Herzfeld and Reubin.[5] Ceresney devotes 95 percent of his time to VW matters; at any given time he is directing the defense of some one hundred products liability and personal injury cases. The parent VW company, Volkswagenwerk, A.G., has empowered Ceresney and his firm to answer interrogatories and other legal queries in VW's name; in a legal sense, Ceresney and VW are indistinguishable. Indeed, Ceresney has even spoken in the first-person singular in responding to questions about VW.

In March 1976 Pittsburgh lawyer Henry H. Wallace was much disturbed by Ceresney's conduct. Wallace represented a client left in pitiable shape after a crash in a VW. John W. Wilson, a Pittsburgh native, served as an army Counterintelligence Corps agent in Germany, graduated from the University of Pittsburgh law school, and then joined the Interstate Commerce Commission in Washington as a staff attorney. A handsome, strapping bachelor of thirty years, Wilson was an archetypical physical fitness enthusiast. On March 30, 1973, he jogged several miles, swam eighteen laps in a Washington pool, and then set out for a drive south through Virginia in a 1972 VW borrowed from his brother's girl friend.

The car overturned on an interstate highway, and Wilson endured horrible agony when brought to Mary Washington Hospital in Richmond. Eleven of his ribs were broken and he could

*The German company is Volkswagenwerk, A.G.; U.S. operations are conducted through a wholly owned subsidiary, Volkswagen of America, Inc. Both will be referred to hereafter as "Volkswagen" or "VW."

breathe with only one lung. Emergency room attendants dared not give him anesthesia, but they had to drain his lungs of blood and other fluids. So Wilson lay groaning on an operating table while attendants hammered drainage tubes into both his sides. A bit later a neurologist confirmed the worst of suspicions. Wilson's spinal column had been severed, leaving him permanently paralyzed from the waist down—no feeling, no bladder control, no bowel control, no sexual function, no means of locomotion. A permanent catheter kept Wilson alive; it also caused a constant urinary infection and low-grade fever; as was stated by one acquaintance, "John feels bad most of the time."

An engineer who inspected the crash car said two of the four bolts used in the steering column loosened because of vibration, fell out, and caused the crash. Wallace sued VW for defective product design on two counts: the steering column and insufficient roof supports. As part of his discovery he demanded that VW produce any tests pertaining to these features, as well as a list of any lawsuits filed against VW alleging defective design of body structure. If Wallace could prove that VW knew that the steering and roof were defective—either through its own testing or through driver experience, as revealed by lawsuits—it would enhance his case considerably.

VW, however, resisted, saying that the request was "unduly burdensome" because "most, if not all, of the requested materials are in the German language, and are physically located in Germany." Wallace sensed great nervousness on VW's part. Several similar cases were pending elsewhere in the country, and VW apparently feared a precedent. At one point VW attorneys—although denying any admission of liability—offered to settle on condition that Wallace surrender the evidence he had amassed on design defect. "I wasn't about to do this," Wallace said. "Too many other lawyers had helped me, and they had clients at stake. Also, I had some information on VW that should go into the record. VW had screwed around too many people."

Still, Wallace worried. The U.S. district judge hearing the case, D. Dortch Warriner, was a conservative in Virginia's truest tradition. He had done corporate work before going on the bench, and plaintiff lawyers, rightly or wrongly, did not consider him their friend. And at early stages of the suit Warriner seemed sympathetic when VW lawyer Ceresney protested that satisfying Wallace's discovery requests would require "truckloads" of documents. At VW's insistence Warriner drastically narrowed the scope of Wallace's demands.

No help. VW continued to refuse Wallace the papers he wanted. "I would call for studies that VW engineers had referred to by name when writing articles for automotive technical journals, and VW would answer, 'They're not available,' or 'We don't know what you are talking about.'" One batch of documents produced were in German. Wallace paid for their translation; they proved totally irrelevant. VW produced eleven films of performance tests—seven of them of U.S. cars. Of the tests showing VWs, none was of a 1972 Beetle, the model in which Wilson had been injured.

Ceresney, on VW's behalf, argued that Wallace himself was responsible for much of the delay. As he pointed out in pleadings, Wallace's original suit did not even specify what defect in the VW caused the accident. When Ceresney filed motions asking Wallace to be more specific, he was ignored. Judge Warriner displayed his exasperation with the plaintiff, exclaiming at one point, "I don't see how defendants can be expected to have prepared a defense when the plaintiff had not even prepared an offense until last month." But this was virtually the last friendly statement VW was to hear from the judge.

"About 15 days before trial," Wallace said, "I saw myself getting into a bind. Judge Warriner had issued an order back in October 1975 specifying what VW must produce. Well, here it was March 15, 1976, and we were coming up fast on the trial date. Under the Virginia rules, discovery must be completed ten days before trial. VW had stalled right up to the deadline and it looked as though they were going to get away with it."

So Wallace wrote Ceresney demanding that he state, in writing, what VW intended to do. Ceresney replied the tests were "not available." Wallace took the letter to a pretrial conference with Judge Warriner, who became visibly angry when he read it. Warriner declared, in effect, "First they say they have 'truckloads' of papers, now they say they are 'not available.' What am I to believe?" He demanded that Ceresney appear five days hence to show cause why he and/or VW should not be held in contempt. And Warriner made plain that he was on the verge of declaring VW in default, telling Wallace that if his charges about VW's misconduct were substantiated, "you win the case. Do you understand that? You win the case."

Wallace understood. Immediately after leaving court he called his law partner, Russell J. Ober, Jr., and told him to search out other cases in which VW's abuse of discovery was a matter of record. "If Judge Warriner indeed was ready to rule VW in default, I wanted to give him any information that might help him toward that decision," Wallace said. "We wanted to show the conduct in our case was not isolated, but a strategy that the VW lawyers—Ceresney and others—used throughout the country.

"We knew that Bill Dobrovir in Washington had taken a default against VW. He gave us the file in his case and some leads on other cases. Byron Block, an engineer from Los Angeles, who has testified in a number of other VW cases, was also helpful. I ran up a phone bill of two thousand, maybe three thousand dollars in less than a week. In those five days we didn't even go to sleep. Lawyers were having boxes of papers air-freighted to us in Washington. Things were rather frantic. Ober got lost in traffic at one point and spent some frantic moments in a phone booth, persuading the Eastern Air Lines air freight office to stay open until he could pick up a shipment."

The last day, Wallace, Ober and a third partner, William P. Chapas, loaded hundreds of pounds of briefs and transcripts into a rented car and drove to Richmond. They worked on their brief until three o'clock of the morning they were due in court at nine, and they put together a damning indictment of VW legal tactics, through the words of three separate federal district judges:

—In Philadelphia, Chief Judge Joseph Lord held VW in default twice in a single case, saying, "It was like pulling teeth to get answers to interrogatories. . . . This client has been a reluctant moose from the very beginning . . . . As long as they continue to use the United States as a market and ergo subject themself to lawsuits, they had better solve these problems."[6]

—In Washington, in Dobrovir's case, Judge John H. Pratt first held VW in default, then reduced the penalty to a fine. He commented, "While for purposes of this memorandum it is not necessary to characterize said conduct as arrogant, contumacious or contemptuous, or the result of indifference, inadvertence or neglect, the record is clear that counsel for the defendants have done a disservice to plaintiffs, have prejudiced them in their rights, and have interfered with the prompt and orderly dispatch of the business of this court." Pratt also noted that the conduct "appears not to have been an isolated instance" but was found in other cases where VW was "represented by the same New York chief counsel."[7] Later, Judge Pratt withdrew the default judgments and reduced the penalty to a contempt fine against VW's local counsel; he specifically absolved Ceresney and his firm of any fault in the case.

—In Kansas City, Missouri, Chief Judge William H. Becker held VW in default for "willful and bad-faith refusal to comply with discovery," and declared, "This case is an example of the frustration of the judicial process that occurs when a defendant corporation refuses to give trial counsel the authority required by the local rules [of court] and attempts to handle matters through house counsel who are either not acquainted with the pretrial rules or not predisposed to obeying them. . . ."[8] In this instance, Ceresney said the failure resulted from a breakdown in communications with local counsel, who failed to advise his firm of a court order.

Put on the stand by Judge Warriner at the default hearing, lawyer Ceresney ran headlong into a rather basic obligation of American law—that is, an attorney who signs interrogatories for a corporation has a duty to furnish the sum total of the corporate information. Ceresney's testimony made plain that either VW chose not to give him the information required to answer Wallace's interrogatories; that he did not choose to ask for it for one reason or another; or that he simply did not divulge what he did know. Whatever the handicap, Ceresney was not an informative witness. In the 145-page transcript of his testimony he used the words "to my knowledge," "I think so," "I don't know," "I guess," or words of that ilk no less than eighty-three times.

Contradictions abounded. One item which Ceresney was ordered to produce was a list of suits involving allegations of defective design of body structure. Ceresney said he had no such "list." But under questioning by Judge Warriner he conceded he did have "cards" showing the cases. Another question dealt with "roll-over" cases. VW responded by listing only one case—although eighteen months previously, during other litigation, a lawyer from Ceresney's firm had listed no less than forty-four roll-over cases. Again, Ceresney denied that VW kept a list of tests conducted on its cars—only to have an engineering witness testify not only as to the existence of a list but its physical dimensions ("the size is perhaps fifteen by fifteen inches and the thickness of that volume may be eight or ten inches").

Judge Warriner did not find Ceresney's testimony credible. He was dismayed at Ceresney's dual role as lawyer and as the corporate personification of Volkswagen.

> It is a gross departure from anything that I have ever known of as an accepted practice on the part of a lawyer. I am not saying, because I don't have proof of it, that it is done with a corrupt motive, but the result of it is the same no matter what the motive might be.
>
> Now, what we have here is as a result of this anomaly a situation in which the person who makes oath to the truth or falsity of certain matters has a perfect out. He can say, "Well, gentlemen, I'm just a lawyer in New York. I can't know what's going on in Germany. I don't know what they've got in their archives. I visited there three years ago and glanced around at filing cabinets and that's all I know about it."

Warriner criticized Ceresney for never saying directly that "those records don't exist. We never ran such tests."

> Instead of that we have evasive type words. We have weasel-type words. And I must assume that these are educated and intelligent people and that they use such words knowing full well what the import of them was, that is to say, that if you use sufficient enough evasions, then you can't be hooked.

Warriner recessed court for half an hour, then returned and declared Volkswagen to be in default. He lectured Ceresney at length. He found that VW's evasiveness "is part of trial strategy that New York counsel exercises," and that it was "contrary to the conduct any lawyer ought to permit himself to be involved in." Warriner continued:

> I am going to indulge the supposition that New York counsel got himself involved in this situation initially at least merely as a matter of convenience and that the proportions that it has now reached were at least initially unintended, and that he has a mistaken zeal to defend his clients by most questionable means. . . .
>
> I want Volkswagen to know that this is not the kind of conduct that is going to be permitted in this court and it is going to be extremely expensive. Whatever you were trying to cover up, it rebounded to your detriment; it's going to cost you, cost you judgment.
>
> It may be that next time you'll be forthcoming . . .
>
> . . . [T]his is extremely distasteful to me . . . that a responsible corporate entity, one with a well-earned good name for quality products worldwide, one that is advertised and properly so with reliability, its unpretentious willingness to give the customer what he's entitled to, that that same company would have either a law department or whatever the department is that engages in anything but a fair and open intercourse with the people.

A week later Volkswagen returned to court to ask Judge Warriner to reconsider. But he was not conciliatory. Using Watergate phraseology, Warriner said that "Volkswagen has participated in a pattern of stonewalling and they haven't seemed to learn." In the earlier default cases, he said, VW lawyers pleaded that they had learned a lesson, and persuaded the judges to reconsider ("waffle, to use another Watergate term"). Warriner would not budge; if VW thought he erred, let VW pursue the matter in the Court of Appeals.

Thus, all that was to be done was for Hank Wallace to present testimony on the damages suffered by John Wilson, his crippled client. Physicians testified to the permanency and severity of the injuries; an economist computed Wilson's lost earnings. But the centerpiece was a videotape of a typical day in Wilson's life—of Wilson wheeling himself around his parents' home in Florida, using ramps and handholds to lift himself in and out of chairs and the bathtub. "When it was shown in court there wasn't a dry eye anywhere," Wallace said.

The jury's verdict: $1,050,000, the largest personal injury judgment ever in the state of Virginia.

"I think," said Hank Wallace, "that we attracted Volkswagen's attention."

Stunned, VW asked Warriner to reconsider his original default order, and the record suggests the judge at this stage had second thoughts about the Draconian results of his action. He offered VW a deal: VW could have a new trial if it would pay all the plaintiff's expenses "reasonably resulting from defendants' failure to disclose, the amount thereof to be approved by the court." VW must pay for two lawyers and an unstated number of automotive engineers "conversant in German and English" who would have "complete authority and right" to go into any VW records they wanted. The new trial would be on the issue of liability only; if VW lost, it must pay the original jury verdict plus interest. And, finally, the firm of Herzfeld and Reubin could not participate in the suit in any way.

VW refused and appealed to the Fourth U.S. Circuit Court of Appeals, which in late 1977 came down heavily on the side of the auto manufacturer, in an opinion that accused Judge Warriner of being biased and arbitrary, in addition to being wrong on the law. Original delays by the plaintiff justified any subsequent delays by VW, the three-judge panel held; it also agreed with VW's contention that the discovery orders were vague and that it had in fact complied as best it could.

The panel criticized Warriner especially harshly for his ruling that Ceresney's behavior in three cases in which VW was held in default for failure to comply with court orders constituted a "pattern" of misconduct. The limited information before Warriner concerning these cases "provide a frail reed on which to predicate a finding of pattern or habit of improper professional conduct," the judges said. And even so, the court said, three cases of the some 200 in which Ceresney and his firm had appeared on behalf of VW did not justify charging a "strategy of deception in discovery on the part of New York counsel."

The appeals court ordered a retrial of the case, starting with the issue of liability. And there the matter rested in the spring of 1978, an embittered Wallace vowing that if the U.S. Supreme Court refused to review the appellate order, "the case will be tried again in Richmond and I plan to give them hell."

* * *

General Motors: "The car was no damned good."

To Chicago lawyer Louis G. Davidson, the scene was unreal, even "sickening."[9] General Motors Corporation, which he was suing in a Corvair accident case, had been ordered by a judge to produce motion pictures of various engineering and safety tests performed on the controversial automobile. The judge also directed GM to have an engineer present to answer Davidson's questions and to provide an index of the data derived from the tests. Davidson had sparred with GM lawyers for long months to get enough evidence to pursue his claim on behalf of a man permanently paralyzed after his Corvair had flipped over, and he felt that "moving pictures of stability tests of 'instrumented' Corvairs would be immensely important."

So he sat in a conference room and watched GM functionaries trundle in five dozen bulky rolls of film. An operator threaded one of the films in the projector and nodded for someone to turn out the lights.

"Hey, wait a minute," protested Davidson. "Before you start, I want to see the index that is supposed to be here, so I can follow what is happening. And which one of you people is the engineer who is to answer my questions?"

The General Motors' staff lawyer told Davidson, "If you have any objections to our procedure, make them in court. I do not intend to argue with you here." The lawyer said GM did not know what the films showed. As to the test data, he said that the engineering calculations had been destroyed.

Davidson turned to the court stenographer who was making a record of the proceedings. "For the record," he began, "I wish to pose an objection—"

"Start the projector," ordered the GM lawyer. The lights went dim and the machine whirred. Images of an auto test danced on the screen.

Davidson, irked, continued reciting his objection, with the stenographer straining to pick up his words.

"Turn on the sound," ordered the GM lawyer. The projectionist complied, and a scratchy, metallic boom filled the room.

The noise was so loud that Davidson had to shout to be heard.

Davidson disgustedly settled back and watched the films for several days, with no indication whatsoever from GM of what the tests were intended to prove—the speed of the vehicles, the G-forces exerted when they swerved on the track or the engineering lessons learned from the tests. A climax of sorts was reached the last day. As Davidson described the sequence later in court papers: "Moving pictures were shown of the Impala and the Chevy II, promotional films with musical sound tracks and bathing beauties. Plaintiffs' counsel [Davidson and an associate] finally left the projection room while movies showing a comedian were being projected."

There was more. On five occasions a judge ordered GM to make employees available for deposition. Not a single one ever appeared. GM delayed by repeatedly asking for postponements or by refusing to produce documents that Davidson needed for his questioning.

Another order compelled GM to produce design layouts for production models of the 1960 to 1965 Corvairs. GM brought in some seventy design layouts, "some of which were forty feet long," according to Davidson. "Using the table where counsel were working, it took a number of minutes to unroll, inspect and then properly roll up each layout." But none of the layouts were what Davidson had requested. He protested frequently, "Give us what we need and let's stop wasting everyone's time." GM stalled for ten days and finally produced what Davidson wanted. Had it been complied earlier, he noted, "GM could have saved itself and plaintiffs the time and expense of examining approximately sixty others of the design layouts."

Davidson repeatedly demanded—and the judge repeatedly ordered—that GM surrender tests on Corvair stability. GM filed countermotions, GM asked for delays, GM objected to "vague" language and to the "relevancy" of Davidson's requests. And then suddenly it inundated Davidson with paper, more than 34,000 engineering and tests reports. "It was as if," he recounted later, "they had taken me to a warehouse of documents, opened the door and said, 'Help yourself.'" But as Davidson and associates began plowing through the papers they realized GM was not being generous at all. The test records did not relate to any issue in their case. GM had given Davidson reports on bucket seat installation, on fuel pump leaks, transmission rattle, fuel economy, seat belt installations and a host of other irrelevant subjects. But, as Davidson said, records "for stability were conspicuous by their absence."

General Motors, Davidson concluded, was "engaged in a sham and deceitful course of conduct to prevent effective discovery by the plaintiffs and to deny to plaintiffs" evidence needed for their case. He called GM's conduct "brazen . . . and unparalleled."

Lou Davidson's frustrating experience occurred in 1965, and what happened to him was no accident. The film incident and his other problems in getting evidence from General Motors, stemmed directly from a coldly calculated strategy in which the nation's leading auto manufacturer squirmed to avoid liability for a multibillion-dollar mistake—the Corvair automobile.

The story of GM's defense of the Corvair is at once a tribute to the nimbleness of the company's lawyers and to the inability of the American legal system to provide justice when one of the litigants—the richer one—refuses to play by the rules. GM's strategy has never been spelled out in law review articles or in speeches to legal symposia; there are some episodes about which even lawyers do not boast publicly. It must be pieced together from scores of files held by plaintiff lawyers across the country, and from fragments of evidence that have crept into the public record.

But a good starting point is at 3:30 P.M. on September 2, 1970, a Wednesday, when Gary Sellers called a number in Buffalo, New York, and asked for Carl Thelin.[10] Sellers identified himself as a lawyer working on Corvair research for Ralph Nader, and he said he hoped that Thelin, as a former engineer for the General Motors Corporation, could be of assistance to him.

Thelin certainly could. He told Sellers that from 1965 to 1967 he had worked on what he called GM's "cloak and dagger operation," a special corporate unit charged with keeping adverse Corvair engineering and test data away from the hordes of litigants—including lawyers such as Davidson—who were howling after Corvair. Thelin laughed. *You know,* he said, *if Ralph Nader hadn't jumped into the Corvair case when he did, GM would have given up the car sooner. Our internal memos said the car* *was no damned good at all. These were written before late 1965, when I arrived.**

The year 1965 was not a happy time for GM and its prized Corvair. After five years of more or less popular acceptance (with sales of half a million annually), drivers found the compact car subjected them to a congeries of problems, ranging from deadly fumes seeping from the heater to a propensity for sudden flips during turns at low speeds. Nader brought together his own voluminous research and that of other auto experts in a book, *Unsafe at Any Speed*, that propelled him into fame and quickly toppled the Corvair into the industrial dustbin. Concurrently, GM found itself defending Corvair suits with a conceivable liability of millions of dollars.

Thelin's story, told from the viewpoint of a working-level engineer executing high-level strategy, was not complete. No GM executive ever called him into a conference and said, "The following is our grand scheme for thwarting the people suing us. We are going to lie and hide documents and give evasive answers." But Thelin had been around GM for eight years, and he knew GM procedures. He had a knack of asking seemingly naive questions of his superiors and remembering what they said. So he was precise about what he knew, and he had the acumen to squirrel away some supporting documents. As Sellers listened to Thelin, he decided the engineer's story had that elusive, undefinable quality known as credibility. What Thelin had to say on that Wednesday afternoon and in subsequent interviews was as follows:

In 1965 GM decided the Corvair suits could not be defended on an individual, *ad hoc* basis. Literally dozens of lawyers had been retained around the country to defend GM, and they were pitted against some of the shrewdest personal injury attorneys in the country. The Association of Trial Lawyers of America had already staged at least one "seminar" on how to litigate a Corvair case, and its members were actively seeking out potential plaintiffs.

A basic rule of defending multiple cases is to make sure that the same story is told in every court. The Corvair suits were

*The italicized quotations are from notes Sellers made during their conversation, later put into memorandum form.

complex, and each was based upon interpretation of intricate engineering data. Thus GM had to ensure that each of its witnesses told the same story, regardless of whether he was testifying in Tampa or Philadelphia. Otherwise, plaintiff lawyers could seize upon differences and try to make them appear to be major inconsistencies.

But according to Thelin, GM went a significant step further. Key executives—and lawyers—knew that the company's internal test reports would damn the Corvair as an unsound automobile if the reports got into the hands of plaintiff attorneys. Further, the documents would show that GM made no effort to warn purchasers of the 1961–63 Corvair of the dangers, even though later models were modified to shed some of the deadly bugs. None of this was to be revealed to the opposing lawyers, however. As Thelin told Sellers: *The secret that GM used, or the trick, was that none of the secret stuff was ever given to anyone who had to testify, so that they could claim ignorance. Chief witnesses never knew the data they should have known.*

The "cloak and dagger operation" was hidden away in General Motors as a unit with the innocuous title "Products Analysis Group."

At first Thelin had no qualms about the assignment. He felt the Corvair, after the 1964 modifications, was a good car, and he distrusted the plaintiff attorneys suing for persons injured in Corvairs. As he told the *Washington Post*'s Morton Mintz, who sat in on one of Sellers' interviews, "We felt that some of these guys were planning to screw GM just because it had billions of dollars."

So Thelin happily conducted "background seminars" at which he gave GM and outside defense lawyers crash courses in such arcane subjects as crash dynamics, and coached them in cross-examining expert witnesses called by the plaintiff. He searched out printed material adverse to Corvair, including proving ground tests that had gotten into the public domain, and compiled it into loose-leaf briefing books along with suggestions as to how defense lawyers could refute criticisms.

GM chose engineers for the Products Analysis Group with care. It avoided what Thelin called "the old fogies who designed this car" because "we were told that some of these guys had to be kept off the stand because they would look like fools. . . . Our witnesses were very knowledgeable, very expert; more than that, they had good rapport with jurors. They would avoid engineering words; talk to the jury, not past them. They were anxious to testify and had good speaking voices."

The Products Analysis Group witnesses also benefited from guidance of the GM legal staff. On November 18, 1965, R. W. Gallant, the group director, asked the GM corporate legal staff for "some guidelines to assist the men . . . in responding under oath to proper questions by opposing counsel about their current duties at Chevrolet."

Aloysius F. Power, the GM general counsel, responded that "questions during cross-examination relating to an engineer's present and prior work assignments . . . *should normally be answered generally.*" Then Power proceeded to list "hypothetical questions and answers which could arise either upon deposition or cross-examination in court, which may assist you in this regard."

Attached to Power's letter were eight pages that can only be called a script, and one in which the answers were designed to be as uninformative as possible: A sampling:

> *Q.* Please describe in general the work performed by the Products Analysis Group.
>
> *A.* There are a number of men in the group and I am not aware of all of the activities.
>
> * * *
>
> *Q.* How long has the Products Analysis Group been in existence?
>
> *A.* I don't really know how long, before I joined the group in ______.*
>
> *Q.* Isn't it true that the Products Analysis Group was expanded in 1965 because of the large number of lawsuits alleging negligent design of the Corvair car?
>
> *A.* I really don't know.

In subsequent Senate testimony, Sellers, the then-Nader attorney, asserted:

*Why could not GM general counsel Power as easily have supplied the date?

. . .[T]he reprehensible character of the script is that in drafting these questions and supplying the answers, the attorneys were providing the answers for the witnesses. The law prohibits this—even where the answers are truthful, since the plaintiff is entitled to the witnesses' own testimony, not the attorney's testimony. . . . As such, the answer is not only *not* the witnesses'—it is the attorney's view of what facts should be provided to the opposing parties on matters of some importance.*

GM wanted tight control over what its expert witnesses would say from the witness stand as well. A memo written June 6, 1966, by an executive in the Products Analysis Group urged that "we attack the problem with a step-by-step editing process" of transcripts of what the experts testified in other cases. Working from transcripts, the editor would delete extraneous and duplicated material and the "by-play" between the lawyers that marks any lawsuit. The executive wrote:

When all the witnesses have had their testimony reduced to the Stage 3 form, a final summary can be made. *All the testimony would be combined into "The Party Line". . . edition.* This edition would consist of the best answer to all the questions asked by the plaintiff to date. This edition would be used as the reviewing and teaching tool for future witnesses.

GM also alerted the Products Analysis Group to be careful about what went into internal reports, since they could be subject to examination by plaintiff lawyers. On February 11, 1966, an education and training officer in the group wrote in a memo to staff engineers that "recent experience in the courts has pointed up the need to review Chevrolet engineering procedures that relate to work order control and technical report writing." If a "question is raised or an opinion expressed about product deficiencies, either in development or production, these must be an-

*As the "best explanation of the harm that arises when an attorney leads a witness," Sellers cited *In the Matter of Eldridge*, 82 New York 1961 (1880), in which the New York Court of Appeals suspended a lawyer for writing out answers for a witness. "Such conduct is inexcusable," the court wrote. "The witness did not answer at all. Eldridge answered for him. We get neither the language nor the memory of the witnesses; we get only that of the teacher. . . . Grant that the answers are not yet shown to be false, and that Eldridge believed them to be true; yet he corrupts justice at the fountain by dictating the evidence of the witness."

swered and made a matter of record." The officer warned the group to cultivate a "new awareness . . . for words and phrases that are vulnerable to misunderstanding or misinterpretation." In other words, don't use language that would be difficult or embarrassing to explain from the witness stand.

Thelin described another stratagem devised by GM's lawyers. First, the lawyers would have the plaintiff, during deposition, describe exactly how the Corvair accident occurred. Then, using the deposition as what Thelin called "a shooting script," he would take a camera crew either to the actual accident site or a re-created one. Other manufacturers' compact cars would be driven over the route as the camera whirred. Then would come the Corvair. Thelin said the tests were not rigged, that the Corvair would go through the curve without incident. On repeat runs, however, the driver would deliberately drive recklessly, bringing the car to the point of a crash, although his skill would keep the car upright. Thelin said, "Our defense was, principally, almost always, that you had to drive in a very reckless manner in order to take the Corvair beyond the 'limit of control,' and that the limit was higher for the Corvair than for competitive models of the same year. The camera was in the back seat, viewing over the driver's shoulder, with a wide-screen lens giving close to normal vision. The movies would knock your eyes out, they were so good."

But Thelin knew all these machinations were hollow, the contrivance of a phony defense. During his first conversation with Sellers he said, *They [GM] knew in January 1965 and even in 1962 how bad the Corvair was. Legal people kept us from revealing this.* Because of his knowledge of GM procedures, Thelin sensed that proving-ground reports existed that he had not seen. After persistent inquiries a GM superior went to a back closet in the Products Analysis Group offices and pulled out a three-inch-thick stack of documents. The papers covered skid and roll-over tests of Corvairs dating back to 1961, and Thelin called them "dynamite." The superior permitted him to read them, but ordered him not to make copies or notes, nor to show them to engineers who might be witnesses in Corvair cases. Thus the witnesses could truthfully say they knew nothing of the reports.

One report in particular caught Thelin's attention. It concerned roll-over tests on 1961 Corvairs—a model that plaintiff lawyers charged was grossly susceptible to unexpected flips—and it indicated that minor engineering changes could eliminate the flaw.

But something mysterious had happened. Under GM's numbering system, the report should have carried the file number "PG 17103." Somehow the report had acquired an extra digit, and the copy Thelin saw was numbered "PG 17*0*103." The source of the extra digit, Thelin did not know. But the "misidentification" gave GM lawyers justification for denying knowledge of the existence of "PG 17103"—which was requested specifically during discovery during several Corvair suits.*

Thelin jumped off ship at this point, psychically if not physically. "That's when my stomach began to churn," he said. "That's when I knew I was getting into deep water. Ignorance is a wonderful thing." His work at GM, he said, was beginning to sound "a little bit hollow." During one of their conversations, attorney Sellers asked Thelin, *How could these results be suppressed?* Thelin replied, *Who says all the crooked people are in small businesses?*

In late 1966, when the Corvair court crisis began to ease, GM cut back the Products Analysis Group and assigned Thelin to a lower-status job. He eventually quit and joined a research laboratory in Buffalo. And somehow his name drifted to the Nader organization as a potential whistle-blower.

During his talks with Gary Sellers and Morton Mintz, Thelin at one point brought up an anecdote that should have special significance for Louis Davidson, the Chicago lawyer who asked for movies of GM tests, and who instead saw bathing beauties and comedians. In this case, Thelin said, GM decided to "pile on the answers, snow them, bury them under material." So his Products Analysis Group produced a veritable roomful of technical documents that the opposing lawyers "couldn't understand and would leave them glassy-eyed in two hours."

So, one may ask, can not Louis G. Davidson fend for himself, glassy-eyed or not? He is a plaintiff's lawyer who chose to work in a scratch-eye world, one in which neither side is totally ignorant of ways to give the opponent a swift kick when his attention

*After Morton Mintz told of this switch in a *Washington Post* article, GM said in a formal statement that it had not produced the document because "in the opinion of our counsel, it had not been called for."

is diverted elsewhere. Davidson is renowned as a shrewd, competent trial lawyer, one of the best in the Midwest. To GM, however, Davidson's motives in seeking out the test documents were not totally clean-handed. GM charged that Davidson was using his suit "in the hope of turning up evidence to be used in other suits or prosecutions," and that he intended to "give nationwide exposure to documents they hope will provide a basis for present and future claims against defendant." (A lay observer wonders why Davidson did not sue GM for libel, for its language was tantamount to a charge he was committing barratry, a violation both of bar canons and most state criminal codes.)

But Davidson held his temper, and he asked the Illinois trial judge, Nicholas J. Bua, of Cook County Circuit Court, to impose draconian sanctions and enter judgment against General Motors on the issue of liability. Illinois rules of civil procedure permit such action against a defendant who flouts court orders, and Judge Bua used stern language in his decision. He held that GM's conduct was designed and calculated to "harass and oppress the plaintiffs" and that it had the effect of "jeopardizing and prejudicing [their] . . . rights to try their cases on the merits and to obtain justice in the courts of this state." Judge Bua ruled that GM in effect had forfeited the lawsuit.

GM escaped on a technicality. In his order, Judge Bua, in careless language, wrote that GM was in "contempt" of court. Illinois procedural rules do not permit a default to be entered as punishment for contempt, so GM went to the Illinois Supreme Court and claimed that it was entitled to another day in court. Judge Bua, through the Illinois Attorney General, said he did not declare GM in default because of the contempt, but because of its failure to comply with his orders. The distinction is a thin one, but important nonetheless. The Illinois Supreme Court ruled for GM. Davidson eventually settled the case out of court.

On August 18, 1966, the U.S. House of Representatives approved a bill giving the Department of Transportation authority to examine auto manufacturers' customer complaint files. The bill, bitterly opposed by Detroit, had a simple rationale: Buyers logically would complain to the manufacturer if their car developed a defect, and therefore the complaint file would be a rich repository for federal safety experts. The Senate had already approved the bill, and the House action meant it would soon go into effect.

Also on August 18, 1966, Walter E. Ludwick, the assistant manager for customer relations of General Motor's Chevrolet Division, issued an order. He told an office functionary to have laborers pick up some twenty-nine crates of microfilmed customer complaints representing more than 150,000 letters from Chevrolet buyers, and store them in a warehouse near Chevrolet's Detroit headquarters. The cases were stacked alongside signs and props that Chevrolet had used in auto shows.

A few months later someone in GM called Morris Levine, owner of Levine Scrap Metal Company, in Detroit, and asked him to cart away the auto show material as surplus junk. Levine sent over a truck, and his workers took away the twenty-nine boxes of microfilm along with the other items.

Eventually Levine sold nineteen of the twenty-nine cases to Harold Keshner, a partner in Sam's Radio Electronic Surplus, also of Detroit. Keshner thought the plastic microfilm holders could be recycled. He didn't bother to look at what was on the film.

Concurrent with Davidson's problems, plaintiff lawyers pursuing Corvair cases elsewhere in the country encountered consistently puzzling conduct by GM lawyers. PI lawyers learn to live with dilatory tactics, for such are the stock-in-trade of defense attorneys. But the Corvair cases were marked by machinations that one lawyer said, "with all respect to Detroit, seemed to be a sit-down strike, and with the auto companies doing the sitting."

One case, aspects of which still remain murky, involved a Philadelphia area man who drove his 1961 Corvair about one hundred miles daily as an appliance repairman for Sears Roebuck & Company.[11] The first year he had the Corvair, he developed headaches and nausea. He took his Corvair to the dealer and complained of smelling gas fumes as he drove. Repairmen tinkered with it and told him the heater was working properly. In early 1962 he developed tremors and had trouble walking and using his hands. The diagnosis: permanent organic brain damage from carbon monoxide poisoning.

The man and his family retained Edward L. Wolf, a Philadelphia personal injury lawyer. Investigating, Wolf found the

1961 Corvair heater shockingly primitive. Air was heated by being passed over the hot manifold of the engine and drawn into the passenger compartment. Wolf read numerous patents in the U.S. Patents Office that stated that this type of heater created hazards because if the manifold leaked, carbon monoxide would mix with the heated air and pass into the vehicle. "This caused many of what used to be known as lovers' lane deaths, where a couple would leave their car heater running when they parked, and be found dead the next morning," Wolf explained. Recognizing these dangers, in the 1940s auto makers switched to other types of heaters.

Through its own words, GM recognized the dangers inherent in reverting to the old manifold heater. The shop manual for the 1961 Corvair stated:

> Because of the inherent characteristics of the heater, objectionable fumes in the engine compartment may be taken into the passenger compartment and result in owner complaints . . . complaints of objectionable odors in the passenger compartment, whether the heater is on or off, *should be traced immediately and promptly corrected.*

During discovery Wolf tried to find out whether customers other than his client had complained of botched heaters. If so, he could claim punitive damages on grounds of recklessness. He directed the following interrogatory to GM's Philadelphia attorneys, the upper-crust firm of Schnader, Harrison, Segal & Lewis:*

> Q. Were there any comments and/or complaints concerning any problems with the presence of noxious fumes or carbon monoxide in other 1961 Corvair model automobiles?
>
> A. Of the 15,806 Greenbriar station wagons manufactured in 1961, defendant has received a written comment or complaint concerning the presence of fumes in respect of only one vehicle other than the vehicle owned and operated by plaintiff.
>
> No written comment or complaint concerning the presence of carbon monoxide, other than the complaint of plaintiff, has been received by defendant.

*One of the name partners, Bernard Segal, was later president of the American Bar Association.

Defendant has no knowledge or record of any such oral comment or complaint.

Ed Wolf did not think GM's answer credible, for he thought the manifold heater was such a piece of engineering junk that other Corvairs *must* have developed trouble. He considered asking W. Bradley Ward, of the Schnader firm, to check back with his clients to see if some mistake had been made, that GM had really not searched that diligently in its files. But he and Ward, who was handling the case for GM, were already on raised-voice terms, and he knew that Ward's answer depended upon information supplied by GM. But he did tell Ward that he was considering asking further explanation of the lack of customers' complaints about the heater.

Concurrently, Wolf tried to force GM to return an engine part that had been taken off the man's Corvair before the suit had been filed. GM alternately couldn't find the part, or didn't think it relevant, and at any rate was not about to turn it over.

Then, to Wolf's surprise, Ward offered a settlement. GM wanted to get rid of the suit. GM did not think the man had much of a case, and GM would not concede that the Corvair heater was inherently defective. Perhaps, however, one bad heater did slip through GM's quality control inspectors. Wolf and Ward haggled over dollars a few days, and then settled for $125,000—not as much as Wolf wished, but nonetheless a respectable amount. No other Corvair heater case had gone to trial, Wolf had obtained little to support his case during discovery, and he was nervous about risking the man's future with a jury.

But GM insisted that the settlement agreement include extraordinary terms. All the depositions Wolf had taken of GM engineers were to be surrendered to GM. So, too, was the engineering data he had obtained from automotive specialists at the Massachusetts Institute of Technology whom he had intended to use as witnesses. So, too, were medical files on the man and "particularly reports on the causal effect" of carbon monoxide on Petry's condition. GM also took the Corvair. Perhaps most significantly, GM forced Wolf to rewrite history. He was required to withdraw his original complaint alleging defective design and file new papers basing the suit on manufacturing error.

So far as the formal court record was concerned, Petry was hurt because of a crack in a cylinder, not a poorly designed heater.

"In other words," Wolf said, "my whole file was taken as a condition of settlement. And in addition to that we had to sign—my client and my law firm, myself—[an agreement] that we would not talk, write, or otherwise advertise or promulgate the facts of the Petry case, and particularly the theory of liability relative to the defective heater."

Later, in response to Senate queries, GM offered a pragmatic reason for imposing a gag order on Wolf. One Los Angeles lawyer alone, David M. Harney, was handling forty-eight Corvair cases, and he and other attorneys were "collaborating, exchanging information and conducting organized litigation against General Motors in several states." Harney, in June 1964, had won a $70,000 settlement in a case involving Corvair handling design. GM said, "Although the settlement did not constitute an admission by either party . . . within two hours . . . [Harney] appeared on a local TV newscast and the settlement was proclaimed as a victory in the first of a number of Corvair cases. . . . The wire services picked up the story of the settlement and it appeared in a number of newspapers throughout the country the following day."

Prospective jurors read newspapers and watch television, and GM's lawyers said they did not want a "recurrence of the exaggerated publicity." GM said it insisted on buying Petry's car "to eliminate the possibility of claims by a future owner of the car."

The silence agreement had considerable local value to General Motors. By the time Wolf negotiated the settlement he had become associated with the Philadelphia firm of Richter, Lord & Cavanaugh, then one of the toughest personal injury offices in town. A common—and ethical—practice for PI lawyers is to develop expertise in a particular category of case and rely upon word of mouth to bring in clients with the same complaint. The client benefits from the past work, and the law firm makes more profit because it does not have to repeat the basic investigation. Defense lawyers, with their reliance on attrition and delay, think this procedure unseemly.

It can and has been argued that an agreement such as that signed by Wolf "has the same substantive effect as would an agreement by that attorney not to take any other carbon monoxide cases," as Gary Sellers told a Senate subcommittee in 1971. The American Bar Association has held that it was unethical for an attorney to make a prior agreement not to represent a member of the public in these circumstances.[12]

Ed Wolf is now dead, as is B. Nathaniel Richter, the lead partner in the firm at the time of the settlement. Thus, no direct explanation is available as to why the GM strictures were accepted. But one lawyer who talked about the case later with Wolf said, "This is a lot of surmise, but it came down to the old dilemma of taking sure money or going before a jury of twelve people and getting zip. The lawyer is obligated to making the best deal possible for an individual client and not insisting on settlement terms that will please Ralph Nader or some editorial writer."

In early 1971 Sam's Radio Eletronic Surplus went out of business.[13] The owner sold the entire stock (mostly junk and salvage items) to scrap dealers Floyd E. Avery and Kenneth A. Simpson, of the Detroit suburb of Wyandotte. Although they did not notice it at the time, their purchase included nineteen cardboard boxes marked "General Motors." In April 1971 a browsing customer went into the boxes and came out with a handful of microfilm holders. He bought 200 to 300 of them for six cents each.

Shortly thereafter, Avery said, he received a collect call from Ralph Nader's Center for Auto Safety, in Washington. The director, Lowell Dodge, supposedly offered Avery $25 and shipping costs for the entire files. Irked at the collect call—Nader's people do tend to be presumptuous—Avery rummaged through the boxes himself and saw that the microfilm came from Chevrolet's customer relations office. He stalled Dodge and eventually refused to accept any more collect calls.*

Re-enter the original stranger, according to Avery, this time with an offer of $6,000 for all the microfilm. Let me think about it, Avery said—and once the man left he called General Motors. Eventually he got to Walter E. Ludwick, the Chevrolet official who had ordered the files into storage in 1966. Avery described what he had, and Ludwick came to Wyandotte in a hurry and

*Dodge's version is that Avery called the Nader organization first, rather than the other way around. Nader associates surmised that the junk dealer thought Nader would pay handsomely for files of his archfoe. "Unfortunately," one of them said, "those were the years when we had trouble paying for a subscription to the *Washington Post*."

looked at them. "He was sure surprised," Avery said. Ludwick "didn't haggle or bargain," he offered $20,000 on the spot, and Avery accepted. "We used Nader as a hammer, let's face it," the scrap dealer said. "It's like so much gold. It's like hitting the Irish Sweepstakes."

Avery and his partner were so happy at the coup that their bragging reached the Detroit newspapers. Nader and a number of lawyers suing GM in Corvair and other Chevrolet cases demanded that the files be opened for inspection, in view of GM's repeated reluctance to admit the existence of customer complaints in court suits.

GM refused, but the *Detroit News* and WWJ-TV, a Detroit television station, managed to obtain 250 of the records. About one fourth of the complaints dealt with the Corvair, and Edward Wolf, reading news accounts in his Philadelphia law office, felt his jaw tighten as he remembered GM's denials in 1965 that it had received complaints about heater fumes.

—A woman from Washington, D. C., sent several letters to GM about gas odors in her car before her dealer solved the problem. She liked the car's overall performance, despite the bugs, and bought another in 1965; it, too, had the gas fume defect.

—A man in Wayne, Nebraska, with a Corvair Greenbriar station wagon (the same model driven by Wolf's client Petry), wrote that the "warm air heater is causing the car to be filled with fumes to the point where it is dangerous to passengers. We asked the dealer to work on this several times but have no results."

—A citizen in Tams, West Virginia, told GM that "fumes from the motor through the manifold heating system cause great discomfort even in summer when the heater is not turned on."

—A man in Cos Cob, Connecticut, said the smell through his heater was so strong "that it is possible to distinguish a change in odor with changes in the brands of gasoline. . . ."

Reflecting on the case at the Senate hearings, Wolf said that he felt W. Bradley Ward "was most candid with me at all times. Any of the problems which I had with General Motors were certainly not caused by him." Nonetheless, he said, when GM's answers to the interrogatories were weighed against "the information which you know was available at the same time [the microfilms] I think that you are going to find that there . . . is a credibility gap."

Ford Motor Company: "He said we had been screwed"

One of the great undiscussable subjects among PI lawyers is the inordinate number of times that pure luck enables them to win a case. "Sometimes," said a man who practices in Cleveland, "I think that Jesus or the Deity keeps a running score, and balances out the good breaks with the bad ones. If you have a run of rotten luck, suddenly gold falls in your lap." Leonard Ring of Chicago tells of winning an action against the manufacturer of gymnastic equipment because a defense witness, during deposition, unwittingly surrendered a key document that previously "did not exist." A Dallas lawyer comments, "During discovery in one personal injury case I began receiving bootleg copies of letters being exchanged by the two law firms defending the case. The letters candidly discussed some rather raw stuff being performed by this other crowd. I was worried, because there was a real possibility that someone was deceiving me, because by any stretch of the code of ethics I should have returned them forthwith. Well, I didn't, and I sweated, and the information contributed materially to my victory."

This lawyer, understandably, is not able to boast publicly of his use of under-the-table material. But the importance of luck, and the surprise friendly witness, is spelled out in the record of a case that became a minor *cause célèbre* among Detroit lawyers. This is what happened:

Three country and western musicians finished a club date in Moline, Illinois, in 1967, and were driving home when they stopped at a railroad crossing to let a train pass. [14] Another vehicle rear-ended their 1965 Ford Galaxie, whose gas tank erupted into flames. One musician was incinerated; another suffered third-degree burns over 95 percent of his body and died the next day; the driver, although severely burned, survived.

Detroit PI lawyer Richard M. Goodman, after analyzing the crash investigation, decided to sue Ford Motor Company, the manufacturer. "There were 200 feet of skid marks before the other car hit the Galaxie, indicating a considerable diminishment of speed. My expert estimated the other car was going no more than thirty miles an hour when it crashed. I based my case on the theory that the Galaxie gas tank was of inadequate construction and design—that Ford was negligent in building a car that wouldn't withstand such an impact. If the other car is going ninety miles an hour, you have to build a Sherman tank to survive the impact. But when the speed is twenty-five or thirty, as we maintained, it's a different ball game. Ford should have built a car strong enough to stay intact." (Another obvious, although unspoken, reason for suing Ford, rather than the driver of the second car, is that Ford is a wealthy corporation, and hence Goodman would be able to collect any amount awarded by the jury. Seldom does a private motorist carry more than $100,000 in liability insurance, and Goodman was thinking in terms of ten times that amount.)

Goodman brought the suit in Wayne County Circuit Court in Detroit, so as to have ready access to Ford personnel and documents. "We wanted test films showing the way Ford vehicles behaved when rear-ended. The auto companies, we've learned from experience, are test-crazy. They want to know everything about a car before they put it on the market, and their test records are complete: they supposedly never throw *anything* away. Using the manufacturer's own testing data is good strategy for two reasons. First, it saves you money. If a PI lawyer tries to stage tests himself, the cost can run up to $5,000 to $10,000 per vehicle. Also, I'd a heck of a lot rather throw someone's own data back at them; they can't challenge technical information from their own tests."

In November 1970 Judge Blair Moody ordered Ford to produce "all reports relative to barrier crash tests performed on 1965 Ford sedan vehicles of the same general design" as the Galaxie; and "all high speed or standard films relative to barrier crash tests performed on a *gas tank of the same design characteristics relating to this case*." [Emphasis added] Judge Moody agreed the test results were essential to Goodman's case "and should be made known for a full and fair evaluation by the fact finder."

Three months later the Ford lawyers wrote Goodman, "Ford Motor has *no reports or films relative to barrier crash tests per-*

formed on 1965 Fords, [emphasis added] or on vehicles with a gas tank of the same design and characteristics of the 1965 Ford."

Goodman was skeptical. He had tried enough auto cases to know the manufacturers' mania for testing, and he could not believe that Ford had marketed a popular car without knowing how it would behave in a crash. Shortly before trial, his suspicions were partially confirmed. A Ford engineer, in depositions, revealed that Ford had made crash tests of its 1966 and 1967 models, and that films and records of these tests were available. Goodman asked for the test data. Ford refused, saying "there were significant and substantial differences in design characteristics . . . of the 1965 vehicle and the 1966 vehicle." But Goodman persisted, and on the opening day of trial, after reviewing what he had learned on discovery, he asked for yet another order on access to test results. Judge Moody's order this time was more inclusive. He directed Ford to produce:

> 1. *All reports relative to crash tests* performed on 1965 and 1966 and 1967 Ford Custom, Galaxies, Galaxies 500 and Galaxies 500 LTD vehicles made prior to December 3, 1967 [the date of the accident].
>
> 2. *All motion pictures, films and still photographs* taken of crash tests or crash-tested vehicles or components thereof on 1965, 1966 and 1967 Ford Custom, Galaxies, Galaxies 500 and Galaxies 500 LTD vehicles made prior to December 3, 1967.

Ford's lawyer denied in open court that any tests had been made on the 1965 models. A few days later Ford did produce ten films of crash tests of 1966 and 1967 models. Thus, during the trial Goodman was forced to rely upon an expert witness who could say only that based upon "his general experience" and his examination of the burned-out Ford, he estimated the speed of the rear-ending auto at thirty miles an hour. The expert opined the death car had not been designed in accordance with current auto safety knowledge and standards, and that the design defect caused the gas tank to rupture and burn.

Ford countered with its own expert, who estimated that the rear-ending auto was going about fifty miles an hour, and that the 1965 design was "well within safety standards available to the [auto] industry at that time."

The jury agreed with Ford, and threw out the case.

"A couple of weeks after the trial," Goodman related, "I received an anonymous phone call from a man who claimed to be a former Ford Motor Company engineer. He said that we had been screwed, that Ford had films of tests of the 1965 models, the very things we wanted. At first he wouldn't give his name, but he would give numbers of a pay booth where he would be at specified times so I could telephone him.

"The procedures were very cloak-and-daggerish and I admit that I was skeptical as to whether he was a nut or playing me along for some ulterior purpose. Then he gave me the clincher. He produced more than one hundred pages of computer printouts showing Ford test material—the date, the model years, the type and purpose of the test, and the internal control number."

After more than a decade of contesting the auto manufacturers in court, Goodman does not surprise easily. But he admits to being "stunned" as he skimmed through the printouts. The information was coded, but following a key included in a covering memorandum, Goodman found startling information.

For instance, on November 1, 1966, Ford engineers conducted a "movable-barrier rear-end test" on a 1965 Galaxie two-door sedan at a speed of thirty miles an hour. The purpose, in Ford's code, was cited as "FTST"—more fully defined in the code sheet as "fuel tank studies." Goodman poked through the printouts for hours and found several such tests on 1965 Galaxies *cited in Ford's own words as fuel tank studies.*

Anger is a luxury PI lawyers rarely allow themselves. A trial attorney must think on his feet, and a common courtroom strategy is to goad an opponent into making foolish or rash statements in the heat of emotion. So wise men learn to breathe slowly and count to ten. But Goodman admits to a mood that went somewhat beyond pique when he realized what Ford had done to him. Even by the most charitable interpretation he could see no justification for Ford withholding the gas tank tests—much less denying their very existence.* He persuaded the former Ford

* Under rules of civil procedure in Michigan and most other jurisdictions, a party who is uncertain as to whether documents are covered by a discovery rule is entitled to submit them to the trial judge in private. The judge determines whether they are relevant. According to one authority on procedure, "An order for production of documents is not complied with by assuring the moving party that the desired information is not contained therein, nor may the party edit the documents before production or withhold what it deems not pertinent."[15]

engineer to shed his anonymity and give an affidavit about the tests, and then he filed a motion asking that his clients be granted a new trial and that Ford be cited for contempt.

In response Ford submitted an affidavit by George Kabot, its senior attorney, who admitted that he had examined the tests of 1965 Fords before the trial. But he determined—on his own—that the tests were not on vehicles "of the same general design or on gas tanks of the same design characteristics" as those covered by Judge Moody's order. He so advised the Ford trial lawyer, Perry Seavitt. Seavitt, however, never advised Judge Moody nor Goodman of the existence of the tests.

Further, Ford maintained that the films of the tests on the 1966 and 1967 models provided Goodman "all the information as to rear-end crash tests which could have been obtained from the test films of the 1965 Fords." Thus "no prejudice had resulted" to the plaintiffs.

During the arguments for a new trial, Goodman finally saw the 1965 test films and analyses. Unsurprisingly, they confirmed what he had tried, unsuccessfully, to prove during the trial: " . . . [T]hey reveal that, on thirty miles per hour rear-end impact, frame buckling damage occurred of a character similar to that which appeared on plaintiffs' vehicle. The effect of such evidence at the trial as supporting the opinion of plaintiffs' expert [witness] is self-evident."

Goodman also scoffed at Ford's claim that since some of the 1965 test models were modified or specially equipped, they did not fall under Judge Moody's order. He noted that the 1966 and 1967 test vehicles had also been modified, and that Ford nonetheless had turned over test data on them.

In an angry conclusion, Goodman argued that "the evidence compels the conclusion that the 1965 tests were deliberately withheld," and that the record

> . . . strongly suggests that Ford's senior attorney [Kabot] charged with the responsibility of measuring these documents against the language of Judge Moody's order would have recognized not only their relevancy but their potential damage to his company's case.
>
> It is difficult to believe that his decision not to reveal this data to his company's trial counsel was unaffected by loyalty to his employer's interests.

> Indeed, it is apparent that had it not been for plaintiffs, counsel's fortuitous meeting with [the former Ford engineer] this evidence would soon have been irrevocably buried in Ford's immense paper files and plaintiffs' opportunity of recovery of their damages would have been irrevocably lost.

Judge Moody denied Goodman a new trial, on grounds he found no "willful violation" of his discovery order. The ruling surprised Detroit PI lawyers following the case. (One of them commented to me: "Talk about double standards! Boy, if any of us was ever caught doing such a thing we'd be driving a hack on the street. But nobody touches Ford Motor Company or its lawyers.") So Goodman went to the Michigan Court of Appeals, where he found more sympathetic ears. On July 22, 1974, a three-judge panel unanimously ordered a new trial, finding the Ford lawyers in fact had not complied with Judge Moody's order.

Dick Goodman talked about the case months later. "Mad?" Oh, I wouldn't go that far. Anger is a wasteful emotion. But what *disgusts* me—I like that word better—is that we were forced to go in circles for so many years. This is wasteful—to the courts, which are supported by the taxpayers; to the plaintiff lawyer, who is being paid by the injured party; to the defense lawyer, who is being paid, in this instance, by the people who buy Ford automobiles.

"Call me naïve, but I'd like to practice law under a system where justice didn't depend on how good you were at playing hide-and-seek."

Epilogue

Many Christmases ago, John V. Lewis, a San Francisco lawyer, paid a courtesy call on Frank Hogan, a former president of the American Bar Association. Lewis found his friend sitting in front of a fireplace, surrounded by magnificent presents, but nonetheless looking rather glum.

"What's the matter, Frank?" he asked. "You don't seem to like your presents. Just suppose, to make you happy, you could have any present that you, one of the leading lawyers in the United States, would want. Just what would a lawyer wish for as his finest present on Christmas Day?"

Hogan thought for a moment, and with a facetious grin replied, "A very rich man, very solvent, walking up to my door in a very great deal of trouble."[1]

The book had been read, and thoroughly. Crude black pencil scrawls marred perhaps one-fourth of the 676 pages—question marks, exclamation points, underlined sentences, unreadable private notes someone had made to himself. I sat down on an old wooden box—I was in Mrs. Anita Groves' antique store in Luray, Virginia—for a closer look at the volume.

How to Be Your Own Lawyer: An Encyclopedia of Law and Forms had been published in 1876, exactly a century earlier, by the Philadelphia house of J. C. McCurdy & Company. The flyleaf credited the author, "The Hon. Hugh M. Spalding," with earlier treatises on the laws of Ohio, Kentucky, Indiana and

Kansas. In the preface, Spalding explained his reason for the book. "No species of knowledge is more in demand, or confers more real and constant usefulness than that of the law and its practical application in both the private and public affairs of each individual." Unfortunately, Spalding lamented, "no species of knowledge is more difficult to obtain at the desired moment." He listed some reasons: "There are times and circumstances which render it advisable to be one's own legal counselor [or involve] matters of minor importance which may not justify . . . the expense or formality of a legal consultation." There are "private matters which it may be neither prudent nor desirable to disclose, but which require some legal light for satisfactory solution or adjustment." There are "business difficulties . . . [and] controverted and vexed questions which constantly demand some knowledge of the law to successfully master, and which are otherwise fruitful of annoyance, distress and doubt."

Spalding hoped his volume would help the lay reader avoid impaling himself on the ancient but universal rule, "Ignorance of the law is no excuse."

The frontispiece of this particular copy bore the handwritten inscription, "R. Alger, Rileyville, Virginia, January 1877. His Book." I knew some of the latter-day Algers, for at the time I lived among them on a farm near Rileyville, in an isolated curl of the Shenandoah Valley that is shielded from outside intrusion by the bordering Blue Ridge and Massanutten mountain ranges. Rileyville, as we liked to say, was 100 minutes and 100 years from Washington.

Isolation gives the people of the Page Valley, as the area is called, a special self-reliance. They do not bother outsiders for solutions to a problem, be it a sick cow, a broken tractor, or a misplaced property boundary. As a longtime lawyer-watcher, one often skeptical of the usefulness of much of what the legal profession does, I noted with satisfaction my first days out there that in the Yellow Pages of the Luray phone book, veterinarians outnumbered attorneys six to five. Legal business there surely must be in the Page Valley, for real estate hounds are sweeping through the area with a rapaciousness not witnessed since Major General Nathaniel Banks' Union troops marched south in 1862. But what lawyers there are keep out of sight, and have no discernible impact on the workaday lives of the populace—a relaxing contrast from Washington, where the ubiquitous lawyers outnumber even the tourists.

There is a reason for the difference, one told tartly in scribbled words beneath R. Alger's signature:

> *Too drat complicated. Why dont they write in plain words so people know what to do. Whol idea is to make people give the drat lawyers money. Dont like lawyer or what they do or what they written This book no good to nobody but another lawyer.*

Why, and how, have the lawyers hooked their professional claws so deeply into our collective backs? Can we ever be free of them? Some weeks after finding Mr. Alger's old book I read comments on lawyers by another Virginian who was even more Naderish. Chief Justice Warren Burger, who has the ex officio status that forbids him being dismissed as a village crank, warned that we "may be well on our way to a society overrun by hordes of lawyers, hungry as locusts, and brigades of judges in numbers never before contemplated." (I mildly demur: we are not "on our way"; the locusts are in the streets.) Burger noted that the United States has more practicing lawyers per 100,000 population (55) than any society in the world—"fourteen times the ratio of modern Japan, which is also a highly complex, highly developed society." Burger does not feel this statistic to be complimentary to the legal profession.[2]

Indeed, a few months before making the cited speech, Burger entertained the Shah of Iran, who begged guidance in modernizing his country's court system. "What do you do now?" Burger asked. The Shah explained that each village had a body of respected elders to whom citizens took their disputes. The claims were resolved under a form of binding arbitration, with no appeals, no review—and no lawyers. Someone had suggested to the Shah that a team of American legal experts be recruited to survey Iran's "problems" and recommend a more sophisticated system of courts.

"My honest answer to him," the Chief Justice said, "was to let well enough alone."

But Americans cannot "let well enough alone" save at the onerous cost of permitting lawyers to continue to dominate our society to a degree that many of us find repugnant. To put it most directly, Americans have about had it with lawyers. The legal system they contrived for us does not work. It satisfies no one (save, on occasion, the lawyers who earn comfortable livings under its aegis). Half a century ago Judge Learned Hand exclaimed, in a bar association lecture, "I must say that as a litigant I should dread a lawsuit beyond almost anything else short of sickness and death." In public-opinion polls lawyers constantly turn up with a "respected" rating lower than even that timeless rogue, the used-car salesman. Signs of the lawyer's loss of esteem are easily found. From a single issue of *Newsweek* I tore out two full-page ads:

> —"Who needs a life insurance policy only a lawyer can understand?" So asked the American Council of Life Insurance, the industry trade group, which answered its own question, "In plain English, no one." The council announced a policy of putting policies into "plain talk" so citizens would know what they bought without resorting to a lawyer.
>
> —"Why Major Reynolds Will be Virginia's Next Lieutenant Governor" declared another ad. The reason: "He's a businessman, not a lawyer."*

Lawyers rule us because they dominate the legislatures which write our laws, because they shape the courts that interpret the laws, and because (given factors one and two) persons in trouble have no recourse but to turn to them. A citizen angry about his plumber or his car repair agency can buy his own wrench or check an auto manual out of his local library, and do his own work. Not so for someone aggrieved with a lawyer, for the profession protects itself in ways that are demeaningly petty. For instance, a decades-old Maryland law prohibits court clerks in the Washington suburban counties of Montgomery and Prince Georges from helping the public fill out routine legal forms needed for such uncomplicated proceedings as the probate of a simple will, or a divorce decree, even when both parties agree to the split and the property settlement. Probating wills is especially

*Reynolds deserves indictment for wishful thinking. He lost in the Democratic primary to Charles Robb—Lyndon Johnson's son-in-law, and a member of the cloutish Washington law firm of Williams & Connolly.

simple, done on fill-in-the-blanks forms that the county registrar of wills—a public servant—supplies to lawyers. According to Leo Cornfield, of *Trusts and Estates Magazine*, probating most estates is "cut and dried. . . . Most of the work is done by the lawyer's secretary, problems are solved gratis by the clerks of the probate court, and very little of the lawyer's own time is consumed."[3] Since most probate fees are based upon a percentage of the value of the estate, this sort of work is so lucrative that lawyers literally pant over the obituary pages. In 1977 a Maryland lawyer could earn—well, *receive*—$5,000 for a $100,000 estate, his physical effort being nothing more demanding than completing standard forms handed him by a bureaucrat.*

There is a reason for lawyers building such protective fences around their practices. It is called money. Lawyers like money, and they pursue it unabashedly, as a matter of right. As the Illinois Bar Association said in 1960, "The respect for the legal profession and its influence in the individual community will be raised when the lawyer occupies his *proper place* at the top of the economic structure." (My emphasis.) At an ABA meeting in 1972 a Texas attorney declared, "It is in the public policy of this country that you [lawyers] be prosperous." A few years earlier another ABA convention delegate was even more direct; he urged his lawyer audience to "come right out at the beginning and sock him [the client] hard."[4]

Understandably, supporting the locusts of the legal profession (the word is that of Chief Justice Burger) sucks immense amounts of money out of the pockets of the citizenry, and immense amounts of patience from the national psyche. Society has been so arranged (by the lawyers) that we need them as navigators at every turn. The tolls are high. In a survey of 321 U.S. and Canadian law firms in 1976, the management consulting firm Altman & Weil, Inc., of Philadelphia, discovered the median earnings for partners were $55,000 annually. The associates, generally persons with less than five years' experience, earned $20,000. Altman & Weil found great regional variances, with

*Maryland State Senator David Scull, himself a lawyer, moved to repeal this outrage in 1977. He proposed a law removing the ban on court clerks helping the public. Another Scull reform would require registrar clerks to help lay citizens fill out probate forms—a service now confined to lawyers.

partner earnings highest in California, at $63,000, and lower in other Western states, $51,000.[5]

These figures, it must be remembered, are *median* income. Move into the higher strata of corporate law, or the big-city firms, and the digits spin upward like the score counter on a crazed pinball machine. Consider Joseph W. Califano, Jr., partner in the Washington firm of Williams, Connolly & Califano, before President Carter brought him into the Cabinet as Secretary of Health, Education and Welfare. Under the Carter Administration's show-and-tell policy for high appointees, Califano made public his 1976 income: $505,490. His Cabinet colleague, Secretary of State Cyrus Vance, reported 1976 earnings of a quarter of a million dollars from the Wall Street firm of Simpson, Thacher & Bartlett, a level considered more or less standard for ranking partners in the larger firms of New York, Washington, Chicago, Los Angeles and Houston. There is ample money for younger persons as well: by the time this book is published, the starting salaries for associates at such New York offices as Cravath, Swaine & Moore will be $30,000—for a person fresh from law school without a day of professional experience.

Further, instances abound where lawyers and firms earned windfall fees amounting to more money than many Americans see in a lifetime. Some striking examples from among scores in my files:

• "Old friend, I'll look into it and call back." So said Frank Fitzsimmons, the Teamsters Union president, to Richard Kleindienst, the former Attorney General of the United States, on the golf course of Washington's Burning Tree Country Club in 1976. The subject Kleindienst raised involved a contract to provide 185,000 Teamsters with health and accident insurance. The person who asked Kleindienst to approach Fitzsimmons was Thomas D. Webb, Jr., a well-connected Washington lawyer who served as an FBI agent before entering private practice. The person who approached Webb—this is getting complicated—was an insurance wheeler-dealer named Joseph Hauser (later convicted of fraud) who felt he needed inside help in obtaining the Teamster business. Kleindienst's approach worked, for Hauser in fact received the insurance contract. In return, Kleindienst received what he described to the SEC as a finder's fee of $125,000 for "five to seven hours' work." The fee is roughly twice the average annual income of an American lawyer. Lawyer Webb split another $125,000 with a public relations man, I. Irving Davidson, who was also involved in the deal. (Kleindienst later told a Senate subcommittee looking into Teamster insurance and pension matters, "I didn't ever ask Mr. Fitzsimmons to use his influence. But in the context of our friendship it was assumed he would use his influence and I certainly hoped he would.")[6]

• In the late 1960s, Chris-Craft Industries, Inc., tried to take over the Piper Aircraft Company, only to encounter bitter opposition from the Piper family and First Boston Corporation, an investment banking firm. Eventually, the Pipers sold out to another corporate suitor, Bangor-Punta Corporation. Chris-Craft sued, charging that Bangor-Punta, First Boston and some Piper family members violated anti-fraud provisions of the securities law in fending off Chris-Craft. Lower courts sided with Chris-Craft, which at one point won a $36 million damage award, largest ever under federal securities laws. But the U.S. Supreme Court in 1977 ultimately sided with Bangor-Punta and First Boston, holding that Congress never expressly gave losers in proxy fights access to the courts, regardless of fraud by the winning side. All this wrangling brought an exasperated sigh from Justice John Paul Stevens, who called it "monumental litigation . . . [with] three trials, three appeals and three groups of . . . petitions" to the Supreme Court. No such lament was heard from the swarms of lawyers in the case, whose total fees approached $5 million—an amount roughly equal to annual earnings of Piper, subject of the takeover fight.*[7]

• Lawyers can keep their eyes on the equivalent of a taxi meter even when "doing good." Consider Arnold & Porter, the Washington superfirm. A & P is large enough, rich enough—yes, even socially conscious enough—to designate one lawyer annually, of the hundred-odd on the premises, to work full-time on public-interest cases. In 1972, a coal company refuse-pile dam collapsed in West Virginia, sending water cascading over sixteen small towns in the Buffalo Creek Valley and killing some 125

*Lawyers in the case included Sullivan & Cromwell, of New York, and Louis Loss, Boston, for First Boston; Wilmer, Cutler & Pickering, Washington, Webster & Sheffield, New York, and Charles A. Wright, Austin, Texas, for Bangor-Punta; Paul, Weiss, Rifkind, Wharton & Garrison, New York, Chris-Craft; and Chadbourne, Parke, Whiteside & Wolff, New York, for the Piper family.

persons. In due course, survivors and family members asked A & P's *pro bono* partner, Gerald Stern, to represent them. But the people had no money, and the firm's executive committee balked at making such an investment of time and money for nothing. So a deal was struck: A & P would take the case on a contingent-fee basis of 25 percent of any amount recovered, plus expenses.

But other lawyers eyed the case as well, deducing (as did A & P) that any accident involving so many persons ultimately would produce some damage money. When Stern visited West Virginia he heard that a local plaintiff lawyer, Amos Wilson, who frequently represented miners in black lung and other cases, was accusing A & P of "soliciting" the Buffalo Creek cases. Stern called on Wilson. As he related later:

> He [Wilson] said he felt he was entitled to at least one-third of any of the business [sic] from this disaster in his home county, since he was the county's leading plaintiff's lawyer. He was quite upset that Arnold & Porter might be retained by a large number of survivors. He said they might have come to him instead if we hadn't come on the scene.

Stern tried to persuade Wilson that A & P had done nothing unethical. Nonetheless, the ethics committee of the state and county bars looked into the matter, causing the Washington firm embarrassing newspaper publicity. After several years' work (by himself and other A & P lawyers) Stern got an out-of-court settlement of $13.5 million. Arnold & Porter's fee was almost $3 million.* "Sometimes," Stern wrote later, "you do well by doing good."[8]

• In 1963 the Washington-New York law firm then known as Dickstein, Shapiro & Galligan** sued a batch of drug companies for allegedly fixing prices on sales of antibiotics to hospitals and

*Another $500,000 went to Steptoe & Johnson, which has offices both in Washington and West Virginia, and which served A & P as local counsel. A & P also received $378,000 for expenses. So the lawyers' total share was almost $3,860,000. The typical plaintiff received only $8,000 to $10,000 for mental injuries, while families received from $20,000 to $50,000 for loss of real estate and personal property and wrongful death.

**The name changed several times thereafter. After former Nixon aide Charles Colson joined the office in 1973 it was known briefly as Colson & Shapiro. Then came Colson's Watergate troubles, and the name shifted again, this time to Dickstein, Shapiro & Morin. Colson played no part in the drug case and did not share in the fee.

other public agencies. During the next ten years the firm spent some 50,000 hours on the case, "a considerable portion of its professional life," in the words of a federal court special master. The firm received no compensation for the first seven years of the suit, and its partners borrowed money to keep it alive. Eventually, in 1973, the drug firms settled for around $100 million. The Shapiro law firm received a court-awarded fee of $6,388,834, a record for private antitrust litigation ($2.5 million of this amount went to other firms around the country that assisted). A Chicago father-son lawyer team, Lee A. Freeman and Lee A. Freeman, Jr., received a separate fee of $2.5 million. Fees to other attorneys brought the gross legal bill to more than $10 million.[9]

I stopped writing at that point and tried to think of the position I wished to argue in the last several pages of this book. I re-read the prologue. Yes, I do like lawyers—individually. Yes, I do believe that men such as Scotty Baldwin and Franklin Jones improve our society, if only by making it dreadfully expensive for manufacturers to risk putting faulty products on the market. Yes, I am pragmatic enough to accept that our nation needs a mandarin class to administer the laws under which we live. Yet . . .

I found myself killing time, moving file boxes to the basement, running across a note or a clipping and wondering why I had not found a place for it in my manuscript. I called a friend who lived with me much of this book.

"I'm stuck," I told her. "As you know, I'm not anti-lawyer—I just think they foul up a lot of things for the rest of us."

"Well," she replied, "why not just say that? Call them 'barnacles on the hull of society,' something like that."

"Yeah, but when a ship gets barnacles, someone scrapes them off. I'm not prepared to argue that, just yet. I closed out *The Superlawyers* with that Dick the Butcher quote from Shakespeare, 'The first thing we do, let's kill all the lawyers.'

"I wrote that with tongue in cheek, but the wife of some Washington lawyer caught me at a cocktail party later and said, 'So you are the son of a bitch who recommends assassinating my husband.' It took me an hour to persuade her I was not advocating class murder."

"Well, why not just say they'd better get off our toes and stop making society so damnably complex? The way I read what you've written, they're more interested in their damned fees and their little courtroom games than they are in justice. For one, I'm tired of it.'' She paused. ''Damned tired of it, and I think lots of other people are also.''

I thought about that statement for a while. ''You're right,'' I said. ''So I think I'll leave out the ersatz political philosophy and say just that.''

Chapter Notes

Chapter One

1. Michael Wheeler, *No-Fault Divorce*. Boston: Beacon Press, 1974.

2. Ibid.

3. Ibid.

4. Rose DeWolf, *The Bonds of Acrimony*. Philadelphia: Lippincott, 1970.

5. Wheeler, op cit.

6. Ethical Considerations 7-1 and 7-10, *Code of Professional Responsibility*, the American Bar Association.

7. Raoul Lionel Felder, *Divorce*. World Publishing Company, New York, 1971.

8. Herbert A. Glieberman, in *Illinois General Practice Workbook*. Springfield, Illinois: Illinois Institute for Continuing Legal Education, 1970–71.

9. The case is summarized in Ivan Barris' brief in *Rose* v. *Rose*, Court of Appeals #8866, Supreme Court of Michigan.

10. DeWolf, op cit.

11. Herbert A. Glieberman, *Confessions of a Divorce Lawyer.* Henry Regnery Company, Chicago, 1975.

12. DeWolf, op cit.

13. Herbert A. Glieberman, "How to Negotiate a Divorce Case Settlement," *Chicago Bar Record*, December 1963.

14. Wheeler, op cit.

15. *Paonessa* v. *State Bar of California*, 43 Cal 2d 222, July 1954.

16. *In the Matter of Javits*, 35 AD2d, 1971.

17. Raoul Felder, letter to author, July 8, 1976.

18. Opinion 558, New York City Bar Association, December 4, 1940.

19. Informal Opinion 869, American Bar Association, October 1965.

20. Opinion 183A, Arizona Bar Association, January 27, 1966. (These three opinions are also cited in Olavi Maru and Roger L. Clough, *Digest of Bar Association Ethics Opinions*, 1970. Chicago: American Bar Foundation.)

21. Background on no-fault divorce was derived in part from Doris Jonas Freed and Henry Foster, "Taking Out the Fault But Not the Sting," *Trial Magazine*, April 1976; and Wheeler, *No-Fault Divorce*.

22. Wheeler, ibid.

23. Ibid.

24. Judge Ralph B. Maxwell, "Divorce Without Trauma," *Trial Magazine*, April 1976.

25. The discussion of the evolution of the Uniform Act is based upon annual and semiannual reports of the Family Law Section and the National Conference of Commissioners on Uniform States Laws, made to the House of Delegates of the American Bar Association between 1971 and 1974.

26. Wheeler, op cit.

27. Charles Sopkin, "The Roughest Divorce Lawyer in Town," *New York* Magazine, July 17, 1975.

Chapter Two

1. Some of the more detailed workings of the Federal Employers Act are drawn from a speech, "The FELA Down to Date," given by Franklin Jones, Sr., at a bar meeting in Houston, May 30, 1959.

2. The Gandy suit is formally styled *Steven Paul Gandy* v. *Verson Manufacturing Company*, Civil Action M-75-9-C, United States District Court for the Eastern District of Texas, Marshall division.

3. Melvin Belli with Robert Blair Kaiser, *My Life on Trial*. New York: Morrow, 1976.

Chapter Three

1. "Personal Damages." Injury Proceedings of 1970 workshop, Practical Law Institute, New York.

2. Edward Tivman, "When You'd Rather Not Do It Yourself," *Juris Doctor*, July–August 1975.

3. The facts of this case are in various pleadings in *Sabrina Pluvinage et al. v. Commings, MD, et al.*, Civil Action #2264-71, U.S. District Court for the District of Columbia.

4. The opinions of the DC Bar Association committees on legal ethics and on unauthorized practice of law are in a letter to Judge Howard Corcoran from Lawrence J. Latto, chairman of the legal ethics committee, March 22, 1974.

Chapter Four

1. Pegler in the *New York World Telegram*, January 24, 1923.

2. Paul E. Steiger, "SEC Enforcers: Are Hit-Run Tactics Good?" Los Angeles *Times*, October 30, 1975.

3. The task force study is formally titled "Report of Special Study of Securities Markets." SEC, April 1963 (mimeographed).

4. Bialkin to a symposium of the ABA Committee on Federal Regulation of Securities, "SEC Injunctive Actions," August 15, 1974; proceedings in *The Business Lawyer*, July 1975. Much of the criticism of SEC procedures was drawn from this symposium and an ABA National Institute, "Advisors to Management: Responsibilities and Liabilities of Lawyers and Accountants," October 1974, proceedings of which are in *The Business Lawyer*, March 1975.

5. Bialkin quoted in *The Business Lawyer*, July 1975.

6. Warren quoted in *The Business Lawyer.*

7. Bialkin quoted in *The Business Lawyer.*

8. *The Wall Street Journal*, February 27, 1974.

9. Monroe Freedman, "Professional Responsibility in Securities Regulation." *New York Law Journal*, April 24, 1974.

10. Monroe Freedman, "A Civil Libertarian Looks at Securities Regulation," *Ohio State Law Journal*, July 1974.

11. Personal background on Randell is from *Time*, May 31, 1968; and Andrew Tobias, *The Funny Money Game*. New York: Playboy Press, 1971.

12. The intricacies of the National Student Marketing case are drawn from various pleadings and depositions in *Securities and Exchange Commission* v. *National Student Marketing Corporation et al.*, Civil Action 225-72, U.S. District Court for the District of Columbia. Especially valuable are the pre-trial briefs of the SEC and White & Case and Epley (the latter submitted by Arnold & Porter).

13. Paul Hoffman, *Lions in the Street*. New York: Saturday Review Press, 1973.

14. Pollack to a panel discussion at the 1977 ABA convention, August 1977; quoted in the *Washington Star*, August 14, 1977.

Court Recess Four

1. *Personal Injury Damages*, proceedings of 1970 workshop, Practicing Law Institute, New York, 1971.

Chapter Five

1. Robert J. Flaherty, "IBM: This Tiger Is No Pussycat," *Forbes*, November 1, 1976.

2. *Business Week*, February 17, 1975.

3. The White study is reported in James Kilmer, "Where You Stand in the Legal Caste System," *Barrister Magazine*, fall 1976.

4. The Industrial Reorganization Act, hearings before the Subcommittee on Antitrust and Monopoly of the Senate Judiciary Committee, Part II, 1974.

5. *Administration of Public Law 89-306, Procurement of Automated Data Processing Resources by the Federal Government*, report by the House Committee on Government Operations, October 1, 1976.

6. IBM internal documents quoted hereafter are exhibits in a variety of antitrust proceedings against the company, especially *The United States* v. *International Business Machines*, civil action 69 Civ 200, in the United States District Court for the Southern District of New York. For ready access to these documents I am grateful to Jack and Stephanie Biddle, of the Computer Industry Association, Rosslyn, Virginia, who maintain an archive of testimony and exhibits from the far-flung IBM litigation. Many of these internal papers are to be found in Rex Malik, *And Tomorrow the World? Inside IBM*. London: Millington, 1975.

7. The market analyses are dated as follows: Smithers, June 14,

1971; Goldman, Sachs, June 3, 1971; du Pont, December 16, 1970; and Merrill, Lynch, November 11, 1970.

8. Bob Foresman, "Telex Lawyer Easy-Going Tulsan," *Tulsa Tribune*, February 21, 1975.

9. Quotations from pre-trial proceedings are from depositions and pleadings in *Telex Corporation and Telex Computer Products, Inc.*, v. *International Business Machines Corporation*, civil actions 72-C-18 and 72-C-89, in the United States District Court for the Northern District of Oklahoma.

10. Marik, *And Tomorrow the World?* Millington Ltd, London, 1975.

11. Maxwell M. Blecher, "Private Antitrust Actions," *The New York Law Journal*, July 7, 1972.

12. *Business Week*, September 22, 1973.

13. "Liberty and Justice for All?" Biddle to EDOS Users Conference, Richmond, Virginia, May 26, 1976; text from Computer Industry Association files.

14. *Fortune*, October 1973.

15. The Walker action was *Floyd L. Walker* v. *the Telex Corporation and Telex Computer Products, Inc.*, number 50,571, Supreme Court of the State of Oklahoma. The Lasky action was *Brobeck, Phleger & Harrison* v. *the Telex Corporation et al.*, number 77-1419, United States Court of Appeals for the Ninth Circuit.

Court Recess Five

1. Judge Bruce Littlejohn, *Laugh with the Judge.* Lexington, S.C.: The Sandlapper Store, Inc., 1974.

Chapter Six

1. Details of the Sciutto case are in various pleadings, deposi-

tions and trial testimony in *Silvio J. Sciutto et al.* v. *Melvin M. Belli et al.*, number 659-706, California Superior Court, San Francisco.

2. Melvin M. Belli with Robert Blair Kaiser, *My Life on Trial.* New York: Morrow, 1976.

3. Belli in the *NACCA Law Journal*, May 1953.

4. The *Washington Star*, November 20, 1974.

5. *Barrister Magazine*, spring 1976.

6. The *Philadelphia Inquirer*, February 14, 1976.

7. "President of Sacramento Valley Bar Association." *Smith* v. *Lewis*, Sup., 118 Cal. Reporter. 621.

8. The *Washington Post*, May 30, 1977.

9. *Fort Myers Seafood Packers, Inc.* v. *Steptoe and Johnson*, 381 F.2d 261 (D.C. Cir.), *cert. denied*, 390 U.S. 946 (1967).

10. Belli, *My Life on Trial.*

11. "$200,000 Verdict Against 'King Torts' Firm," *Medical World News*, June 14, 1976.

12. *Gambert* v. *Hart*, cited at 7 *American Jurisprudence* 2d, "Attorneys at Law," Section 168.

13. The volume of *American Jury Trials* cited in the text is an invaluable compendium of the law of attorney malpractice. Also useful for background information were David O. Haughey, "Lawyers' Malpractice: A Comparative Appraisal," *48 Notre Dame Lawyer* 888, 1973; and Otto M. Kaus and Ronald E. Mallen, "The Misguiding Hand of Counsel—Reflections on 'Criminal Malpractice,' " *21 UCLA Law Review* 1191, 1974.

14. In addition to an interview, information on Freidberg's personal and professional background is found in Robert Kroll, "First Doctors, Now Lawyers," *The Nation*, November 27, 1976; Kroll, "Suing Lawyers for a Living," *Student Lawyer*, May 1976; Russell Roth, "The Malpractitioner—Who He Is and How He Works," *Modern Medicine*, September 15, 1975; Roger Rappoport, "Dr. Nork Will See You Now," *New Times*, August

22, 1975; "Lawyers v. Lawyers," *Time*, January 12, 1976; "What You Haven't Read About the Nork Case," *Medical Economics*, July 22, 1974; and Marlene Adler Marks, "Stalking the Culpable Counselor," *Juris Doctor*, December 1975.

15. *Lewis* v. *Kromidellis*, Sacramento, California, Superior Court, January 17, 1975, cited in 19 ATLA Newsletter 3, April 1976.

16. *Neel* v. *Magnana*, 6 Cal. 3d 176.

Chapter Seven

1. William B. Spann, Jr., president of the American Bar Association, to the North Carolina State Bar, Charlotte, North Carolina, October 27, 1977; text from ABA Communications Division (mimeograph).

2. *Hickman* v. *Taylor*, 329 U.S. 495, 1946.

3. *Bollard* v. *Volkswagen of America, Inc. et al.*, 56 F. R. D. 570, 1971.

4. *Stapleton* v. *Kawasaki Heavy Industries, Ltd.*, 69 F. R. D. 489, 1975.

5. The VW case is discussed in briefs and transcripts in *Wilson* v. *Volkswagen of America*, United States District Court for the Eastern District of Virginia, verdict returned April 7, 1976. At the appeal level, the case is *Volkswagen of America Inc.* v. *John W. Wilson*, number 76-1883, United States Court of Appeals for the Fourth Circuit.

6. *Richardson* v. *Volkswagen*, civil action 70-3260, United States District Court for the Eastern District of Pennsylvania.

7. *Christian* v. *Volkswagenwerk A.G.*, civil action 2215-75, U.S. District Court for the District of Columbia.

8. *Bollard* v. *Volkswagen of America, Inc.*, 56 F. R. D. 570, 1971.

9. Davidson's version of the movie sequence is in his "Brief

and Argument for Appellees,'' in *Delmar et al.* v. *General Motors Corporation*, numbers 39380 and 39556 consolidated, Supreme Court of Illinois, November term 1965. Other events in this litigation are from the court file.

10. Gary Sellers, a Washington attorney who did research on auto safety for two and one half years for the Ralph Nader organization, gave me access to the intraoffice GM documents cited in this section.

11. The Philadelphia case is *Petry* v. *General Motors Corporation, Chevrolet Division*, civil action 32,119, United States District Court for the Eastern District of Pennsylvania. Attorney Wolf testified about his handling of the case before the Antitrust and Monopoly Subcommittee of the Senate Judiciary Committee in hearings in late 1971.

12. American Bar Association, informal opinion 19680.

13. The finding of the GM microfilm records was detailed in the Detroit *News* and the Detroit *Free Press* from April 28 through May 8, 1971.

14. The Ford case is *Rock Island Bank & Trust Company* v. *Ford Motor Company*, civil action 128-101 Wayne County, Michigan; the decision in the Michigan Court of Appeals is 54 Mich App 278. The contested test results are in a Ford memorandum dated June 10, 1968, and signed by F. B. Capalbo, supervisor, safety test operations section, vehicle safety and emissions test department.

15. *Moore's Federal Practice* 2d Edition, Volume 4A, 34-39. citing *U.S.* v. *National City Bank*, 7 F. R. D. 68, 1946.

Epilogue

1. Melvin Belli, *Modern Trials*, Volume One. New York: Bobbs-Merrill, 1954.

2. Burger to the American Bar Association National Conference on Minor Disputes Resolution, Columbia University, May

27, 1977, text from public information office, U.S. Supreme Court (mimeograph).

3. "Cut and dried." Cornfeld quoted in *Washington Post*, October 10, 1977.

4. Quoted in Ralph Nader, "Limits for Lawyers' Fees," Washington *Star*, June 21, 1975.

5. *Journal of the American Bar Association*, February 1977.

6. Washington *Post*, March 15 and November 2, 1977, the latter reporting on testimony before the Senate Permanent Subcommittee on Investigations.

7. Washington *Post*, February 24, 1977.

8. Gerald M. Stern, *The Buffalo Creek Disaster*. New York: Random House, 1976. The $500,000 payment to Steptoe & Johnson and $378,000 of Arnold & Porter expenses were revealed by Robert Walters in "Superlawyers of Washington," *Washington Newsworks*, September 16–22, 1976.

9. Washington *Post*, December 21, 1973.

Index